Czeching My Roots

A Heritage Saga and Autobiography

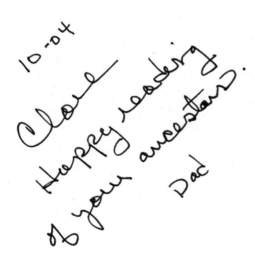

10-04

Claire

Happy reading
of your ancestors.

Dad

Leona Sprinclova Choy

Czeching My Roots

A Heritage Saga and Autobiography

Leona Sprinclova Choy

Golden Morning Publishing
Winchester, Virginia

Czeching My Roots: *A Heritage Saga and Autobiography*

© 2002 Leona Sprinclova Choy

Published by *Golden Morning Publishing*
P.O. Box 2697, Winchester, VA 22604

Produced by Richard Choy

Library of Congress Cataloging-in-Publication Data
Choy, Leona
      Czeching My Roots: A Heritage Saga and Autobiography
Library of Congress Control Number: 2002092304
ISBN 1-889283-16-9
      1. Non-fiction—Autobiography—History—Christianity
      Includes bibliographical references

Printed in the USA by

MORRIS PUBLISHING
3212 East Highway 30 • Kearney, NE 68847 • 1-800-650-7888

Contents

A Tribute

I dedicate this heritage search to my paternal grandmother, Frantiska Plachy Sprinclova. She lived with our family in Iowa and took care of me from my infancy. She was the pivotal person in my life. When I began the serious exploration of my roots in 1990, it was 50 years after her death in 1940.

I also dedicate this story to my father, Frank (Frantisek) Spryncl, and to my mother, Marie Rompotlova Spryncl. I want to honor all three of them in a way I may not have honored and fully appreciated them during their lifetimes. They would be surprised to know that late in my life I repeatedly visited their ancestral villages in the Czech Republic and truly came to value my heritage.

The word for grandmother in the Czech language is "Babicka," phonetically pronounced "Buh-bee-tchka." Accents in Czech always fall on the first syllable. In its shortened form it is "Bubi," phonetically "Buh-bee." But since I already had one Bubi, my maternal grandmother, my live-in grandma taught me from babyhood to call her "Baba," pronounced "Bah-bah." (In speaking to her, however, I would use the direct address form "Babo," phonetically "Bah-bo.")

In my innocence, I used that term with deep affection. But as a child of three or four, I remember certain relatives criticizing my parents and grandma for letting me call her Baba. The reason was that another common meaning of the Czech word Baba is "old lady," which sounds somewhat disrespectful. Grandma laughed away the criticism, although I was in tears. I felt that people were scolding me for insulting my precious grandma.

"Never mind, Leonko," pronounced "Lee-ong-ko" she said in Czech, enfolding me in the comfort of her lap and drying my tears. "We know how much we love each other. You keep calling me just what I said." So she was cherished Baba to me for the rest of her life and mine.

I truly bonded with her. I was extremely shy and always stayed close enough to her so I could hide from strangers behind her cotton, flowered apron, which she always wore over her European style long dresses.

Although Baba was a literate woman in Czech, she didn't know how to speak English. She declared upon arriving in America, "I won't live long enough to make it worthwhile to learn." She was in her mid-fifties when she came to the "New World" from the "Old Country," as immigrant Czechs referred to America and their homeland. God surprised her, however, to let her live another quarter century in her adopted land. I, too, spoke only the Czech language during my first few years because that was the language of our home in deference to Baba.

I treasure two old books with crumbly, brown and brittle pages written in the 1800s by a famous Czech lady author, Bozena Nemcova. The title is *The Grandmother*. One book is an English translation (1891) of the original Czech version published decades earlier. The author's depiction of country life in Bohemia, a province of Czechoslovakia, reflects some of the background of my grandparents.

The first two paragraphs of the book echo my feelings toward Baba. I reproduce them here as my tribute to her:

> *"It was long, long ago, when last I gazed on that dear face, kissed those pale, wrinkled cheeks, and tried to fathom the depths of those blue eyes in which were hidden so much goodness and love. Long ago it was when, for the last time, those aged hands blessed me. Our Grandmother is no more; for many a year she has slept beneath the cold sod.*
>
> *"But to me she is not dead. Her image, with its lights and shadows, is imprinted upon my soul, and as long*

as I live, I shall live in her. Were I master of an artist's brush, how differently, dear Grandmother, would I glorify you! But this sketch—I know not, I know not how it will please. But you used to say, 'Upon this earthly ball, not a soul that pleases all.' If, then, a few readers shall find as much pleasure in reading about you as I do in writing, I shall be content."

I reproduce the same paragraphs below to show my readers how the Czech language appears. I also want my readers to understand that when I have inserted Czech words into the text of the following chapters, I have not been able to add the correct diacritical markings above certain letters.

Dávno, dávno již tomu, co jsem posledně se dívala do té milé, mírné tváře, co jsem zulíbala to bledé líce, plné vrásků, nahlížela do modrého oka, v němž se jevilo tolik dobroty a lásky; dávno tomu, co mne posledně žehnaly staré její ruce! — Není více dobré stařenky! Dávno již odpočívá ve chladné zemi.
Mně ale neumřela! — Obraz její otisknut v duši mé s veškerou svojí barvitostí, a dokud zdráva zůstane, dotud bude žít v ní! — Kdybych štětcem mistrně vládnout znala, oslavila bych tě, milá babičko, jinak; ale nástin tento, perem kroslený — nevím, nevím, jak se komu zalíbí!
Ty jsi ale vždy říkala: „Není na světě člověk ten, aby se zachoval lidem všem." Dost na tom, když se najde jen několik čtenářů, kteří o tobě s takovou oblibou čísti budou, s jakou já o tobě píšu.

Preface

Why does anyone write an autobiography? Why have I dared to do so? Is it because I think I am *somebody?* Not in a proud or conceited sense, but *I am somebody*—and so is my reader. Each of us is somebody special and important to God and to our family and friends. Because God invested life in me, He expects me to be a good steward by passing on to others the valuable things I have learned. By writing my life story, I am creating an extension of myself that I hope has some permanency.

Speaking of the death of her maternal grandmother, Paula D'Arcy wrote in her book, *The Red Bird,* "I was stunned that [the family] barely knew her, although she visited us often. We knew names, dates and places...but we didn't *know her.* She hadn't let us in." Paula said she was sad because no one would ever be aware of her grandmother's true feelings, needs and loves because she lived and died and was never deeply known. Paula felt that her family was the poorer because they never realized their grandmother's dreams, hopes and hurts or benefited from her accumulated wisdom.

I definitely don't want that said about me. In this book I take you with me on the journey of my life and times and the generations before my life began. I haven't white-washed my failures or down-played my triumphs because it was God who led me all the way. I take responsibility for my failures. The triumphs or successes are because of God's grace. I tried to be honest. *I want you to know the real me*, imperfect and vulnerable as I am. I want you to understand my dreams, hopes, feelings, needs, loves and hurts. I want to share my acquired wisdom. When you finish reading, you will know me even if we have never met. Those who do know me may discover some surprising things.

For whom did I write?

I wrote for my grown children and their spouses who are busy with their own lives, careers and families. I've written and published many other books. Perhaps my children haven't had time to read them all. But I want them to read this one. I poured our common heritage into the pages. I answered questions they may not be asking now but may want to ask some day. I wrote about times and history and events that I wish my parents and grandparents had shared with me. They didn't. Now they can't. But I *can* do that for those who come after me, and I have done so.

I regret knowing absolutely nothing, not even dates and places and basic facts about two of my grandfathers who died before I was born. They lived but they are lost to me, although their blood flows in my veins. Each of my children knows me in a unique way but only in part. We interact at different levels and through varied relationships. Reading my entire story, they will be able to put some pieces together and know me better.

I wrote for my grandchildren, some of whom are still young children, others are young adults, some are not yet born. When they grow up, I won't be here. They may not remember me well. But when they are mature enough to read this book, they will be able to know the real me and may come to know themselves better through me.

I wrote for my great-grandchildren yet unborn. I won't know them, just as my great-grandparents could not have known me. But future branches of our family tree will be able to know me through my story and get a taste of the times in which I and our ancestors lived.

I wrote to pass on generational blessings to my family, as my husband, Ted, did through his autobiography, and to pass on cautions against hereditary tendencies. For the former, I hope my heirs embrace those blessings eagerly and gratefully. For the latter, the power of God is sufficient to overcome and cancel inherited negatives.

I wrote for readers who share some of the same backgrounds, experiences or heritage—or whose parents or grandparents did. I wrote also for those to whom my life and times are entirely unfamiliar—I hope they will, nevertheless, find my story of value. The researched historical material may prove meaningful to a wide readership. I hope that the account of my own spiritual journey will inspire and encourage others in their personal walk with God.

I wrote for myself. I needed to look at my life in its totality from the top of my present chronological mountain. It was enlightening to look back at my climb—all the way back to the foothills and even underground to the history of our forefathers. I wanted to trace with gratitude the loving hand of God in the details of my journey. *I am the one who has benefited most from this writing.*

Introduction

Digging for Treasure

I am who I am not only because of my heredity but also because of influences upon me in the past. When I look back, I seem to see myself as a series of different people—a child, a teen, a student, an adult, a wife, mother, missionary, writer, career person and eventually a grandmother. I am still in process—so is my reader.

Of course, I met my dad and mother only after they were adults. I related to them as their child. What fun it would have been to know *them* as children and teenagers!

At this writing, I am 18 years older than my dad was when he died and nearly 40 years older than both my grandfathers were when they died. My dad only knew me from infancy to age 21 when I was a newlywed. Even after I was married, he still called me his "kid." He didn't live to know me as a mother because he died while we were living in Hong Kong.

My grandmother, Baba, was already in her sixties when I was born. I always thought of her as "old," although now I'm older than she was when she died! I wish I had known her when she was a child growing up in a peasant family in Europe. I try to visualize her as a young bride, young mother and then a young widow.

Baba knew me as a baby and a child. We last saw each other when I was a young teen. Now that I'm a grandmother, would she recognize me? Would she see herself in me?

My children and grandchildren never had a chance to meet the people and know about the events that influenced my early life so profoundly. *But I'm trying to do something about that by writing this heritage narrative.* Through this story they and my other readers will be introduced to those people and walk with me through those events.

I find it exciting that my children and grandchildren, whether they realize it or not, are who they are and who they will become, in part because of my parents and grandparents, and the forefathers of my husband, all the way back to the beginning of time. That's awesome! Through this story I hope they discover some things to inspire them, as I have, through exploring our roots.

The above realization has motivated me to dig, while I can, for the treasure of our past so that my children and grand-children will be able to pass on that wealth of knowledge to their future generations.

Two of my granddaughters, Kelly and Kara, when they were pre-teens, sent me the following words in a Mother's Day card. This gave me further incentive to live up to the expectations of those who come after me.

> *Grandma, you have a way about you that I someday hope to have.*
>
> *You seem to have found the answers to so many questions that life brings.*
>
> *You accept life for what it is, and you accept me for who I am.*
>
> *From you I learn what wisdom really is.*
>
> *You give me a sense of family—not just my immediate family, but the family I never met.*
>
> *Your firsthand accounts of how life was for you growing up are things I could never get anywhere else.*
>
> *Grandma, you've added so much to my life...and you give me so many reasons to love you.*

I tried to work some magic by going back in a "time capsule" to my childhood and beyond that as far back as I can to introduce the people who are part of the genetic and cultural background of my children and grandchildren.

I introduce myself as a child, then as a teenager, as I invite the reader to see life through my eyes scores of years ago. What a different world it was then, as it was for Ted in his early years in China!

I want you to know the grandmother who imprinted her character and faith so indelibly on my life. Ted's grandmother did the same for him. I already chronicled my husband's roots and life legacy in his biography, *My Dreams and Visions.* That book is also partially my autobiography because I interwove stories of our 46 years of life and ministry together. I didn't repeat those memorable events in detail in this book because I wanted to concentrate on the *distinctives of my story.*

I tried to unearth the factors that motivated and molded the lives of my grandparents' generation and our previous generations in Europe. What fun I had searching for our unique "hidden treasure!" No one's treasure is exactly like our family treasure, and it belongs equally to each one in our family.

What pick and shovel did I use? I dug into my own memory and discovered some things I thought I would not even remember. There they were—stored and still available in the hard disk of my mental computer! I never before consciously called up some of them on my memory display screen. I literally relived my life through this writing.

I dug into musty family records and crumbly photo albums. Unfortunately, many gems in our treasure chest were lost through the years because most photos weren't identified or dated.

I tried to tap into the memory banks of others who knew our families and who might shed light on the generation of my grandparents. Few such people were left when I began my belated search. I wish I had started much earlier while they were alive.

I dug into history sources and reference books to research the times and places in Czechoslovakia where my forefathers lived and loved and worked. I wanted to know what motivated them to sail late in the 19th century and early in the 20th century to transplant their family trees to the New World of America.

Finally, I went to see for myself some of the things—ancient castles and bridges, villages and landscapes on which their eyes actually gazed. I wanted to share those experiences with my family and descendants because they are part of our common heritage.

Ted and I had the rare and wonderful privilege many times to walk the roads, see the historic and cultural sites and visit villages of *his* birthplace and childhood in China. We were delighted to meet the present generation there, especially those who survived political revolutions, persecutions and imprisonments to remain true to their Christian faith. *But I was eager to also see places and people of my own ethnic roots—I wanted equal opportunity!*

At last it was my turn! God surprised me with the fulfillment of that dream to visit my grandparents' homeland. My first trip to the Czech Republic was with Ted the year before he died. In the years following, I was delighted to take more journeys to that land. A happy bonus was to find several generations of living relatives I never knew existed and establish a warm bond with them. We spent weeks together during several years. I surprised myself and them by still being conversant in the language of my childhood.

In all this digging, I have at times been fascinated, sometimes surprised, startled—also dismayed and disappointed—to find out some things *about myself.* I gained insights into some reasons why I am like I am. In part, it is because of whose genes I have, but it is also because of early experiences and influences I still carry within my mind, body and spirit, all of which I pass on to my children and grandchildren.

When I look in the mirror, I can't change the fact that I am a full-blooded Czech. I have Czech body structure, features and characteristics. I have a confession to make, so I will get it over with, although I will go into further detail in the chapters that follow.

In my childhood and youth, I rebelled against my ethnic background. I wanted to hide my roots so deep that no one would see them. I'm now ashamed of my attitude, but at that time I disliked being part of a minority cultural group. Sometimes unkind people would refer to Czechs in a derogatory way as "Bohunks." I think such experiences contributed to making me shy.

I desperately wanted to blend in with my schoolmates who, in my eyes, didn't seem as outstandingly different as I perceived myself to be. In reality, they too were products of a melting pot society. I know now that my perceptions were warped. I even refused to speak the Czech language when I reached late childhood and teens. I was embarrassed in front of my friends when my dad spoke English with a Czech accent. I was ashamed of my ancestry, although I knew almost nothing about the wonderful heritage I discovered years later and of which *I am now justifiably proud!*

I realize that I must have unkindly distanced myself from Baba in her final years. She seemed to be an outsider, not part of my new world of young American friends. I no longer spent time with her or confided in her. I didn't listen to her or know how she felt. I understand this more clearly and sympathetically now that I am a grandmother myself.

In the diaries I kept during my early teens, some of which I still have, I made scarcely any reference to Baba, although she lived with us and I saw her every day. She died at age 76 when I was a mid-teen. I hope that in her wise and gentle way she understood the reasons for the widening generation gap between us. I have uncomfortable memory flashes of occasionally seeing tears trickle down her aging face and hearing her say, "No one needs me anymore. I'm just in the way." I had busy teenage things to do, friends to invite for sleep overs and school activities to attend. I was living in a modern world that was moving faster and faster. Baba did not feel a part of my young life, and I didn't make any effort to include her.

I never consciously stopped loving her but neither did I express my love. I thought I no longer needed her warm embrace which had been my comfort zone as a child cuddled up in the big apron on her lap.

I sincerely regret being a thoughtless, self-centered (but typical) teen, not only impolite toward my grandmother but also rude to my parents. I didn't honor my father and mother according to the commandment of God or even observe common courtesies toward them. Later in life, I became more aware of that, especially after I became a parent.

I can no longer ask for forgiveness in person from Baba and my parents, but I asked God for forgiveness and received the assurance that He granted it. God, in His mercy and love, has nevertheless added to me the long life which He promised to those who keep that commandment.

Such memories became painfully clear to me as I followed my search into the past to write this personal saga. Since I can't undo or redo the past, why should I bring up such things? I want to be realistic and honest. I don't want to record our roots-record by viewing it through false or rose-colored glasses.

Since I have frankly revealed my shortcomings and cleared my conscience, I am deliberately putting aside the regrets of the past to move on. Even as a grandmother, I'm still in process, growing and becoming more like what Baba surely prayed I would become.

I hope, through God's tender mercy and sovereign plan, to have another chance to express the depth of my love and appreciation to Baba and my parents in person when we are together in heaven, which Jesus called "My Father's House." A God-prepared eternity is *my* assurance in Christ as it was *hers and theirs.*

Perhaps this book is partly my opportunity to express that love and appreciation in print.

Leona's paternal grand-mother, Frantiska Plachy Sprincl, affectionately called "Baba"

Parents: Frantisek (Frank) Spryncl and Marie Rompotlova Spryncl

1
What's in "the Trunk"

My husband and I were the *trunk* of our family tree and our four sons, Richard, Clifford, Gary and Jeff, are the *branches*. Our grandchildren and the children they will have and the generations to come are the spreading *branches*.

Suddenly, so it seems, I find myself "the matriarch" in chronological age and the only remaining part of the trunk of my family tree.

Some of our branches are offspring from our own biological trunk—authentic *Chinese Czechers*—our sons and some of our grandchildren. But we have also enthusiastically welcomed the grafting of some new branches into our tree by extended family relationships—marriage, blended families and adoption. I embrace grafted branches just as warmly as branches sprouting from our original trunk. We treasure them equally because they were lovingly chosen. They enrich our family tree and bear wonderful varieties of fruit that our original tree could not have produced.

Our trunk is unique because it is made up of two people

from two geographically and culturally separate root systems. My husband, Ted, was from the continent of Asia, from the ancient historic land of China. My heritage is from the continent of Europe, from what is now The Czech Republic. We met and married on still another continent, North America, to which my forefathers came to seek a better life.

Soon we who are part of the present main trunk will be the roots of those who come after us. Some of our branches have already become trunks in their own right and their young, extended branches before long will mature into trunks too. An entire human forest will spring up around our main trunk!

Although my generation calls itself the main trunk at present, we are the offspring and descendants of the branch systems of the past generation, in fact, of all generations that have gone before. I believe all of us are here in the plan of God and in His foreordained continuity stream of life, and our posterity will be part of God's unfolding plan.

The Christian heritage passed to my husband and me from each of our grandparents, who spoke different languages and grew up far apart on this planet, was no coincidence. Ted and I believed it was appointed by God. We, in turn, have the joy and obligation and privilege to pass this treasure on to our children and to our children's children as a Christian legacy throughout what remains of human history.

TRUNK DESTINY

I have roots and also branches.
I am part of what has been
and what is yet to be.
In between is *me:*
the *trunk* of the family tree.

2

Through me pass
generations from antiquity
who have determined
what I have become.
They are my history.
They have molded me.

From me new branches spring.
They are my posterity.
Some choice I have
to assist and incline them
toward the best
of what they might become.
Still, they are free
to grow and change
within the range
of their heredity and opportunity
and God's special plan
arranged from Eternity.

For me, the trunk between,
I pray that I might be
a planting strong against
the inevitable storms
yet bending with the wind
passing on the best
from roots unseen
but giving branches room
to stretch and reach
upward to new heights
because I fulfilled
with the help of God
my trunk destiny.[1]

Unfortunately, neither my husband nor I could trace our roots back very far. Both of us regret that we didn't ask our parents and grandparents more questions about their early lives and what they remembered of their roots. It is pointless to feel guilty—

children rarely care about their roots when they see their more exciting futures stretching out seemingly open-end ahead of them. It rarely seems to matter to youth where they came from. They are usually concerned only with where they are going after school tomorrow.

In your youth, you view daily events up close, as through a microscope. Usually it takes the seasoning of life, the more mature years, before you think about and value your roots. Eventually you begin to see your life in a broader panorama, on a wider screen than you did in your youth. You can see further when you've climbed some of the higher hills of life and experienced the valleys between. You have the advantage of looking back over your shoulder to see where you've come from and forward to where you are going.

I embarked upon this creative and nostalgic adventure of writing my story in order to leave a heritage. God handed me the baton in life's race only for my lifetime. Now I am responsible to pass it on to the next generation.

The words of a song by Jon Mohr express it well for me:

> "Surrounded by so great a cloud of witnesses,
> Let us run the race, not only for the prize;
> But, as those who've gone before us,
> Let us leave for those behind us
> The heritage of faithfulness passed on through godly lives.
>
> Oh, may all who come behind us find us faithful.
> May the fire of our devotion light their way.
> May the footprints that we leave lead them to believe,
> And the lives we live inspire them to obey.
> Oh, may all who come behind us find us faithful."[2]

Our descendants may not fully appreciate this historical saga now, just as we would not have valued it when we were younger. But it will be available when they, too, reach the summit of some of life's hills and long to search for and find the gold of the past.

Time passes so quickly. The stages of life focus in and fade out as the spotlight shines on changing dramas and new characters. How enriching are all our experiences, both difficult and joyful, if we learn to savor each moment as we live it!

STAGE OF GENERATIONS

I've greeted many mornings like this one:
fresh, spring mornings, year after year.
They may appear the same
because nature's garments never go out of style
but *I* am not the same as I was
in those bygone springtimes.

As a child
I walked on tiptoe, wide-eyed in wonder
as if I were the first to discover nature.
Everything was new to me
although ancient as time and creation.

In my youth
nature seemed to be a setting for the private stage
on which *my* emotions played the leading parts.
I could hardly wait to turn another page
in the thrilling script of my life.

Then, *at summer's noonday,*
I saw spring approach again
with hushed and measured steps
taking off her verdant cloak and laying it down
under the sun in my garden

5

so that *my own son*
still bundled in winter wear
could poke at the peeping crocus in the soft soil
and laugh at the chirping robin
with anticipation in *his* new eyes
to see *his* pristine world.

Soon, ah, too soon, *at prime of life*
I watch *my grandson* stomping his toddler feet
bouncing innocently in my tulip bed
bubbling with unsullied delight
over *his* chaste, new world.

And now, *in life's autumn time,*
I still welcome spring's approach
with open arms and eager heart.
Generations focus in, fade out—
and what of me?

I see at last life's harmony
in perfect panorama:
the CREATED, the CREATION, the CREATOR—
the world a splendid stage
the changing season-scenes
both neophyte players and the pros
some hiding behind gilded masks
others garbed in tattered costumes
or flaunting sequined velvet.

The stages of life may alternate
between dim, shadowy scenery
and klieg-lighted brilliance.
But over all
producing and directing
perfectly orchestrating
the ever-cycling dramas of my life
IS MY GOD! [3]

2
Checking Out the Czechs

Because my ethnic heritage is interwoven throughout my life story, let's dig first at those cultural and national roots to briefly examine them. I am a Czech and our *branches* are part Czech. Who are the Czechs? Are they the same as Bohemians?

The word *Bohemie* is somewhat demeaning slang. Some use the word *Bohemian* to characterize a free and easy or careless way of living or to describe an unconventional person. That use is derived from the French word *boheme* which really does refer to French gypsies.

The Kingdom of Bohemia existed about one thousand years ago, the Kingdom of Moravia even earlier. When the royal House of Hapsburg ruled the Austro-Hungarian Empire for almost 300 years, there was a Province of Bohemia which lasted until after World War I.

Some of the older generation remembered living in the old empire where some were soldiers, many were farmers and others worked in factories or government jobs. Those people re-

7

ferred to their former homeland as Bohemia and called themselves Bohemians. My grandma, Baba, and my dad did, along with most of the early immigrants in Iowa. People would say they spoke *Bohemian*. Actually, there is no such language. Since 1918, after Baba and her family left their homeland, the word Cech (Czech) has officially been used rather than Bohemian.

Humans lived in the Czech and Slovak lands for thousands of years. Archeologists confirmed that primitive farmers populated the area some 5000 years before the birth of Christ. Those prehistoric people made decorated pottery, lived in wooden longhouses and organized themselves into small farming settlements. The first inhabitants of the Czech and Slovak lands to appear in recorded history were the Celts, a people mentioned by the ancient Greeks and Romans. The original homeland of the Celts was the area of Bohemia, western Austria and Bavaria where the Celtic peoples emerged during the 7th century B.C. The Celts spread to Moravia and Slovakia during the 4th century B.C., and by the birth of Christ had dispersed across wide areas of Western Europe, Italy, Spain and the British Isles.

The Cechs are descendants of an ancient Slavic tribe which migrated from the region of the Vistula River to the central part of the European continent between 400 and 500 A.D. Legend tells that the leader of some of these people was a chieftain named Jan Cechus. His followers were called Cechs and lived in Central Europe for over 1300 years.

When Julius Caesar was the leader of the Roman Empire, his armies gained victories in Gaul, (France) in Britain and in many other lands. One of the tribes he defeated was the Alpine Boii, a Celtic tribe. From then on through the centuries, historians recorded the name of the lands of the Boii as Boio-hemia or Bohemia, even after it became the homeland of the Slav people. The Boii spoke a form of Celtic whereas the Cechs spoke a Slav language.

The history of the Czechs from the 5th to the 17th century is a record of recurring wars with German and Magyar invaders. The culmination of their struggle came with their defeat by the Hapsburgs in the battle of "Bila Hora" (the White Mountain) on November 8, 1620. That famous battle marked the end of Bohemia's independence as a nation and the subsequent collapse of Protestantism there. As a result, 3600 families went into exile scattering to different countries. Probably the first Czech came to America to the colony of New York in about 1633, but it wasn't until about 1848 that Czechs began to emigrate to the United States in large numbers.

Wars were the dark side for the peace-loving Czechs. Throughout their history, Czechs and Slovaks were dominated by their more powerful neighbors. Czech territory was a favorite battleground for the wars of other nations. They have been forced by political or military circumstances to be on one side or the other. But like people everywhere, Czechs yearn for security, peace, freedom from fear and a chance to be their own creative and contented selves. They tend to be idealists with a strong sense of justice.

The reader may be confused by different names for this country. *In the 20th century the name changed five times!* There was no country called Czechoslovakia before 1918. During the period from 1620 to the eve of World War I in 1914, the country was ruled by a series of Austrian kings named Hapsburg. When my dad came to America in 1907, his passport indicated *Austria* as his birthplace and citizenship, although he was born in the region of Moravia in what is now called The Czech Republic.

The *Czechoslovak Republic (Czechoslovakia)* was established in 1918 when the old Austro-Hungarian Empire was dismantled after World War I. Included were the provinces of Czechy, Moravia, Slovakia, Silesia, and Ruthenia. My dad's family came from Radlice, Moravia and my mother's family from Siroky Dul

9

near Policka, also in Moravia. Baba's family left their troubled homeland only a few years before this event, but my mother's family emigrated several decades earlier.

"Democracy, tolerance and independence" was the slogan in 1918 for the formation of new Czechoslovakia. Thomas Masaryk, the founder and first president of the Republic of Czechoslovakia, intended his nation to be free. Not only the most industrialized country of Eastern Europe before World War II, it could also claim the longest tradition of parliamentary democracy.

Fifteen years after Czechoslovakia was founded, Adolph Hitler came to power in Germany. Within five years, the Fuhrer had consolidated his position and built the defeated Germany back into a formidable military power. Then he began his quest for more *Lebensraum*, "living space," for his Third Reich.

The lands confiscated from Germany after World War I, as well as other areas of the Continent which had sizable German populations, were his first territorial goals. High on his list of priorities was to take Czechoslovakia. In 1938, Hitler insisted that the Sudetenland of Western Czechoslovakia, with its three million German-speaking people, should be "allowed to become" part of his Third Reich. The Czech government understandably resisted, which led to confrontation and retaliation against the Sudetenlanders.

Czechoslovaks knew that to let Hitler have his way meant the eventual dismemberment of their nation, and they were determined to resist his invasion. However, Czechoslovakia's Western allies, Britain and France, anxious to avoid another war, yielded to Hitler's power-hungry demands in a final gesture of appeasement. The Czechs and the world soon found out what giving Hitler his way would mean.

The Munich agreement of September 29, 1938, resulted in the Sudetenland passing over to Hitler's Germany. The Czech government had absolutely no say in the matter and were compelled to bow their necks to him. Less than half a year later, the dismemberment of the remainder of Czechoslovakia took place. I was 13 years old at the time, and I remember my dad sitting close to the radio listening to every evening's news of what was happening to devastate the homeland that was once so dear to him. He tried to explain to Baba how the Nazis were forcibly occupying Bohemia and Moravia, the very area where their home was located, while Slovak fascist sympathizers were setting up their own puppet state in what was left of the country. Baba often retreated to her room after such conversations and silently shed tears to think that her homeland, after less than a quarter of a century of nationhood, was ripped asunder again.

No area of Europe escaped unscathed from World War II, but the conflict in Eastern Europe was waged with exceptional brutality. Armies on both sides fought to the death, giving and asking no mercy. Soldiers and civilians alike were victims of atrocities rarely paralleled in the history of wars. It is important to understand the frame of mind Czechoslovaks and other Eastern Europeans have been in for so long. That terrible time still looms large in the memory of the older people and has been retold to the younger generations. We need to know about that dark period of our roots in order to appreciate current events there.

Loss of life was measured by the millions. The Soviet Union alone lost more than 20 million of her people. Poland, Hungary and Czechoslovakia suffered proportionately devastating casualties. Most were not slain in battle but in the brutality that accompanied the Nazi occupation. Few families escaped the loss of relatives and friends. Many names of places still strike fear, anger and grief in Czech hearts, names like Treblinka, Auschwitz—and Lidice.

When I was a senior in high school, a tragic event in Czechoslovakia rocked all Czechs abroad. Lidice was a small village 20 kilometers west of Prague. The resistance movement against the Nazis was strong in Czechoslovakia. They were determined to do their part and demonstrated uncommon bravery and defiance. In May 1942, Czech freedom fighters assassinated Hitler's personally appointed Reich protector, Reinhard Heydrich. Hitler, infuriated, took ruthless revenge and ordered the death of 10,000 Czechs. He targeted little Lidice in revenge.

One morning in June 1942, the inhabitants of Lidice woke to find themselves surrounded by Nazi Storm troopers who confiscated their valuables and seized all property. Every adult male over age 16 was taken in groups of 10 to the orchard of a Czech farm and shot to death. All women were trucked to the concentration camps at Ravensbruck or Terezin where many of them died of starvation, disease and exhaustion. Ninety-four children were gassed in mobile gas chambers but those with Nordic features, who looked like good Aryan specimens capable of being "Germanized," were sent to live with German families. Then the Nazis burned and bulldozed Lidice to the ground. The soldiers plowed over the ruined site. When a stunned world received the news of such deplorable, brutal acts, it firmed global resolve to defeat the Nazis at any cost. The slogan "Lidice shall live!" spread worldwide.

Baba died in 1940. My dad often said he was so thankful she died without knowing what happened at Lidice because our family knew people there. The name Lidice was on everyone's mind in Cedar Rapids because of the high concentration of Czech people in its population. Terror, disgust and anger were vented in gatherings of Czechs. Their emotions turned into grief when news came of relatives listed among the dead.

When the few women who survived Ravensbruck returned after the war, they found only a field of corn where their precious little village once stood. A new town was eventually built a few hundred yards away, but the field that was the village of Lidice is now a national monument. I had the sad privilege to visit that site on one of my trips.

In 1945, during my second year in college, Czechoslovakia was finally "liberated" from the Nazis by Russian and American troops, and the Republic was reestablished. For the first three years, the country was governed by a democratically elected coalition government. During that period, the Communist party enjoyed wide popular support because of its grand promises, especially to throw out the Germans. Communists hoped to gradually take over the Czech government through the democratic process. However, those plans never got beyond the first stage. Czechs found out that the situation only became much worse under communism.

In 1948 the communists seized power after a group of non-communist ministers resigned in protest against communists receiving the important police posts. When the president also resigned, the communists seized complete control. They took away virtually every freedom from the people along with all personal property. At that point, the country was renamed the *Czechoslovak Socialist Republic,* the name of the country when Ted and I made our first trip there in 1991.

The Yalta Conference determined that Czechoslovakia should become a socialist state within the Warsaw Pact. During the 1950s, under the Stalinist regime, a wave of mock trials and executions rocked the country. The Czech people remained suppressed and most citizens became listless under their Russian captors, their democratic spirit only a wistful echo of past hopes and dreams.

A valiant attempt at some reform and a break for freedom of sorts called "The Prague Spring" took place in 1967 when Alexander Dubcek tried to introduce reforms. The excited people rose up with a glimmer of hope. Dubcek, although apparently a sincere communist, did champion freedom, and some considered him even to be sympathetic to Christians. Unfortunately, his liberal reforms did not please the Soviet Union, and the following year Czechoslovakia was invaded by members of the Warsaw Pact forces.

Whatever puppet Czech leader was put in power was obliged to follow the Russian line to the letter. Would-be escapees from the country were shot with no questions asked, and the land was virtually a prison state under direct Russian military occupation. Economically, the nation was in much worse shape after the rigid, centralized, communist planning system was introduced, although industry remained stronger than in neighboring communist countries.

A few fierce protests bubbled from the underground. They were desperate gestures of a freedom-loving people whose spirit, though suppressed, remained unbroken. They got nowhere in their attempts at defiance against Russian domination. It continued until the remarkable ground-swell of a peaceful people's revolution after the Berlin wall came down.

In 1989, in what is called "The Velvet Revolution" because no shots were fired and no lives were lost, the country was dramatically freed from communist control and Soviet troops were forced to leave the country. Vaclav Havel, playwright and former political prisoner, became the elected president. At that point the name of the country was once again changed and called the *Czech and Slovak Federal Republic (CSFR)*.

On January 1, 1993, the Czechs and Slovaks peacefully divided into two separate countries, renaming them once again as *The Czech Republic* and *The Slovak Republic*. Some called it "The Velvet Divorce" because it was done democratically, peacefully and quietly.

Does this sort out all the names for the reader? For convenience and simplicity, regardless of the era I am describing in the chapters that follow, I use the name *Czechoslovakia* for the homeland of my ancestors.

Looking at a map of Europe, you will see that the Czech Republic is not so much an eastern as a central European nation. The capital, Prague, is actually farther west than Vienna, capital of Austria. Hitler once called Czechoslovakia a "dagger aimed at the heart of Germany," and took terrible action to make sure the point was blunted.

Because of its geographical position, this small country has been on center stage during much of Europe's turbulent history. It is presently squeezed in by five countries touching its borders. Starting from the northeast, clockwise, is Poland, Russia, Hungary, Austria and Germany.

The two newly renamed countries together cover about 49,371 square miles (127,869 square kilometers)—only about the size of New York State. The population of approximately 16 million is also about that of New York State.

The major cities are *Praha* (Prague) the capital, population approximately 1,173,031; *Brno*, 361,561; *Bratislava*, 345,515; and *Ostrava*, 302,111.

The chief ethnic groups are Czech (65 percent), Slovak (30 percent), and Hungarian (4 percent).

Major churches are Roman Catholic, 8 million; Slovak Lutheran, 430,000; and The Evangelical Church of Czech Brethren, 270,000. In summary, 77 percent of the people are Roman Catholic and 20 percent are Protestant in the two countries.

As to economy, steel, coke, iron, cement, fertilizers, textiles, chemicals, vehicles and weapons are produced or manufactured. Potatoes, sugar beets, wheat, barley, oats, rye, corn, cattle, dairy products, hogs and sheep are agricultural products. Great reserves of coal lie beneath its soil. The country also mines iron ore, uranium, mercury, antimony and magnesium. About 14 percent of the people engage in agriculture, and nearly 40 percent work in manufacturing. It is, in fact, a major industrial power.

Ninety-nine percent of the people can read and write and

60 percent of the population between the ages of five and 19 are in school. Teacher-to-student ratio is 1 to 33. At this writing, the per-capita income is about half that of the United States.

The Czechs and Slovaks today have a working week of 42 hours and can look forward to a paid vacation every year. Consumer goods and luxuries are expensive by Western standards, but nearly every home has a television set. A surprisingly large number of workers own automobiles. It is also surprising that a large number of ordinary Czechs—not just the top officials—have small, usually very rustic getaway homes in the hills and forests away from the city. There is a rapid exodus from urban areas on weekends.

Medical attention is both cheap and readily available to all. A fair assessment of the Czech nation today is that they are a cultured, talented and friendly people, living in what can only be described as one of the "have" nations of the world. If we compare their situation with the lot of the average person in the Third World, the Czechs are well off. All children can receive an education. The nation has been rated as one of the three most literate countries in the world.

Geographically, the two countries are among the most beautiful on earth. The land has just about everything—high mountains, deep valleys, dense forests, rolling plains, rivers, lakes and caves. In fact, everything except a coastline. Few places can rival them for architectural treasures. More than 2,500 "real" castles still dot the landscape, and although time and innumerable wars have taken their toll, there remain more than 25,000 other buildings of historic note.

There are 1,300 mineral springs and health spas. Czech handicrafts, especially crystal ware, are famous around the world for their beauty and quality.

A similarity exists between the two homelands represented by the generational *trunk* of our family tree. Communism was gaining the upper hand in both countries at almost the same time—in China and in Czechoslovakia. Communists seized power in Czechoslovakia in 1948, the first year Ted and I spent in Hong Kong, after we graduated from college and Ted from seminary. We were prevented from going into the China Mainland at that time because communists were also taking control there, and all missionaries had to flee within the next year or so.

Czechs have always preferred to live in peace rather than die as military heroes, but wars were continually forced upon them. That is true of the Chinese people as well. Both valiant peoples have suffered greatly through many wars over thousands of years. The Czechs, as do the Chinese, admire men who stand for culture and freedom. Both the Czechs and the Chinese are proud of the heritage of their nations. I hope that our *branches*, our children and grandchildren and future "grands" and "greats," though their identity may become blended, diluted and intermingled with other admirable cultures, will always be proud of both their Czech and Chinese ancestry.

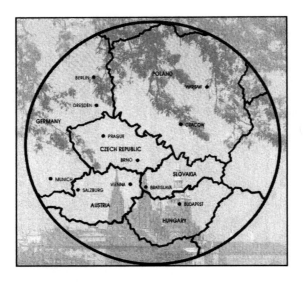

Location of the Czech Republic in relation to surrounding countries of Europe

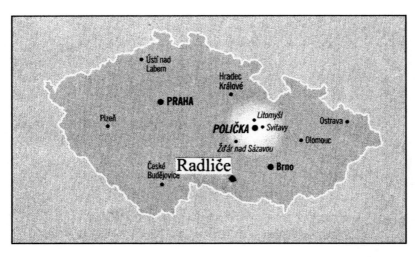

The Czech Republic with the location of Leona's two ancestral towns: Policka and Radlice

3

Voyage to the New World

    If my ancestors had not come to America, I would not have been born in Iowa. I might have lived my life in Czechoslovakia and the *branches* of my family tree would certainly have different heredity. Before I begin the story with my birth, it is important to find out why and when my forefathers came to America.

    Various motives caused Czechs to leave their homeland for a new life abroad. Desperation from continued bad times, poverty, famine and little hope for the future influenced many to cut family ties of centuries, pull up their roots and strike out for the New World.

    Those who left for America had high hopes that they could work for themselves instead of for the state and be free from constant fear and pressure. The discovery of gold in California was mentioned in Austrian and Czech newspapers as early as February 1849. During the period shortly afterward, 25,000 Czechs emigrated to the United States. Fantastic stories circulated that in

America the streets were paved with gold and roast pigs, complete with knife and fork, were running down the streets! At the same time, articles appeared in Czech papers warning prospective emigrants to America. One published in 1883 declared:

"America is a land of plenty, but it is not such a fabulous paradise that with no effort whatever life's necessities are provided. America honors hard work. Older people would be better off staying at home because they are too accustomed to old ways, and it would be hard for them to adapt. The best prospects lie with young, strong, healthy, industrious and capable people. Day laborers, farmers and tradesmen can expect earlier employment than writers, shopkeepers, etc. who do not know the English language. If at first you can't find work in your trade, don't be ashamed to latch on to any other work. Be careful of swindlers. Don't trust strangers. If you are determined to go and seek your fortune, travel there as fast, as safely and as inexpensively as possible. But don't forget that when you come to a foreign land, you are sacrificing your native land in the process. Straighten out your business affairs and don't plan on returning. Sell all your possessions. Take linens, clothing, shoes and featherbeds, which in America are expensive. The smaller your expectations, the smaller the possibility of disappointment. As soon as you are settled, apply immediately for citizenship...."

Such cautions give us insight into what was involved for them. I'm sure my relatives were aware of such things.

Poverty was real in my grandparents' village. Often my dad told of their daily food being "brambori and zeli" (potatoes and cabbage) cooked first one way and then another, but always the same ingredients. Sometimes there was goat's milk for a treat, he said. A little meat only on special occasions. They kept geese, and his job as a boy was to round up the geese and close the gate at night. One roasted goose would provide food for weeks during a holiday season.

Local misfortunes such as floods and droughts and the resulting failures of potato and other crops also motivated many Czechs to seek new homes abroad. They heard that land was cheap in America and wages were higher than in their country.

Some left in order to escape compulsory military service in wars with Italy and Prussia. They feared conscription into the Austrian armies, but not because they were disloyal or unpatriotic. Their country was constantly ruled by outside tyrants who cared little for the lives of the people. Czechs were simply unwilling to fight and die in battles not their own. They knew they probably wouldn't survive army life because their rulers considered them expendable. Their policy was to send Czech boys directly to the front lines. My dad and two of his brothers each left before they reached draft age of 17.

Oppressed people dream of freedom and risk everything to obtain it. It was a time of czars, kings and emperors. East and central Europe was dominated by autocratic empires. Because they were part of Austro-Hungary, they were under the cruel heel of the aging Emperor Franz Joseph. Dad told me that even children in elementary school heard tales of the great man, Mr. Abraham Lincoln, who had led a war to free the slaves. Such stories were eagerly circulated and fed the dreams of the oppressed peasants, offering hope to the hopeless.

The authorities, of course, did all they could to keep young Czech men from fleeing the country. Because they refused to grant them permits to leave, many simply left without permits. Authorities threatened the families of those whose young men fled the country. They tried propaganda. "In America the Indians will *getcha!* You'll be slaves like the black people. Americans will exploit you, and you will be sorry if you leave." Many young men left on the very eve of possible draft into the army. Baba wanted her youngest son, Charlie, not yet draft age, to go safely to the New World before he reached maturity.

It was common practice for an adventuresome older son to come to the New World first, work hard, save money and then buy a ticket to bring another member of the family over from the Old Country. One after the other was brought over until most of the family was in America. Usually they didn't send money, only tickets.

The fare was ridiculously low compared to today's rates. From Hamburg, Germany to New York was typically $28 per person for steerage class, $72 for second class and $120 for a berth. It sometimes took years for a new immigrant to save enough money to send for even one member of his family, let alone to get all of his brothers and sisters and parents to America.

At this point, I must rely more heavily on research and probability, because I don't recall Baba or my dad talking about their experience of making the dangerous voyage from Europe to New York. Once they were in the land of their destination, Old Country hardships seemed to fade. Probably not in their memories but from their conversations. As far as I know, they never looked back, never wished they had not come, never regretted leaving their roots of centuries to risk life in a strange country.

After they left and in their lifetimes, their country went through two world wars on their soil, and those who remained there suffered poverty and oppression from a number of tyrants and dictators. How could they not be thankful they escaped to America?

Yes, America had its shortcomings. The immigrants, including my immediate relatives, had countless economic hardships because they arrived with virtually no money, no skills, no promised jobs, no security awaiting them. But they were not afraid of hard work and determined to make the new country their permanent home. They applied for citizenship as soon as they could understand the English language and learn enough of the workings of the U.S. government to pass the exam. Whatever adversities and reverses they suffered, they worked hard, saved their money and helped to build America into what it has become.

I always heard them say, "There's just no place like America!" Didn't they ever want to go back? Even for a visit? Certainly not during the military occupation and suffering under Hitler and the devastation afterward. My relatives expressed no such desire, not even during my teens when some Czechs in my hometown were traveling back "for a look" and to find out whether their relatives survived the horrors of war. Neither Dad nor Baba nor any of our other relatives seemed to have any pull back to the land they left. They came for peace, freedom, bread and hope for the future. They were busy in the pursuit and enjoyment of these, and most of them attained some measure of their dreams during their lifetimes.

Uncle John apparently came first, then he bought a ticket for my dad, and later both of them saved enough to bring Uncle Joe over. Their sister, Antonia, was already married and had a son, so their family came over separately, as did Dad's sister, Mary. Baba and teenage Charlie were the last ones to come over together, after all the brothers saved enough money to send for them. Most of the family arrived shortly after the turn of the century, although most of Mother's family came in the late 1800s.

When it was Baba's turn, she undoubtedly sold their small property and house and possessions, gave away what she couldn't sell and turned the proceeds into money that would be needed in America. It was customary to tie the money in a bag hung around your neck and tucked under your clothing. It was all you had in the world. You were making an irrevocable choice. You were exchanging your past for a shiny dream of the future in a faraway land of uncertain opportunity.

What did they bring along from the Old Country? Many took feather quilts, bulky as they were, sometimes home-cured sausage, smoked ham and small mementos of the past. Baba doubtless gathered whatever they could carry in bags and bundles. Per-haps she sent a steamer trunk or two ahead. She tied her "satek" (scarf) on her head, and said a tearful goodbye to relatives and friends whom she never expected to see again. Perhaps they were fortunate enough to have a good neighbor take them in his horse-drawn wagon to the nearest larger village as they set off for their long journey.

From that point, they probably traveled to Prague on the "immigrant" train, which was considered 4th class, with hard benches along interior walls. All their possessions would have been deposited beside them in the aisles. It must have been congested because most people took as much as they could carry in their arms and on their backs.

Those fleeing military conscription often did so by "night flights," not on planes, which were not even invented yet, but under cover of darkness. Sometimes they had to bribe officials with money to facilitate their exit. Many dangers lay between leav-ing their home village and actually getting on board a ship bound for America. Thieves lurked in unlikely places to mug those who were leaving because they knew about the money hung around their necks. Some were assaulted on the trains and robbed. Some who lost all they had while en route were forced to turn back. They would now be destitute and could never leave the coun-try—they had sold everything and returned to their home village with nothing.

Upon reaching Hamburg, Germany, their final land con-veyance was a slow shuttle train to the dock where their ship lay anchor. Once their tickets were confirmed, each person was given a large tag to pin to his clothing with a number, his name, the name of the ship and his destination.

My understanding is that each of our family members went by steerage class, which the dictionary defines as "a section in a passenger ship for those paying the lowest fares with inferior accommodations located in the lower part of the ship near the rudder." Why was it called "steerage?" In old-fashioned ships, a large wheel was located deep inside the ship at the stern so that if the steering control on the bridge failed to work during a storm, the ship could be steered by hand from below deck.

Between 1872 and 1932, 85 to 95 percent of all immigrants went by steerage. The price of the ticket covered everything including food, such as it was. Immigrants were hustled with their bundles and baggage to the lowest deck in the bowels of the ship.

Imagine a large room about seven feet high, as wide as the ship and one-third its length. Floor and ceiling were iron or wood. Through the center was a shaft to the hold. The bunks, usually two or three tier, were made of metal strips with mattresses of burlap stuffed with straw. Sometimes three or four people occupied one bunk and took turns sleeping. The sexes were separated, sometimes on separate decks, but more often by a strung wire on which blankets were hung like a curtain to make a divider. Children stayed with their mothers. Each room was crammed with about 300 people.

The lowest part of the ship would experience the most violent motion, and dirt filtered in from the smoke stack. People ate from shelves or benches in passages between the sleeping compartments. Toilets and washrooms were primitive, and only salt water was available for washing. The inadequate ventilation, foul air, smells from the galley, vomit of the seasick, odor of unwashed bodies and the stench of the nearby toilet rooms made nearly everyone nauseous.

They only place for fresh air and fresh water was on a very small upper deck where people could stagger out, if they could stand the violent motion of the ship and blasts of whipping winds. On deck, they were in danger of being washed overboard, especially the small children who could slide away under the railings when the ship heaved. Mothers wouldn't let children out of their sight or grasp. The boat would rock and creak, and in violent storms would sometimes split open. Some of the voyages were never completed because whole ships went down, and many lives were lost at sea. The smaller the ship, the higher the waves, the worse the motion. It was tossed like a cork on the ocean.

Each person was given a plate, cup and spoon. Thin soup and stringy beef, barrel after barrel of herring fish, the cheapest food available, and garlic on dry bread kept people barely alive for voyages that could last up to three or four weeks, depending on the weather. Many either didn't or simply couldn't eat. Only water sustained their lives. They washed their utensils in cold salt water in the same basin or barrel in which they washed their faces and hands.

Many people became seasick and stayed seasick for the whole voyage. Crying and screaming and moaning filled the air day and night, although it was hard to tell the time of the day in the dark hold without portholes. The constant pounding of the engines muddled many people's minds into a state of semi-consciousness. They laid in a stupor for most of the voyage because of the polluted air and continual babble of conversation day and night.

In addition, the long, powerful blasts of the ship's steam siren day and night must have been terrifying. How could people have survived under those conditions? Many didn't. Often children got measles or other diseases which would spread rapidly. Baba and her son probably saw bodies being slipped into the sea at night, mostly of old people, the weak or young children who could not stand the journey. The ship's crew would bundle the bodies up and simply toss them into the water after jerking off the name tags and giving them to family members. Mothers would scream when their dead children were taken from their laps. There was no other way.

According to sources, the fatality rate for steerage ran about 10 percent. One of the twin daughters of my mother's aunt died at sea. As far as I know, all the rest of my relatives on both sides of my family somehow survived and were eager to face life in the New World—whatever it would bring.

*Baba and four of her six children in Moravia
before coming to America. (Leona's father at left)*

Baba's husband, Jan Sprincl, Leona's grandfather

4

At Last—The Promised Land

Clutching feather quilts, suitcases, bundles of clothes and their children's hands, thousands of immigrants from many countries, including Baba and her son Charlie, finally emerged from the stench of the ship's steerage onto the decks. This was the day their ship steamed into New York harbor! Illness had devastated many but as the ship drew near shore, the big waves abated and queasy stomachs settled down. Tears, cries and shouts of jubilation filled the air. They were survivors! They were part of the 5000 a day who were "processed" into America during the second peak of immigration between 1892 and 1924.

How happy they must have been to peer through the heavy morning fog to see that grand lady—the Statue of Liberty—long talked about symbol of freedom. They already endured much to reach this point. "Give me your tired, your poor, your oppressed...." read the welcome inscription. Yes, they were, all of that, but full of hope. And New York was their Golden Door to a new life.

Their first view of Ellis Island was ornate, shining copper

domes, vast windows and vaulted ceilings. Perhaps the architects wanted to live up to the immigrants' image of "streets of gold."

Many were surprised and bewildered to find that the first and second class passengers, some of whom may have actually enjoyed the voyage since they traveled in reasonable comfort, slept in cabins and ate excellent food in private dining rooms were allowed to disembark first. They did not have to go through the excruciating, time-consuming "formalities" of Ellis Island.

All steerage immigrants, still tottering under all their worldly possessions, were taken *en masse* from the ship by ferries to the famous Ellis Island processing point. It was a good thing that each wore a tag with his name and manifest number because most of them didn't speak English and couldn't otherwise be identified.

From 1855 until the opening of the federal immigration station at Ellis Island, the arrival center for immigrants to New York was Castle Garden at the Battery, the foot of Manhattan Island. Ellis Island, only 27.5 acres, was chosen for its isolation and purchased for $10,000 as a landing point for immigrants. Little more than a small, flat island in upper New York harbor, it was actually one of three nearly joined islands. The island was named for an early owner, Samuel Ellis, who farmed there and operated a tavern. It is about 1300 feet from the Statue of Liberty.

The immigration station opened in 1892 after the federal government took over the registration of immigrants. The first large, two-story wooden main station burned down in 1897, and all early immigrant records were destroyed. In 1900 a new one was built. Some of my relatives who came in the late 1800s were processed through that early station, but Dad, his siblings, Baba and other relatives in the later one. It stands to this day, although no longer used for immigration. It has been restored as a national landmark.

Baba and Charlie were herded like cattle into the imperial red-brick building lying almost level with the surrounding water. They streamed up the stairs into a large Great Hall with its soaring, barrel-vaulted ceiling which served as the Registry Hall. Ordered to line up four abreast, they began the many hours of waiting in lines, being shoved from one section to the next for inspection. The building was divided into a maze of passageways with iron-pipe railings called "the pens" separating them by ship or manifest number. They waited sitting on long lines of wooden benches and gradually slid along them until they got to the end and heard the shout "Next! Next!" at last. The call was for the checking of their documents. Interpreters, available for 15 languages, helped them through their physical examinations.

On a single spring day in 1907, approximately the time my dad came through Ellis Island at the age of 17, records show that 11,747 immigrants were processed. It had expanded in 20 years into a miniature city on an island, now tripled in size by using landfill. A staff of some 700 doctors, nurses, interpreters, matrons, clerks, maintenance men and night watchmen worked up to 12 hours a day, seven days a week. The Red Cross, YMCA, Salvation Army and dozens of other welfare and religious groups served coffee and doughnuts, offered used clothing, helped find luggage and wandering children and assisted in locating American relatives. They even organized impromptu concerts and parties to give the immigrants some light-hearted diversion while waiting for their turn to be processed.

During the three-day processing routine and quarantine, baggage was disinfected and everyone examined for possible "loathsome and contagious diseases." One by one, the newcomers filed past doctors who tried to detect hints of illness. If they found any suspected irregularities, they put a large chalk mark in their own coding system on the coats of those who failed this "60-second physical." But the immigrants struggled to endure anything, no matter how difficult, at this final juncture on their way to a new life in the New World.

At one point, doctors would turn the eyelids of immigrants inside out looking for symptoms of trachoma, an eye disease. The examination was painful. Their scalps and nails were examined for fungus. Sometimes their hair was cut or their heads were shaved to determine the extent of suspected diseases. If inspectors found lice, immigrants were sent to the bathhouse for disinfecting and delousing. Men and women were separated behind screens, asked to strip to the waist for examinations. Inspectors looked for symptoms of heart disease, tuberculosis, lameness, deafness, general weakness, physical deformity, mental problems and poor eyesight.

If some diseases were thought curable, the persons were sent to clinics within the building for treatment or directly to hospitals before they were certified and allowed to stay in America. If the inspections were not finished by evening, immigrants had to stay overnight and continue the next day. The complex included a hospital, dormitories, kitchen, laundry and recreational facilities. From 1900 to 1954, 355 births and 3500 deaths, 1400 of them children, were recorded in the immigrant processing complex.

The major dread and anxiety for families was that some member would not pass inspection. If that happened, he or she would be sent back immediately to the country from which he had just come. Imagine the trauma and the prospect. He would return landless, jobless and in poverty, certainly in disgrace for being rejected. If a child was rejected, a family adult was forced to return home with him. Families would become separated, perhaps never to be reunited again.

The ordeal the immigrants went through was frightening for another reason. They had looked forward to landing in a free, open America. Instead they found bars, high wire pens, locked gates and uniformed guards. Because of their background, they thought that anyone wearing a uniform was a soldier, although that certainly wasn't the case at Ellis Island. They had just come from lands where they were persecuted, mistreated and oppressed. They didn't understand what was happening to them, and no one actually explained the need for such strict processing.

After the lengthy physical inspections, they were required to show their papers and answer questions asked by other officials. Interpreters were provided as needed. They asked the immigrant to add 2 and 2, then 4 and 4 and to try reading a paragraph from a book in English to ascertain the extent of their literacy. Unable to read English, a university professor might have been labeled as illiterate! Later, literacy laws were passed to determine knowledge of their own language, but in early years that was not the case.

Then followed questions about where they were going, whether they had a *bone fide* sponsor, was a relative meeting them and did they have a job or family at their destination. The American government wanted to be sure the immigrant would not become a public charge. Single girls were not allowed to be picked up by any single gentleman. This was an effort to prevent illegal procurement of girls for prostitution. Finally, each individual was asked to show that he had $25 in American money and a ticket to his destination by train or other conveyance. Those departing to a certain part of the country by train had another placard hung around their necks with the train connection number, date and time.

During the processing of an immigrant's papers, each was asked his name. Often the person didn't understand the question in English and had, at most, only a few English words in his vocabulary that he used indiscriminately. That is one way, so the story goes, that surnames became changed and entered as part of their permanent record. Sometimes when asked his name, the immigrant would answer with the name of the place from which he came. "Berlin," for instance. His name was recorded as Mr. Berliner. Stories circulated that sometimes names were deliberately altered or shortened by the ship's officers because some names were terribly hard to spell and pronounce. Other times, it was simply through the carelessness of the authorities or their handwriting or spelling. It was common to drop the "-witz" and the "-ski" and the "-son" at the end of a long foreign surname. The practice was an attempt to Americanize the names. Sometimes a first name was mistaken for a surname and the immigrant was stuck with it for the rest of his life. This presented serious difficulties later when proof of landing was required to obtain American citizenship.

I don't know at what point my dad's and uncles' and grandmother's name was changed from the original Sprincl to Spryncl and whether it was deliberate or through carelessness on someone's part. But I don't think it helped the pronunciation. On the contrary, it left the surname without any regular vowel. Nor do I know the circumstances when the final "l" was dropped from the end of all my mother's family's correct surname of "Rompotl." Only one uncle retained the "l" in his surname in America, which was and still is the original spelling in Czechoslovakia.

Having finally passed through all the foregoing procedures, immigrants had to wait until someone arrived to claim them or money and directions were received indicating where they were to go. If the persons coming to claim them had not arrived yet, or they could not find them or other unexpected delays occurred, they often had to spend a day, a night or longer just waiting. They slept on benches, on the floor leaning on their bundles and luggage or in simple dormitories where they slept fully clothed with their hands on their luggage so it would not be stolen.

The American authorities provided food for the immigrants, if they experienced unavoidable delay. That was the first time many tasted white bread and butter and encountered the strange food called "sandwich." Milk was provided and sometimes bananas with the skin on, of course, but which they didn't know how to eat. Dad told me of his comical experience of trying to eat a banana with the skin still on, green and very puckry, because no one told him it was necessary to peel it first. Coffee was available, but they were introduced to the strange new custom of putting sugar in it. That was unheard of by peasants in the Old Country!

When they were ready to board their train, vendors offered them the opportunity to buy a box lunch for the journey to Iowa which would take several days. Dad said it cost a whole American dollar and contained only a small loaf of bread, some salami, an orange, a green banana and some large biscuits. Vendors made a great deal of money taking advantage of the immigrants, since a dollar was a lot of money for them in those days and the food was sub-standard.

Ellis Island officials helped the new immigrants exchange their country's money for American currency, got them to their train connection on time and instructed the conductor to notify them where and when to get off. They rode special immigrant trains that were not as good as ordinary passenger trains. Often they were delayed and the cars put off on side rails, while other trains got priority. Although they traveled lower class, they were unfairly charged first class fares. They could do nothing about it. The immigrants didn't complain and overlooked those final inconveniences and hardships because they knew they were nearing their destination.

Jews and Italians usually headed for the large cities. Norwegians, Germans and Czechs were mostly bound for Midwestern farms and small towns. Doubtless Baba and Charlie had prepaid train tickets sent by my dad. An interpreter saw that they and their bundles got on the right train to Cedar Rapids, Iowa—the promised land at last!

In the mid-1920s, a change took place. Federal laws stated that immigrants must be processed in their country of origin, and the United States enacted laws setting limits on the number of each ethnic group allowed into the country. Ellis Island retreated into obsolescence and closed officially in 1954.

The buildings fell into shambles, deserted and not maintained, an object for vandals. Ten years later, the property came into the hands of the National Park Service. In the fall of 1990, after many years of privately funded renovation and restoration costing $156 million dollars, its doors opened to the public as a grand Immigration Museum. The complex includes theaters and exhibits depicting the early American immigrant experience of 12 million hopeful people who passed through the Golden Door. Visitors can now retrace the footsteps of their ancestors. More than 100 million living Americans can trace their U.S. roots to a man, woman or child who came through Ellis Island between 1892 and 1954—*and so can we!*

5

Settling in Cornfield Country

As nearly as I can figure, my maternal grandfather, Antonin Rompotl, was the first of our families to leave the Czech lands (a part of Austria at that time) to come to America about 1880. When he came to Cedar Rapids, the population was slightly more than 3000. He died at age 39 so I never knew him or anything about him. Unfortunately, I never asked my mother about the circumstances of his untimely death. She was only 11 at the time, the oldest of three children. My grandmother, Anastasia, whom I called "Bubi," then married her first husband's nephew, Joseph, who was about the same age as she. I was in my teens before I learned that Joseph was not my biological grandfather since, coincidentally, his surname was the same as her first husband. With Antonin's arrival, my family tree was planted in American soil, and the stage was set for my eventual birth.

By and large, Czechs didn't come to the New World for freedom of religion nor were they asylum-seekers. They were not political radicals because they never had any opportunity for active participation in the government of their homeland. They came more often for freedom *from* religious oppression. I will discuss the attitude of the Czech *freethinkers* in a later chapter. Most of the immigrants came from economically depressed rural areas, which accounts for some lack of cultural sophistication. They emigrated primarily for economic reasons. They were settlers, not seekers of dollars who were waiting to be repatriated.

Usually when one immigrant or a family settled in a certain area of America, they sent for or invited others in their home village to settle there as well. That was the case in many communities in the United States where Czechs, Slovaks and other Slav speaking people put down their roots in the early years. Sometimes they named their settlements after villages or cities in their homeland. In Texas, Oklahoma, Kansas, Nebraska, South Dakota, Wisconsin, Minnesota and Iowa there are clusters of Czech people.

The fertile soil of Iowa was the biggest attraction for Czech settlers. Many brought seeds to plant in their gardens and fields and tools to build their houses. In Iowa, there are communities around Tama, Chelsea, Belle Plaine, Elberon, Vining, Clutier—all within a 20 mile area. Spillville, Cresco and Protivin are also Czech settlements. Another prominent Czech cluster of towns includes Fairfax, Swisher, Ely and Solon, just south of Cedar Rapids. That was the destination for both sides of my family. I don't know the occupation of my maternal grandfather, but my dad worked on a farm in Ely for a family named Lorenc when he first arrived in 1907 and where he saved his money to start bringing over the rest of the family.

Czechs, along with other immigrants, had adjustment problems in a new land. Often they faced frightening situations they didn't anticipate, so blinded were they with anticipation to come to a "land flowing with milk and honey." They had to find a place to live, a way to make a living, learn a new language and get an education. Most of them arrived with their money nearly used up on the long journey to America.

They not only faced different customs but new economic standards. Many came from farm and peasant backgrounds but were now trying to settle in cities beginning to buzz with developing industries. Most Czech immigrants came from the cottager class, not the poorest, because they did own tiny fragments of land that hardly supported a family. Their children would inherit still smaller fragments when divided among them. Such farmers had little hope of self-improvement because the richest land barons amassed more and more land and put small farmers out of business.

Some new immigrants stayed with members of their families until they could become independent. Many were young and unskilled. New factories needed workers, and many Czechs found work in mills, canneries and the meat processing plant in Cedar Rapids. Often older children or under-age teens went to work in factories, since child labor was not yet illegal. Those with skills such as dressmaking or tailoring pursued those. Some worked for others on farms and lived as hired hands with the farm family. Farms in America had larger acreage than in Europe and required machinery to make the ground productive. Some Czechs went into food service.

Czechs are known to be hard workers and thrifty. They entered all kinds of professions and occupations. Some years ago, the city officials in Cedar Rapids, the major, councilmen, many heads of departments, the Fire Chief, the Chief of Police and county supervisors were all of Czech ancestry. Some of Czech descent are now congressmen, judges, governors, mayors and other elected officials. At the time I graduated from high school, it was estimated that about one-fourth of the city's population were of Czech ancestry, and that Cedar Rapids had the largest percentage of Czechs of any city in the United States.

Historians record that the first settlement of Czechs in Iowa was probably near the Iowa River in Johnson County about 1850 since they usually tried to settle along the banks of rivers and streams. Travel was by wagon with oxen, and land had to be cleared to erect log homes. At first some built houses of sod with thatched roofs like the houses in villages in their homeland. When they found that timber was plentiful, they were happy to make even their roofs of wood shingles, sometimes four feet long. In the early days, furniture was scarce and people slept on bundles of straw on the floor, covering themselves with feather comforters brought from the Old Country.

New arrivals were always amazed at the immensity of America, having come from such a small country in Europe. Wildlife was plentiful, the cost of living was modest and there were not the social class differences they experienced in their homeland. Rich and poor were respected equally. No one was afraid to express his opinion publicly. Some wrote to relatives back home, "People don't carry heavy burdens on their own backs here. They have animals for that purpose. Cattle are kept outside throughout the year, and only horses stay in barns in the winter. Imagine, they even burn forests to gain more arable land! Women can get jobs in town and *all they have to do* is laundry and cooking and clean the house!"

Czechs who arrived after the Homestead Act of 1862 took advantage of available land. But before long, free land was no longer available, and at the height of Czech immigration in the 1880s, when my early ancestors arrived, a prospective farmer had to have between $400 and $1000 to get started. After brush was cut away and stumps cleared, they planted either beets, potatoes, corn, wheat, oats or barley along with summer vegetables. Their wise farming approach was to diversify to guard against crop failure. Eventually they found that corn was easier to grow than wheat and provided better yields in the Midwestern climate.

The tradition of neighbors lending or borrowing equipment and helping each other was a positive custom they brought from the Old Country. They pooled their labor for threshing and harvesting. Women prepared food, children played games and everybody gathered in the evening to drink home brew. Women generally wouldn't be working in the fields as they would have in their homeland. Milking cows were a man's chore in America. In the old country it was exclusively a woman's job. Boys were kept busy on the farm and girls helped with indoor chores. When they were no longer needed at home, girls often became maids to Cedar Rapids families, returning home only to assist with work at harvest time. Living with established families helped them learn English more quickly.

Cedar Rapids was a town of only about four hundred people when the first Czechs arrived about 1852. They settled mostly in the southeast and southwest sections of the city. The population of Cedar Rapids mushroomed in the next few decades. When my dad arrived in 1907, it was already over 30,000. Horse and carriage traffic was becoming common. The first train reached town in 1859 and local residents were proud of their impressive train station downtown. I grew up during the days when Cedar Rapids was a regular stop on the route from Chicago going West. In fact, after Ted and I were married and packed to leave for China in 1947, we left by train from there to the West coast. The station was demolished in 1961. The first airfield, Hunter's Field, was built in 1924, a year before I was born. Now the modern airfield outside of town attracts major airlines.

Because the Czechs are such a thrifty people, their first ambition was usually to own their land and their homes. To own a family farm that could be passed down to one's children was the Czech-American dream. This was in contrast to the way people were locked into their economic system in the Old Country. There, the rule was, "once poor, always poor." In America they found

41

that anything seemed possible with hard work. The transition from village peasant life to frontier farming, however, was difficult and complex. On the plus side, the Czechs had a lot of experience coping with adversity, so they generally did well under the harsh conditions of the Midwest.

The Czechs started their own Savings and Loan Associations, some of which continue to this day with branches throughout the country. Soon followed their own insurance companies to secure their properties against fire and lightning. My parents always bought their insurance from the Czech companies, dealt with a Czech bank and patronized Czech people who had all manner of businesses.

Czech people were reluctant to carry mortgages—somehow it seemed disgraceful to them. Early songs and dramas and movies often had plots about the wicked landlord with the big black mustache who foreclosed on a mortgage and threw the poor, shivering family with children out in the street in freezing winter. The Czechs wanted no part of that. They usually waited until they had saved enough to buy a home by paying cash or they carried a mortgage only for a few years. In the 1940s, when I graduated from high school, it was estimated that about 75 percent of the Czech families owned their homes and had paid off their loans usually within five years if they had to borrow.

Before I was born, my parents started to save money to build their own home. By the time I was five, in 1930, they bought the house in town where I grew up. It was still being built when they signed the deed, and was quite an achievement toward their American dream.

Many of the early homes in Cedar Rapids still stand and are occupied. Czech homes, even the modest ones, are usually kept in excellent maintenance with neat yards, shade trees, fruit trees and shrubs. No matter how small the yard, Czechs continue to succeed in growing lovely flower gardens and usually a vegetable patch, no matter how small.

    A distant relative who came as a five year old boy to Cedar Rapids from the same home village in The Czech Republic as Baba's family, wrote a nostalgic piece about the early Czech settlers.

In Memory of Our Czech Ancestors Who Settled This New Land

    "They did not give up and leave when misfortune and nearly insurmountable difficulties assailed them. They stayed, persevered and surmounted the adversities. If they could return and walk again the place where they built their first log home in this new land of promise, they would not believe the contributions they made to the success of this land, America. I think they might have said:

    'When we first came to this prairie, the sun shown bright with promise in the vast blue sky. We marveled. The wind blew the tall grasses gently like ocean waves. We hoped for harvests soon to displace them. We listened to birds sing a welcome song as if to cheer us on to get started. The vastness of the rolling land surpassed all our imaginations when we left our small native Czech villages. Eagerly we worked with the sod, chopped the trees, sweating to build at least a temporary home for our family. A roving Indian or two struck fear into our hearts. We had heard such blood-curdling stories before we came!

    'But nothing could compare to enduring the trials of scorching hot summers followed by the fierce snow and bitter cold of winters. From before sunrise to dusk, day after day, we toiled with calloused hands to break the sod and make it into the fertile land it is today. Life was harsh, not only for us, but for our children. We buried many of our precious ones in small graves on the prairie. In spite of all the hardships, our harvests grew with the country. So did our hopes.

'You are a new generation. You have not seen nor shared our early hopes and dreams or silent weeping, nor the immeasurable sacrifices that are buried with us in the soil of this land. Though we now lie in the ground of *America the Beautiful*, the wind still gently blows, and overhead new generations of birds still sing optimistic songs.

'And though the tall prairie grasses and the Indians are long gone, and skyscrapers, industries and freeways are in their place, we, your ancestors, pray that you will remember the toils and the hardships we bore to help build this great country *for you to enjoy and share* with your children and the children to come.'"

Joseph Robert Doupnik (By permission)

6

Iowa in the "Early Days"

What was my hometown like at the time my earliest ancestors arrived and a few decades before?

The first white settlers found a pleasant place in Iowa with its gently rolling terrain dotted with streams, rivers and ponds, much like their Czech homeland. Wild game was plentiful, with deer, elk, turkeys, prairie chickens, pheasants, quail, rabbits and a few buffalo. The winding river with its tributary streams was full of fish—bass, pike, buffalo and catfish. In season, there were plenty of wild plums, crab apples, blackberries, wild currants, gooseberries and nuts. The land was fertile, ideal for growing crops or vegetables.

While I was growing up, I didn't understand the reason my dad was so eager to go fishing whenever he had a spare hour. Scores of years later when I went to Czechoslovakia, I found that every village had its fish pond. He often took me along to fish, although I didn't really care for fishing as a child. I would bring a book to read on the bank while he fished or as I sat with him in his rented rowboat. He would take Baba and mother and me to hunt mushrooms, nuts and wild berries in the woods in the fall. Whenever they discovered an area that yielded abundantly, that place became a family secret. Dad was also a small game hunter—rabbits and squirrels for food not sport. (I didn't like the taste of either so I refused to eat them.) I could understand the reason for the eagerness of my parents and Baba to pursue those things after I saw that was what they did in their homeland.

Iowa land was ideal for the Indians and for their style of living and culture. Two relatively friendly tribes of the Sioux nation, the Sac and the Fox, wanted no trouble with anyone. Their desires were only to fish, hunt, play games and enjoy their tribal family life. Although they never understood the white man's way of living, they were friendly and cooperative when early settlers arrived. Similar to the experience of the Pilgrims at Plymouth, many of the Midwestern immigrant settlers wouldn't have survived had it not been for help from local Indians. Indian men would show white men the best places to hunt and fish. Indian women would show white women where to gather roots and herbs to combat prairie illnesses.

At least 17 historic tribes previously lived in our part of Iowa. Some were the Kickapoo, the Kichigami, the Ottawa, the Miamis, the Missouris, the Pawnees, the Chippewas, the Omahas, the Dakotas and the Ioways, for whom Iowa was named. Many were eventually decimated by other Indian enemies, by smallpox, the plague and the white man's whiskey.

The oldest folks in town told about roving Indians who learned a few words in Czech and would come to the door and ask for "cukr" (sugar), "maslo" (butter), "mouka" (flour), "vejce" (eggs) and "kava" (coffee). They held sacks open in which to put the items. The children were always warned to run home, if they saw Indians, and hide under featherbeds when Indians knocked at the door.

I was fascinated with Indian lore as a child. A children's radio program called "The Singing Lady" was my favorite because she told stories of Indians. I would roam our nearby woods looking for Indian burial mounds, and occasionally I even found an arrowhead. My imagination went wild. I would borrow books from the children's library about Indians and dream about how things were in the days of early settlers. I asked for an Indian costume for Christmas one year, which my indulgent parents ordered directly from the Montgomery Ward catalog. When I unwrapped the box and found it complete with feathers in the head dress and a rubber tomahawk, I ignored every other gift I received to parade around in my Indian outfit. Cowboys and Indians was a favorite neighborhood game, and I always championed the part of the Indians, pretending to take the scalps of the cowboys.

The fact that Indians were deeply religious impressed me. They believed in a Great Spirit who created the earth and all good things in it. The Indian was a true environmentalist. The braves killed no animals needlessly, only for food and skins. Indians cut no trees except to use for fuel or shelter. They dumped no garbage into streams, instead they buried their refuse and waste.

The Indians were pushed further and further west, eventually surrendering all their lands and reluctantly moving to government reservations. I heard that the last big group of Indians returned in 1859 to see the first train come into Cedar Rapids— they called it the "iron horse." After that, they disappeared from the area. But in my imagination, I still "saw" them sometimes at dusk or in the smoke of a burning leaf fire.

The railroad apparently affected commerce and transportation greatly. After their ships docked at various ports of entry, the trains carried goods to their destination. In Cedar Rapids, the Union Station was built in 1897 patterned after Flemish Guild Halls of the 14th through 16th centuries in the Gothic Revival

47

style. A red brick structure trimmed in blue Indiana stone with a clay tile roof, it was 400 feet long and 40 feet wide with a tower in the center standing 102 feet high. The long seats were much like solid church pews with armrests between. Richly stained woodwork, a fireplace at each end and marble floors made it a pride to the city and a gateway to many Czech immigrants for 64 years. Because the train went through the center of town, huge traffic jams built up several times a day into the 1940s because of trains stopping, switching rails, backing up, then pulling forward, back and forth. The station was purchased for demolition by the City of Cedar Rapids in 1961 for more than it cost to build it. Many were sad to see a nostalgic landmark disappear. Old timers remember the belching, coal-burning engines that would be considered an environmental hazard today. Two large parking ramps connected by a skywalk have replaced it now.

Not long before my ancestors arrived, a meatpacking plant located in an icehouse on the Cedar river was built in 1871 by an Irish immigrant, Thomas M. Sinclair. Many of my unskilled relatives including both grandfathers, most of my uncles and many of my aunts and cousins, along with thousands of other Czechs, were employed at "the packin' house" most of their lives. The job carried a relatively high wage scale and an important benefit package. Because of the mass employment it provided the community, the stench was tolerated, but not without much complaint. In those days, there was no method of using the waste parts from the butchering process, and it was dumped into the river down a long chute. The plant was rebuilt as a large installation with monstrous slaughter houses, curing factory, smoke house, sausage factory, refrigerated storage, packaging buildings and its own railroad connections.

One summer during my college days, I worked there for a few months of manual labor cutting meat off bones with a slim, sharp knife (which I was squeamish about using), and later on I worked on the assembly line in the refrigerated department. Garbed in my winter coat, gloves and ski cap, for eight hours each day my job was to catch the frozen carcasses of huge hogs as they came swinging through the door hanging on a hook from a pulley. I had to turn them around to flop belly down on the conveyer belt. I kept from going stark crazy with the monotony by singing at the top of my lungs, since no one could hear me—and also by looking forward to meet a certain young man during lunch break who worked in the shipping room!

Many Czechs, among them my relatives, worked at the Quaker Oats Company, the largest cereal mill in the world. Its predecessor was the National Oats Company established in 1910. It produced not only oat cereal but flour, animal feed, corn meal, corn oil, grits, pancake flour and pet food. I also worked there one summer on an assembly line putting bonus premiums into boxes of oats. I didn't have to count sheep jumping over a fence, if I couldn't fall asleep at night. The boxes kept coming faster and faster even in my dreams.

The Douglas Starch Works was established in 1903 and among its products were corn syrup, corn starches and other corn products. In May 1919, the entire plant blew up and disappeared in a pillar of smoke sending debris more than a mile high. My parents still talked about it with relatives who worked there but who escaped harm because they were at home eating dinner when the tragedy occurred. About 50 people lost their lives in the fiery blast. It was believed that a spark of static electricity in the dusty interior caused the explosion. Penick and Ford Ltd. bought the site and built a new plant on it which diversified into more than 200 products for industrial and food use.

When Czech immigrants arrived in town, and after they found some job that would enable them to survive, they started to attend night school. Usually the immigrants' school was held three times a week at Washington High School to provide adult students an opportunity to learn to speak, read and write the English language. Many met their spouses-to-be during those sessions. The school building was built in 1891, and my mother attended high school there graduating in 1911 or 1912. Graduation exercises were held at Greene's Opera House. I have photos of mother in 1911 lined up with girl classmates all wearing identical long dresses with tiny waists (held in by corsets), puffed sleeves, broad-brimmed hats and boot-like high-laced shoes.

Some random dates and statistics of early Cedar Rapids follow to give the reader a feeling for the times in which our fore-fathers lived. When founded in 1841, the same year Iowa was admitted to the Union, the town was called Rapids City and was incorporated in 1856 when it held the first election. There must have been an obvious need for the jail since it was completed before the town was officially founded! The first schoolhouse was erected in 1846. The first dam was built across the Cedar river in 1841 at a cost of $600, and the first steamboat arrived in 1844. The first bridge was built across the Cedar River in 1856. Rev. Williston Jones opened a school of higher education in his home in 1851 which later became Coe College. That same year the First Presbyterian Church building was constructed near the center of town.

The first phones were installed in 1877 shortly before my grandfather Antonin arrived. The first street car started its route the year he arrived. Although the city started its first fire department in 1869, in 1894, when my mother was two years old, the first professional fire department was established. The engine was horse drawn. The horses were so conditioned to react immediately to the sound of the fire gong that they knew just where to step under the harness. When a horse was to be retired from fire duty, it was best sold to someone in a small town or on a farm. If the horse were sold to someone in the city, the person was sure to have a runaway every time the horse heard a gong in the distance.

It would even break through the stall. In 1893, the police and fire department shared one horse. If a fire occurred, police had to wait their turn until the horse returned.

In 1860, communication by telegraph connected Cedar Rapids with the rest of the country. The first water mains were installed in 1875. The first phones was installed in 1879, and by the following year there were 28 phones in the city. The earliest ones simply connected two specific locations by lines strung over the roofs. As the number of phones increased, or people were added to the circuit, the tops of roofs began to look like spider webs. There was no switchboard at first, so when you wanted to call the person on the other end of your line, you would tap with a pencil on the speaking hole, hoping he was in earshot. When you listened, you had to put your ear to the same hole! We've come a long way, baby! No one would have dreamed of cell phones.

Electricity for power and light came to Cedar Rapids in 1882. The year my mother was born, there were only 6000 electric lights in town, and power was only available part-time. In 1894, electricity became available full time and many new things began to be possible.

A year before mother was born, professional baseball began in Cedar Rapids. The year the Great Depression began, 1929, was also the year the biggest spring flood in the city's history occurred.

The population in 1860 was about 1600. The city had a bank, a livery stable and a hotel. About 80 Czech families were already living in the area. Most of the land at that time was covered with native prairie grasses. There were no bridges, and roads were only paths in the sod cover. There was enough timber to supply lumber and fuel for the taking. When trees were cut down for building, they were squared off to make log homes, and plaster was used to fill spaces between the logs and to cover inside walls. $175 would supply any young couple starting out with enough money for a team of horses, harness, plow, harrow and a cultivator.

Sales were not always in cash but often in barter. Hogs sold for $2.50, the same amount as a pound of coffee. Sugar was 50 cents a pound. Trade was in necessities such a bolts of yard goods, shoes, nails and hardware. Women usually sewed trousers and coats for the whole family. Enough food was raised in most family gardens to sustain the family through winter. Corn was ground into meal and cooked for breakfast with a spoonful of molasses made from the farm's own crop of sorghum cane. Barley was parched in the oven and ground for a coffee of sorts. If the family was fortunate enough to own a cow for milk, the cow roamed the prairie but came home to the sound of the horn flute. Everyone's cow recognized the family flute and returned to the right barn.

In 1900, at the turn of that century, the population of our hometown was approximately 11,000. When I was born, the city population was about 50,000.

An original sales ticket from a grocery story in 1912 shows that 10 cents was the cost of a wash basin, 65 cents bought a tea kettle, slightly less was paid for a pail and about the same for a dishpan. A salt and pepper shaker was five cents, a dozen china dinner plates were one dollar, and a cuspidor (an essential bowl-shaped receptacle in which to spit or deposit ashes) was 25 cents.

The first street cars were drawn by horses or mules. After electricity came, electric trolleys or street cars were propelled by being attached to overhead power lines and ran on tracks. The trolley could go in both directions. At the end of the line, the conductor-engineer would shove a long steel pole through a hole in the floor of the trolley and switch the car's direction for the return run. Then he flipped the backs of all the straw-woven seats to face the opposite direction and took up his position as driver from the opposite end of the trolley. You deposited your nickel in a see-through metal and glass box beside the driver. He didn't make change and tokens were also used. There were no regular stops at first. Passengers simply pulled an overhead cord to indicate when they wanted to get off, otherwise the trolley wouldn't stop. It did stop to pick up passengers if someone standing by the street raised a hand to hail it. You never could tell when one would arrive because schedules were uncertain. When the trolley really got up to speed, it would sway back and forth as it clattered down the tracks, and you had to hang on to the back of the seat in front of you. During my elementary school years, street cars were still in service, and we happily rode to town on them.

The first "horseless carriage" was a steam car built before 1900. A fire had to be built underneath it for a half hour before starting so the boiler would be hot enough to create steam to drive it. Electric cars were experimented with—they were quiet, didn't emit any pollution, their interiors were plush including upholstery and curtains, but batteries had to be charged every 70 miles.

In 1900, people became excited about gasoline powered cars that would run at the breath-taking speed of *25 mph*. Women passengers wore veils over their hats and faces and covered their faces with cold cream because there was no windshield to protect them against that incredible speed. Men wore caps and goggles and gloves to protect themselves. The first cars that came snorting and rattling down the dirt roads were said to cause havoc among the horses and carriages. Frightened horses often set off at a wild gallop, dragging people in carriages over rough roads, sometimes upsetting them.

Leona's maternal grandparents, Antonin and Anastasia (her mother in center)

Leona's maternal grandmother's family (grandmother, Anastasia, back row on right)

7

The Sprouting of My Roots

I was born on June 22, 1925, in Cedar Rapids, Iowa, about six years after my parents married. I grew up as an only child but with a deep longing for a brother or sister, sort of a sense that there was a missing person in my family. Years later in my teens, my parents told me that they lost their first child, a son, at birth. Perhaps I missed the brother I never had.

I experienced a mysterious and poignant moment recently when shuffling through a box of old photos. I found a truly beautiful picture of my mother in her thirties. It was mounted in a large cardboard folder, actually pasted in firmly. I had a strange feeling, almost a tap on the shoulder, to tear Mother's picture out of the folder and look behind it. The idea seemed unreasonable. I didn't even think of doing that with many other such folders I had been looking at. I followed my impulse, although it was difficult to do without destroying the picture. To my amazement, I found a yellowed-with-age, folded note behind the picture written with pencil on tablet paper. I recognized Mother's handwriting, although

it was nearly faded. I read, "Hurry home for lunch, honey. Baby
and I will be waiting for you. Love, Marie" It was dated five years
before my birth. *The baby wasn't me.* I don't know the reason for
my brother's death. I wonder why I was meant to discover that
secret note, or why Mother kept it hidden so securely. It was a
touching moment.

My mother was 33 and my dad was 34 when I was born.
Dad was working as a shipping clerk in a furniture store, a job he
took soon after he returned from military service in the U.S. Army
in World War I.

Dad came to America from Czechoslovakia at age 17 in
1907. He farmed for a time near Ely, Iowa with his brother John.
At some point, he worked in Detroit, Michigan, but I don't know
at what kind of job. According to an original document I have, he
became a U.S. citizen at the age of 26 in Linn County, Iowa, at
the Superior Court of Cedar Rapids. His previous citizenship was
listed as "Subject of Austria" and his Naturalization Number was
1358966, dated December 28, 1916.

Dad enlisted in the army on April 30, 1918. The participation of Cedar Rapids Czechs in the First World War was a noted
achievement. Terrible devastation was going on in Czechoslovakia at that time because of continuous wars fought on its soil. A
Bohemian Relief Society was organized in Iowa to raise money
for destitute widows and orphans in their homeland. Through other
organizations and alliances, money was raised to aid Czech pris-
oners, women sewed for the American Red Cross and the Czech
Red Cross in Prague, garments were knit for soldiers and civilians
and huge bundles of clothing were sent to help war orphans of
Bohemia. To raise funds, bazaars were held with merchandise,
animals, poultry and agricultural products donated by citizens.

Caught up in the spirit of patriotism for the United States,
Dad said he felt it was not only his duty but his privilege to defend
his adopted country in appreciation of the freedom he was enjoy-

ing. After brief basic training at Fort Dodge, Iowa, he was sent by the Army to France where he was assigned to Company G , 313th Ammunition Train. He left the U.S. on August 17 of that year, became a corporal in September, then sergeant in December at Pont du Chateau, France. His tour of duty was short because the armistice was soon signed and the war was over.

Jubilation echoed throughout the world, especially in our hometown, because the liberation of Czechoslovakia also took place when the armistice was signed. The celebration in Cedar Rapids lasted for seven days with Czech bands and orchestras playing every day in connection with a big bazaar for fund raising to help the war effort. Dad was one of 2,541 men from Cedar Rapids and Linn County who fought in World War I, of whom a significant number were of Czech descent.

Dad returned to Iowa on May 29, 1919 and was discharged on June 11. His official papers list him as "5 feet ten inches tall, dark brown eyes, dark hair and ruddy complexion." His character reference was listed as "excellent." I remember his hair being slightly wavy and he eventually had the beginnings of a receding hairline.

Dad told me he liked the name of the village of Leone in France and decided that if he ever had a little girl, he would name her Leona. Apparently he met my mother very soon after returning from the war. They must have had a whirlwind romance and were married on December 6, 1919 at Waterloo, Iowa. Maybe they eloped? Only two strange named witnesses signed their marriage certificate and there are no wedding pictures with a group of people.

Mother's name was Marie Rompot, although people sometimes called her Mary. She was born in Cedar Rapids on January 28, 1892 and spent her whole life there. Her father, Antonin, born in 1865, and her stepfather Joseph (the nephew of Antonin) were both born in Czechoslovakia, as was her mother, Anastasia Drapela.

All of them came to America on the ships as I have described, went through the Ellis Island ordeal and settled in Iowa. Mother was the eldest child. She had a brother, Anton, born in 1893 and a sister, Frances, born in 1895. I don't know where she attended elementary school, perhaps Jackson, but her high school education was at the old Washington High School located at that time on Greene Square downtown. Mother was very short, only five feet two inches, with hazel eyes and slightly wavy brown hair.

Mother's first marriage was to a handsome young man named Ralph Warner who was a baseball player. I don't know anything about him except that he became ill shortly after they were married. I remember hearing that mother spent many months faithfully commuting back and forth daily to Oakdale, a small tuberculosis sanitarium where he was hospitalized. She cared for him until his death. I don't know how long they were married or how much time elapsed before she met my dad. Mother didn't talk about that period of her life, or perhaps my young ears weren't listening.

My parents were living in town on 8th Avenue at the time I was born, and Dad was proud of being able to purchase his first car, a Model "T" Ford. I have a photo of my parents by their rented home, posing by their car with their pet dog.

Shortly after I was born, my parents moved from Cedar Rapids to a location about eight miles east of town at a bend in old Highway 30 by the Marion cutoff. Dad named his new business "Midway Inn," probably because it was midway between Cedar Rapids and Mount Vernon. Dad's dream was to go into business for himself, and the small lunch room was a start. Dad's brother John joined in the business for a time until he established his own location. Our two families lived together in a small, old house behind the lunch room.

In this chapter I recount memories of the first few years of my life when I knew only the small world around the Midway Inn.

I have tried to recreate some of the atmosphere from the dusty reaches of my mind. I knew nothing of the business struggles of my parents which I will share in the following chapter. Almost all my memories revolve around my precious grandmother, Baba, who must have come to live with us soon after I was born. Because my parents both worked, Baba was my primary care giver.

The first thing I remember being aware of as an infant was the wallpaper design beside my crib. There were gaudy, bright-colored parrots all over it. Strange that I should recall such a detail.

I remember lying in my crib and watching the shadows on the wall made by the trees outside the window in the moonlight or on a sunny day when I was put down for my nap.

As soon as I could sit up, I remember Baba pulling me around in a little red wagon everywhere she went in the house so I could be with her as she attended to household tasks. In the winter of my first year, my dad bought me a little sled with a long rope. What fun it was to be pulled around in the snow by the people who worked for my parents and by Baba when she went to the barn to feed the chickens and milk the cow!

The house had an old-fashioned bay window with a wide indoor seat that opened up for storage. I would sit on Baba's lap as we watched the rain outside, or the snow in winter, or the people driving into the parking lot to go into the lunch room. Baba showed me how to follow the raindrops with my finger as they trickled outside the window. She would draw pictures on the steaming inside of the windows on humid days and ask me to guess what she drew. When Jack Frost coated the windows inside, I would try to scrape my own pictures on the frosted glass with my little finger nail.

Baba taught me many Czech words as we pointed through the window at different things. Because I was with her constantly, my first language was Czech, although I picked up some English words at the same time from customers in the lunch room or friends of the family.

In my babyhood, Baba would rock me to sleep on her lap singing a little Czech ditty that went something like this, in phonetic spelling: "Ho-pee, ho-pee," (rock, rock) while rocking me back and forth in her arms. "Kotch-ka sned-la kro-pee," which means, as near as I can remember, (The cat ate the rice pudding.) Whenever I felt out of sorts or tired, I'd pull at Baba's dress and plead, "Ho-pee, ho-pee."

We'd play other little children's games. Baba would take the palm of my little hand and trace circles on it with her index finger as if she were stirring food in a pan. She would say, "Varila myska kasicku, Na zelenem rendlicku," meaning (A mother mouse was stirring the porridge in an iron pan.) Then she would pinch the tip of each of my little fingers in turn while repeating (please understand this is not an accurate Czech rendering, and I can't type the diacritical marks above certain letters!) "Tomu dala, tomu dala, tomu dala, tomu dala." (She gave some to this one, and some to another, some to another and another). Then, for the pinky finger, Baba would say rapidly "Tomu nedala nic, nic, nic, nic, nic" which means, (But to this one she gave none, none, none, none)—while tickling her fingers up my arm as if the mousie were running up under my armpit. I would squeal with delight.

I passed that on to my four sons and now to our grandchildren.

I didn't like the attic. I was afraid of being there. The steps would creak on the way up and frightened me. I refused to take a nap by myself in the big, iron four-poster bed in the attic room because the wind whistled in such a scary way through the cracks in the eves and under the window frames. I developed a fear of attics because they seemed to be isolated from the rest of the house and the rest of the family.

Some of the young ladies whom my parents employed,

often my older cousins, took turns to baby-sit me when Baba was otherwise occupied. They didn't tell me the pleasant stories Baba did—they teased me by scaring me with ghost stories, especially when they were in charge of putting me to bed in the creaky attic room. They seemed to think it was funny when I cried and screamed for Baba. With a straight face, stifling laughter, they pretended not to know why I was so upset.

My cousin, Frances, who lived with us in the Midway house with her brother, Jerry, and parents during my first year, gave me my first dolly for Christmas. I simply called her "Panenka" which means dolly in Czech. I wouldn't go anywhere without her. My parents bought me a small wicker doll baby carriage for my second birthday. It had a top over it so I could keep my dolly in the shade while I pushed her around the yard. Baba made dolly several outfits of clothes and a tiny patchwork quilt from pieces left over from the big quilts she used to make.

Baba raised a flock of chickens, a couple of geese, and had a sizeable garden she tended mostly herself. I trailed her everywhere. I "helped" her plant the seeds, water the long rows, harvest the green peas and beans and look for the ripe cucumbers Baba said were hiding from her on the vines. She would pick a fresh cucumber, wipe it on her apron and give it to me to munch on. (No pesticides were used in those days.) My mother was upset with Baba because she thought eating a cucumber hot from the garden would give me a tummy ache. So Baba never gave me one unless we were sure Mother wasn't around.

Baba showed me how to open the pea pods and zip out the young, tasty peas by running them across my teeth. Nothing tasted as delicious as vegetables fresh from the garden that "we" planted together from seeds. Ever after, when I sniff fresh pea pods, I remember those first garden experiences. I have the same memory sensation when I sniff the silks from sweet corn in the husk right from the garden. Pure nostalgia.

When I was old enough to care for a little garden myself, Baba tilled a plot for me, and we planted in my plot several seeds of anything she planted in her big garden. Dad bought me a miniature rake, shovel, bucket and wheelbarrow. With my small watering can, I watered my garden at the same time Baba watered hers. What fun to see my seeds grow! (After I learned not to keep digging up the seeds to see whether they were really growing.)

Baba showed me how to look for potato bugs on the leaves and told me how she earned money as a little girl by doing that all day long in the potato patches in the Old Country. She provided me with an empty glass soda pop bottle to drop them into. Cabbage worms were even more fun, because I had to look carefully for them under the green leaves where they camouflaged themselves. These creatures were my friends, Baba told me, but we didn't want to share our vegetables with them.

Near dinner time, we'd fill my little basket with lettuce leaves, rinse them well under the hand pump over the well in the yard and Baba would make sour cream dressing for the lettuce at mealtime.

I loved the smell of the dill patch Baba planted for her specialty, "koprova omacka," a thick, creamy soup with dill, potatoes, hard boiled eggs and milk—a Czech favorite. I ate my soup in a special porcelain bowl Baba said she brought from the Old Country. It was decorated with blue and yellow flower designs. I learned to eat with a small silver spoon with a looped handle that Baba also brought from her homeland.

Tomatoes eaten right in the garden, cantaloupes and watermelons, unchilled of course, even hot from the sun, eaten next to the vine where they grew, were unsurpassed for flavor.

We had one black and white Holstein cow that occupied a stall in our barn behind the house. Baba called her "Bossy." At milking time, Baba squeezed hot, raw, full of cream, unpasteurized milk right into a little tin cup she bought for me at the hardware store. An unforgettable taste! That indulgence probably contributed to my chubbiness as a toddler. I would run for my cup when Baba started for the barn. Baba asked my dad to make a miniature stool for me to sit on that was just like the three-legged one she used when she milked Bossy. Dad painted it red, and Baba traced a white flower on it with a paint brush.

The smell of the hay and the cow's warm body, the lowing sound Bossy made while being milked, the sound of the streams of milk hitting the side of the tin pail, the drone of flies trying to land on Bossy, which she deftly shooed away with her tail—such first impressions of my life never fade.

We both walked barefoot as we gardened. I can still feel the squish of the mud between my little fat toes after the rain when we went out to inspect how much the garden grew from the shower. I loved the smell of wet plants, laughed at the shower I got when I tried to shake the rain drops from the tall sunflowers as I reached for the bending faces of the big brown and yellow blossoms.

Of course I got my share of bee stings and slivers and other "ouchies" from going barefoot, but that didn't take away from the fun of it. Baba always knew how to take care of such things.

Before we went into the house, Baba and I would stand on the cement slab in front of the hand pump at the well and take turns pumping the icy cold water on our muddy feet to clean up. A blue enamel cup always hung by a wire at the side of the pump shaft where anyone could pump themselves a cool cup of well water on hot days. Truck drivers, delivery men, anyone could help themselves to our well water with its slightly irony taste. No one worried about fluoridation, pollutants or whatever. The taste of fresh, cold, well water is unequaled for its thirst-quenching qualities.

Indoors, we had a large, clean white bucket which Baba

kept full of drinking water. A long-handled dipper floated in it for use at the sink since we had no running water indoors.

Baba and my mother cooked on the iron top of the wood stove. A woodbox stood in one corner of the kitchen, and a basket of dried corncobs for starting fires was in another corner. You lifted the round iron top off the burners with a removable iron handle, put the wood inside, and replaced the flat top of the burner. The stove heated the pails of water for laundry and bathing.

The top of the stove also warmed the flat iron used to iron clothes. We had no electricity so no electric iron. I think we had two flatirons. While one was in use at the ironing board, another was heating up on the woodburning cookstove. The assembly-line procedure worked quite well. There was no such thing as wash and wear clothing yet, and no respectable family, no matter how poor, would think of wearing clothing that was not ironed. A flatiron was multi-purposed. It made a good doorstop, and a warmed iron wrapped in newspaper or a blanket removed the chill from bed linens on a freezing winter night. You had to snuggle under the feather comforters in a hurry and lie still until the warmth of the iron spread its comfort. At Christmas, wrapping paper was carefully removed from gifts, folded and put away for use again. A flatiron could press the creases and wrinkles away—but you had to be careful not to scorch the paper. I saw Baba test the iron by quickly touching its heated surface with her moistened finger. If it sizzled, it was ready. When I was three, I received for Christmas a tiny flatiron and miniature ironing board to play with. I still have the iron and use it as a paperweight.

Oven heat may have been hard to control, but the most delicious homemade bread and baked goods came forth. Baking was much more an art than it is today with our measured heat and precise recipes. Electric bread makers? Not even in their dreams! For cooks of that era, it was "a pinch of this—a handful of that—enough, but not too much—knead it until it feels right." Directions like that would drive a modern housewife to the point of buying fast food.

Gathering "vejce" (eggs) from the hen nests in the barn was a responsible job I couldn't do alone when I was very young because I had to reach up to the nests in the hay. The boxes were elevated so they would be safe from a hungry fox or other predator. The mother hen was usually unhappy and vocal with her squawks when I tried to take away eggs on which she was still sitting. Even Baba got pecked occasionally. Sometimes Baba put a solid, milk white, artificial glass egg in a young hen's nest to encourage her to start laying. Baba explained that the hen would notice that there was already an egg in her nest and think, "Oh, did I lay that? I guess I really can do it. I'll try to lay another one."

Every once in awhile, a non-laying hen disappeared. When I questioned Baba, she would just smile. I found out in a few years, when I was old enough to handle such facts of life, that Dad and Baba had a tried and true routine for the first stage of fried chicken. Baba would shoo the selected chicken toward Dad who stood ready with a heavy wire hooked at one end to snare the bird. When it was in his hands, he cut off its head with one whack of an ax on a stump and let it flop around for a few minutes to bleed. Baba was ready with a bucket of scalding water for loosening the feathers before plucking it clean, down to those pesky pinfeathers. Then it was plunged into a bucket of ice cold water to cool thoroughly. Baba gutted it, removing the heart, liver and gizzard. Intestines were thrown in the garbage. Baba cut it deftly into single serving pieces. Salted and peppered, each piece was dredged in either cornmeal or flour and pan fried to a delicious brown. The taste and aroma of fresh fried chicken can't be compared to today's frozen chicken wrapped in plastic from the supermarket.

I didn't dare go into the barn without Baba because the "kohout" (rooster) would ferociously run after us to peck us in the back of our ankles—or higher, in my case, because I was a little person. Baba would chase him away with a stick.

Nothing can beat the taste of an egg scrambled within minutes of being laid, eaten with a slice of homemade rye "chleba" (bread). But bread *without* caraway seed, thank you, which is typically Czech but which *I* still don't like! Spread home-churned butter on the bread, accompany it with a cup of "mleko" (milk) straight from the cow, and you have a meal fit for royalty.

In the evenings, Baba and I would sit on the back porch facing the lunch room and the highway and look at the stars. As a small child, I was sure some of the shooting stars fell to the ground, and I would run through the wet evening grass looking for them. "They are fireflies," Baba explained, "little mirror images of the stars God made for us to enjoy."

Assured that it was all right to catch them, fireflies provided simple fun for me on hot summer evenings. An empty glass pop bottle came into use again into which I gently dropped in the ones I finally learned to catch. I wanted to save them until I could see them better in the morning light. If naughty boy cousins were visiting, they would snatch away my precious fireflies and squish them on the cement to make a phosphorescent streak. Oh, how I cried!

We would count cars coming along the highway. That was how Baba taught me to count in the Czech language. "Jeden, dva, tri, ctyri, pet, sest, sedm, osm, devet, deset..." In those early days, there were not many cars on the road at night, and they didn't whiz by at high speeds as they do now. We made a game out of trying to guess whether or not the car was going to turn into the parking lot of the lunch room. Mother and Dad usually wouldn't finish their work until long after Baba put me to bed.

There were always plenty of cats and kittens around the house and barn. My dad suspected that nearby farmers sometimes came by in the middle of the night and dumped a gunny sack full of their unwanted, newborn kittens in our yard. They knew we had a cow and expected that the kittens would adopt us—or we would adopt them. A number of them hung around the barn especially at milking time, but most of them were quite wild. Baba managed to tame an occasional nice one as a pet for her Leonka, and I had an endless supply of purring friends most of the time. I gave them all Czech names of one kind or another, but they universally responded to "kitty-kitty-kitty" no matter what else I called them. I'm sure they must have been heavily flea-infested since no flea powder was available in those days.

Sometimes, a new batch of tiny kittens whose eyes weren't even open yet were dumped on our property, but strangely, they disappeared again overnight. I didn't learn until I was older that Dad had to drown them or else we would have been overrun with cats. I shed tears of grief when I found out about that.

I also had a constant supply of dogs. I still remember a very fat black and white mutt that "suddenly appeared" on our porch one morning. I was sure it had eaten too much because it had a round, distended tummy. Baba knew a little secret and prepared a large cardboard box with old rags to make a doggie bed. I was delighted to have another pet.

The next morning I screamed with delight to find five darling squealing puppies in the box with my new pet. I concluded the obvious—she must have vomited them up during the night. That's why she had been so fat! I didn't want to give up any of the cute puppies until I was sure they went to people who would love them as much as I did.

Baba and my mother and sometimes an aunt or two would have a cottage cheese making party. Whole milk was allowed to set for six or eight hours. When the cream was skimmed off, the milk was used for cottage cheese. A stoneware crock was filled with the milk and set on the back of the cookstove where there was very little heat. The crock was loosely covered until curds developed—from eight to 24 hours. A wooden spoon was used to stir and test for readiness. Then it was poured into a large, square cheese cloth or clean flour sack. The whey (the remaining liquid) was poured away, and the curds were squeezed in the cheesecloth, tightly tied and hung on a clothesline to dry for up to eight hours. Delicious and nourishing! Maybe you didn't know that was what Little Miss Muffet in the nursery rhyme was eating as she "sat on her tuffet." I doubt that the spider who sat down beside her really wanted her snack.

Homemade noodle making was a process that continued throughout my childhood and goes on today among my Czech relatives. The proportions are: 1 ½ cups of white flour, 2 eggs, well beaten, 1 tsp. oil or melted shortening. Put the flour in a small bowl and make a well in it. Into the well pour the eggs and oil. Mix to a stiff dough. Turn out on a floured surface and knead until very stiff. With a rolling pin, roll dough out until almost paper thin. Spread it out on a clean, dry cloth to partly dry so the dough doesn't stick together when cutting the noodles. Cut dough in about two inch wide strips, stack them on top of each other and with a sharp knife cut noodles to desired width—wide or thin as you like. Noodles can be boiled in broth or salted water and served in soup or as a side dish. Season as you like. If not used immediately, noodles can be dried and then frozen in an airtight package. The taste beats those in plastic packages from the supermarket!

Sauerkraut making was great fun! Baba and my parents and relatives did things the way they were accustomed to in the Old Country. They stomped barefooted in big, usually wooden containers of the processing cabbage! The proportions for about 15 quarts of sauerkraut are: 40 pounds of cabbage, a scant cup of sugar, a scant cup of salt and a handful of caraway seed (optional). Remove outer leaves from cabbage heads, cut in half, remove hearts. Dad had a special metal kraut cutter that looked like the bottom of a miniature rocking chair with which he shredded the cabbage over a large washtub. After the other ingredients were added, the more sanitary way was to mix and squeeze with your hands until juicy. Then pack loosely into stoneware crocks, if you planned to use it in two or three months, or pack loosely into glass jars, adding juice about level with the top. Add one or two cabbage hearts into each jar. Screw lids as tightly as possible and store in the basement or similar area. Set jars on newspapers and cover with more papers in case the juice leaks out while the sauerkraut is working. Do not disturb for at least four to five weeks. Leaking is ok but *the aroma is another matter!* Why would anyone want to buy sauerkraut in a can?

I'll refrain from describing other traditional Czech dishes because that would only make your mouth water.

Tornados seemed to be more frequent in the Iowa countryside years ago than they are now. We had a storm cellar under the house. Just the hint of the first dark, foreboding clouds on the horizon, accompanied by an increasingly howling wind, would drive us all down there. Sometimes there was an eery, sudden stillness that interrupted the screaming wind. It struck terror in my little heart because it signaled a tornado's sure approach.

After running from window to window, slamming each one shut and throwing water on the fire in the stove, Baba would sweep me up in her apron and carry me to the outside cellar door leading underneath the house, where she would light the kerosene lamp. By that time my parents and the lunch room employees (and sometimes a few customers) joined us, after they were sure they had battened down all moveable things outside. The door would be firmly shut, and the howling wind was subdued in our ears as we'd wait out the storm against the farthest inner wall.

I can still smell the damp cellar and the fumes of the kerosene lamp. I didn't like the spider webs in the corners and on the ceiling. I imagined all kinds of scary things in the dark because the lamp cast weird shadows. In my memory, I can hear Baba singing hymns softly as she held me close and rocked me on her lap, while I buried my head in her breast and clung tightly to her.

However quickly we had to get down to the cellar, Baba somehow never forgot to bring along a slice of bread with jam wrapped in a hanky, stuffed in her apron pocket for little Leonka— to pacify and distract me while we rode out the storm.

Sometimes the tornados touched down on nearby farms, along the highway or in the fields and caused much destruction. I can't recall tornados doing any substantial damage to our house, barn or restaurant property. But usually tree branches would be scattered everywhere and trash blown against the buildings. Once we did lose some large trees, completely uprooted, in our picnic park along the highway. Baba would always whisper "Djekuji, Pan Buh" (Thank You, Lord God) when we all crawled out of the cellar after the storm. Baba never forgot to acknowledge God's care in any situation.

By the time I was born, Dad and Mother had to have a primitive phone installed because they conducted a business. The rectangular box hung on the wall of our house. You had to turn the crank on the side quickly several times to summon "the operator." Then you told her the number you wanted, or the name of the people or where they lived. I can't remember whether there were phone books in the 1920s yet, probably not. The operator was a friendly person who seemed to know everything. Because you were on a party line with several other families on the same circuit, the phone would ring at everyone's house at the same time. Each family with a phone in the same area was assigned a code of a certain number of rings, some combination of short and long rings. You had to listen for your particular combination. You also knew the code for some of your neighbors, so there was nothing to keep you from quietly lifting the receiver and listening in on their conversation.

We didn't have indoor plumbing during those early years.

I remember the white porcelain pails with lids that served as chamber pots for nighttime use so people wouldn't have to go to the outhouse (outdoor toilet) in the dark. I had a small one with a handle and lid decorated with flowers. It was by my bedside for use during the night.

Wooden outhouses, several times the size of modern phone booths, were common in rural areas. One would be lettered on the side "Men" and the other "Women," unless one served for both. As I remember, ours had a white latticed sort of foyer with vines or morning glory flowers growing along the latticework which hid the doorway. A simple hook and eye locked the wooden door from the inside. Two round holes were cut in a wooden slab that served as a seat. I really can't remember that two adult occupants ever used the facility at the same time, but with some of my little girl cousins, we would go in two at a time, since there were two holes to sit on.

One of the holes was smaller—for children. I always had scary thought that if I sat on the big hole, I might fall in and *die a dreadful death!* Usually there wasn't even toilet paper, as we know it. Newspaper torn into squares served the purpose. You could sit there in the dim light (no electricity of course, but some daylight filtered in through the eves) and look at the old newspapers and magazines—if you wanted to stay that long.

But who wanted to? The smell of chemical lime that my dad threw down the holes occasionally to stifle the odor and disintegrate the contents at the bottom of the deep holes in the earth are unforgettable smells that you want to forget. They motivated you to finish as soon as possible. I practiced holding my breath as long as I could. I remember sometimes running out the door before I even pulled up my panties all the way!

Another thing that motivated you to hurry was the wasps that often made nests under the slanted roof. You had to keep quiet not to disturb them. Plenty of flies were on hand to buzz around you while you were occupied.

Our walkway to the "privy," as it was sometimes called, was made of planks laid end to end, and if it rained, they could be slippery. You were in danger of falling, if you were in a hurry. In winter, the planks were often icy and one had to step lively but carefully to make the visit on time. Then you had to unwrap the layers of winter clothing, watch your mittens and scarf so they wouldn't fall down the holes and perch on the cold seat. You tried to finish in record time and not make the trip very often. At least no wasps zoomed after you in winter.

For pranks on Halloween, the "big kids" sometimes tipped over a few outhouses, and they had to be righted again in a hurry so they could be used. The little buildings had no permanent base, and a strong wind could even blow them over.

I can't remember having a regular bathtub at the Midway house. I do remember a big, oval tin tub with handles in which Baba bathed me. She would fill it with water heated in buckets on the stove. In the winter, I took my bath near the woodstove that kept the big kitchen warm. I guess the rest of the family bathed in the same fashion.

Baba asked Dad to get her a big barrel to collect rain water from the spout that came down from the house roof. She used that soft water to wash our hair and to do laundry. She rinsed our hair with vinegar to make it soft and shiny. We always conserved water by using the same water from washing vegetables or people to throw on the flower beds. Leftover coffee and tea was used for house plants. Water from the sink drained into a bucket underneath and was given to the chickens. After doing the laundry by hand on a washboard, the water was useful for mopping the wooden or linoleum floors.

Baba brought many customs and traditions from the Old Country, some of them having to do with cures for illnesses or injuries. I remember her brewing up some kind of concoction resembling tea that I was forced to drink as a remedy for stomach ache. It was hatefully bitter, but Baba would sweeten it with honey and feed it to me with a spoon. I tried not to complain of a tummy ache very often in order to avoid the cure. She would also gather the large leaves from the Plantain plant or weed in the yard and apply them as a poultice to injuries, aches or pains. Cuts and skinned knees were doused with kerosene or turpentine or painted with iodine, all of which smarted intensely. For bruises, boils, and other skin problems, she applied hot flaxseed poultices. For sore throats, Baba saw that the family gargled with salted vinegar or swallowed honey.

Chest congestion was helped by Vick's Vap-O-Rub or goose grease rubbed on the chest and covered with flannel. In the spring, she administered sulfur and molasses to "thin" the blood. For a cough, she made onion syrup by slicing onions and brewing them with sugar until a thick liquid formed. Fletcher's Castoria was an awful tasting mild laxative, so you had to wash it down quickly with water. Hoarhound candy was for a cold and so was breathing steam from a boiling tea kettle. Vaseline was not only good for chapped lips but for rough skin on elbows and heels. Watkins salve came in a round, gold box and its creosote base was orange or amber. Advertising claimed "Good for man and beast." I looked upon Baba as the original "Doctor Mom" and tried not to get sick very often, so I wouldn't have to endure any of her potions.

Rhubarb grew plentifully in a special patch and rhubarb sauce and rhubarb pie were summer delights that Baba made for the whole family. Sometimes rhubarb pies were on the menu at the lunch room, if Baba had time to help Mother make them.

Dad bought me two little red chairs and a child's table with fold-down sides on which they gave me my meals on the porch in the summer. It was set up in the big kitchen by the stove in cold weather. My cousins and I shared many picnics on that table under the trees. The many kittens and puppies would come around begging for food. Our meals were usually sandwiches from the lunch room and soda pop to drink. My favorite flavor was strawberry.

There was a sort of open-walled, latticed pavilion between our house and the lunch room in the early years where we also took our meals on hot summer days. Baba would put a white oil-cloth on the table and I'd help carry out our picnic in my little basket.

Where it came from, I don't know, but we had the skeletal metal body of an old black Model "T" car in our yard. It was a piece of junk, minus wheels and most of its other parts. No doors either, but it had seats with the stuffing hanging out and a steering wheel. The gas and brake pedals were intact, so when my cousins visited, we spent many hours "driving," playing "trip to town," and making the whirring noise of the motor while waving to imaginary passing cars.

I must have been only two years old or so when my Aunt Anna, Uncle John's wife, was sitting on the porch on a quiet summer's eve with Baba and me. For what reason I can't remember, she removed her false teeth. Shocked and frightened, I ran to hide behind Baba's long skirt! Everyone laughed at my fear, but no one bothered to explain the reasons for false teeth. I remember trying for days to remove my own teeth unsuccessfully. When my baby teeth began to fall out, I was afraid that was the beginning of the end—I would soon lose them all like Aunt Anna and have to get removable ones!

Many birds roosted in our trees and in the picnic area, and I like to watch them. Baba had Old Country stories about birds and bugs personified with names, and I listened with rapt attention to many a tale. My favorite was the Czech classic children's book, "Brocci," (Insects) with illustrations by a famous Czech artist. I begged Baba to read it over and over to me. It was about a little firefly family and a whole neighborhood of firefly relatives. Their adventures thrilled me, and the little characters became as real to me as human friends. It had a sad ending, and I cried every time she read it to me.

Apparently the book had never been translated into English. Baba, of course, read it to me in Czech. In years to come, I went on a search to find a translation and looked in vain even when I went to bookstores in Czechoslovakia. I still have the original book in Czech from which Baba read to me. To my delight, 65 years later I finally found a newly translated edition in Czechoslovakia with identical art work!

If birds and insects could fly, I reasoned, why couldn't I? My childish mind devised a scheme. There was a rather steep side to one part of our porch that had no railing. One day when I was by myself, I decided to try jumping off. I figured that if I flapped my chubby arms like the birds did their wings, I might be able to fly. I tried it.

I fell with a thud onto the dirt, screamed with fright and suffered a skinned knee and bruised elbow. I needed a lot of comforting and kisses on my "boo-boos" from Baba. It gave her a chance to explain how God made people different from the birds and insects who were meant to fly because God gave them wings. People were meant to walk on their two feet, and I had better stick to walking on mine and not try to fly again.

*Leona's parents' first business and house in the country,
called "Midway"*

Baba's little "Leonka" at Midway

76

8

Great Depression Memories

Unfortunately, Dad tried to launch his dream of being a small business entrepreneur in the most difficult years before and after "The Great Depression" which began in the late 1920s and continued into the 1930s. It was a "best of times and the worst of times" period in my parents' lives. I was too young to be aware of it.

During the few years just before the Depression, my parents seem to have done very well in their first business venture of the lunch room. It was sort of a golden interval, a pre-Depression success. People often told them they should be charging much more for their homemade specialties. Nevertheless, they were thrifty and must have saved in the bank every dollar they could spare toward the goal of buying their own little house in the city. Their hard work paid off, and they must have wisely withdrawn their money just before banks crashed in 1929, because they did achieve their dream.

From that point, however, it was rough going. As far back

as I can remember, Mother and Dad seemed to be entirely occupied with working hard day and night just to make ends meet. I guess I could be called "a Depression era child" because I was left with a "Depression mentality." That isn't an emotional condition, but rather a spending perspective. Because money was hard to come by during my growing years, my parents never had much available for luxuries. They were frugal with everything. As a result, all my life I have been reluctant to spend money on anything that wasn't absolutely necessary. In fact, I still feel guilty about purchasing anything that seems extravagant or luxurious, and I always search for bargains.

I record this slice of my parents' working life as a vignette of the times that are past, a bit of Americana that can't be repeated. It is a piece of family history that is also part of my roots.

Early photos show that when my parents bought Midway Inn, it was only a tiny shop scarcely big enough for one or two customers at a time to come in and buy some snacks. Two gasoline pumps stood near the little shop, and early signs read "Drahos Gas Station." That must have attracted Dad to buy the place. Gas stations were just coming into prominence. When Dad arrived in America, there were only 800 cars in all of Iowa. Another factor which probably drew him to that location was its proximity to the "Seedling Mile" six miles east of Cedar Rapids. In 1918, that was the very first paved stretch of old Highway 30 in Linn County. It was really only a mile long and 16 feet wide, a demonstration strip to show people what the county hoped to do in years to come. It was near the location of their little lunch room. By the time I was born, that highway was newly paved all the way from Cedar Rapids.

At first, there were no service stations, even when cars were becoming popular. Gas pumps were installed in front of general stores and the newly established repair and sales garages. Most of those garages were converted livery stables. When a customer needed gasoline, a store clerk or mechanic came out and pumped it by turning a handle on the side of the pump. The gasoline went up into a glass container on top of the pump. That was the kind of pump Dad had, according to photos. When the number of gallons ordered was reached on the marked container, the hose was put into the tank and a lever released the gasoline. The early Model "T" had a gravity-flow tank which was only a little higher than the engine. Gravity flow was fine on level ground and slightly hilly areas, but on steep hills, the driver often turned around and backed up so the tank would remain higher than the engine. Dad said the car had more power in reverse!

After some research on how cars ran in those early days, I learned that because there was no gas gauge at first, men carried a little black metal ruler to measure the gas in the tank. Nor was there a dip stick to check the oil. I remember seeing my dad down on his knees turning something underneath the car to find out if it needed more oil. It usually did. The early cars had no water pump either, so you had to keep adding water just to be sure.

In later years, I remember Dad comparing notes with some of my uncles about their first cars. His first Model "T" was not new, although by 1916 the price had fallen to $360 for a new one because the number coming off the assembly line increased. He said his first car had no door in front on the driver's side.

Because the first models didn't have starters, there was a hand-turned crank in front below the radiator. When Dad cranked it, he had to quickly run around the car and jump in so he could adjust the levers on the steering wheel. The tall lever was the emergency brake. Two levers controlled the gasoline and the spark. If he didn't adjust it fast enough, the motor would die. Cranking a Model "T" was tricky and dangerous. If a man wasn't careful, it would backfire and often break the cranker's arm or even hit his face and knock out his teeth. This was called "kick." As a child, I often heard the loud sound of a car backfiring and mistook it for a gun shot. The gasoline tank was under the front seat. To fill it, Dad and Mother had to get out and remove the front seat cushion to reach the gas cap.

When the knob on top of the horn was pushed down, it made a terrible squawk, like "oh-oo-ga." When the car started, it would vibrate, rattle and shake. Maybe that's why it was often called a "tin Lizzy," "jalopy" or "flivver." The early headlights were like carriage lights, lit with a match and burning a liquid fuel. Later models had lights that became dimmer when going up a hill until they were barely a glow, and as one drove downhill they became brighter.

Henry Ford made his last Model "T" two years after I was born. Dad and his brothers would often laugh about it being "the farmer's friend" since it could be used as a portable power plant. With rear wheels jacked up and a power takeoff attached, a Ford could saw wood, grind feed and shell corn. It could also plow fields. And after the day's work was done, the family could all load up into the machine and go see a silent movie.

Early tires were of solid rubber. In later ones, the inner tubes had to be patched, and Dad repaired many a tire at Midway. Jacks had to be manually pushed up, and air had to be pumped into tires by hand, too. Bad roads gave Dad lots of business. He served as a mechanic when needed and stocked the parts that frequently wore out, although each car was sold with its own metal toolbox containing tire tools. In low gear, a car could dig its way along through the mud for miles, its radiator steaming and puffing. In winter, the frozen ruts of one lane country roads were hard on cars. They needed a lot of attention after such trips. The Model "T" was called the common man's car and was a unique contributor to the history of transportation.

I wondered why Mother never learned to drive, even in later years when we got newer cars. (Dad always bought Fords.) Perhaps it was because most men told their wives and daughters they could learn to drive when they could change a tire by themselves. I'm glad Dad didn't require that of me when he taught me to drive at age 15.

My parents must have added on to the original building to provide seating space in the lunch room for more customers. They moved the gasoline pumps at a distance from the lunch room and renamed it "Spryncl's."

Midway Inn, tiny though it was, turned out to be a favorite drive-out-for-dinner place for people from Cedar Rapids in the days when not many families ate out. People usually invited friends and relatives to their homes for a meal, and of course did the cooking themselves. They would never have suggested, "Let's meet at a restaurant." But with modern ways fast becoming popular and motor cars taking the place of horses and carriages, it became a pleasant excursion to drive eight miles out of town through the countryside to enjoy the delicious food for which Spryncl's became famous.

Customers liked to take the food they bought in my parents' lunch room and eat it in the fresh air on picnic tables under huge shade trees in an adjoining field. Cows grazed nearby, and the scene was peaceful and typically rural.

According to my childhood recollection and old photos, inside the little eatery was a counter with eight rotating top stools (screwed to the floor by their iron base) in front of the counter. An iron foot rail ran along the floor for the comfort of people who preferred sitting at the counter to eat. A waitress would write their orders on a pad and bring the slip into the kitchen where mother would prepare the food. No "fast food," only food prepared fast. Nothing was started until ordered, so it was hot from the grill.

Two or three wooden tables without table cloths or place mats were arranged to seat four people. Napkins, salt and pepper shakers and sugar bowls were kept in the center of the table. A long glass showcase displayed boxes of candy, gum, mints and the like. An old photo showed O Henry, Milky Way and Hershey candy bars, caramel lolly pops, gum and Life-Savers. Camels and Lucky Strike cigarettes and boxes of unwrapped cigars were on display. Budweiser and Falstaff beer signs were tacked on the walls. Bottles of soft drinks that everyone called "pop" were lined up on the shelves for display, but those the customer ordered were pulled from a refrigerated cooler stocked with ice and replenished daily.

Photos show home baked pies behind sliding glass front shelves, and a chalkboard menu hung behind the counter on the wall. A wooden hall tree stood beside the front screen door entrance, and there were hooks along the wall for customers' coats. Several bare light bulbs hung from the ceiling, and a few other simple shaded ones lit the table area.

The kitchen ran along half of the back of the small building, and the other half was storage area where I was allowed to play with empty boxes and tins to amuse myself when my parents and Baba were busy.

Signs on the windows in old photos advertised soft drinks, cigars, candy, hot coffee, fresh potato chips, chicken sandwiches, chicken noodle soup, tenderloins and hamburgers. "Pop 5 cents" was prominent, always *Hur Mon* brand. Painted on the wooden siding in large lettering was "Barbecue" and "Lunch." Dad built a tall brick barbecue fireplace outside at the left as you faced the front door where he barbecued the ribs and the pork that was used for sandwiches. *Peter Pan* bread was the brand they used exclusively. A piled high barbecue pork or beef sandwich sold for 15 cents, a breaded pork tenderloin cost 20 cents. A hot dog, which we always called a "wiener," was ten cents and so was an egg fixed any way you liked it. Coffee and milk were ten cents, so was a generous size ham sandwich. A three-dip ice cream cone in a variety of flavors was five cents. A metal sign outside read "Ice cold Coca Cola sold here" in characteristic scroll lettering identical to the trademark today. A glass Coke bottle in the still recognized traditional shape was pictured.

Mother made the chicken noodle soup from scratch, including the noodles, and it was famous far and wide. They made potato chips from fresh potatoes and hand-cranked them out in curly-cues with a gadget fastened to the edge of the table. They were deep fried in hot oil daily. Chicken sandwiches were made from freshly killed chickens, since frozen foods were not yet available. Coffee was brewed fresh many times a day and served with heavy cream.

My parents' specialty was pork tenderloin sandwiches. Dad would buy the whole boneless loin and cut it up in rather thin slabs. Mother pounded it with the back of a meat cleaver to tenderize it. She dipped the slices of loin in a batter she made from flour, milk and eggs and then into a specially seasoned breading before frying them. Slices were put into buns or between bread for a sandwich. Some preferred to put catsup on it, others didn't want to spoil the distinctive taste by adding anything. My parents had a large grill stove on which many orders could be prepared at once.

Mother baked the homemade pies far into the night for the next day's customers. Lemon, banana, coconut cream, chocolate, cherry and apple pies were among the customer favorites.

Awnings above all the windows could be cranked back and up when not needed. Bare light bulbs were strung along the roof edge to attract customers at night. Neon lighting was not yet invented. Several trees provided shade between the house and the back of the shop, which was only a few steps from the house.

As the nation tried to struggle out of the Depression years, everyone was having a hard time. At Midway the summers were hot because air-conditioning wasn't invented yet. Circulating table fans whirred constantly. Winters were bitter with frequent blizzards. Dad had to shovel by hand the entire parking lot and the access area by the gas station before any customers could be expected to stop. Snow plows weren't invented yet either.

Dad had a license to sell beer on the premises with the meals and that convenience brought a lot of customers in the early years. During the years of Prohibition, starting about 1930, no beer could be sold, and their customers sharply decreased. When beer was permitted again in 1933, but could only be sold within the city limits, Dad was discouraged and ready to give up the rural location. He felt he couldn't succeed in any business outside of the city limits.

The country as a whole didn't fully recover from the Great Depression for the next decade after its official beginning on October 29, 1929, when the stock market crashed. The East and West coasts and more populated industrial cities felt the dreadful impact first.

Already a thriving city of 50,000, Cedar Rapids was connected to the rest of the country by rail and boasted a small, new airport. Because the economy was based largely on small industries and the production of basic foodstuffs, the Depression didn't affect our town until a couple of years later. That probably accounts for my parents to have fortunately purchased their little dream homes in 1930.

I was only four when the Depression occurred and didn't realize how much Dad was affected by his financial reverses. Mother confessed to me in later years that perhaps he never fully got over that trauma.

Dad was nearly 40 at the time of the Depression. Although he continued to work hard, he never regained the momentum of business success he seemed headed for in his early years. During my childhood years and into my high school years, my parents managed a succession of small restaurants in the city. Mother always worked long hours at Dad's side doing most of the cooking. Later she got jobs in other restaurants to add to the family income. He kept changing locations with the hope that his ventures might finally take off. But they never seemed to. His continued business failures were a great personal disillusionment for him. He had come to the New World of America in his late teens full of idealism and grand dreams of success. Most immigrants were told that anyone could do anything or be anything he wanted, if he worked hard. It didn't work that way for Dad.

Eventually, Dad even tried his hand at the tavern business, which he disliked intensely because of the rude and rowdy clientele and late hours, but he had no experience other than food service. As time went on, Dad seemed to give up and put aside his earlier dreams and ambitions of owning a business. He settled for somehow just making ends meet and taking care of his family as best he could.

As long as I can remember, Dad and Mother had a simple, and I presume workable, budget system. In Dad's desk they kept about a dozen long envelopes labeled groceries, gas bill, light bill, phone, clothing, gasoline, Dad's pocket money, etc. When Dad brought home his slim pay check, he had already converted it to small bills. They divided all the cash into the envelopes in whatever amount they previously decided was necessary, and they limited their spending until the next pay day. They did have one envelope labeled "Emergency," but it was usually empty by the next pay period. There was no such thing as credit cards to tempt them. I don't think they even had a check book in those days. All transactions were in cash. They certainly wouldn't have dreamed of borrowing money from the bank. They lived on what Dad earned.

Their lean budget must have been a large factor in limiting our family from taking vacations. I remember only twice in the 17 years I lived at home that our family took what you could call a vacation. Once we went on a two-day trip to Wisconsin Dells, and the other time to Chicago for the 1933 World's Fair when I was eight. Dad went fishing on Sundays mostly by himself to unwind after the stress of his job all week. There were occasional weekend picnics and get-togethers with relatives, but my parents never seemed to be in a financial position to take off from work to go anywhere. In those days, vacations were not the "urgency" for ordinary people that they seem to be now.

9

New Experiences in the City

The new little house my parents purchased in Cedar Rapids just before the Great Depression was nevertheless a tangible and satisfying symbol of my parents' early success. It was a brick, two-bedroom house at 935 26th Street, Southeast. An old deed lists $5,500 as the total price for their newly built house and lot. They paid cash. That was my happy home from the age of five until I left for college. The following is a slice of life from the early thirties to stir similar memories in those who lived through such days and perhaps cause modern, young readers to wonder at such simple times.

I remember that during the first year we lived there, many friends and relatives came to visit us, and each time, my parents followed the ritual of "showing them through" so they could see what a modern place we had. Quite an upward move from the drafty, old farmhouse. Not only did it have electricity, but central heat, city water, indoor plumbing, two bedrooms with a modern bathroom between—a bathroom with *lavender tub and washbasin and toilet!* That, apparently, was the ultimate in those days—to have color tinted fixtures. Mother and Dad's bedroom had an alcove where the new vanity fit. They bought almost all new furniture just before the banks crashed.

There was a modest size dining room with a table that had three big leaves to add when we needed more seating space at holiday times. The small living room had a real fireplace and on the mantel Dad placed a new clock that chimed not only the hours but every quarter hour throughout the day and night. Baba's job was to wind it daily, a happy task she never forgot each night before climbing into bed. My parents bought new carpets for each room, not the installed wall to wall kind, which were not in style yet, but those that covered most of floor. In the spring and fall the furniture was moved aside, the carpets and rugs were rolled up, taken outdoors and hung over clotheslines. Baba, Dad and Mother would take turns beating the dust out of them by whacking them with a large, looped, wire carpet beater with a handle.

We had a modern kitchen with a new Roper gas stove and an "ice box" placed on a platform near the side door, so the ice man could deliver cakes of ice without walking through the kitchen. Dad asked the carpenter to add on what they called "a summer kitchen" adjoining the main kitchen toward the back of the house. That room was unheated, but in the summer it was a pleasant place to do ironing and other chores.

We had a full, unfinished basement and a monster coal burning furnace with big ducts leading into the ceiling like outstretched arms that connected to the heating registers in each room on the main floor. There was a separate room called a coal bin along the wall toward the driveway from which Dad shoveled out coal early each winter morning and each night before bedtime. There was a high window near the wall of the bin that opened out to the driveway. The coal truck delivered several tons of coal at one time, letting it slide down a coal chute directly into the coal bin.

Mother made sure the carpenter built a "cold cellar" like a large closet along one wall underneath the ground level where home canned goods in jars were kept. Throughout the summer and early fall, Mother and Baba would harvest our garden and buy produce in season from the city market. Certain mornings of the week, farmers brought their fresh fruits and vegetables to market, and housewives would buy in quantity to put up for the winter. When cucumbers were plentiful, they filled many pint and quart jars with dill pickles, bread-and-butter pickles and "chunk" pickles. The aroma of vinegar, bay leaf, cloves, dill and other spices lingered in the kitchen for days. Mother had a large canning kettle with a wire rack that held about eight quarts at a time. She would can tomatoes, beans, peas, carrots, corn and beets. She used Mason jars with glass lids and rubber rings in the early days. Later, when she used metal lids, we would listen for the ping! as they sealed after canning. If a jar didn't seal, it was considered unsafe and the contents discarded. It was such a pretty sight to see the glass jars with their multi-colored contents all lined up on shelves assuring abundant winter eating.

Some things weren't canned but kept in the root cellar. There was a special bin for potatoes. Onions were hung from the ceiling in string bags. Parsnips, beets, carrots, turnips, squash, pumpkins and heads of cabbage were stored loose for the winter.

Ordinarily the basement was a nice place to play, but on Mondays, Mother took over the basement. Every Monday was laundry day. All around our neighborhood housewives strung clotheslines from metal hooks either screwed into the backs of their houses or garages or from steel "T" poles imbedded in cement. Our clotheslines were wire. You could look through the back yards from one end of our block to the other and see nearly identical collections of laundry: flat white sheets, towels, dress shirts, children's clothing and nightclothes.

Some of the ladies seemed to be in friendly competition to see who could have her wash on the line first. I believe some must have hung their duds out by the light of the moon before they went to bed. How else could their immaculate laundry have been shamelessly waving at daybreak?

Even before I went to kindergarten, I helped my mother. The double metal tubs stood ready to fill with hot water from a black hose connected to the faucet. Mother would wheel over her new Maytag electric washer on its castered legs, and plug the cord into a socket near the shower faucets on the wall. She filled the washer drum with steaming hot water. When we first moved to the city, Baba still made her own lye soap and still went the extra mile to boil the whites in a big vat on an old double burner gas cook stove in our basement. She'd occasionally punch the clothes up and down with a wooden dowel. The lye solution was hard on the hands and eyes but tough on dirt. The steam from the soapy water tickled my nose. Mother used Fels Naptha soap, later Duz detergent from the grocery store because each new box had a pretty cup, saucer or dish tucked inside as a special premium.

We had a little door in the wall of our main floor bathroom into which we stuffed our dirty clothes during the week. They would fall down a wooden clothes chute to the basement. On laundry days, Mother let me open the lower chute door and let the clothes tumble down into the basement into a clothes basket at the bottom. She taught me to sort them carefully into colored and white piles.

I helped her load the whites into the hot suds and used a long wooden dowel to push them under the surface. Mother started the agitator which beat so hard that the Maytag would move around the basement, until Dad figured a way to stabilize it with wooden blocks. Splashed water would flow down the drain in the cement floor. After the timer on the washer went "ding," mother used the wooden dowel to pull out each piece of laundry. Taking one corner, she fed it into the automatic wringer. The soapy water fell back into the washer, and the flattened piece of laundry emerged on the other side. My job was to catch the clothes coming out of the wringer. I had to be careful not to get my fingers caught. I dropped the clothes into the first metal tub of scalding water and swished them around with the dowel to get the soap out.

Mother moved the wringer between the two laundry tubs and followed the same procedure to transfer the clothes from the first tub into the cold rinse water tub. For whites, bluing was added to the final rinse. Then she put them through the wringer for a third time, and they fell into baskets ready on the floor.

For such things as Dad's shirts and white blouses that had to be crisp when ironed, there was another rinse with Argo starch or Satina rinse to help the iron glide smoothly.

After each load, Mother carried the clothes basket up the stairs and out into the back yard. She took a hot, wet rag and ran it over our four wire clotheslines. A bag of wooden clothespins hung ready for us to pin up the clothes, which we had to shake out because they were flat. Towels first, sheets on the outside lines and underwear on inside lines, so the items wouldn't embarrass us before the neighbors. When the lines became too heavy, we'd prop them up with wooden poles on the end of which Dad had fastened a bent nail to catch the line. Dish towels, wash cloths and small items I would spread out on the grass.

Folding the dry clothes was fun for me in the beginning, but got to be a chore as years went by. To crawl into bed on Monday night between crisp sheets scented with breezes and sunshine was a pleasant sensory experience. Mother laundered all bed linens weekly because we had only one set per bed. Towels dried stiff and scratchy but absorbed well. We never lost one sock from a pair as people claim they do now with automatic washers and dryers.

When the first snowflakes appeared or it was obvious that

the wet clothes on the line were freezing so stiff they could stand up by themselves, Mother announced it was time to start hanging the clothes on lines in the basement where they took much longer to dry.

I gave the details above to motivate the reader to be incredibly thankful for our labor-saving appliances today!

We had an unfinished attic full of stored things. Trunks, seasonal clothes, all kinds of interesting things. When I got a little older and somewhat over my fear of attics, I spent many hours rummaging in boxes and discovering old photos, a dress form, hat boxes with "antique hats" from my mother's single days, mementos of my mother's early life and of Dad's army days—including his old uniform which fascinated me. There was an immense old sea chest with a rounded top and steel bands around it. Inside were compartments and drawers. Dad told me he used it to ship to America everything he owned in the Old Country.

I found an old zither, a lap musical instrument with 40 or so strings stretched over a flat, guitar-like sounding box. No one seemed to know anything about it or knew how to play it. I had fun just strumming on it. I wish I had kept it because it would be an antique now.

We had a modest size lawn in the back and another in the front that we had to mow with a hand push mower. Dad spaded half of the back yard for Baba's garden of vegetables and flowers. Each year as Baba got older and her strength declined, Dad spaded a little less space for her to garden and seeded more in lawn so she wouldn't overdo. She spent much time watering with a garden hose now. She didn't have to carry buckets of water from a pump as she did when we lived in the country, because we were tapped into city water and sewage. Plastic garbage bags had not been invented, so we burned trash in a sort of brick fireplace in the back yard. We made a compost pile for garbage.

Our single car garage was just big enough for Dad's 1928

Hupmobile, quite a step up from his first "Tin Lizzy." Dad built a workbench along one inside wall of the garage for his handyman tools. Our garage had enough space for my tricycle and later my two-wheeler.

Because our small new house had only two bedrooms, Baba and I slept together in a double bed from the time I was a baby until I was about 13 years old. In the winter, we would snuggle under her homemade feather comforter called a "pezova deka." In the hot summer, there was no air conditioning, and in the early days we only had one electric fan. I recall Baba fanning me on hot nights with one of the cardboard "funeral fans" with a stick handle, commonly used in churches. One side was printed with advertising from a local funeral home and the other side had a Bible scene in color.

Baba made the feather comforter at one of the feather-stripping gatherings of family, relatives and friends from Czechoslovakia. Such parties were at least an annual event during my early childhood. Czech women learned the craft in the Old Country. If there was a forthcoming wedding, the bride's mother would traditionally provide the new bride and groom with a down featherbed and pillows. A featherbed is a huge pillow-like cover over the entire bed. It was warm and cozy in a day when many folks slept in unheated bedrooms. Families saved, washed and dried goose and duck feathers each time they roasted a goose, the traditional Czech holiday entree. Then the women gathered at one or another of their homes to strip away the soft, fluffy parts from the center core or quill of the feathers. The soft feathers were divided among the ladies who worked on them. Usually the stripping bee took place in the kitchen because early kitchens, especially farm kitchens, were large with a long table.

Baba took me along to those "drachky " (feather stripping) parties commonly held in the winter. Because I was shy about playing with other children, I stuck close to her and looked

93

at a picture book or just listened to the merry chatter of the women. This was a social event for them where they exchanged gossip, talked about nostalgic times in the Old Country and swapped recipes or some advice for a home remedy. Always the fragrance of coffee brewing filled the air as pot after pot was consumed with the ever-present "kolaches" (traditional round, open-faced, fruit-filled yeast pastry) or yummy apple strudel.

Sometimes the ladies laughed until they sneezed—it was more cause for laughter when the feathers from the individual piles took off across the room in every direction. Usually, however, they put the stripped feathers under big overturned bowls or dish pans to prevent sneezing catastrophes. When the bowls were full, the hostess came around with a large flour bag to collect the feathers. Most of the women wore dusting caps to keep the fine downy feathers out of their hair. In fact, both my grandmothers wore such caps most of the time at home, a carry-over custom from the Old Country. For Baba, who had sparse hair, a cap was a necessity.

Pillows and comforters stuffed with such feathers lasted a lifetime. A business in town had special equipment to wash and dry the feathers, restore them to like-new condition and replace the ticking. They were handed down as heirlooms from generation to generation.

On my later trips to Czechoslovakia, I found that feather-beds are still almost universally used. In the early morning you see them being aired on balconies of high rise apartments. They are sometimes stitched in squares to prevent the feathers from shifting, although I experienced sleeping under some without stitching. In the middle of the night, you found the feathers all bunched up at one end and none keeping you warm! You had to get up and shake the comforter to redistribute the feathers.

Even Czech people who lived in town would raise two or three geese every year in preparation for holidays. Geese were preferred to turkey. Everything from the goose was put to use. Women caught blood from the goose to cook with onions and caraway seed as a sandwich filling, to make blood pudding or for use in other recipes. The lard from the goose was used for cooking, and grease was smeared on the chest of someone with chest cold. Often when I had a cough, Baba would rub me with it, and then cover my chest with a flannel cloth before she dressed me in my warm nightgown and tucked me into bed.

The largest feathers from the goose were only partially stripped for the soft, downy part, but some of the flaring top feathers were left on. Eight or more of the heavier ones were stitched or woven together with heavy thread and made into "perotky" or pastry brushes. They were used to baste a roast, grease the tops of pastries and the like.

One of the first things Baba asked my dad to make when we moved into the new house was a long, wooden flower box attached to the house under the front windows. She and Mother never failed to plant red and pink geraniums and petunias in that outdoor box year after year. My mother continued the tradition until her death. (You see such flower boxes at the windows all over Czechoslovakia today.) When I visit my hometown and drive by our brick home, the box is no longer there. I miss it. The present owners (the house has sold and resold many times since my parents died) may not have time to care for flowers.

Baba put my dad to work bringing top soil to plant flowers in areas along the house at the sides of the driveway. Her favorites were multicolored petunias, marigolds, "zeleznacki" (moss roses) and tall hollyhocks—pink and red and white. I can never see a hollyhock without thinking of Baba.

She took me by the hand in the early morning when the dew was still on the grass, led me to the flower borders and reminded me that we should say "dobre jitro" (good morning) to the "kvetiny" (flowers). I would stoop down and nuzzle my face into the sweet smelling, wet blossoms and laugh with delight. Baba's evening custom was to take her galvanized tin watering can, fill it from the faucet at the side of the house and dutifully water each plant after the sun went down in the hot summer. When we moved into the new house, Baba bought me a small, brightly decorated, tin watering can from the dime store, so I could join her in the evening ritual.

Then we sat on the back step of the porch to watch the sun set and count the stars as they came out. Baba wanted to be sure I remembered how to count in Czech, but my childish tongue got all mixed up on the higher numbers. When it got chilly, I sat on her lap and she wrapped a shawl around my shoulders, as I snuggled against her. "Babo, tell me a "povidka" (story) from when you were little," I would beg in Czech. Baba had a memory full of stories from the Old Country.

Often I asked for the one about the "Kozlatka a vlk" (The Kids and the Wolf). A wolf was prominent in many Czech stories, as it is in some American folk tales. In Czech, Baba would tell me, with lots of sound effects and change of voice for each character:

"Once upon a time, a mother goat had seven kids (baby goats) and they all looked alike. Whenever she went into the woods to work, she told them, 'Dear children, beware of the wolf. Don't let him in the house or there will be trouble.' Then she put the basket on her back, took the rake in her hand and went off to the woods to work.

"After a while, the wolf arrived at the house. He had seen the mother goat leave. He knocked on the door and called out, 'Open, open, little ones! Mother has returned from the woods.'

"The kids knew that the deep, rough voice was not their mother's. 'Our "maminka" (mother) doesn't have that kind of voice. We won't open the door.'

"After a while, the wolf knocked again. This time he spoke in a softer voice. 'Open, open, little ones! Mother is back from the woods now.'

"This time the kids looked through the window of the door. They saw two black legs. 'Ah! Maminka doesn't have black legs.' They didn't open the door this time either.

"As soon as the wolf heard that, he dashed away to the mill. He jumped into the flour bin to whiten his legs. At once he returned to the house and lifted his legs to the window at the door. In a high voice he called, 'Open, open, little ones! Mother is back from the woods.'

"When the kids saw the white legs and heard the high voice, they really thought their mother was home this time. They opened the door—and—the wolf leaped into the room. Oh! How frightened the unhappy kids were when they found they had been fooled. It wasn't their maminka. It was the wolf!

"Quickly all of them ran to hide. One crawled into bed, and one went under the bed. One hid under the table. One ran behind the stove, and another crawled under the stove. Still another jumped on top of the cupboard. The last one crawled into the oven. (I was always astonished at that!) However, the wolf found all of them and swallowed each one. Then he went into the garden and fell fast asleep under a tree.

"In about an hour, the mother goat came out of the woods. When she saw the open gate by the house and found the house empty, she knew something terrible had happened. She searched for her beloved kids. She looked into every corner. She searched all over the place but didn't find even one of her seven little kids. When she called, not one voice answered.

"She ran out into the garden and there—she saw the wolf fast asleep under the tree. He was snoring so hard that the leaves on the tree were shaking. (I would want to add the snoring noises when Baba came to that point in the story.) On tiptoe she walked to the side of the wolf. What was that moving inside the wolf's stomach? She knew at once that her kids were inside the wolf!

She was happy, too, because she knew they must be alive since they were kicking.

"Mother goat hurried into the house for a pair of scissors. While the wolf was in deep sleep, she slit open his stomach. Out jumped her seven little kids, alive and happy! They all got busy collecting rocks to put into the wolf's stomach. Then mother goat sewed up the cut. (The implausibility of all this never bothered me at that early age!)

"At last the wolf woke up. He felt so thirsty. He got to his feet and started to walk over to the well. Hardly had he taken a step when the big stones in his stomach began to roll around. He said to himself, 'What is knocking in my stomach? I did eat some kids, and now I must have indigestion.'

"He crawled over to the top of the well and leaned over to get a drink. This made the stones roll forward into his chest. He lost his balance and tumbled into the well. There he drowned.

"Maminka goat and her seven little kids were very glad that the old wolf could never bother them again. They made a circle by holding hands and they "tancily okolo" (danced around) the well, singing merry songs."

Then Baba and I would laugh, jump up and join hands and "tancily okolo" until we were out of breath.

From the time I was a toddler, Baba let me help her gather seeds from the dry hollyhocks and other annual flowers to save for next year's planting. We put them in used envelopes that Baba retrieved from my dad's wastebasket, and she wrote the Czech names of the flowers on them. She kept the packets in the deep drawers of her heavy oak bureau in our bedroom, under her neatly folded clothing.

She often kept a "jablko" (apple) tucked in among her clothing to "fragrance" them. It was long before the days of aerosol sprays and all those unnatural chemical room deodorizers. The fragrance of a ripening apple stirs my memory.

On her bureau, Baba kept her button box. I was fascinated by the bright colored glass and shiny silver, gold, brass and pearl buttons. I must have played with the buttons as much as I did with other store bought toys. Every thrifty homemaker had a button box. Ladies would cut buttons off worn and outdated clothing and save them for homemade dresses and shirts or to replace lost buttons. When I was about five, Baba gave me a large blunt needle and allowed me to pick out the most colorful buttons to make a string necklace. Today there are even Button Clubs and books on the history of buttons. I understand there are more than 50,000 button collectors. Buttons go back to 2,500 B.C. when primitive people used them as money and to ward off evil. For me, they simply provided hours of fun.

Baba, along with my mother and some other relatives, skillfully sewed quilts in beautiful patterns. They saved pieces of cloth from old aprons, dresses, shirts and even trousers. They also bought new material by the yard, sharing the different piece goods with each other to cut into the triangles, stars, octagons, hexagons and other shapes that went into the making of a crazy quilt. Baba made a special full size quilt for me in lavender designs, my favorite color since I was a child. That quilt and other embroidered linens were stored in my new "Hope Chest" made of fragrant cedar. Supposedly, the accumulated contents of this chest and the chest itself was prepared for the day I would get married. That certainly seemed far away to an eight year old girl. When I grew up and did get married and moved many times across the country and across the world, I took that quilt along and used it until it actually wore out. It was always a reminder of the loving care Baba had invested to make it for me.

At times when I was sick from one thing or another, Baba made a favorite "comfort food" for me that I still associate with not feeling well. She would toast a slice of bread, butter it, cut it into bite size pieces, pour hot milk over it, then add a dash of cinnamon and sugar. That was sure to stay down and calm a queasy stomach. If any family member became really ill, the doctor actually made a house call within a few hours, arriving with everything he needed for the patient in his black bag. The first thing I wanted to do whenever I was sick was to climb into Dad and Mother's double bed. There I surrounded myself with favorite books, lots of pillows and the comfort of my pet dog by my side. I knew Baba or Mother would serve me my meals in bed, and I could stay home from school.

Baba saved string and wound it into an ever larger ball. She saved all birthday cards, Christmas cards, gift wraps and ribbons in her bureau drawers. Anything can be used again, she would say, and you never know when you will need something and there it will be. She especially saved aluminum foil from Hershey chocolate bars. Foil had just been invented and was scarce. No one dreamed that someday we could buy it in rolls. Baba made pretty pictures with bits of foil, coloring parts of it with paint, making flower designs or scenery and putting them behind glass in a frame.

Because the house was still in process of building when my parents signed the contract to buy it, they knew the Czech carpenter pretty well. He asked whether he could make something for Baba. She said she would like two things: a low wooden stool to sit on and a wooden cutting board for the kitchen. He made both. He drilled some holes in the center of the stool so Baba could carry it. He made the bread cutting board in the shape of a pig—I kept it to this day.

In the fall, my parents and Baba and I all went nutting. Some relatives joined us when we went to the private woods of our relatives in the country. From experience, they knew the areas where nut trees grew wild. We gathered hickory nuts, walnuts, hazelnuts and chestnuts. Baba would spread them on newspapers in our attic to dry thoroughly. In the winter, before the holiday season, she would crack nuts to use in baking Czech goodies.

She asked Dad to find her just the right kind of very hard rock, one with a slight indentation along the top, on which she could lay the nut without having it roll off. She had a special hammer to crack nuts. Dad did find exactly the right big stone after much searching in rock piles. Baba kept it in the basement near the bottom step where she would sit and crack nuts. I was with her, of course, sampling the best of the nut meats. One for me, one for the nut jar, one for me..., etc. When I became more coordinated, Baba taught me exactly how to tap the nut carefully so the nut meat would come out in wholes or halves and how to use the nut pick.

Hunting mushrooms is a Czech tradition, more than a hobby, and continued among the Czech immigrants, including our family. You had to know exactly when to go looking for them because mushrooms have a short growing period of a few weeks. Certain ones only grow in the spring, others in late summer or late fall. A good time to hunt is when the woods are steamy on warm days following a rain. You have to know where to look in a particular section of the woods. If you can find an undergrowth with moss, you can usually find a special kind of mushroom.

In Iowa, popular varieties are morels with round or conical heads and sort of large pock marks all over them, the rooster comb variety, and the parasol or grass mushrooms. Another likely place is in thickly carpeted woods of mixed oak, aspen, elm, and maple. Certain ones can only be found near birch trees, others where the ground is covered with decaying leaves and crumbling logs. Some, like "kozibrada" (goat's beard), are a large, edible fungus found right on trees.

Baba taught me that it was important to behave properly in the woods and respect the environment and wildlife. I was told not to scare animals and birds. I was not to kick out mushrooms that I chose not to pick but leave them for someone else. She told me to pick only those she definitely recognized. Baba used to say "All mushrooms are edible—*but some only once!*" Some lookalikes are poisonous and one has to know the difference. To avoid breaking the spawn in which they grow, she showed me how to carefully pick them and then cover over the little hollow where they grew. I shouldn't throw them in the basket or stifle them in a bag but gently place them there.

As soon as we returned home, they had to be cleaned and sliced to separate possible worm eaten parts. Mushrooms are full of water and become moldy quickly, so Baba dried them by spreading them loosely on window screens Dad laid flat on the floor for winter storage in our attic. Baba and Mother canned or pickled some. It was before the days of frozen foods. Fresh mushrooms, especially the little "buttons" or morels, sauted lightly in butter, scrambled with eggs, salted and peppered are a tasty delight.

Baba was apparently a literate woman. She read everything in Czech she could get her hands on, though there was little available. There were no Czech libraries in our hometown at the time. Immigrants had access only to the books they brought from their homeland. She subscribed to a weekly or monthly newspaper in Czech called "Krestanski Listy," a Christian journal, which she read from cover to cover as soon as each issue arrived. I treasure several of her books in my library, among the very few things I have as memories of her. Besides her big black Czech Bible, I have kept her prayer book and hymn book along with several small story books she read over and over to me.

If I recall correctly, Baba said that her maiden name "Plachy" could also be pronounced and spelled "Palacky" and that she had some well-known ancestors. That was why her parents named her Frantiska, why she named my dad Frank or Frantisek, and why "Frances" is one of the names that our family has passed down to many of us, including my middle name. In researching my heritage in later years, I wonder if it is possible she was descended from Frantisek Palacky, also from Moravia, 1798-1876. He was a famous educator, writer, editor of the journal of the Bohemian Museum. He compiled the history of the Czech nation in Bohemia and Moravia in five volumes. Apparently he was active politically, well-known in the Empire, chairman of the 1848 Prague Slavic Congress and a deputy in the Reichsrat. I wish I had asked Baba. Of one thing I am certain, Baba must have come from a well-educated though poor family. I have no way to verify her ancestry, but it may be that I inherited my inclination toward writing from this illustrious ancestor through Baba's blood line.

Baba liked to read even late into the night. To do so, she would go into the kitchen, close the door so she wouldn't disturb anyone, and read her books by the light of an old goose neck lamp. Sometimes I would hear her get up and I would tiptoe into the kitchen after her. She permitted me to stay awhile and sit on her lap as she read aloud to me. I loved to listen to the gentle sound of her voice, even though I didn't understand the big words. When I got drowsy, she led me back to our bedroom and tucked me in.

As a very young child, I remember being impressed with the colored illustrations in one of her books that showed people wearing costumes of other lands. I was fascinated with it and asked Baba many questions. Why do they all dress differently? What are "countries?" Do the people speak the same as we do? How far away are other countries? Do they all have little children? Baba was patient to answer my questions at my level. She said the story was about certain people who knew God and went to other countries to tell people about Him because those people never heard of God.

I remember her saying, "Someday, Leonko, perhaps you will go to many different countries and see people who dress differently, and you will have many new adventures. Maybe you will

103

tell the people about God, too." I could not imagine such a thing at the time, but in the providence of God, what Baba said came to pass. Her words were prophetic. I have had the privilege of traveling, living and working for God in many different lands—yes, where they wear different costumes and speak different languages.

10

My Widening World

Although I was already five when we moved to the city, I really didn't know how to play with other children because I spent my early years mostly around adults. I remember my mother asking June, a somewhat older girl (all of 11 years old) who lived two houses away, "Please teach Leona how to play with other children." June took me under her wing and introduced me to the give and take of neighborhood kid relationships. I trailed her around watching how she interacted with other kids and picked up on her interests. She subscribed to a children's magazine, *Wee Wisdom*, from which she would read stories to me and explain things. She showed me how to play tunes on her piano with one finger.

My first "city friend" after we moved to 26th Street was Dorothy, who was a year younger. We spent most of our next few years calling each other best friends. She lived "catty-corner" across the street in a big white house with a spacious front porch. A wide, wooden swing hung by chains from the ceiling of the porch where we spent much time talking and playing games.

"Dot," as I called her, went faithfully with her parents to the Catholic church. Our family, except for Baba, didn't go to any church. My parents never allowed me to go to church with Dot but never explained why. I was permitted to go with her to the annual ice cream socials held at her church, St. Wenceslaus. Lights were strung overhead on the parking lot at the side of the church. Card tables covered with oil cloths were set up with folding chairs around them, and tickets were sold in advance for dishes of ice cream and cake. We always looked forward to the socials, and on those occasions I usually stayed overnight at Dot's house.

Dot was an only child, too. Not having siblings, we had to find our friends outside our family circle. We stayed overnight at each other's homes a lot. We didn't have group slumber parties like girls do now, but it was common practice among kids we knew to stay over night with good friends. Sometimes we had supper with each other's family, then the whole evening stretched ahead of us for fun and games and reading until it was bedtime. Pajama clad, we would jump into the double bed, and talk and talk and talk until one or the other wouldn't answer because sleep overcame her. It was a game to see who could outlast the other in resisting the sandman.

In our younger years, we played with dolls and eventually learned to make doll clothes. Dot was really good at it, but I had to learn from her even how to thread a needle. We would beg scraps of cloth from our mothers or from Baba and sew outfits for our dolls. We pretended shoe boxes were doll beds and pretty scraps of cloth were blankets. Some of that activity we did in Dot's attic. She had a "friendly" attic that didn't scare me, probably because Dot and I were there together. We played many games in our private attic playroom.

Dot and I had vivid imaginations. We often acted out dramas and made up our own characters and plots. She would play one person's part, I would play another. And in voices that suited the characters, we would wing it. Sometimes we made up additional "episodes" of some of the serial stories which were aired on the radio, similar to our TV soap operas. "Gail and Dan" were a favorite character couple on the radio, and we got them in and out of a lot of predicaments that the writers of the series would never have dreamed of.

As soon as I was able to read, books became my close companions. I read a book over and over, enjoying it as much the sixth time as the first. We were children in the era of the "Big-Little" books—cheap kids' books about 1 ½ to 2 inches thick and about 5 by 6 inches in size. Some had cartoon type plots, some were early Disney characters, pirates, mad inventors and Buck Rogers science-fiction. Those were great for trading with our friends. We'd sit on Dot's porch swing or under our apple tree in the back yard reading them independently or to each other.

I had a young aunt Margaret who gave me nothing but books for Christmas and birthdays when often I would rather have received toys. But hers was a long-term investment in me. She was a country school teacher who knew the value of good reading. I am indebted to her for starting me on a lifetime of reading by stimulating my imagination and appreciation of literature, ultimately becoming an author myself.

I accumulated entire sets of "The Curly Tops," "The Bobbsey Twins" and other series of children's books. A few years later, Dot and I read the "Elsie Dinsmore" series that she collected. Still later, there were mystery books featuring Nancy Drew, a girl detective, and in my teens, the Grace Livingstone Hill novels which have even made a comeback today. I read anything and everything I could lay my hands on. I always borrowed the limit of books from the school library. I don't recall using the public library during my elementary school years, but I did during my teens. Books took me to faraway lands, opened new horizons for me, introduced me to new people and places. Among my friends, we loaned books back and forth.

One Christmas when I was seven, Aunt Margaret gave me the thick, illustrated volume of Stevenson's *A Child's Garden of Verses*. It sparked into flame a desire to write poetry. I memorized many poems effortlessly because of their singsong format and my repeated reading. I recited poems while pumping up on my rope swing under our old apple tree in the back yard.

After I saved enough nickels and dimes to buy the paper-back edition of *One Hundred and One Famous Poems*, Wordsworth, Longfellow, Byron and Dickinson became my friends. My favorite card game was "Authors." Poets' portraits and their literary works were pictured on the playing cards. *The Cedar Rapids Gazette* published Edgar Guest's whimsical poetry. I devoured his books on folksy topics which I understood more easily than the more obscure themes of the classic poets. I can recite his poem, *Myself*, to this day:

> I have to live with myself and so
> I want to be fit for myself to know;
> I want to be able as days go by
> always to look myself straight in the eye....

Our family was not inclined toward literary pursuits. I don't remember Mother ever reading a book or Dad either. The most they had time to read after hard days of work was the newspaper. My beloved live-in grandmother Baba, however, loved poetry in her own language. She taught me to recite a few traditional Czech poems which I still remember.

Before long, I tried to write my own poems. Because I was so shy, I never let anyone see them. None of my classmates wrote poems, and I was afraid of being teased. I thought the other children would call me the equivalent of a "nerd" in today's slang. I longed to meet a live poet who wrote about ideas in my world.

I hid my "collected words" in a musty suitcase in our attic. When I reached my teens, I decided to burn all my childhood poems in a ritual of relinquishment because, to my newly grown up mind, they were too juvenile. Nevertheless, I couldn't keep from writing poetry because it bubbled up from somewhere inside. I found it more natural to express my emotions in poetry than prose. I was excited when we started to study poetry in a high school literature class. But when my interpretation of some classic poem differed from the teacher's explanation, she told me it was "wrong," and I felt humiliated. I wondered how she could really know what the poet meant. Her remark kept me hiding my poetry efforts so that no one would criticize them. I was afraid to expose my inner thoughts and show my vulnerability.

Newspapers were delivered by "the paper boy" who carried them in a big canvas bag on the front of his bicycle. He would roll his own papers, tuck in the pages against the wind and ride along the street giving them a heave toward everyone's front porch. Sometimes he missed and we'd have to search in the evergreen bushes. Most of the time the paper hit the front door with a thud, my signal to run out and get the *Cedar Rapids Gazette*. Once every week the boy would come around in the evening to collect the money from his customers. He only wanted one week's pay at a time and with his paper punch he made a hole signifying "Paid" on the card we always kept on the fireplace mantle. My mother kept change in a jar beside it to pay the boy in coins.

On Sundays, the newspaper was thicker and included colored comic strips we called "funny papers." It came early in the morning, not in the evening like the daily paper. I'd grab the funny papers before my parents were awake, spread them out on the living room floor, and after I learned to read, read absolutely every comic strip. Among my favorite comic strip characters were the Katzenjammer Kids, Buck Rogers, Happy Hooligan, Joe Palooka, Popeye, Blondie and Dick Tracy. I particularly liked Alley Oop, Tarzan, Maggie and Jiggs and antics of the bald kid named Henry.

Children who couldn't read yet tuned to our local radio station KWCR, broadcasting from the fifth floor of the Paramount building, to hear a nice person reading "the funnies" aloud strip by strip. Our parents could sleep in without being bugged to read the comics to us. That was a terrific way to learn new words. The reader also explained what was going on in case we didn't understand the reason for the actions or words of the characters. He or she used different voice ranges for each character, and we let our imaginations carry us along. My older cousin, LaVerna, was one of the readers.

In the weekday *Gazette,* I would look for the children's corner on the comic page called "Tales of Uncle Wiggley." He was a smart rabbit dressed in a suit who had many very human-like adventures with his rabbit family and woodland friends. Before I could read, Mother or Dad would read Uncle Wiggley's stories to me.

When I was six, Dad and mother gave me a little roll-top desk and chair, which I have now passed on to my grandchildren. From the time I was a toddler, I loved to sit at Dad's big desk in the gas station and "pretend-write" on scraps of paper he would supply for me from old invoices or order blanks. I loved to sharpen pencils in his hand-cranked sharpener screwed to the wall (which my eldest son Rick still has) from Sanford's Stationery Store. When Baba couldn't find me, she knew I would be at Dad's desk "doing work."

I was thrilled with my new "real desk," its cubby holes for my "important things," and its one drawer. Dad put it in the corner of our living room, a tall lamp beside it and bought me my own early model radio. I had favorite late afternoon and dinner hour children's programs, and usually got my way to eat my dinner at my desk. Being an only child, I got away with a lot. I would generally stamp my feet and pout until I got anything I wanted.

Among my favorite programs were The Singing Lady, Jimmie Allen, The Aldrich Family, Jack Armstrong and Little Orphan Annie. I begged mother to buy Ovaltine (which extra nourishment I certainly didn't need to build up my already chubby body) because I needed to send in the inner foil seal with a letter and 25 cents to get a decoder badge or special code ring. Each night the announcer gave some clue as to what was going to happen in the next episode by spelling the words using numbers. Only those "in the secret circle" who had the decoder ring would be able to decipher the hidden message.

Other programs our family listened to were Jack Benny, Eddie Cantor, Charlie Chan, Amos and Andy (Dad's favorite), George Burns and Gracie Allen and Paul Whitman. One Man's Family was a Sunday night tradition. Then there was Fibber McGee and Molly, the Lux Radio Theater and the very scary mystery shows, The Shadow and The Green Hornet.

Our very first radio was like a large, rectangular metal box with dials in the front and headphones which meant that only one person at a time could listen. The next model had a big horn speaker above it. I think it was an Atwater Kent with tubes that I liked to see light up and glow in the open back of the cabinet. You had to adjust the sensitive dials on the front very carefully to dim the *whee* and *whoo* whining noises and tune the crackling static down to a minimum.

Later we had a wooden "Cathedral" tabletop radio and still later Dad got a really big, fancy console model as high as his shoulders with doors that closed like a cabinet to hide its controls. It was extra special because it had an electric phonograph on top, revealed only when you lifted the lid. Our first phonograph had been the hand crank style, and this was a great leap forward. Our Uncle Frank in Chicago worked at the company that made them. Although it must have cost quite a bit, Dad probably got a good deal through his connections.

We had only a few 78 rpm records—a few waltzes, some Czech polkas and a few of Dad's favorite songs. He said he would pay me a whole dime if I memorized all the words. One was "There's an Old Apple Tree in the Orchard." I did, and he was good to his promise. Another of his favorites was "The Big Rock Candy Mountain." Two other classics were Czech records with singing and recitations in two voices called "Dedecek and Babicka" (Grandpa and Grandma) on which the two carried on a comical domestic dialogue.

Basically I was a lonely child. My parents, sensing that, were happy to buy me a pet dog as a companion. I think I had only two dogs during my childhood and teens. They were truly my best friends. The first was a mottled brown little mutt named Jeep whom I dearly loved. After two years, it was killed on the highway when it strayed from home, a sad day for me. I remember Dad burying Jeep under the newly planted Blue Spruce tree in the back yard. I thought of Jeep every time I looked out my bedroom window at that tree on moonlight nights and pondered what it meant to die and would I die too. My parents replaced my loss with a tiny black and white Boston terrier pup that I named Penny. She was my companion until I left for college, sleeping at the foot of my bed and following me wherever I went around home.

It was before the convenience of dog food in cans or boxes, so Mother cooked a week's worth of food for Penny at one time. It was a concoction of fresh liver and other giblets cooked with corn meal until it congealed into a thick mass. Not a nice smell while being prepared! Mother would keep it in the refrigerator, and every day scoop off a portion for Penny, who thrived on it. Penny finally died from complications of old age after I was married and living in Hong Kong.

My actual classroom years in Buchanan elementary school were somewhat eclipsed by the simple childhood things that I preferred doing in the neighborhood after school. I endured school hours by dreaming of what I would do after I hurried home, changed my clothes and jumped on my bike to join my chums.

When I was old enough for kindergarten at Buchanan School, Mother happened to meet a neighbor along Mt. Vernon Avenue who said her son was just starting kindergarten too. The mothers made an arrangement that every morning I was to stop by his house, two blocks away, and we would walk to kindergarten together. He was a freckle-faced, red-haired boy named Paul Phillip Perdue, who turned out to be the smartest kid in the class all the way through high school. But at least we started out in step together.

Paul's mother was teaching him to play the piano. I was fascinated to hear him practice. Later he played a clarinet in the band. I envied him and other children who played instruments. Much later, Mother bought an old piano from my aunt Margaret, had it reconditioned and paid for lessons from a young lady on the west side named Roseanne. It was a disaster and a waste of money! I dreaded each Saturday's lesson because I was unwilling to start from scratch and practice scales. I gave up the whole thing. Perhaps if my parents had let me start on a simple instrument, and I could have experienced the motivation of group playing, it would have gone better. As it turned out, I concentrated on singing, no instrument required, and that gave me great satisfaction throughout my school years.

In the first few grades, little girls wore dresses to school and long black cotton stockings or knee socks. We all wanted genuine "Buster Brown" shoes which were so substantial they seldom wore out. We just outgrew them. "For good" we wore shiny patent leather shoes with a strap.

The Buchanan kids made a short cut to school through

part of the pasture behind our houses where it sloped to Mt. Vernon Avenue, the "big street" that adjoined 26th Street. We trampled a path through the weeds in spring and made trails through the snow in winter. Of course we walked to elementary school, a distance of probably eight blocks. Fall, winter, spring—the weather didn't make any difference, everyone walked. In winter we wore galoshes, leggings, snow suits, stocking caps, ear muffs, scarves and mittens. We didn't beg for rides from our dads because we met our friends at various locations along our route, accumulating quite a congenial gang before we got to the school building. At election time, I'm sure our parents would have been amused to hear us kindergartners arguing the merits of different political candidates, echoing whatever we were overhearing at home.

We had to wait for the crossing guard because our particular group of kids lived on the opposite side of Mt. Vernon Avenue from the school building. We knew many of the families by name who lived in the houses along our entire school route. Each house seemed to take on the character of the people who lived in it. Incredible as it sounds, even now when I visit my home town, I can dip into my memory and recall the names of families who lived in many of the houses along Mt. Vernon Avenue.

We walked home again at noon and back for afternoon school session. It was a treat on bitterly cold winter days, when the snow was deep or it was near zero, to take our lunch in a metal lunch box and eat at our desks. Elementary schools didn't have cafeterias in those days. Of course we traded sandwiches, fruit, cookies, whatever with classmates as children have always done. We knew the "peanut butter and jelly" kids and the "bologna or cheese" kids, those who always brought homemade bread and those with store-bought bread. Potato chips and snack foods didn't come in plastic bags in those days. Milk didn't come in cartons either, so we may have had a small glass bottle of milk in our lunch box.

Thirty percent of the labor force was out of work in 1932. But that year I was only seven and was more affected by the pictures on the front page of the kidnaping for ransom and then death of the Lindbergh baby. It seemed that parents hugged their children more afterward. In sixth grade, we were shocked at the blazing crash of the German Zeppelin airship, the *Hindenburg*, as it attempted to dock in New Jersey. In art class, the boys, especially Joe Pugsley, who had obvious talent, were drawing graphic scenes of that catastrophe. The boys would talk about Joe DiMaggio breaking the World's Series hitting records. They played cops and robbers pretending to capture the notorious John Dillinger or Bonnie and Clyde who were robbing banks and gas stations at that time. They all admired J. Edgar Hoover who was getting tough on crime through his newly established FBI. But our childhood world was still serene and benign.

I was far from an outstanding student at Buchanan. My memories of kindergarten are that our class met in a high ceiling auditorium with a stage on one side. I think it doubled as a gym because there was heavy wire mesh over the high windows. My teacher was a tall, gentle, white-haired, soft spoken lady named Miss Harper. Our principal was Miss Phillips.

In the early grades, we always started the school year by bringing a new box of multi-colored, hard-pressed, not wax, *Crayolas* in a metal box and a penny pencil with an eraser at the end. A large *Big Chief* tablet with lines was essential. The Indian pictured wore a huge feathered headdress cascading down his back. Gold lines trimmed the edge of the red tablet, and touches of gold on the chief's buckskin clothing added to his royal appearance. It also appealed to my childhood fascination with Indian lore. (About 60 or more years later, I was amused to see a similar tablet in an office supply store. It was the same large size, red, and pictured an Indian, but the lettered words were "Son of Big Chief." The long black hair of that modern Indian was pulled back with a twisted pink band around his head and hung down behind his neck. He wore a loose-fitting, sleeveless garment and no feathered headdress! He was serving a new "politically correct" generation!)

Learning to read was fun. I was more than ready and learned rapidly because we were taught by the phonics method. The teacher had charts with the figure of a little boy in blue overalls who pointed at the vowels and syllables. We never saw his face, only his back as he pointed. One of my first books was "Millions of Cats" and "The Little Engine That Could." We stretched out on little rugs we brought to school for our nap times.

One incident stands out for me in kindergarten. I walked to school in the rain one day carrying a blue umbrella. After class, I picked up a blue umbrella I thought was mine and returned home with it. Another child was upset because I had taken his umbrella by mistake. Miss Harper told me the next day to be sure to bring it back and pick up my own. Day after day I kept forgetting to do so. Finally she sent me home during classtime to bring it back. I had to walk alone, not accompanied by my friend Paul or any of the other kids. I sobbed all the way home and back, embarrassed, frightened and shamed. Incredible that such a small incident stayed in my memory for three-quarters of a century!

We began every class day by repeating "The Pledge of Allegiance to the Flag." We extended our right arm straight and pointed it toward the flag while reciting. This changed later during the Hitler era because it looked too much like the "Heil Hitler" salute of the Nazis. We were told to put our hands over our hearts after that. Then we sang "America," or "My Country 'Tis of Thee" as we called it. ("The Star-Spangled Banner" was too difficult and "God Bless America" hadn't been composed yet.) I don't remember whether we always prayed, but in some classes we recited "The Lord's Prayer." Some teachers did lead their class in prayer and even taught us Scripture verses in public school. One teacher who did was Mrs. Gray. We always said we had "Gramma Gray for grammar." She taught us a verse from Proverbs I never forgot: "A good name is rather to be chosen than great riches."

At Christmas, teachers openly read the story of the birth of Jesus from the Bible, and we always dramatized the nativity scene in homemade costumes during the Christmas program. In later grades at Buchanan, teachers drilled us in memorizing accurately word for word the entire story from the gospel of Luke for recitation during the programs. I'll never forget it.

I liked art and was quite good at drawing, but I struggled with arithmetic. We had to stand at the blackboard and solve problems in front of the whole class. My mistakes embarrassed me. Arithmetic never made sense. My report card regularly carried the notation, "Leona needs to work harder on being accurate in arithmetic." I learned to count on my fingers for addition and subtraction—which I do to this day. We were forbidden to do that, but I understand from my grandchildren that it is accepted these days in school! The multiplication table and fractions took me a long time to master. Now children are sometimes allowed to use calculators.

Our individual desks had attached seats, and the desk tops had holes for inkwells. The tops lifted up so we could keep our pencils, papers and books inside. Our parents had to buy a certain kind of black ink for us to bring to school, a wooden pen holder and a box of metal pen tips. The teacher showed us how to properly suck off the filmy protection from the pen tip so ink would adhere to it and how to insert it into the slot at the end of the wooden pen holder.

I cheated in the penmanship class when the teacher wasn't looking by using the forbidden finger movements to do cursive writing instead of the push-pulls and oval exercises with full arm movements required by the Palmer Method of Penmanship. Because my cheating still produced the required standard, I qualified to receive the Palmer diploma too. The cheating never bothered me, but my handwriting suffered for the rest of my life because it is hardly legible—even to me! The typewriter and eventually the computer salvaged my writing career in later years.

I don't recall that either of my parents ever came to the scheduled evening P.T.A. meetings or for Parents Night when we displayed our school progress. They always seemed to be busy working. Of course Baba couldn't come because she didn't understand English. I envied the other children whose parents always proudly showed up. I would say that my elementary school days were not really happy ones for me. It's possible that I was a slow bloomer.

11

Neighborhoods—As They Used to Be

The older one becomes, the faster time seems to fly. In my early childhood, however, time seemed to walk at a more leisurely pace. I recall those years in slow motion, and while writing the story of my life, I have savored the memories at length. Time sort of seemed to stand still. Children weren't in such a hurry to grow up as they are now. Life in the close knit neighborhood we enjoyed would be hard to duplicate these days.

The neighborhood of 26th Street had a character of its own. Everyone knew everyone else. Couples with young children lived on both sides of the one block that dead-ended in a fence with woods beyond. Because people didn't seem to move from one house to another or change neighborhoods as much in those days, we children grew up together from kindergarten through our teens. Some lived in the same neighborhood while going to college. In fact, over 60 years later, several families still lived there!

Some of those young couples are now great-grandparents!

Many of the families were of Czech descent, some still spoke Czech at home. Children of various ages all had counterparts in children of other families. Most families had more than one child, and the Smith family at the end of the block had the most children—four. Families all knew each other, and our parents trusted us to go anywhere around the neighborhood, even into someone else's house, if we were invited. It was a warm environment in which to start out in life and provided us experiences in getting along with each other.

The neighborhood children spent a lot of time on porches and front steps. It was before television and before air-conditioning, so everyone seemed to spill out of their sultry houses on summer evenings after the sun set. Whenever you'd see folks sitting on their porch, you knew that was an open invitation to join them. You were always welcome. It was a relaxing time when you could talk about just anything—frivolous or serious. Children seemed to have favorite adults among the neighbors to whom they gravitated and with whom they felt at ease.

We didn't have a front porch. We had a small cement stoop without a covering but we still spent much time sitting on our wide step with other neighbors and friends. But houses with big, covered porches held the greatest attraction, especially when it rained or when the midday sun was hot.

Young children would romp on lawns, wrestle, play games, even after dark if parents were also nearby sitting with other neighbors. For some of us, when the street lights went on, it was our signal to go indoors. More privileged older kids, usually teens, stayed out longer playing in the street, riding bikes even after dark or parking them together under the street lights to talk. I don't recall anyone getting into real trouble. Drugs were unknown, and even the older ones seldom sneaked a smoke. There was some rowdiness, but it never led to any serious confrontations.

When we first moved to the city, I got a rather large tricycle for Christmas. It had a place for another child to stand on the crossbar between the two back wheels. Dot had fun riding on the back, hanging tightly to me. I pedaled as fast as I could on the sidewalk that only ran along the side of the street her house was on. Our side of the street had no sidewalk, and the lawns tapered right to the edge of the street. I gave most of the other younger children rides on my trike, but Dot always had priority.

My friend, June, and another older girl friend, Charlotte, neither of them teens yet, were into "collecting movie stars." They kept immense scrapbooks where they pasted pictures of their favorite Hollywood actors and actresses clipped from movie magazines, which were all the rage in the early 1930s. Of course the pictures were black and white, pre-dating color printing. Clark Gable, Joan Crawford, Betty Grable, Katherine Hepburn—that was the era. They spent hours and hours clipping, pasting and discussing the gossip they read about them in the magazines. Dot and I were given some of their leftover pictures, so we had our own collection.

Often we spread a blanket under the trees either at her house or mine, and did our playing and reading outdoors to keep cool on hot days during vacation. Those were the days of the "ice man" who delivered blocks of ice to our back doors with huge, mean-looking steel tongs. Electric refrigerators had not been designed yet. At our house, the ice man delivered the big ten cent block right into the lower airtight section of our ice box. If the ice melted before the next morning, the food might spoil. Of course, we didn't have much food to refrigerate since fresh produce usually came from the garden. Moreover, nobody kept opening the ice box, as we do the refrigerator, just to stare into it. Who would have dreamed about today's automatic icemakers?

But "stolen bread is sweet" and we kids loved to snitch bits of ice that had been chipped off the big blocks just behind the heavy leather flap hanging over the open back of the ice truck. As soon as we saw the ice man disappear inside someone's back door, we ran to the truck as fast as our legs would carry us, lifted up the flap and grabbed for the bits of ice lying around on the wooden truck bed. We'd shove them into our mouths and then run back to sit innocently on a neighbor's lawn nearby when the ice man returned.

If he looked our way, we might have our mouths full of ice that was freezing our cheeks—but oh, how cooling and delicious those pieces were! Somehow, we always managed to find bite-size ice pieces. My guess is that Mr. ice man generously chipped some off for us and was wise to our innocent game.

Because there was little traffic on our street except for the cars of people who lived there and delivery trucks, we could play right in the street most of the time. We chalked hop scotch squares on the cement and tossed our favorite lucky stones when our turns came.

We played "May I?" in the evenings, where one person was "It" and gave instructions to one after the other of a lineup of kids in front of him. "Take one giant step forward...or one backward...or two to the side...or five baby steps forward." If we failed to say "May I?" we were penalized and told to go back to the starting line. If we remembered, we were given permission to proceed as instructed.

We played "Kick the can" and "Hide-and-seek" by the hour. We girls played a lot of jacks—doing "onesies, twosies, chickens in the coop" and all the variations of jacks and ball. The boys played marbles games. Sometimes they let us girls play, if no other boys were available. We all had collections of favorite marbles in cloth bags with a draw string at the top. We'd find a place where there was smooth, packed dirt and drew a circle in the dirt. Then we showed off our skill by using our favorite "shooter" marble.

There was a several year period where it was all the rage

to collect lead soldiers in various poses—with guns, on horseback, sometimes painted ones, sometimes unpainted. Some of the bigger boys even had home casting kits with lead molds to melt and make the soldiers. The boys were able to recycle their broken and bent lead soldiers, casualties of previous war games, and melt them into new shapes. Beside playing imaginative war games with them, another game went something like this: The person who owned some lead figures would line them up against a wall, sometimes the outside wall of the elementary school on the playground, and anyone could try his luck or skill at shooting or rolling his own marbles at the lineup from a prescribed distance. If he knocked down a lead figure, he could keep it. If he failed, he forfeited the marble he rolled. (I think that was the point—I'm scraping the dust off long ago memories.) But it got to be such an all-consuming fad at Buchanan Elementary that teachers considered it out of control, bordering on gambling and eventually put a stop to it.

Yo-yos were also in fashion. You had to own a Duncan model to really be "with it." We practiced and practiced such tricks as baby-in-the-cradle, over-the-rainbow, and lingering fishline. I was never very good, but some of the neighborhood boys were almost professionals.

A favorite cheap toy was the penny glider. I think it cost a penny. It was a narrow, flat piece of lightweight pine balsa with a metal clip in front to weigh the nose down, and slits for the cross piece that made the tail. You would wind it with a rubber band and launch it to roll, bank and glide.

Most of us had metal roller skates with four ball bearing wheels that clamped on to your hard shoes. They had an adjustable metal platform to make them longer or shorter and adjustable clamps around your shoe. You had to tighten them with a hollow metal key which you wore around your neck so you wouldn't lose it. Those skates contributed to many skinned knees and bruised elbows in my growing years.

One neighbor boy stands out as my first "puppy love." Jim lived three houses away toward the woods on the same side of the street. He was also an only child and my age. He was chubby, cute, had dimples and all the neighborhood girls vied with one another to play with Jim, to get Jim's attention, to get a valentine from Jim, to be invited over to Jim's house, even to sit on the front steps with Jim's Mom—anything that concerned Jim.

I was no exception. When I got to the two-wheeled bike stage, to ride up and down the street with Jim put me on cloud nine. I absolutely had to have an *Iver-Johnson* balloon-tired bike because Jim said it was the best. And I cheered for the Chicago Cubs baseball team because Jim did. I spent hours talking with Jim under the street lights with other kids. I often got lucky when he invited me to his house and to his basement to watch him put together his first crystal radio set. What excitement to actually hear voices and music through the primitive headset he had rigged up! Jim had a basketball hoop on his garage and one in the basement on a pole where we would shoot baskets together.

Jim was a model airplane buff. In those days, you constructed your own from light balsa wood and followed directions to cut the pieces with a razor blade to fit. No ready made fancy plastic models. Jim let me help on many occasions, and I learned a lot about airplanes because Jim knew everything there was to know—so he said.

On special occasions, he invited me over to his house in the evening while his dad read the paper or his mom was sewing. We listened to "Gang Busters," a cops and robbers crime-solver program on the radio. Jim's mom would make popcorn and Koolaid for us, another cloud-nine experience about which I could brag to the other girls. Her corn popper was a long-handled, wire screen box which she kept shaking over a low fire until the kernels popped and plumped up.

When we reached our teens, we neighborhood girls cast

124

even more serious eyes in Jim's direction. Unfortunately, he seemed to think of all of us simply as his long-time pals from the neighborhood and didn't give any of us much attention. He went to Catholic school so was not involved in any of our public school activities. He did earn a bad reputation as a bully, however, because it was reported on good authority by the children on our street that Jim killed a kitten belonging to a little neighbor girl, Marie, by "dropping it hard" on the cement. I'm not sure whether there were witnesses to convict him.

Boys on 26th street were always playing catch with or without a glove. Sometimes they would condescend to play with us girls—if no other fellows were around to see them. We girls learned to play a passable game of softball though, and when the boys were short of players, we were allowed on the teams. We played touch football, too, until we got near our teens and the differences between boys and girls became more apparent. Besides, we girls didn't want to mess up our hair.

The neighborhood was safe. No one locked their doors. Since there was no air conditioning, in summer all doors and windows remained open day and night. Dad always left his keys in his car's ignition.

When we moved to the street in 1930, only a few houses had been built. There were many vacant lots where we played ball and other games. There was an empty lot next to us and one directly across from it next to Dot's house. That was a special favorite place for ball games and other neighborhood kid gatherings.

As each new house was being constructed, neighborhood children had great fun climbing around between the two-by-fours and chasing each other through the house frameworks—often dangerous, but we loved danger, especially if we could keep our antics away from our parents. We climbed on piles of sand to play "King of the Hill" and collected short pieces of lumber to build our own play houses. As each new house went up, we knew we'd have more playmates and speculated on whose friends they would be.

We labeled certain houses as having unfriendly occupants, however. Sometimes they were couples without children, who yelled at us if we came into their yards to retrieve a runaway ball. The Soderlunds were in that category, and we always ran past their house so they wouldn't see us.

One of the fun experiences we repeated after every rain-storm was to take off our shoes and socks, roll up our pants and wade in the cold rushing water along the sides of the street. Some-times one of the more youthful hearted moms would join us and splash along barefooted. The water emptied down a steep cement incline behind the barricade fence at the end of the street and poured down into the pond at the bottom of the hill. Sitting on that big fence was another favorite gathering place for kids.

A large, friendly, oak tree with a thick trunk stood at the edge of the woods by the fence. On one of the sturdy horizontal branches, the Smiths' dad suspended an old rubber tire by a rope and we children would swing way out over the woods below. We played Tarzan and did many risky tricks on that favorite swing. The more daring teens even let go with a Tarzan yell and tumbled down into the woods.

In the very early years, behind the rows of houses on both sides of the street was pasture land. A wire fence ran along behind all the houses so that the grazing cows wouldn't wander into our gardens. There was a secret hole in the fence that all the children knew about behind June's house, and we had a well-worn path to it. It seemed like such a huge pasture then, but I guess that was only because we were little and the world seemed so big.

A large, spreading, weeping willow tree stood in the middle of the pasture behind us in whose low branches some of the older kids built a secret tree house. They formed a club that met in the treehouse, but they didn't let just anyone become a member of their "Willow Club." They remained exclusive with special initiation ceremonies, secret passwords and secret meetings. The older kids considered some of us too young and excluded us from the Club until we became "old enough" to be accepted into their inner circle. By that time, however, some of the parents decided the clubhouse should be disbanded because it posed too great a temptation for "teenage shenanigans," as they called it. The word got around that some of the kids were smoking there, and a few empty beer bottles were noticed.

It didn't seem that even the bigger kids got into too much trouble. At Halloween the most that they did in our neighborhood was to use a bar of soap to mark on windows.

Of course, everyone had a garden in which they planted both flowers and vegetables. Without exception, every house had a narrow, one-car garage with the heavy door opened by hand. No one would have dreamed of such a luxury as a second car or an automatic garage door opener. As the years went by and cars got longer and wider, people often added a few feet to the back of the garage to accommodate the newer models. Dad did the same for the Ford he owned when I was learning to drive.

Milk was delivered to our door according to Mother's order on a note left in the insulated metal milk box at our back door. Before the days of pasteurization, the cream rose to the top of the glass bottle and our parents used it for their coffee. Cottage cheese, butter, whipping cream and eggs were also delivered by the milkman on request. He usually came very early in the morning, sometimes before dawn. Groceries were also delivered to our door. Mother would phone a list of her needs to the grocery store, and a grocery boy would bring them to our house within an hour or so. Neighborhood groceries or mom-and-pop stores were common in those days. Most of them included a meat counter with fresh meat. They served their regular customers on a cash or credit basis. You could walk in, pick up needed items and just say, "Charge it!" No credit cards yet. The grocer wrote it down on a little pad, tore off the page and possibly stuck it on an upturned nail which served as a record keeper.

A couple of blocks down Mt. Vernon Avenue on the way to Buchanan School was a little grocery store called "Rosie's." Rosie was a plump, jolly Czech lady who stocked absolutely everything anyone would need in her little store. When you walked in, the door had a jingle on it to let Rosie know she had a customer, since she lived in the back of her store. Children were especially attracted to the penny candy on display. We made the store a regular stop on the way from school, if we happened to have a penny or two. You could select what you wanted from big jars of candy and gum. It was hard to decide between big red jawbreakers, Tootsie rolls, suckers, pink, yellow and white marshmallow chicks, colored candy balls with gum in the center, round bubble gum wrapped in little papers that had jokes in them and other tempting treats. Rosie would give your purchase to you in a little paper bag, even if you only bought a penny's worth. She didn't make much profit on her little customers, but she loved us and we loved her.

Dot and I were often sent to Rosie's to buy ten cents worth of cold cuts for sandwiches, if our mothers wanted something quick to make for our lunch. A big loaf of sliced, white Colonial Bread was 25 cents. You could also hand Rosie a list of things your mother wrote down that she wanted, and Rosie would select the items and put them in a paper sack for you to carry home. You brought her money tied in a handkerchief, she would take however much the items cost and give you back your change. No receipt, as I recall. Rosie knew the names of most of us regular kid customers and knew our parents, too.

In every season, a favorite place to play was in the woods beyond the end of our street. A steep embankment led to a pond that was always a source of fun. In winter it froze solid, and we skated on it. In spring, we caught polliwogs and sometimes brought them home in glass jars to watch as they hatched into little frogs. The pond was stream fed and swelled over its banks in the rainy season. We had fun following the creek further into the woods in both directions. Dorothy Smith, her brother and two sisters lived in the last house on the block next to the woods. She was "the other Dorothy." I would alternate between the two Dorothys for many years, calling each one of them, in turn, my "best friend," depending on who I was currently mad at or most chummy with. All of us walked freely in the woods from our earliest childhood. Apparently it was safe because we readily obtained permission from our parents. Often I wandered in the woods alone.

We waded through a carpet of multi-colored autumn leaves and watched the squirrels and chipmunks scamper at our approach. We threw rocks at rabbits and tried to find their holes. Several of us would designate a special, favorite tree under which we would meet for secret club meetings that "the other kids" wouldn't know about. We made special marks on such trees, like Indian signs, and made up our own Indian language. Some of the other children were as keen on Indian lore as I was.

We picked violets, spring beauties and tiny yellow buttercups in the early spring in our woods. We put these in little homemade paper baskets to celebrate May Day. When milkweed pods were in full fluffy dress, we would look under the leaves for big caterpillars and return after school day by day to watch them until they turned into gorgeous black and orange monarch butterflies. In the hot summer, the woods gave us shade for picnics in our secret hideaways.

In our own backyard, we had a splendid apple tree that was fragrant with blossoms in spring and bore yellow Delicious apples in summer. It had some easy access limbs to climb, if I got a start with a step ladder. Some of the higher, inner branches made a natural platform where I asked Dad to tie some planks between the branches for me. That was my very own tree house where I could lie on a blanket in the summer and not even be visible from the ground. I would take a favorite book and some Koolaid in a corked bottle up to my secluded hideaway. The hours would pass in pure childhood delight among the swaying branches with the breeze blowing. Who needed air conditioning?

Winter was such fun. When I saw the slate grey sky without definable clouds on a December afternoon and felt a strange yet exciting hush descend over the common noises of the outdoors, I knew snow was on the way. We didn't have the sophisticated weather forecasting we do now, so the radio announcer wasn't able to tell us very accurately if the weather was about to change. We did better at figuring that out for ourselves. Baba was pretty good at forecasting weather changes signaled by her aches or pains.

The loud bang-clang-slam of Dad in the basement shoveling coal into our furnace early in the morning would wake me. I remembered yesterday's grey sky and would run to the window to see a white world lying before me with not a single footprint marring the beauty of the new-fallen snow. A huge Iowa blizzard often descended on us during the night. The howling wind had not even awakened me. Snow covered the evergreens, weighed down the branches and put a round mound over every familiar thing in our yard.

If it was a school day, I still went to school, but I could hardly keep my mind on what the teacher was saying. If it was a weekend, I knew there was fun ahead. Baba insisted on giving me a hearty hot breakfast of oatmeal or Cream of Wheat before she let me go out. After being sure that I put on layers of clothing, which included my snow suit with heavy wool snow pants over regular clothing, high black rubber buckle overshoes, ear muffs, a wool cap and my mittens, Baba would turn me loose.

I loved making the first deep footprints in the new fallen snow with my heavy overshoes. I would run all over the yard making tracks in circles and creative designs.

In the winter, all of us had a sled of some sort. To receive a *Flexible Flyer* sled was the ultimate Christmas gift. Some of the kids had the special deluxe model which was brilliant red with black trimmings and green runners. Mine was a standard model but genuine because it had the eagle trademark. I treasured it and faithfully waxed the runners before a big day of sledding. We were all impressed to learn that these sleds were what Commander Byrd was using on his trip to the South Pole. The expedition took a half dozen *Flexible Flyers* with them to help carry supplies.

We belly flopped down sloping lawns and steep driveways or right along the street when the snow was packed solid. For real thrills, we climbed under the fence behind Smith's house at the end of the block and found ourselves at the very top of what seemed to us as a tremendously steep hill. We'd line up, get a good running start and belly flop at high speed down the snowy hill. The biggest thrill came by going over "the bump" at the bottom before gliding off along level ground right across the frozen creek. Some kids were very good at steering their sled downhill with their feet at the same time others were belly flopping. Often there were sled traffic jams on the hill, if some kids jumped the gun and didn't wait their turn. We did have accidents and bruises, but nothing tragic happened.

There might have been a dozen or two children not only from our neighborhood but from adjoining neighborhoods gathered at the "big hill" after school on winter days—and all day on Saturday. When we fell off the sleds, perhaps because two or three of us were trying to hold on to each other sitting on one long sled, we'd have a grand pile-up in some snow drift and shout with the fun. If the cold snap continued for several days, and it often did in Iowa's sub zero weather, the constant use of our special sledding hill packed the snow down into smooth, hard ice, and we went down the hill like greased lightening.

I'd often arrive home for dinner with my mittens frozen stiff, my cheeks red, snow on my eyelashes, perhaps my stocking cap (as we called ski caps in those days) lost and some bruised muscles. The friendly kitchen noises and the aroma of a hot meal being prepared welcomed me. The smell of my wet mittens toasting on the hot air register—something like the smell of a wet cat—is unforgettable.

There was an early phenomenon that I don't know whether Iowa still experiences in these later years. Sometimes after a deep snowfall, the weather changed quickly to a sudden warmup, and sleet or freezing rain covered the snow that was perhaps already a foot or more deep. Then a sudden freeze gave the snow a very hard crust that didn't thaw perhaps for weeks. We put on our shoe ice skates while sitting on our doorsteps and then skated right out across all the lawns, along the street, on the driveways—endlessly. We didn't need a pond or ice rink. The whole neighborhood was one big ice crust for our skating adventures. We even skated at night over the frozen lawns by moonlight or streetlight.

And time, too, has frozen in my memory those simple, happy childhood days.

12

Family Branches and Twigs

Czech families traditionally spent much time visiting with relatives. That was what they did for diversion, entertainment and for genuine enjoyment. They didn't even have to call ahead to see if a visit was convenient—they just dropped over to someone's house on a whim. Relatives were always welcome, coffee was brewed and there were usually kolaches in the kitchen.

Without brothers and sisters, I often spent time with my cousins, especially my first cousin, Martha. We were together sometimes on weekends and especially at holiday get-togethers of our families and relatives. Our Aunt Fan (Frances, my mother's sister and Martha's dad's sister too) sort of took us under her wing and did many things for us. She generously bought gifts and clothes for us, took us places with her and warmly invested herself into our lives. She never had children, had been divorced early in life, so she poured herself into her nieces and nephews--to our benefit and great appreciation.

One year she bought the two of us identical, huge, brown

Teddy Bears, almost larger than we could carry. Another Christmas she bought Martha and me huge dolls, bigger than life size babies. The dolls were actually able to wear year-old baby clothes. It was the heyday of Shirley Temple films, and Aunt Fan took us to see every one of them. What fun! She bought us Shirley Temple cut-out flat paper dolls and we could put many changes of dresses and costumes on the color paper replica of Shirley. I collected all the books published from the movies of Shirley Temple like "Little Colonel," "Rebecca of Sunnybrook Farm," etc. When we got older, Aunt Fan took us to every Deanna Durbin movie and those starring Jane Withers.

Aunt Fan took us on a major excursion to Chicago on the train. Neither of us had ever been on a train. She bought us new suitcases, we wore our best dresses and hats and our excitement was running high. We were to travel not just on an ordinary train but on one of the first newly designed, sleek "Streamliners" to come through Cedar Rapids. We left on the evening train. Waving goodbye and blowing kisses to our families who stood outside the window, we were finally on the way to our big adventure.

We were hardly seated when a white-jacketed dining car steward came through announcing the last call for dinner. We didn't need to have that experience because Aunt Fan packed some snacks for us. Besides, we were too excited to eat much. I don't remember how many hours the trip took, but we stayed glued to the window watching the lights of every little town whiz by until we got drowsy and dozed off. Aunt Fan woke us in time to point out the lighted Tribune Tower, the Merchandise Mart and other Loop buildings as they emerged from the shadows. We passed slowly into the dark, covered train shed of the station.

"Union Station! Chicago!" the conductor and brakeman shouted as they passed speedily through our coach. Passengers began removing luggage from racks overhead and jostling each other in the aisles. With a slight lurch the train stopped, and we could hear the hiss of steam engines as a fog of steam clouded the train windows.

When we got off, it seemed that we walked almost the length of the train before we got inside the station. We were awed by its cavernous size. It was a scary and intimidating place to small Iowa girls as we looked up at the high ceilings and Rococo architecture. Loudspeaker announcements blared arrivals and departures and reverberated through the expanse of the station. Redcaps moved in all directions carrying or pushing baggage. Newspaper peddlers loudly hawked the *Chicago Tribune* and the *Chicago Herald & Examiner*. We were relieved to see our Uncle Frank and Aunt Helen who came to meet us. For two little girls, seeing the sights of Chicago for the first time was awesome. Aunt Fan continued to take us to Chicago every few years until our teens. We felt like seasoned travelers by then, thanks to the way she generously opened the world to us.

It was always exciting to visit my cousin Martha's house. She had many brothers and a sister, and there always seemed to be something interesting going on at her house. I missed that kind of sibling give and take. A special treat was to stay overnight at her house. There wasn't an extra bedroom so we slept—I don't remember where! Her mom always gave us two nickels so we could go across the street to buy chocolate covered ice cream bars on a stick from a little shanty run by some black neighbors. They cost five cents, but if you found the words "Free" stamped on the stick after you finished, you could go back and get another one without paying again. Ice cream sandwiches were also five cents and so were a variety of candy bars.

Sometimes both Martha and I would stay overnight or for a weekend at our grandma Bubi's house (my mother's mother) on Second Street. Grandma Bubi's name was Anastasia. Step Grandpa Jed, short for "Dedecek" (grandpa) in Czech, was the only grandfather I ever knew. I can't say I really knew him, although I saw him rather frequently since he was still living until I finished college and even after we left for China. I think the reason was because he was probably an alcoholic and I seldom saw him sober, especially at holiday times. My guess is that his lifetime job in the "packin' house" (the meat packing plant) was such a meaningless, routine drudgery that he drank heavily to forget the real world. Bubi was always angry at Grandpa Jed for drinking. She said he didn't know when to stop. He drank alone, he drank with family, he drank with relatives, with neighbors, with friends and with fellow workers. That included hard liquor. I remember Bubi hiding bottles of whiskey she found in their closet so he couldn't find them. It was a bad habit that Grandpa Jed carried with him to his death. It is sad that this is the one thing I remember about him. There must have been a *real* Grandpa Jed under all of that. After Bubi died, my Aunt Fan continued to live with him. She was also quite disgusted and impatient with him, but did her best to cook for and take care of him and household matters.

My memories of Grandma Bubi are not very vivid because I was only eight when she died. I remember her as a quiet, gentle woman, rather reserved. It seemed to me she didn't talk very much, but I could be wrong. Maybe I didn't listen. I think she spoke only Czech. I do remember that she had a big, blue, enamel coffee pot brewing on her stove at all times and an endless supply of kolaches—especially my favorites with sweet cottage cheese and poppy seed filling. My mother recorded in my baby book that my first outing was to Bubi's house, and we spent my first Christmas there when I was six months old.

Bubi raised some chickens in her back yard, and Martha and I were allowed to feed them occasionally. Martha and her brothers and sister spent more time with Bubi and Jed than I did since they lived within walking distance of their house, and for my first five years, we lived eight miles out of town in the opposite direction.

Bubi and Jed's house was not far from the Cedar River and if someone went with us, we could walk to a small park on the riverbank that had benches and shade trees. A butcher shop selling fresh meats was across the street from Bubi's, and when Martha and I reached a responsible age, we were allowed to cross the street to buy chops, wieners, cold cuts, cheese or bologna when they asked us to. Nothing was pre-packaged. You picked out what you wanted behind the big glass showcase, and the butcher sliced or chopped it for you on the spot. Our purchase would be wrapped in butcher's paper and tied with string. The floor had sawdust all over it—I never knew why.

A grocery store called "The Globe" was just around the corner, and it too had sawdust on the floor. It seemed immense to me, and I thought it stocked nearly everything in the world on its many shelves. It was more than a neighborhood grocery, more like a forerunner of supermarkets. Martha and I were always eager to shop there with Bubi, Jed or Aunt Fan.

Across from The Globe was the Olympic Theater where Martha and I loved to attend the cheap Saturday matinee. If we had an extra nickel, we'd stop at The Globe and get a candy bar, sometimes a Powerhouse bar with caramel and peanuts covered with chocolate. Nothing could taste better than that. We even licked the paper wrapper. A dime would get us in to "the show," usually a double feature. Black and white films, of course, because color didn't come in until 1937. Between the main features, they would show cartoons and a continuing series of some sort of mystery or a Western that always left us with a cliff-hanger. We could hardly stand the suspense and begged to come back the following week to see what would take place next. *Flash Gordon in the 25th Century* left us wide-eyed at what might happen in the distant future. Sometimes we saw Charlie Chan, Tarzan and the Apes, Gene Autrey, Ken Maynard, Hop-a-long Cassidy or some young cowboy named John Wayne. As kids, we didn't like movies with "too much mush." Later, as teens, we liked the "mush," the guys kissing girls.

Kids constantly shifted from seat to seat or got up to go back to the lobby where the management sold popcorn and candy. When the background music got louder, we'd run back to our seats so we wouldn't miss anything. Nobody thought of leaving until the screen went dark and the house lights came on. Then everyone rushed out to be the first on the sidewalk. The sunlight nearly blinded us as we staggered out. Some of the big boys would run ahead and pretend to "mow us down" with their thumb and index finger guns.

Dad was keen on Western movies and saw every one he could. One of his favorites was "On the Trail of the Lonesome Pine," and he bought the record of the theme song. He ordered an entire set of twelve Zane Grey Western novels in hardback from some mail order house. I remember Mother being upset with him for being so extravagant. Dad was not much of a reader in English, so I doubt that he ever read them, but he had the satisfaction of owning them.

Bubi's house had only one bedroom and it was separated from the dining room by a heavy curtain. Aunt Fan had a bedroom built in the attic which she occupied even after Bubi died. She worked her entire lifetime at the Quaker Oats plant, walking many blocks to work winter and summer. Every step of the attic stairs squeaked because the wooden steps were not covered with carpet. The rest of the attic was unfinished, full of stored things, but in one corner there was a spare double bed. Martha and I slept there sometimes, but I always thought it was spooky and would sleep with covers pulled over my head. We would tell ghost stories and frighten one another even more. Then we'd snuggle up and giggle at ourselves. We amused ourselves by writing on each other's bare backs with our finger nail and trying to guess what was written.

When visiting my grandparents, I remember one unforgettable sound I heard especially in the quiet of the night. The railroad tracks were not far away, and many freight trains went through town. I recall the mournful, wailing sound of train whistles when windows were open. Every time I hear train whistles anywhere in the country or wherever we lived or traveled overseas, that memory comes back to me because I associate them with my experience as a young child at Bubi's.

Grandpa Jed used to make beer in his basement, and kept the big corked bottles down there because it was cooler. He had the process down to a science. I seem to recall a rubber tube inserted into a hole in the cork of a wooden keg. That allowed gases to escape from fermentation, I guess. The end of the tube was in a gallon jug of water, and I remember the blub-blub sound of the gases. When the beer was ready, he bottled it in dark bottles. He had a device to attach the caps. (Jed also made wine from grapes, cherries, currants, raspberries, rhubarb and dandelion. The above procedure may have been for wine, I'm not sure. Childhood memories are a little hazy!) Jed drank the beer from a large size tin container. It always had a lot of foam on top which would stick to his upper lip and make us laugh at his white moustache. He didn't seem to care whether the beer was hot or cold as long as it was alcoholic. I think some of my uncles called the above process "bathtub gin."

Jed used to get backaches so when Martha and I were very little, he asked us to walk up and down on his back until it cracked. We giggled and made a game out of it. Sure enough, his back would crack, and he said he felt better. Walking on his back often resulted in change falling out of his pockets which he let us keep. That's where we often got our money for "the show" and for candy bars.

The light in our grandparents' bedroom on the main floor was a bare bulb suspended from the ceiling. It was one of the first kind installed after electricity came to town. A long chain dangled from it and depending on how far down you pulled the chain, that much brighter the light in the bulb became—from dim to full shine. I was fascinated by it.

Mother came home one day and said Bubi had a stroke. I didn't know what that was, but I remember she was very sick. Afterward, she would walk very slowly, dragging one foot and speaking in a slurred way. She would sit quietly a lot. I remember going with Mother to take Bubi to Dr. Petrovitsky for a checkup. I vividly recall the doctor asking her to walk across his office. Bubi did, and dragged one leg slowly behind her. The doctor took my mother aside and said in a whisper, "She won't get any better." Mother cried.

Mother insisted that Bubi come and stay at our home during her recuperation so we could care for her. My dad bought a brand new settee swing and put it under our shady apple tree in the back yard where Bubi could rest and cool off from the summer heat. I can't remember whether she actually stayed very long. The next thing I was aware of was that she had another stroke and died. She was only 58.

I remember little about the funeral except seeing lots and lots of floral bouquets in baskets at the funeral home and at the cemetery. The smell of fresh roses was almost overwhelming. Martha and I wore identical, brand new white dresses and white, wide-brimmed hats to the funeral. Our mothers took us to a professional photographer afterward. Some poses were taken of me with Mother and Baba at the studio. I had a scowl on my face in all the pictures because I didn't want to be all dressed up in that stupid dress, and I didn't want my picture taken.

From my babyhood, my cousin Blanche and her parents who lived in the country occasionally visited us, and we visited them. It seemed quite a long drive to their farm in those early days. Every summer from the time Martha and I were quite young, we spent a week at Blanche's house near West Branch, Iowa. She was a cousin to both of us, and we three were nearly the same age. Our parents drove us there and fetched us a week later.

Blanche's mother always sewed identical one piece outdoor pajamas for the three of us, a different color each year, and we had our picture taken by her dad with his new box camera. That is also where I was introduced to the wonder of feed sacks. Because Blanche's dad farmed, he would come home from the grist mill with colorful feed sacks containing baby chick mash, pig feed or chop for the cows. The plain, unbleached, flour sacks printed with the brand names were bleached out with lye soap and a few other ingredients until all the print came off and they became white. They were hung on the clothesline for the sun to finish the job, which sometimes took several days.

Each feed sack was about a square yard after the stitching was removed. The white ones were used for diapers, tea towels, petticoats and even the backing for quilts. The prettiest ones printed with all sorts of flowers or designs were saved until there was enough of one pattern to make a dress, a skirt, aprons, curtains— or a nightgown. I remember that Martha and I wore flower printed feed sack nighties when we stayed overnight at Bubi's house.

We did many interesting things together that Martha and I as "city cousins" didn't normally experience. We trekked with Blanche to round up the cows in the pasture every evening. Watching the milking and then trying to catch the dozen or so cats that converged on the milking process was lots of fun. The smell of a cow's body and the hot milk reminded me of my experience as a toddler living at Midway. We spent hours playing hide-and-seek in the haymow in the barn. (I'm not sure that the word "allergy" had been coined yet, but we did a lot of sneezing.) Feeding slop to the hogs was not so much fun and stinky, to say the least, but I liked feeding the horses. I loved to touch a horse's velvety nose and pet it between the ears while it stood in the stall, careful to avoid the friendly nips from its big teeth.

If our visit to the farm coincided with haying time, it generated a lot of excitement. Haying was usually a cooperative effort among Czech farmers, and men went from one farm to the next. We even got rides occasionally on the mowing machine, if we promised to hang on tight. The mowing machine had two wheels, a gearbox and a long cutting blade which extended out to the right of the wheels. It was pulled by a team of horses. We had to be careful not to get too near that big, scary machine. As the driver guided his team down the field in straight rows, the cutting blade mowed the hay, which remained on the ground. Often the mower blade uncovered snakes and cut them in half. Some quail nests were demolished, as were nests of baby rabbits. We wanted to try and rescue them and keep them as pets, but the men usually discouraged us saying that the little bunnies wouldn't live happily in captivity.

The men and boys took pitchforks and piled the hay into round shocks about six feet high and ten feet in diameter. The shocks had to be dragged to a predetermined location to be stacked. Not everybody could be a stacker, they said. It took special skill to pile and arrange a large haystack so that when winter came, the farmer could climb to the top of a ladder and pitch hay down to feed his cattle. A well-stacked haystack repelled rain and was good for feeding from top to bottom.

At intervals during the hot day, we girls helped to carry gallons of lemonade in jugs from the farmhouse to the sweating workers.

During haying time, Blanche's mom prepared huge breakfasts for the hired hands who had already been hard at work helping her dad since before daybreak. If the weather was hot and sunny, they had to work fast and literally "make hay while the sun shines." A sudden rain would soak all the grass. It would be hard to wait for another window of opportunity because the crew had to move on to the next farm. If we were awake, we girls joined the men at breakfast for mounds of scrambled eggs, piles of bacon and sausage, pancakes and hot syrup smothered with real butter, pan fried potatoes, whole milk, homemade bread and preserves. The men consumed several big pots of strong, freshly brewed coffee with thick cream and ample spoons full of sugar. While they ate, Blanche's mom was already starting preparations for the big midday meal for which they would return at noon.

In late afternoon or evening, we walked a scant block down the dusty farm road to a legendary old store by the railroad tracks at a freight stop called "Oasis." It looked just like the pictures of old country stores in Norman Rockwell paintings—pot bellied stove, big wooden pickle barrel, the smell of harnesses, and farmers sitting around talking farm talk, smoking their pipes or playing cards on an overturned crate.

On Saturday nights, Blanche's dad and mom took us with them into town. We watched outdoor movies in the park while her parents did their week's grocery shopping. The movies were projected on a big white sheet suspended between two trees and tied with a rope. Usually it was a romantic Western movie. We brought blankets and stretched out on the grass to watch the film. Her parents bought us three-dip ice cream cones at the local drug store as we piled in the back seat of their car for the drive home—three very sleepy cousins. We three slept together on an oversize unfolding couch in the living room. I remember hearing the hoot of owls at night and being awakened by roosters at dawn. Sounds I didn't hear on 26th street in the city. Another sound that has stayed in my memory and carries me back to those country vacations is the sad evening call of mourning doves in the trees around their spring house.

I had my first taste of Koolaid on those country visits. It had just come on the market, and Blanche's mom bought several flavors for us girls to sample with her homemade cookies. Blanche's family made home style rootbeer from scratch and cooled it in large, brown, corked bottles placed in a bucket and suspended by a rope into their deep well beside the house.

Drinking ice cold, homemade rootbeer on a hot summer night, sitting on their porch watching for shooting stars, catching fireflies on the lawn—that was simple, innocent fun of an Iowa childhood.

13

Perpetuating a Heritage

Czech ethnic culture was in evidence all around me while I was growing up. I couldn't avoid it, enjoyed some positive aspects of it but refused to consider myself part of it. That may seem strange, but I didn't want to identify myself as a Czech. The further I advanced in my teens, the greater effort I made to distance myself from that culture personally and geographically. By the time I was in college and blended in with the rest of the "regular American" students, I put my Czech ethnicity in a trunk and closed the lid. Perhaps that is typical of many second generationers of other ethnic groups. Not until much later in life did I try to open that trunk, reclaim my Czech-ness and realize what a treasure it was.

In early America, of course everyone except the Indians was an immigrant. The second generation sometimes didn't even seem as enthusiastically patriotic as many of the new immigrants. Those newcomers were 100 percent Americans, almost fiercely proud of their adopted land and their new citizenship. Undoubtedly they placed a higher value on their freedom because they lacked freedom and opportunity in their homelands. Once they arrived here and tasted of America's realities, however, they soon found out America had faults, made mistakes and was sometimes not as good to them as they had hoped—but they defended her proudly in the face of any criticism. I did identify with that—I was an American through and through. I didn't even want to be a hyphenated one, *not* a Czech-American.

Some recent immigrants deliberately try to forget their heritage and assimilate into the American culture with all possible speed. But many, who have had a distinct, rich, cultural heritage elsewhere in the world for centuries, even thousands of years, seek to preserve that culture even while becoming good citizens of the United States. Most Czechs were definitely in the latter camp, proud of their culture and seeking to perpetuate it by various means. Although I rejected my heritage while growing up, I feel it is important to my life story at this point to describe their commendable attempts to retain their heritage—which I now do appreciate

Czechs have always been sociable people who bond with their friends and relatives. The American pioneer individualism they encountered in their new homeland was unfamiliar to them, not even to their liking. They were accustomed to village-centered traditions emphasizing communal and familial values. Pubs, festivals and the like were part of everyday life in their rural Czech homeland. Social beer drinking was for most Czechs an important part of life, liberty and the pursuit of happiness. It was an accepted and enjoyed pastime in their homeland and carried over to the Czech communities in America. Many families brewed and bottled their own beer and made their own wine, as I have described my grandfather and uncles doing. Getting happily drunk with family, relatives and neighbors was not uncommon. They were seldom rowdy, simply congenial.

Drama productions in Old World costumes were presented frequently in the early years in Cedar Rapids—sometimes comedies, operettas or traditional Czech plays. Amateur actors, managers, musicians and ushers donated their time and talents and used the productions to raise money for some worthy cause. Local citizen artists made the props and painted scenery to recreate an Old World atmosphere of familiar houses, village and street scenes and landscapes of old Bohemia. The plays usually followed the European custom of having a prompter's box just below stage level, hidden from the audience by a small, shell-shaped screen. I remember going to such productions with my parents and relatives. But if the dialogue was in Czech, I had a hard time to follow the plot.

Language to the Czech is an integral part of their history and life. Because their ancestors struggled for centuries to maintain a national language and literature, they sought to preserve that language wherever in the world they settled. This, of course, is typical of many immigrant groups and strongly so in the case of Czechs. At the same time, they quickly welcomed opportunities to learn the language of the country they chose as their new homeland. The first generation settlers easily retained their native language through a network of mutual friends and societies, clubs and organizations of their countrymen.

Each second generation usually goes through what is often called an identity crisis and has a more difficult time to retain or learn the language. They may also lack motivation. A live-in grandparent such as I had, always a highly respected member of the family, is a convenient bridge for learning the folklore and language of the homeland. At least this preserves "home-style" conversation, although it usually does not provide a reading facility of the language or any formal knowledge of culture and history. When that family tie is severed and those brought up under such circumstances are out among majority English speaking people, the language lapse is evident. I am a typical example.

Looking back on more than 65 years of not using or even hearing the Czech language that I spoke exclusively for the first four years of my life, I find that I can understand more than I can speak. Since I learned it by hearing alone, I skipped the intermediate step of learning it through written words. The fact that I learned other languages in subsequent years gives me the strange sensation of automatically trying to answer a question posed to me in Czech with a different language coming from my mouth.

At the same time, I found that when I was re-exposed to basic Czech words and conversation, my "mental computer" began to display on my brain screen and through my audio apparatus some language identification that remains in my "hard disc," although it was never used or thought about for scores of years. It was simply never "erased." I didn't have to start from scratch to speak Czech again.

Mother's parents were born in Czechoslovakia, but Mother was born in Cedar Rapids. Early in the 20th century, second generation Czechs growing up in Cedar Rapids had opportunities for Saturday, Sunday and summer classes to study the Czech language. Sometimes classes were held in connection with a church, such as St. Wenceslaus Catholic parochial school where the priests often assisted with the instruction. They taught Czech grammar, composition, songs and prayers.

The first Czech school opened in the 1890s with about 200 students. A three-story Czech School was built in 1901 and was the first building in the United States to be used exclusively as a Czech school. Bazaars and community programs funded its construction and maintenance and Czech lodges and the Sokols also helped. The school was non-sectarian and free. In the early years, the girls were taught outside of regular school hours how to make lace, to knit and to embroider. As time went on, enrollment dropped and fell still further during the Communist regime to about 25 in 1953. It grew again in the 1990s when Communists lost power. A surge of enrollment came with the opening of the National Czech & Slovak Museum & Library in 1995. At this writing, the Czech language summer school has become popular again. It is held annually and attracts some children not of Czech descent who want to broaden their knowledge of world cultures. The school used the classrooms of Wilson School not far from Czech Village. Parents and the public celebrate the conclusion of the sessions with a performance and ice cream social.

When I was a child, a night school for adult students who wanted to learn the Czech language was held in the old Washington High School. Even some prominent Czech professional men of the city enrolled to brush up on their language skills. About 1934, Czech classes were organized as part of the curriculum of Washington and Grant public high schools, but they were later discontinued for lack of enrollment.

The parents of some of my young friends "forced" them to go to the Saturday Czech school. Typical of most second generation immigrant children, they didn't like to sacrifice their free Saturdays for more school. My parents and Baba would have liked me to attend, but as a self-willed (spoiled) only child, I usually got my own way. I never went to a single class. Looking back, I now regret the loss of that excellent opportunity.

For present third and fourth generation Czechs who want to know more about their culture, history, literature, music and art and for outsiders interested for a variety of reasons, language classes became available in more recent years. In 1974, adult evening classes began to be offered by Kirkwood Community College and included audio-visual resources. For some, they served as refresher courses in the language.

Through the years there have been eleven Czech newspapers published or circulated in the Cedar Rapids area, but none is published now. Some are still published in Chicago, Omaha, Texas,

Cleveland, New York City and elsewhere. Some lodges, societies and organizations publish house organs, journals or bulletins both in English and Czech.

To keep the Czech spirit and heritage alive in the traditional Czech shopping area of 16th Avenue Southwest in Cedar Rapids, long known as "Czech Town," a Czech Village Association was established. Buildings were renovated in the two block area, and merchants and businessmen helped to fund, restore and renovate the old cultural influences. New parking lots, pedestrian plaza walkways, the Riverfront Park and Riverside driveway were improved. A village clock tower on an island in front of the bandstand in the middle of the Village was an added attraction as well as a deterrent to fast traffic. Shops, buildings and restaurants are in Czech motif. Recorded folk music sometimes greets visitors and shoppers, and unmetered parking spaces welcome tourists and citizens.

The Czech Heritage Foundation was established in 1973 not only for Iowans but a wider membership from more than 25 states and abroad. It served as the liaison between the Fine Arts Foundation and the Czech Village Association. A quarterly newsletter and various books and booklets including history, music, recipes and traditions were made available.

Libraries of reading material in Czech were established through the years at various locations. Now the library of the Czech Fine Arts Foundation became part of the outstanding National Czech & Slovak Museum & Library which has become a repository for many Czech volumes. The collection includes books on fine arts, literature, poetry, history, music, folk arts, biography, travel, religion, children's books, encyclopedia sets, newspapers, magazines, almanacs and other titles. Although not a lending library, the books are available for research projects.

An outstanding way to perpetuate Czech heritage is the new Museum complex, one of the world's foremost institutions for preserving and interpreting the history and culture of Czechs and Slovaks. Their mission is to collect, restore and display historical materials, artifacts and crafts. Presidents of three countries—President Clinton, representing the host country, Vaclav Havel of the Czech Republic and President Kovac of Slovakia—participated in the dedication ceremony in 1995. It was a gala event that drew nationwide media attention.

Besides the Library, the Museum houses a permanent multimedia exhibition of Czech and Slovak homelands through fine and folk art, a stunning costume section, maps, military information, glassware and ceramics and a 19th century immigrant home. The complex includes a gift shop, exhibits of crafts and art objects from the Czech Republic and Slovakia and provides facilities for group events. It houses one of the largest in the United States authentic collections of costumes from different regions of the two countries. Displays and exhibits change according to the seasons and their international availability and include cut glass, ruby glass, porcelains, ceramic ware, works of art, pictures, handicrafts and tools. Had Baba and my parents lived to see this day of public pride accorded to their heritage in Cedar Rapids, they would be amazed.

Slovo, meaning *word* in Czech, is a professional, slick journal with outstanding photography published biannually by the Museum since Spring of 2000. It reinforces the Museum's mission of interpreting the panorama of Czech and Slovak history and culture, including the immigrant experience, to a very diverse audience. The magazine presents aspects of the Museum's mission in non-scholarly, accessible prose for popular audiences. Contributors of research articles and essays are drawn from a wide spectrum of scholars, community researchers, well-known authors and public figures.

Homemade meat products, baked goods from centuries-old recipes, saddle and leather products sold by folks who have been in the business for decades are still available on "The Avenue," as the Czech area of 16th Ave Southwest is referred to in Czech circles. Other businesses sell glassware, ceramics, antiques, imports from Czechoslovakia and handicrafts. You can find a variety of personal, professional and business services with Czech names serving not only the community but the metropolitan area of Cedar Rapids.

Not too many years went by before Czech settlers realized they needed a cemetery of their own. Before the turn of the 20th century, the Bohemian National Cemetery was established. Later its name was changed to Czech National Cemetery. Baba, my parents, all their brothers and sisters and most of our relatives are buried in the quiet, tree-dotted west side location at the crest of a hill overlooking the city.

While certain of my older relatives were alive, they persisted in following a tradition which seemed to be carried over from the Old Country. Either on Sunday morning or afternoon during three seasons of the year, they brought fresh cut flowers to put on the graves of their departed family members. They spent time clearing away wilted flowers from the previous week or filling the metal containers with fresh water. They generally made things neat around the headstones, although the cemetery has a perpetual care arrangement to keep the grass cut and trimmed. Then they strolled around looking at the bouquets on other graves, sometimes commenting on those that never got any fresh flowers. Sometimes they talked about their memories of the departed ones.

Many or perhaps most of the Czech families purchased family burial plots long before they needed them. It was an important decision to them. They would walk around looking over the grassy areas realizing that someday they would be lying there-- and perhaps wondering if anyone would put fresh flowers near their headstones.

I remember a particular, large chestnut tree that provided

shade on hot summer afternoons extending its branches over the headstones of my maternal grandfather, Antonin. Just for fun, Dad and I would often collect handfuls of chestnuts that had fallen to the ground while Mother did the fresh flower ritual. I tried to hang back from helping her because sometimes she wanted me to dump the stinky water from the metal containers and fill them at the faucets provided at intervals near the grave sites.

My parents seemed to go along with this ritual, although I don't recall that Baba would accompany us very often. "Babo," I asked her when I was a small child, "do the people under the ground know we bring flowers? Do they hear us when we talk about them?"

She answered me, "The real part of them, their spirit, is somewhere else. They don't know whether or not anyone puts fresh flowers on their graves. It is better to remember them in our hearts."

"If they aren't here, where are they? How did they get out of the ground?"

"Their bodies are still here, but the spirits of those who knew Jesus are in heaven with Him. They are not sick any more and are happy forever doing many exciting things with God. The others are somewhere else."

"Then why do people bring flowers?"

"Probably to show other people who are bringing flowers that their flowers are prettier than theirs or that they are more thoughtful," said Baba with a smile and a twinkle in her eye that both of us understood.

That satisfied me, and I took Baba's explanation as my own. I increasingly disliked going along on those too frequent family excursions to the cemetery. When I got old enough to have a choice, I stayed home or went over to one of my friend's homes on Sunday afternoons. My mother continued to follow the tradition, especially after my dad died, if she could get a ride with someone, since she never learned to drive. But she left me written instructions that after she died I should discontinue that tradition, which, because I no longer lived in my hometown, I would not have been able to fulfill anyway.

Before the snows of winter set in, it was the older Czechs' custom to decorate all the relatives' graves with artificial wreathes or evergreens or plastic flowers of some sort that would withstand the winter's gale winds and ice and snow storms.

Memorial Day during my childhood was a special day when grave sites were decorated quite lavishly. In fact, they called it "Decoration Day." Peonies, irises and other spring flowers were in full bloom by that time. On occasion, there were parades to the cemetery, speeches and other events. Because of his military service, my dad belonged to the American Legion and the Veterans of Foreign Wars organizations and often marched in those parades proudly wearing his Legionnaire cap.

When parades and events are held in Czech Village or for dancing groups, people who have authentic, colorful Czech costumes called "kroje," both men and women, wear them proudly. The particular combination of colors depends on the region in the Czech Republic or the specific village from which their ancestors came. There is symbolism to the different colors. White stands for cleanliness and purity and is worn on holidays and important celebrations such as christenings and weddings. Brown and black were colors associated with fertility. In the traditional wedding costume, the bride was to wear something in those colors so the couple would have children. Gold or yellow denoted the sun, harvest and riches. Red was the color of happiness and life. Both yellow and red were colors favored by brides even more than white. Dark blue was the color worn by older people, widows and widowers, and the color of working clothes. Green was associated with spring and summer, fertility and natural rebirth and renewal. It was usually worn by young people as a symbol of long lasting youth and energy. The bluebird, heart, dove and flowers are popular Czech symbols.

The costumes of people in Moravia, the place of my ancestry, are richly colorful and creative, often completely hand-worked with original designs. No part of them was left unadorned. For women and girls, large, puffy sleeves, heavily embroidered and full of lace, collar and decorative apron with bobbin lace, a long skirt, a vest or bolero full of shirred silk ribbons, sometimes with sequins front and back, sometimes laced in front are typical. More broad silk ribbons, also hand-embroidered, are worn around the waist, and they wear elaborate headdresses. Traditionally, unmarried girls wear a band of flowers with ribbon streamers. Married women wear caps of lace and bows or colorful head kerchiefs. The outfit is completed by black stockings and high boots.

Men and boys wear billowy, embroidered, long-sleeved white shirts, heavily embroidered vests, black decorated or embroidered trousers and shiny high black boots. Their leather belts are meant to circle their waists several times. Soft, felt mountain hats with a brim are often embellished with feathers from the tails of a rooster, ostrich or peacock. (Each long feather on a bachelor supposedly stands for a girl friend. After marriage they get clipped!)

One of the early Czech associations transplanted from their homeland was the Sokol organization which originated in Bohemia. The word "Sokol" means "falcon," a bird symbolizing swiftness and freedom. The association is best known for its group fitness training as a gymnastic club, but it stands for more than that. Sokol's aim is to educate people to the highest physical and mental proficiency, to nobleness and to morality. A three-story building, the Sokol Hall, with gymnasiums and gym apparatus was built in my hometown, and much of the training was geared to prepare for performance in massive group exhibitions or tournaments called "Slets." Those took place on a national and international level.

Until political events prevented it, the largest Slet was held in Czechoslovakia with literally thousands of Sokols in their uniforms executing drills, exercises and calisthenics in magnificent coordinated movements on an immense field. Track events, high jumps and broad jumps, shot put and discus were part of the exhibition in addition to the mass exercises.

Ordinary gym classes were also sponsored by Czech Sokols in Cedar Rapids for tumbling, balance bars, rings, leather horses and other apparatus. When I was an early teen, my parents urged me to sign up for classes since some of my school chums were doing so. Why not give it a try? I did, but because I was not very coordinated or eager to take risks, and everyone else seemed to be in good shape already, (and I was well-padded with extra pounds throughout my childhood) my enthusiasm soon wore thin and I quit.

The Sokols built a camp on the banks of a river about 18 miles from the city to which I went each summer for several years during late childhood. It was one of the high points of my year, a group experience for which I longed, since I always had to seek companionship outside my home. We slept in quite rustic individual cabins of about eight campers to one counselor, ate in a common dining hall and swam in the river. That's where I learned to swim and advanced from receiving my beginner's badge my first year to achieving junior life saving my last.

As we sat around the campfire each night, counselors taught us folk songs in the Czech language. I can sing several of them to this day. Group sports, story telling, skits, hiking, flag raising, wood lore—all were part of my first experiences of being away from home with a group my own age and primarily from Czech families. During the early morning flag raising and sunset lowering of the flag, I learned the proper way to fold and unfold the American flag, how to hoist it up the flag pole and properly respect our national emblem.

The Sokols and other Czech organizations held regular bazaars for fund raising, and our family went to most of them. My parents met their friends and relatives there, caught up on news and gossip and took advantage of the raffles for poultry. Sometimes Dad came home carrying a live goose or a quacking duck he won. Your admission ticket had numbers on it, and when they spun the big wheel on the platform, you were on tiptoe to know whether you were a winner. The part I didn't like was when Dad killed the poultry in our basement to the accompaniment of screeches and flying feathers. I held my hands to my ears.

Czech people love music and expressed it by forming numerous musical organizations after they arrived in America. In Cedar Rapids, their bands, orchestras and ensembles played for parades, funeral processions, programs, plays, dedication of buildings and festivals commemorating their special days. Czech music was in demand for parties, election rallies, state fairs, firemen's tournaments and picnics. Choral clubs singing Czech folk songs are still popular. The whole city enjoys their performances.

Music is a major way the Czechs have perpetuated their heritage. Their music is upbeat, quick tempo, suitable for spirited dancing, always in a major key. The polka, written in 2/4 time, is a vivacious dance for couples. It was only introduced in Prague in 1837 but soon spread to the rest of Europe and America. The Beseda, the national dance of the Czech people, is a collection of mazurkas, polkas and waltzes, performed for spectators by group dancers at weddings and other festive occasions.

Typical instruments for Czech band music are accordions, clarinets, saxophones, trumpets, cornets, tubas and drums. Marches and waltzes are popular. Czechoslovakia was not without its famous classical composers and musicians who wrote operas, chamber music, choral works, orchestral works, symphonies and piano pieces. Dvorak, Smetana, Brenda and Janacek are only few of the names familiar to musicians. Another, Martinu, a noted pianist and violinist with the Czech Philharmonic Orchestra, was born in Policka, the Moravian town of my mother's ancestry. Years later I was privileged to visit his birthplace.

The Czechs were a dancing people in their homeland, and their delight in kicking up their heels carried over to their adopted land. On Saturday nights during my childhood, Aunt Fan would take me along with some of my cousins to the C.S.P.S. Hall or one of the lodge halls where we children sat in the balcony looking down on the dancers. Sometimes it was polka dancing with partners, somewhat like square dancing, sometimes it was the Beseda. Later they included ballroom dancing of quite a lively sort. Much merriment—and drinking—characterized such gatherings.

Even an attempt to list the most famous of the traditional Czech dishes and what goes into making them would be a selection dilemma. Food has been a major way to perpetuate their culture. Kolaches, of course, the most popular yeast pastry, are distinctively Czech. The word comes from "kolo" which means round or wheel. They are tasty and welcome everywhere from formal weddings to intimate family gatherings. I grew up thinking they were always about three inches in diameter, open-faced, (although occasionally covered) with fruit fillings like prune, cherry, berry, poppy seed and sweet cottage cheese. Not until I traveled in Czechoslovakia was I introduced to the original size and shape. It is like a large pie or a pizza, and is sliced and served like a pizza. Each Czech woman seems to have her favorite recipe for them. There are as many variations are there are dumpling recipes.

Staples are roast pork, goose, duck, rabbit, sauerkraut, potatoes, cabbage and dumplings—but oh, the variety of ways to fix those common ingredients! Meals wouldn't be complete without serving dense rye bread, usually with caraway seed. Egg noodles in many different shapes and consistencies beckon you. Czechs serve soups, thick and thin, in infinite variety, always tasty and before nearly every meal. Mushroom dishes abound.

When it comes to desserts, an apple strudel sends me swiftly back to my childhood. Kneaded dough stretched until paper thin at least the size of an open newspaper is piled with apple slices, raisins and nuts, sprinkled with melted butter, cinnamon and sugar. Then it is gently rolled like a huge jelly roll. The process takes more than one pair of hands. It always stretched across our entire dining room table like a gigantic worm before baking in the oven. Eaten warm and topped with real whipped cream or ice cream...well...!

A discussion of foods that perpetuate the Czech heritage would be incomplete without revealing some of the marvels of "knedliki" (dumplings). A dumpling doesn't look glamorous beside the rest of the attractive stuff on your dinner plate, but it is the true test of a cook's proficiency. Too much flour, they say, and you have a "bomba"—a cannonball. Too much liquid and you have noodles. Boil it too long and you get pond sludge. Don't boil it long enough and you get raw pond sludge. A good "knedlik" is never hard, heavy or soggy. However, potato dumplings are dense and moist, bread-based ones are somewhere in between and yeast ones have the consistency of feather cushions. Supposedly there are 14 categories of them—some are steamed, boiled, served in sauce, plopped into soup, covered with gravy. The dessert variety is filled with fresh fruit, dropped into boiling water, and when fished out, smothered with butter, sugar and cinnamon, sometimes grated cheese. (Some fruit dumpling lovers have been known to eat 30 or more at a sitting!)

Not only are the right ingredients essential for making dumplings, but the right proportions, the right touch by the cook in folding, jabbing, shaping, beating to incorporate just the right amount of air and handling them with the proper implements are the secrets. Family recipes live on and points of technique are debated. Good Czech cooks say it takes "a trick"—whatever that means—all the way to properly slicing the fluffy kind of bread dumplings with a thread slipped under the finished product and crossed over the top. It is never cut with a knife!

Some herbs which show up in many Czech dishes are caraway seed, poppy seed, rosemary, sage, marjoram, saffron, dill and the ever-popular garlic. Some herbs are used for medicinal purposes. There are Old World remedies for many ailments. I know, because Baba "inflicted" many of them on me!

14

Czech Festivals and Celebrations

A major way of perpetuating Czech heritage is the celebration of Czech customs and traditions through festivals held throughout the year. Their importance demands a separate chapter. Some of them are still celebrated on "The Avenue" in the Czech part of my hometown as well as in Czechoslovakia. They are happy times for those of Czech descent and likewise enjoyed by the community. Perhaps some of the celebrations will diminish in years to come. On the other hand, they may increase since it has become more popular to acknowledge one's ethnic roots.

"Houby Days" (mushroom days) in May feature Czech folk art and customs, Czech music and dancing, mushroom hunting contests, parades and more. The breakfast menu, of course, features mushrooms. Our family's search for mushrooms is described elsewhere in this book.

The Czech Village Festival in Cedar Rapids, the largest of the yearly events, traditionally takes place the weekend following Labor Day in September. Featured are carnival entertainment, music, dancing, contests, a flea market, a "Bake-Off," kolache eating contests, a beer garden, a parade and other fun events for children and adults.

St. Joseph's Day, the Czech version of St. Patrick's Day, is celebrated on March 19th to commemorate Joseph, the adoptive father of Jesus and patron saint of working people. Everyone with the name Joseph or any derivative, one of the most common Czech names, is honored—a day for fun and merrymaking. In Czech Village, the taverns serve red beer, the bakery sells red bread, the Village is decorated with red banners and a late afternoon parade circles The Avenue. This event also signals the beginning of spring.

The Czech Christmas calendar started on December 4th (St. Barbara's Day) when girls brought the sprig of a blossoming tree into the house and placed it in water. They believed that if this "Good Luck Branch" blossomed on Christmas Eve, good fortune was in store. If unmarried, the girl would find a good husband during the coming year.

St. Nicholas Day is celebrated on the Saturday before December 6th. The "real" Saint Nicholas was born about 270 A.D. in Patara, Lycia, a small country along the Mediterranean Sea, now a part of present day Turkey. The legend of his generosity and good works spread and at the beginning of the 12th century, the custom of bringing gifts in connection with it originated in France. Nuns in a convent began the practice of leaving gifts secretly at the homes of poor families with small children on St. Nicholas Eve, December 5th. The gifts were fruit, nuts and oranges from Spain, which in those days were luxuries. The legend spread all over Europe and was observed by rich and poor alike. Street parades were led by a man representing the saint. He was mounted on a white horse, dressed in a red bishop's robe, wore the traditional mitred hat and carried a shepherd's crook. He became the patron saint of children throughout the world and was known by other names like Svaty Mikulas, San Nicola, Pere Noel, Sinterklass, Sonnerklass and Kriss Kringle. We finally transformed him into Santa Claus in America!

Legend has it that St. Nicholas descends from heaven on a golden cord. He is accompanied by an "andel" (angel) in white and a "cert" (devil) dressed in black with his face painted red. The wicked devil carries a switch and rattles a chain, while the sweet angel consults her book which lists the name of all good children. The children are asked whether they have been well-behaved and whether they say their prayers. The angel writes the record in her book. If they nod honestly, they are given gifts of apples, nuts, gingerbread and candy. The devil, lurking in the background, rattles his chain and stands ready to punish mischievous children with his switch and to give them his gift—a piece of coal. This drama is reenacted on the streets of Czech Village annually with costumed children playing the parts of the angel and devil. The event marks the official start of the Christmas season which ends with a visit of the Three Kings on January 6th.

As a child, I never had a problem with believing in Santa Claus because I understood that Saint Nicholas was a real person in history. I avoided the disillusionment of my young friends who eventually "found out there was no real Santa Claus." I maintained that there *was* one, and I could prove it!

On the day of Christmas Eve called "vanoce," everyone is supposed to fast until evening. Legend has it that anyone who successfully does so will see the "Golden Pig" and have good luck all year. (Perhaps their hunger gives them hallucinations!)

Czechs admit that the custom of decorating a Christmas tree came from Germany. Traditional decorations included real candles, hand-blown glass ornaments, gingerbread cookies, wrapped candies, nuts, honey cakes and ornaments crafted from straw or cloth and baked dough. When I was born, Mother and Dad bought a little artificial tree about four feet high whose branches they would unfold when they took it from storage. It became our family tradition. Such trees were called "feather trees" and were popular among Czechs. We had authentic Czech hand-blown ornaments in various shapes and colors with which we decorated it until I left for college. I remember the shapes of those ornaments to this day—birds, flowers, animals, stars, bells—having handled them and treasured them year after year. Tinsel rope garlands, foil icicles and a tinsel star at the top completed the adorning of our little tree.

When I was young, I didn't realize the special tradition connected with little "feather trees." As a teen, I begged for a "real tree like everyone else" which my parents finally consented to buy each year. Mother still decorated our "feather tree" throughout my college years. I don't know what happened to it after my husband and I left for China, but if I had it today and kept those ornaments, it would be a priceless collector's item. I would have been delighted to pass it on to my children and grandchildren.

The tradition of eating carp on Christmas Eve dates back many centuries. A fish was the symbol of Christ from the days of the Early Church. I asked Baba about it. "Is that the same kind of fish Dad catches in the Cedar River?"

"Your dad catches river mud carp which tastes much different from fresh pond carp. In Czechoslovakia, nearly every village has a community pond which all families contribute to stocking with baby fish in the spring. The fish grow big during the summer. Each year before winter comes and the pond freezes, families take nets and catch all the big fish and divide them among the families. Then the pond is drained dry until it is filled again next spring. The carp they plan to use for their traditional Christmas eve dinner must be kept alive until use."

"How did they do that, Baba?"

"The carp was put into the bathtub to swim around until time to prepare it, sometimes many days later. That was fun for the children."

"Could the children take a bath with the carp?"

"Of course not, Leonko!" Baba laughed. "They may be permitted to skip their baths until just before Christmas. In winter, people didn't take as many baths as in summer."

The tradition was to fix the big carp in four different ways. Best cuts were covered with flour, dipped in egg, then bread crumbs and fried. Other cuts were steamed and then smothered with a thick black sauce of prunes, nuts, raisins, carrots, parsley, celery, hard gingerbread and spices. That was served with dumplings made with butter-fried cubes of bread or rolls. A third portion was made into sort of a gelatin and chilled for appetizers later. The head and tail were wrapped in a cloth and boiled with herbs. They used that stock for soup with finely cut carrots and other garden vegetables.

For Christmas Eve dinner when she lived with us, Baba always made pearl barley soup with some of the mushrooms she had dried. That was the traditional appetizer. Some parts of the carp prepared as above were then served along with fruit and some of the goodies she and Mother would have been baking for weeks. That included the "pernicks," gingerbread, kolaches, apple strudel, "vanocka" (braided Christmas sweet bread), decorated cookies and sweet, nutty Christmas crescents. From early childhood, I was allowed to help spread the frosting on the cookies and put "the sprinkles" on them. Later, I learned how to use cookie cutters in different shapes to cut out the dough.

"What did you do on Christmas Eve in your country when Dad was a little boy?" I asked Baba.

"We had a big family and not much money, but we followed as many of the traditions as we could. As it began to get dark, we all went outdoors to watch for the first star to come out, which reminded us of the star that led the wise men to Jesus. When we went indoors, we would say a prayer of thanks to God, then eat our Christmas Eve meal for which some relatives usually joined us. Afterward, we would gather around the wood stove and sing Christmas hymns like "Ticha Noc" (Silent Night). Under the Christmas tree, which we cut from the forest ourselves, we had a little wooden manger scene called "Betlem." Someone secretly tinkled a little bell on the Christmas tree to signal that "Jezisek," the Christ Child, who was traveling through the countryside, had brought gifts. Then it was time to open the presents. When your dad was a little boy, the gifts were mostly new homemade things to wear or homemade toys, maybe a new pair of shoes or boots for each child.

"I remember one more custom," said Baba. "On Christmas Eve, we would put down a bedding of straw or hay on our wooden floor (we didn't have rugs or carpets) near the Christmas tree, and if the children wanted to sleep on it, we reminded them that they were participating in the poor and humble birth of baby Jesus.

"On Christmas Eve, most families went to a candle light service in our church. But it was a very long walk for us, several miles through the deep forest and over many hills from our little village of Radlice to our church in the bigger town of Velka Lhota. Often the snow was deep and drifted. We would have had to carry our lanterns in the dark. The bitter wind might blow them out. So we usually waited until Christmas morning, and after we ate our hot carp soup and cooked porridge and "vanocka," we would all bundle up and go to church singing carols along the way, perhaps joined by other neighbors as we walked. Sometimes we got a ride with a neighbor who had a sleigh pulled by horses."

In Czechoslovakia, on Christmas Day, "Hod Bozi" Baba called it, dinner might include giblet soup with noodles, roast goose with dumplings and sauerkraut, lots of bakery, fruit, nuts and coffee. The day was spent visiting and receiving relatives and friends and eating more goodies. It was the custom for those who had quarreled during the year to forgive each other publicly.

The day after Christmas was St. Stephen's Day, a time for children to go caroling. If someone invited them in from the cold, they received rewards of candies, fruit and cookies. Sometimes children carried miniature Bethlehem scenes with them.

"Where does Good King Wenceslaus fit in, Baba? Our teacher at school said it was a Czech carol."

"Vaclav, or Wenceslaus, was a good king who lived long ago in our country. He is known as the patron saint of Bohemia. Legend has it that in the cold winter, the king himself would cut wood in the forest and secretly carry it to needy widows and orphans of his kingdom on Christmas. The carol tells about his good deeds. He was killed when still young. The Catholic Church called him a Saint, and there is a big statue of him on his horse in Prague overlooking a section of the city named after him."

December 31 was called "Sylvestr" after a saint by that name. Czechs serve a drink of eggnog with cognac and eat "chlebycky" (little open-faced sandwiches heaped with potato salad, ham, eggs, sliced pickles and cheese).

The Christmas season officially ended for Czechs on January 6, "Tri Krale" (Three Kings) Day. Three men would dress up in costumes like kings and go caroling. To give a blessing to the families in the community, with a piece of chalk blessed by the local priest, they would write above the doorway of each home the traditional name of one of the kings who brought gifts to Jesus--either the words Kaspar, Melchior or Balthazar or just K or M or B. That day was the signal to take down the Christmas tree.

Easter was a more important holiday than Christmas among the Czechs, and a joyous one because it commemorated the death and resurrection of Jesus Christ. To attend church services is high on the agenda for most families, although a sunrise service is not traditional. A typical Easter dish in the past, when sheep were kept in large numbers in rural Moravia, was baked lamb. (Lamb symbolized Christ who was called The Lamb of God.) Later, other delicacies replaced it with a pastry baked in the shape of a lamb either of leavened dough or sort of a sponge cake.

The tradition of decorating eggs has been passed on from generation to generation for over 2000 years. The egg represented rebirth in the spring of the year, new spiritual life now and future hope in the life to come. "Kraslice" (decorated eggs) became a long time special skill of Czechs since the 14th century. They prepared the natural dyes themselves by using onion skins, flowers, berries, bark, leaves, seeds and even moss. Each village had its distinctive motifs and colors with different symbolism.

The eggs that were to be eaten would be colored after being hard boiled and cooled. For the unique, creative decorating of ornamental eggs that would last for years as souvenirs, the white and yolk were blown out through a small hole at each end of the raw egg. When Baba lived with us, she colored eggs the former way. When Easter approached, she would boil onion skins she had been saving. That provided a rich, reddish brown dye. She used melted wax from a honey comb to draw designs or names on the egg shell with a large needle or wooden match stick. Then she dipped the egg into the dye. After drying, she wiped off the wax and the design was left in white. She had various other color dyes, but I think they were already store bought. Red and purple are the most common colors symbolizing the passion of Christ and His victory over the grave. Red and purple flower designs are favored. True folk artists use several phases involving a number of dye baths and using batik techniques. Some involve pasting bits of straw or other fabrics or lace designs or cut outs before multiple dipping.

Baba said that in her village a small, leafless tree would be cut down and adorned with colored eggshells, flowers and ribbons. Girls would parade their decorated trees around the neighborhood competing with one another for the prettiest one. This Easter Egg tree would be like the Christmas tree and kept either outdoors or in the house.

In Czechoslovakia, one custom on Easter Monday was for village boys to plait willow twigs into switches and playfully chase and lightly lash the girls with those whips. They were appeased by the girls with gifts of Easter eggs and lots of laughter. But on Easter Tuesday, the girls had the right to whip the boys in return! In some regions of Moravia, young people drench one another with cold water. That was said to give them good health!

*Leona's childhood home on 26th Street
in Cedar Rapids, Iowa*

Baba and Leona (age 8) and her mother

15

Religious Life Among Czech Immigrants

This chapter is important to set the stage for my own spiritual journey. I wish I had known earlier the complexities of the religious situation among Czechs in my hometown. When I was a child, of course I didn't understand it. I didn't know the historical background in Czechoslovakia, and I wasn't a Christian. I doubt that my parents really understood it either because I'm sure they weren't aware of the whole picture. Only my later research and the perspective of the "rear view mirror" enabled me to sort it out and understand its effect on me.

It has been said that among no other immigrants have so many people professed *religious liberalism*. I was vaguely aware of that while growing up, but I didn't know how to label it. It might have originated in the attempts in the 15th century by followers of Jan Hus to correct the abuses of the Roman Catholic Church and to offset Austrian autocracy with Czech democracy.

For the two centuries following, Protestantism was the dominant religion of Bohemia. Then the Czechs were defeated in that much-talked-about battle of the White Mountain in 1620, after which the Catholic Church was solidly back in power under the rule of Austria.

Many Protestant Czechs fled to other countries at that time. More than 150,000 people, including 80 percent of the nobility, went into exile within six years. Among them was the great educator, Jan Amos Komensky (Comenius). Those who remained, worshiped in secret at the risk of their lives, still clinging to the evangelical faith of Jan Hus.

When Baba and her family left the country, it was 96 percent Catholic. Her fellow worshipers were definitely in the minority, and often less than happy relationships existed between the two religious groups. Therefore, Protestants, Catholics and many free-thinkers made up the Czech immigrants to this country.

Who were the free-thinkers? In large part, they were anti-Catholic because that religion represented to them an association with the Austrian autocracy which they hated. It gobbled up all the best of their land, three-fourths of the country, beheaded 27 of their leaders in one day, levied high taxes and repressed the people. As a result, Catholicism was proclaimed the state religion. The free-thinkers gladly welcomed what they thought was the American idea of the separation of church and state. At least they understood it to mean that there would be no state religion here to impose itself upon the free rights of the people. They were right about that.

Not all free-thinkers were atheists, but many were. They believed life is what you make it right here for yourself and your family, and there is no existence beyond death. Others believed vaguely in nature as some kind of guiding force for mankind. Still others had faith in a Creator, but they didn't approve of an organized church, so they avoided any church contacts.

Among the early Czech settlers in Cedar Rapids, many had liberal ideas or were militantly anti-Catholic because of what they suffered in the Old Country. They gathered to debate new thoughts concerning liberalism, published a paper and arranged educational lectures. The members of the Sokols and the fraternal organizations were largely free-thinkers in practice, though there were notable exceptions. Because they officially organized themselves as a society and became incorporated, their leaders were authorized to conduct marriage ceremonies, funerals and the like. As a movement, it did not gain momentum, especially among the young. Some members eventually joined very liberal or Unitarian churches or simply continued to stay away from organized religion. Because some Czech people preferred not to have a minister or priest conduct a funeral service, there were "speakers" available from among the free-thinkers to perform that service. Many of the Czechs I knew as relatives and friends during my growing years were wonderful, industrious, honest, warm-hearted people and good neighbors, but they stayed outside of the organized church and gave little thought to what would happen to them when this life ended.

We had a Czech neighbor who was one of the warmest, most loving and accepting ladies I knew. She was my favorite and my confidant, and I spent many evenings hanging out on her porch talking about anything and everything on my young mind. I admired her above all the grown ups on our block. She came from Czechoslovakia as a young woman, married and had two children younger than I. My spiritual life was beginning to dawn and I was seeking after God. Because she was such a wonderful woman, I was almost certain she must know a lot about God. Still shy and insecure, I decided to write her a private letter to ask her some serious questions. "Do you believe in God? If you do, why? If you don't, why not? Can you tell me about God?" I gave my note to her secretly, sealed with some wax!

She took several days to answer me, then called me over one evening for our porch chat. "Leona, I'm sorry to tell you that I don't believe in God. If you only knew the terrible things we went through in the Old Country at the hands of the church and the priests in the name of the established church, you would understand. I can never forgive or forget that persecution. They said they did it for God. So I don't believe in God."

I was deeply disillusioned and somewhat set back in my search for God for awhile. She was such a good woman in every way and remained my close friend throughout my high school years. I was personally disappointed and baffled. No, I didn't know anything about the persecution she talked about. I couldn't believe God would have inspired that abuse. Surely she must have misunderstood her oppressors. In hindsight, I believe she and her family were among the free-thinkers who wanted to keep as far away from the organized church as they could.

A number of Czech Catholic churches were established in my hometown, and there was a sizeable Catholic community whose people had strong bonds with each other. St. Wenceslaus, Immaculate Conception and St. Ludmila churches each sponsored schools in which Czech priests and nuns taught. Eventually they bought a cemetery of their own, Saint John's.

St. Ludmila's Church was only a few blocks from my "Teta" (Aunt) Slavik's house on J street Southwest. She was Antonia Slavik, one of Baba's married daughters, who lived there with her husband, Uncle Jake, and college student son, Godfrey. From early childhood, I looked forward to the fun of the annual Kolache Festival in June at that Catholic church, an event enjoyed by the whole community, Czech and non-Czech. A money-raiser for the church, it included a bazaar and a carnival with drinks and kolaches served with each paid admission.

The Protestant community affected me more directly because of Baba's personal faith and regular church attendance, although in my high school years I joined a Presbyterian Church that had no ethnic connections.

Baba was a member of the Czech Evangelical and Reformed Church that met in a small brick building at the Southwest corner of Second street and Fifteenth Avenue Southwest. It was built not long before Baba came to America. The need for a church arose because many members of the Independent Reformed Church of Ely, Iowa had moved to Cedar Rapids and wished to organize a branch of their mother congregation. The Ely church, organized in 1858, was the first Czech Protestant church in the United States. The small congregation in Cedar Rapids borrowed other buildings and even met in a tent for their worship in the Czech language from 1907 until their church was built and dedicated debt free in 1911.

I was baptized as an infant in that church by the minister, Rev. Frank Helmich, who came to the pastorate in 1922 and served until 1939. Baba's funeral was conducted by the minister who followed him, Rev. Milo Filipi.

During my early childhood, all sixty-some members were of Czech descent and morning worship was conducted in the Czech language. Later, the Sunday School and youth societies began to use English. From our home on the east side of town to Baba's church on the west side seemed a great distance to me in the early days. She was unable to attend unless my dad gave her a ride and arranged to pick her up afterward. That was an inconvenience for him because Sunday was a work day in the restaurants that he and Mother managed during most of my childhood into my teen years.

Baba took me to church with her from the time I was a toddler, and I sat beside her during adult worship. I was too shy to be left alone in Sunday School, therefore I received no Christian training at my age level. I remember being fidgety and trying to pass the time by watching the fascinating colors of the biblical scenes in the stained glass windows as the sun shown through, by

thumbing through the Czech hymnbook or looking at an occasional picture story paper a teacher might give me.

Baba's habit was to stand in reverence with bowed head
for a moment of silent prayer when she first came into the row of
pews, then bowing slightly (genuflecting) before sitting down. That
impressed me. When I was old enough to talk, I asked her innumerable "Why?" questions.

"Baba, why do we go to church?"

It satisfied my childish mind when she simply replied, "To
worship God and His Son, Jesus."

It was much later that I asked, "Is God that tall, fat man
with the round face and black suit who stands in front and talks to
the people every Sunday?"

She laughed and set me straight. "No, Pan Helmich (Rev.
Helmich) is just a wonderful man who studies the Bible a lot and
knows God better than some of the rest of the people. He tells us
many things about how God made the world and how we can live
to please His Son, Jesus." Neither of whom, she explained, could
we see with our eyes because they were invisible.

I was relieved to know that the minister's son, Dan, also a
husky young man with a round face who taught a Sunday School
class and raised chickens on a farm was not the Son we came to
worship—nor was his dad God!

In the hot summers before the days of air conditioning,
we were sticky-hot and had to fan ourselves with cardboard "funeral fans" like the one Baba fanned me with when I was a baby.
When I close my eyes, I can still see the hard, polished oak pews
and the tall palm plants at the sides of the platform. I can hear the
tiny, wheezy organ and continuous drone of the small oscillating
electric fans that attempted to circulate the hot air. I can smell the
damp, musty odor coming up from the cool basement. They are
vivid memories. In my mind, I can still hear the friendly, whispered Czech chatter after the service as members took advantage

of being in church to socialize and catch up on the news of one another's families in town or still in the Old Country. I must have made a nuisance of myself tugging at Baba's dress, begging to leave quickly because I was impatient to do something else.

Sometimes we walked what I realize now must have been a long way for Baba—all the way from church to my Teta Slavik's house. We often spent the rest of the day there until my dad had time to come and take us home. All those distances that I remember as being so far are actually so short when I visit my hometown now and retrace the distances. Teta Tony and Uncle Jake had a small cherry, apple and pear orchard behind their home and raised chickens and ducks. They rented the large vacant lot next to their home for a large garden and grew many vegetables and rows of sweet corn. Apparently they shared the garden with my parents because when Dad came for us, both he and Mother would spend a few hours working in the garden and bringing home some of the produce.

When I was older, I would accompany Baba on the street car that ran on trolley tracks. I was her interpreter when we needed to transfer to a second street car that took us to her church.

Baba brought me to Christmas celebrations at this little church from the time I learned to walk. I was intrigued by the costumes in the nativity play, the carols, the recitations by young children—all warm and friendly sights and sounds. I was wide-eyed at the Christmas tree that reached nearly to the ceiling and captivated by the many decorations brought from the Old Country by families of the congregation. I remember the pungent fragrance of the pine branches mingled with the burning smell of real candles in dishes on the window sills casting shadows against the stained glass windows. The small congregation sat in semi-darkness for the Christmas program. I can visualize the sparkling, lighted star at the top of the tree almost brushing the ceiling. My childish eyes took it all in and I was full of "Whys?" for Baba when we were alone and it was tucking-in-bed time.

She took her time to explain in simple Czech the story of the birth of Jesus, the shepherds, the wise men, why they rode on camels instead of in motor cars and why they wore funny clothes. I asked her whether all the angels were named Harold. It puzzled her because she didn't understand the English words of the Christmas carols the young children sang. "Hark, the *herald* angels sing" would have gone by her. She asked Pan Helmich to explain that one and they had a good laugh at my expense.

When I began learning to read in school, Baba gave my mother some money to buy a Bible in English as her gift to me at Christmas. She asked mother to write the date in it, then she carefully wrapped it for me under the Christmas tree. I still have that first Bible—a precious treasure from my Baba.

Often Baba and I stayed at Teta Slavik's for days at a time, especially during vacations. Sometimes I invited my best friend, Dot, from our neighborhood to come along, and we spent many summer afternoons on the porch swing or climbing trees in the orchard. Prickly red raspberry bushes grew in the orchard. In my estimation, nothing can beat the fragrance and taste of soft, ripe raspberries smothered with heavy sweet cream. Teta Slavik was a good cook of Czech delicacies, and our family enjoyed many savory meals there, especially on holidays. As a small child, I enjoyed eating chicken brains! Baba always saved that sweet delicacy from the fried chicken to indulge her little granddaughter.

Around the time of the monthly meeting of the women's Lydia Circle from Baba's church, we came again to Teta Slavik's. The meeting was conducted in Czech with singing, prayers and Bible study and the ladies would linger on into the afternoon. After the traditional coffee and kolaches, they busied themselves working on quilts or other projects to raise money for benevolent works of the church.

"Why do we always visit Mrs. Nezerka?" I asked Baba as we walked the short block from Teta Tony's to the house of Baba's elderly friend.

"Because Mrs. Nezerka is afraid to die. We go to pray with her and tell her about heaven."

"Is everybody going to die?" I asked, wide-eyed. "Are you going to die, too, Baba?"

"Yes, everyone dies. In the cemetery there are big graves and little graves. But Baba isn't afraid to die because she will be in heaven with Jesus and God. Remember that, Leonko, and don't be sad. It will be a happy time."

I didn't understand fully. All I could think of was how sad I would be if I couldn't hold Baba's hand anymore.

Baba had a very special friend we visited often when we stayed at Teta Tony's. Mrs. Loyka had been Baba's friend ever since they were little girls in Czechoslovakia. Baba and Mrs. Loyka spent a lot of time praying together and reading their Bibles when we visited, but she always kept a closet full of books and toys for me to play with, so I didn't mind going with Baba on those visits.

Summer picnics in the park with the little congregation from Baba's church were also times when Baba would take me with her. I never participated in the contests or sports because in my early childhood I didn't know how to play with other children. So I just hung around with Baba and her often quite elderly friends.

I understand that by the 1970s the church no longer held Czech worship services because most members transferred to English speaking churches with their families. Since the second generation didn't understand Czech, it did not seem practical to continue a Czech church. The old brick building still stands but is now occupied by the Redemption Missionary Baptist denomination.

The other major Czech Protestant church was the Jan Hus Memorial Presbyterian Church. Organized in 1880, the small congregation met for years in homes to study the Bible and sing hymns in Czech in long meter to the accompaniment of a violin. They met for two years in a room in a packing plant where boxes served as seats, then for several years thereafter borrowed the facilities of other churches. It took many years before the mostly poor, early Czech settlers could afford a church building. Sometimes those Cedar Rapids Czech Christians would walk the incredible distance of nine miles to the nearby town of Ely to hear sermons by a Czech pastor—and walked nine miles back the same afternoon!

In 1889, the church was officially incorporated. They purchased the frame structure of the First Congregational Church for $1600, including the pews, and literally moved it in one piece to the corner of Ninth Avenue and Seventh Street Southeast—a monumental feat.

The congregation continued to grow for the next decades, and in 1915 that old church building was sold and for a second time moved away to another location, making room for a new structure to be built on the same spot. I have an old photo of the move with my dad at about age 25 standing in front as part of the labor crew. The new building was dedicated debt free in 1916.

In the beginning, they used only the Czech language. Later, some sermons were delivered in English, and eventually two separate services were held every Sunday morning. Ninety percent of the congregation were of Czech descent as late as 1942, but no Czech language services were held after 1959.

My parents began attending that church during the time I was in college and were active in the Mariners Anchor Club for couples. Mother was involved in the Tabitha Women's Society which assisted overseas missions and community work. Dad was a deacon at the time of his death.

Ted and I were married in that church in 1947, after we both graduated from Wheaton College in Illinois the same year.

We sailed for Hong Kong several months after our wedding.

The church building on that location was eventually sold to the New Jerusalem Church of God in Christ, and the Czech congregation built a new church building in 1973 at Schaeffer Drive and Twenty-ninth Street Southwest. They brought along the large pipe organ from the former church. A large percent of the church members are still of Czech descent, although not many are able to speak Czech. The ministers who serve the church now are no longer ethnic Czechs.

Leona (age 14) with parents

16

My World in High School

Life continued normally for me as I made the transition from Buchanan to McKinley, a combined junior and senior high school at the time. I had to walk a longer distance to school and often biked in good weather, even coming home for lunch occasionally. No bussing in those days. In winter, unless snow fell more than a foot or two and drifted, we were still expected to get to school. We loved school closing days after a serious ice storm.

Approaching my teens, I was a tomboy and enjoyed doing outdoor things with Dad because that seemed to be the only time I could have him to myself. I thought he probably missed having a son, so he taught me to fish, bought me my own pole and showed me how to dig worms in dirt where he previously dumped coffee grounds. I learned to make bait out of dough, cotton and vanilla extract. He taught me to shoot a 22 caliber rifle, whistle through my teeth and spit cherry seeds to hit a target. He bought me a genuine Red Ryder BB gun by Daisy Company for $2.95 from the Wards catalog. I got to be quite expert at target shooting.

Dad and I liked to go to the Palisades on the Cedar River to fish from a row boat. The Palisades-Kepler Park is some miles out of town where the Cedar River carved its way through layers of limestone leaving some bluffs 90 feet high. They come straight down into the water with nooks and crannies that looked spooky to me. When I got into high school, I read that geologists claim this part of Iowa was at one time repeatedly covered with water from floods, along with most of the land west of the Mississippi river. Huge mammals probably roamed the land at the same time as amphibious creatures but died off in the later glacial drift. By the time the ice reached this area, it began to melt and washed down good, fertile top soil to benefit Iowa's future agriculture and formed Iowa's rivers. In its wake, it left behind some gigantic boulders like one deposited in Bever Park down the hill from the bandstand. Children liked to slide down from it into the soft sand at the bottom of the boulder beside a little stream. I had fun hunting for fossils at the Palisades and managed to have quite a collection.

Dad and I had a special ritual we enjoyed sometimes when he came home late at night from work. He was fond of stinky but delicious Limburger cheese and pickled herrings from a wooden tub with spices floating in it. We'd hang out in the kitchen with the door closed so we wouldn't wake anyone, spread the cheese on crackers and just talk about stuff. Dad and I were close, and he was not reticent about hugging his daughter at any age. I liked it when people called me "Daddy's girl." Ours was a satisfying, comfortable, healthy relationship.

I remember having a relatively happy childhood. No family is perfect, of course, but I don't think we were a dysfunctional family. Scores of years later, it seems popular to call most families of the past dysfunctional as an excuse to blame all one's problems on parents. We didn't yell at one another, no one abused anyone else, my parents didn't criticize me or put me down with any verbal abuse. I don't remember outbursts of anger—except my own. Admittedly, I was a spoiled child accustomed to having my own way. The dictionary definition for "sullen" describes me: "showing irritation and ill humor by a gloomy silence; sulky, moody." I had a critical disposition toward myself and others, including my parents. Nevertheless, we were all still civil to one another and kept our emotions largely under control. In front of my friends, however, I guess I appeared to be cheerful and forced myself to be out-going because I wanted them to accept me.

I didn't have as much time to do outdoor things with Dad after new things like gym classes, sports, music classes, social studies, history, literature, sewing, cooking, biology and chemistry began challenging me to explore a new world. I studied Latin, later French, sang in the chorus and participated in musical dramas throughout high school. My friendships expanded and some of my shyness began to disappear. Academic classes were where I finally came into my own. I studied hard, earned good grades and was eventually elected to the National Honor Society. Algebra and Geometry, however, were my downfall, and I had a difficult time getting passing grades. My brain simply didn't grasp those concepts. In English and literature I excelled.

I didn't like the stupid, misfitting, one piece gym suits we girls were required to wear for sports. They were usually yucky green or "prison blue," as I called it. And I didn't like the lack of privacy in communal showers. Sewing was a bore. Who wanted to make aprons? Cooking was a time to goof off. I can't remember making anything except "eggs goldenrod" and cocoa. When I took a career aptitude test in the counselor's office, the results showed that I should consider becoming either an opera singer or a social worker. Laughable! I did like to sing, but I certainly didn't have a solo voice or talent.

The hallway walls were filled with row upon row of individual lockers, and we were assigned different ones in different hallways each semester. Moreover, they had locks with combina-tion you had to memorize and definitely not forget. Scores of years later, I still have occasional nightmares of wandering through the school halls unable to find my locker, not being able to re-member my combination or finding it full of moldy towels and smelly gym suits..

When I was in grade school, the nurse gave eye exams in her office annually at which time we were also weighed and mea-sured. I tried to hang back to the end of the line when our class was called because I was so embarrassed to weigh more than anyone else. Those were the days of strict instructions by your mother to eat everything she put on your plate. And take a second helping. Chubby is healthy. Think of the starving children in China. I could never understand the connection. The Chinese wouldn't have access to my food even if I didn't eat it and they might not even like it.

I was aware from kindergarten days that my vision didn't seem to be as good as that of my classmates. I couldn't see the blackboard clearly, but I was too embarrassed to ask for a front seat. Who wanted to sit right under the teacher's nose, anyway? My left eye had some kind of spot in it that almost obscured my vision. When we had eye exams, I couldn't even read the largest "E" on the eye chart with my left eye. I cheated on the eye exam when the nurse told me to cover my right eye and to read the chart with my left eye. I peeked around the cardboard and read it with my "good eye." No one ever picked up on my problem. As a child, I felt I was somehow flawed and didn't want to let anyone know. I simply struggled with poor vision. As a result, my grades were not very good, with the exception of classes where reading or close work was required.

Finally when I was 13, I became desperate and confessed to my parents that I thought I should have an eye exam. The doc-tor discovered that I had a congenital cataract in my left eye, possibly from an injury at my difficult birth. Surgery had not yet developed to the point of even attempting to deal with it. (Not until I reached my mid-fifties was cataract surgery able to correct my problem.) I got my first pair of glasses as I entered junior high. The prescription for my impaired left eye was still not much more than window glass—nothing could improve the sight in it. Suddenly, however, wearing glasses opened a whole new world to me that I had not been seeing, and my grades took wings. I received some teasing from classmates who called me "four eyes" because I wore glasses, but I endured it because of the benefits.

With money saved from baby sitting jobs, I bought a little square Brownie camera that took 127 film and I pursued a new hobby. I filled several albums with black and white snapshots of my dog, my friends, classmates, the neighbors and all our teen activities. Color film had not come on the market yet.

When I was about 14, I was delighted that Dad built a bedroom for me in our attic. It was getting too difficult to share a room with Baba since I had homework and too many clothes for our tiny mutual closet. I decorated my room with wall paper and put up a border of pictures from the National Geographic magazine. I'm not sure why, perhaps because I always had dreams of exploring "far away places with strange sounding names." Finally I could stay up as late as I wished without bothering anyone when I listened to The Hit Parade on the radio. I could also invite girl friends to stay overnight. A major problem was that the room didn't have a heating duct, and I had to snuggle under mountains of quilts to keep warm in winter. Frost heavily painted the inside of my window. In the morning I made a dash for the stairs through the rest of the cold attic. I could see my icy breath before I reached the stairs.

What was my world like in 1940 when I was 15 years old?

That was the year Mother had major surgery, the removal of a breast from suspected cancer. That shook my sheltered world because the word "cancer" struck terror to everyone. Her cancer did not recur, however, and she lived more than 25 years after that and died of a stroke. Mother had long term high blood pressure, and in her last year she had adult onset diabetes. In our extended family, everyone died of strokes, not heart attacks and not usually from cancer. (Dad was so healthy that I never remember him ever having a cold or seeing a doctor, and he didn't have a single cavity in his teeth his entire life. But he died of a stroke at age 59.)

Baba died in 1940. She had been struggling with late onset diabetes and her condition was growing steadily worse. My mother bought a little kitchen scale and weighed all her food according to a diet prescribed by her doctor. I don't think insulin injections had been developed yet. The final blow to Baba was the untimely death of her daughter, Teta Tony, scarcely a year before. Baba grieved deeply, cried frequently and kept repeating that she wished she had died in her place. She had been so close to her daughter and spent more and more time at her house in her later years. Baba eventually became delirious from her illness and finally lapsed into a coma. She didn't even recognize her Czech minister when he came to pray with her. Her illness was complicated by diabetic sores on her foot which left her bedridden. Had she not died, her foot would have been amputated.

I have deep regrets that somehow I was not there for her when she needed me. I recall staying away from her room. I didn't know how to cope with her dying condition. I had been so close to her from infancy, so bonded in every way, but gradually, as I became older, I drifted away to follow my own interests. Baba didn't fit into my new world. I am so sorry. Hindsight is painful. I let her down and realized it too late because I could no longer do anything about it.

The day my precious Baba died was a blur in my memory. The funeral director came to put a floral wreath on our front door, according to the custom in those days, to announce a death in the neighborhood. I shut myself in my attic bedroom and wrote a poem to express my feelings about her. I was hardly aware of the murmur of many voices downstairs. I stayed away from the gathering of family, friends and neighbors who came to offer sympathy around a potluck meal with everyone bringing in food. I remember thinking that it somehow wasn't right for people to be doing such normal things—eating, chatting together, even laughing—as if Baba were still alive. I couldn't imagine that anything would ever be normal again, since the person who had meant the most to me was no longer living. I remember nothing, absolutely nothing, about her funeral or the burial. I can't even visualize it.

My memories didn't resume until about a week afterward when Dad and Mother finished cleaning out Baba's bedroom and disposing of her personal effects, including the furniture she and I shared. They announced that they would be buying an entire new bedroom suite, desk, new carpet and curtains—all for me. I could choose everything myself and could now move down from my attic room. My feelings were mixed—I was stunned with sadness at never being in that room with Baba again, yet thrilled with the anticipation of having my very own private bedroom. Life resumed its normal teenage pace.

What was happening in the world at large in the 1940s? People were either dancing to Tommy Dorsey's big-band swing or jitterbugging. Every Saturday I listened to the "Lucky Strike Hit Parade" for the countdown of popular songs. Ronald Reagan was playing in "B" movies. Tyrone Power, Loretta Young and Alice Faye were my favorite stars. Lana Turner, Ann Sheridan and Ingrid Bergman were escalating toward stardom. For my birthday, I wanted a 78-rpm record of Ingrid's latest hit song "Intermezzo" from her latest movie. It would cost fifty cents. *Gone*

With the Wind was breaking box office records. My cousin, Martha, and I saw it twice and were spellbound by the dramatics. We also sat through Walt Disney's *Pinocchio* twice (you could do that in those days—you just stayed in your seat for the next showing) and we came out singing "When You Wish Upon a Star."

One of the first Technicolor movies was *The Wizard of Oz* with Judy Garland. She and Mickey Rooney were co-staring in teen movies. Adults paid a quarter for admission and kids under 12 got in for a dime. Mother always went to "Bank Night" on Tuesday nights after her work when sets of dishes or a cash prize would be given away through a drawing of a number from admission ticket stubs. *Superman* with reporter Clark Kent and *Bat-Man* were popular comic books. Knock-knock jokes were all the rage.

Something called "country music" was just becoming popular but we called it "hillbilly music." Most families tuned in on Saturday nights, if you could bring in WLS from far away Chicago, to hear the National Barn Dance. If you were lucky and your Philco or Zenith was really good and atmospheric conditions were just right, you might get WSM from Nashville and hear the Grand Ole Opry.

The "World of Tomorrow" exhibits in the New York World's Fair predicted that someday we would have television—pictures would actually come through the air and be captured on a private screen in your home. Sounded unbelievable. Moreover, someday homes would be air-conditioned, there would be a cure for cancer and traffic congestion and—such a daring forecast—someday women would have a life outside the home! At that point in time, a woman's weekly schedule looked like this: Monday you did laundry, Tuesday you ironed, the next few days you cleaned house, perhaps spending an additional six hours a week sewing, you spent 12 hours cooking and eight hours washing dishes and doing kitchen work.

Dad bragged that his new suit not only came with two pairs of pants but they had zippers not buttons on the fly. Dad and most men wore hats or caps but were clean shaven. Beards were rare. *Burma Shave* signs lined the sides of the highways with their shaving cream rhymes.

I remember when the incredible news hit the streets that the new A & P supermarket in town actually had shopping carts in which to collect your groceries and a check-out place to pay. All agreed that this would soon put the "mom and pop" neighborhood grocery stores out of business. The chain stores were here to stay because they saved money for customers. That was important.

Most people earned less than $2000 a year and a married couple with a net income of between $3000 and $4000 paid only $8 in income tax. Average income for a doctor or lawyer was about $5000. In the entire country, only 280,000 families had incomes over $10,000.

When I was 15, I got my learner's driving permit, and my dad taught me how to drive his Ford. There were no driver's education classes in schools. I learned on a clutch drive and killed the engine on more hills than I could count. It was scary when you started to roll backward with cars behind you honking and drivers yelling! Soon Oldsmobile would come out with "a car that never needs shifting, the most modern car in the world." It would have a Hydra-Matic Drive, they said. I got my driver's license the month I reached 16. Dad was proud that I passed the test for my license the first time, but then he realized there would be a struggle for the car keys from then on. But he was happy because of one of the perks—he wouldn't have to drive me everywhere. Dad reminded me, however, that gasoline cost 15 cents a gallon at the filling station now, and if I wanted to use the car, I'd have to earn money for gas.

We paid three cents for a postage stamp, a penny for a

postcard, and the mail man (there were no women mail carriers) delivered letters twice a day and on Saturdays. We paid 12 cents for a quart of milk delivered to our door, 21 cents for a pound for coffee and 36 cents for the best cut of steak. Bargains? Not when you considered that the average wage was $22.30 a week. You could buy a new car for under $800, but it would take a long time to save up that much. No family we knew had two cars or was even thinking about it.

I wore saddle shoes and bobby socks to school but silk hose on Sunday by the time I was a teen. A seam ran up the back of the stockings which was hard to keep straight. It would be decades before panty hose were on the market, so you had to hold up your stockings with a garter belt or "girdle" to which they were hitched. Ready-made dresses were coming into style, and from the Sears catalog you could order a cotton casual dress for $2.98. Skirts and sweaters or blouses were usual school attire. Only laborers or cowboys wore jeans. People dressed up to go "down town," and a hat and gloves were expected for church attendance. For sports or after school play we wore over the ankle "gym shoes" that we could buy for 79 cents a pair, if we ordered them through the Sears catalog. We did have to pay an additional 11 cents for postage.

A shampoo every week or two was considered frequent— no female dashed for the bathroom every morning to shower and shampoo her hair. Although I was an only child and we had one bathroom, my dad still installed a sink and shower in our open basement so he wouldn't have to compete with three females in the morning before work. He shaved with shaving cream and a straight razor. Electric ones weren't invented yet.

From the time I turned 13, I got a twice-a-year permanent wave with hot metal curlers clamped on to rolled hair and connected to a huge octopus-like machine. There was always the danger of your hair burning or singeing. If the clamps were left on too long, your hair would turn out "frizzy," and you were stuck with it until it grew out. The acrid stench of the curling solution was almost unbearable. Men kept their hair under control by adding hair oil and slicking it back.

Summertime brought a growing controversy about topless swimsuits—but the debate was about *men's suits!* Two out of three Americans polled felt that men should not hit the beach barechested! Of course, girls had one piece suits, usually with skirts over the bottom half.

There were many things we didn't have because they weren't developed, designed, invented or even dreamed of in the 40s. We had no antibiotics, frisbees, frozen food, nylon, Xerox, radar, fluorescent lights, credit cards or ball point pens. No dripdry clothes, icemakers, dishwashers, clothes dryers, freezers, plastic, FM radios, tape recorders, synthesized music, disco, Cheerios, instant coffee or McDonald's. It was long before plastic contact lenses, laser beams, day-care centers, nursing homes or artificial hearts. No fax machines, root canals, disposable diapers, Velcro, scotch tape, Internet, microwave ovens, powdered milk, boxed cakes, canned pet food or pizzas. We didn't have any DDT, vitamin pills, food processors, home movie cameras, videos or exercise bikes. Somehow we got along all right without them!

In the 40s, thousands of children still died from measles, whooping cough, diphtheria, chicken pox, small pox and especially from polio. Milder cases were crippled for life, more serious cases tried to survive by living in big contraptions called "iron lungs" which kept them breathing. Polio shots were still in the future. If children caught any one of the contagious diseases, a nurse from the city health department came to the house and posted a big, red cardboard sign "Quarantine" on the door. No one was to enter or leave for 21 days.

Segregation of restrooms, restaurants, water fountains, buses and theaters was practiced nearly everywhere in the South, although it was not as noticeable in the North. We had several Negroes in our high school and there were Negro neighborhoods, often near the railroad tracks. We wouldn't have dared call them "blacks" because they considered the term insulting. Several were my good friends in high school. One tall boy did really well on the basketball court. It was long before famous black sports stars commanded astronomical salaries. Integration was not even an issue or a goal yet.

President Roosevelt gave regular "Fireside Chats" on the radio telling citizens the state of the country. He was starting his seventh year as president, and there were rumors he would run for an unheard of third term. He warned us about the dangerous future "if the world is ruled by force in the hands of the few." His words proved ominously true. The period 1939 to 1940 was a watershed time for world events, but they still seemed far away to high school students preoccupied with social events, boy friends, the latest movies and doing homework over the phone with friends. (I still remember our simple phone number, 4868, no prefixes or area codes, and 8044 was my grandma Bubi's number. We rotary dialed the numbers and of course the phone was stationary in one place.) Who could ever imagine someone walking around in the house with a phone that had no wires? Go outside or in your car with one? In your dreams!

Despite the wars going on elsewhere in the world, my world continued as usual. I walked home sometimes alone quite late at night from school events, feeling perfectly safe on dark streets lit only by an occasional street light. I swam at Marion pool in summers and went to Camp Hitaga sponsored by the Camp Fire Girls. Sleeping in cabins and tents, singing around the camp-fire, learning crafts, boating, horsemanship—all were part of group experiences that helped bring me out of my isolated world as an only child. The friendships I made at camp impacted my life deeply. Local chapters of Camp Fire Girls held meetings in homes of members. When my turn came, Mother outdid herself in providing lavish refreshments. She meant well, but that embarrassed me because I felt it was overdone.

I played Monopoly and card games for hours with my friends, sweated as I mowed our lawn with a push mower and baby sat with Dickie, the little boy who lived directly across the street. His mother paid me 15 cents an hour and 20 cents after midnight. I was impressed with the stars and constellations his parents painted on his bedroom ceiling with luminescent paint. They glowed after I turned the lights out for him. Dickie's parents always left good snacks for me, and I could listen to the radio while I did my homework.

Dad, some of my uncles, grandpa Jed and sometimes their friends played Poker in our basement and filled it with choking smoke from their cigars and cigarettes. I hated that smell. It would be decades before it became a public health issue to smoke, and most men pursued the habit without any qualms. I don't remember any adult women who smoked cigarettes, however. Although he was a cigar smoker, Dad would put on his smart-looking "Smoking jacket" and light up his pipe when he was in the living room listening to the radio or reading the newspaper. I didn't find the smell of sweet briar all that bad. He kept his Prince Albert tobacco in a little "Smoking Cabinet" lined with metal.

I wasn't popular in high school and only had a few casual dates. A lot of us girls hung out together even at sports events. Most of the boys I knew were just good pals. I guess I would have been considered a "wallflower" because I didn't attend the school dances or "Mixers," as we called them. The first reason was because no one asked me for a date, second, because I didn't learn to dance. Mother almost forced me to take a few ballroom dancing lessons from a lady she met at work who said she gave lessons in the living room of her home. She had removed the carpets, waxed the wooden floor to a shine, used a blaring old record player for the music and put a sign on her door, "Lily's Dancing School." She was fat, middle-aged and should have used deodorant. After two lessons, I absolutely refused to return. I didn't go to the proms. I didn't have a "crush" on anyone in particular, well, maybe my biology teacher, Mr. Kelly. I guess I was the studious type since by the time I graduated, I was voted by my classmates in the yearbook as "Most Likely To Succeed."

I avoided the business courses but did take one semester of personal typing which stood me in good stead as a writer for the rest of my life. Dad bought me a vintage Underwood standard typewriter at a pawn shop which cost next to nothing, and it opened a whole new world of writing to me. I had to pound hard on the keys to get action, and I covered the letters on the keys because we had been taught by the blind touch system. To see the letters just confused me and slowed me down. Electric typewriters were still in the future, and no one even dreamed of such a thing as a computer-word processor. At this writing, I even have a computer that is programmed for voice activation, although I haven't had occasion to use that feature.

My first real job at age 16 was in the gift wrapping department of Craemer's Department store downtown. With my friend from school, Margaret, we applied for our Social Security cards and landed the jobs. We were excited to get our first pay checks, small as they were, and promptly spent all our money on new clothes.

Soon world events began to impact us too. At first we hardly noticed the pictures in our newspapers of the arrogant, mustached German leader in a military uniform with his arm extended in a stiff salute, yelling at his goose-stepping soldiers. My dad said that he was threatening the peace of the whole world. He was right. Soon Adolf Hitler ruled Europe from Paris to Warsaw. Only Britain stood between his fanatical Nazis and the American shore. On the radio we heard Winston Churchill urging his nation never to give up, while our president, Franklin Roosevelt, was struggling to keep the U.S. from getting involved in "other people's wars." But 1940-41 changed all that.

Leading up to this period, in the middle and late 30s, Mussolini was pursuing his illusions of conquering Europe from his domain in Italy, and eventually he became an ally of Hitler. Joseph Stalin had taken control of the USSR and was killing millions of his own people in political purges. The Communist leader, Mao Tse-tung, was rising to power in China. Japan was inching its murderous way into China. The stage was being set for the world war which was to follow, but the United States continued to feel secure because we had never experienced direct attack to our shores. After all, oceans separated us from those events.

In 1938, everything accelerated. The Nazis took Austria, then swallowed up Czechoslovakia, followed by Poland. In 1940, they smashed Denmark and Norway in April, conquered Holland and Belgium in May and occupied Paris in June. Turning their massive air attacks and bombings on Britain, the Germans pounded London until 45,000 Londoners were killed or wounded and countless thousands were left homeless. Extensive areas of London, including Parliament, the financial district, cultural edifices and many buildings of the Royal family were bombed. One and a half million children were evacuated from London to the countryside to protect their lives. People were sleeping underground in the subway or in air raid shelters. Winston Churchill used every measure he possibly could to draw the United States into the war which he said was "for the survival of the civilized Christian world." But Roosevelt was determined to keep our country out of war. Typical of the anti-war slogans was, "The Yanks are *not* coming!" It was someone else's war, not ours.

Until December 7, 1941, that is. When the Japanese bombed Pearl Harbor in Honolulu, I was at the home of my friend, Ione, on Sunday afternoon singing around the piano with some other friends. Her dad rushed in shouting, "America is attacked!" We were shocked into silence and disbelief. We couldn't have envisioned what that would mean for our ordinary lives from that day on. Now it became *our* war, everyone agreed. Both anger against the enemy and resolve to defend our nation took over. We were energized by President Roosevelt's declaration that "We have nothing to fear but fear itself." We would win this war no matter how long it took or how great the cost!

Ione's two brothers immediately enlisted in the Navy as did many of my cousins and uncles and friends and the older boys in high school. Defense plants were hiring every worker they could find, women were taking jobs to release men for the armed forces and war production peaked by the time I graduated from high school in 1943.

Everyone's life was affected. The government issued ration stamps to buy meat, cheese and sugar. We used Oleomargarine on our bread instead of butter, coloring it yellow with little color packets that came in the package with the off-white, lard-like spread. The ration coupons limited our driving to three gallons of gas a week. That certainly curtailed my use of Dad's car. He got a factory job at a defense plant and had to use the car to get to work. Everyone who could, planted "Victory gardens" in their back yards to supplement their diets. We saved tin cans for scrap drives. We took our worn shoes to the shoe repair shop for new soles and heels. By the time I was a senior in high school, many fellows in my class skipped the graduation exercises and enlisted in the service or were drafted.

High school girls volunteered to roll bandages for the Red Cross, and we were encouraged to knit sweaters to send to the front lines for our service men. Such a task was out of my line, but I optimistically bought knitting needles and yarn and spent the next two years trying to knit *one* sweater. It was such a disaster that I had to keep it myself! We recycled our clothes by dyeing them a new color with Rit or Tintex dyes. We used newspapers for cupboard shelf paper and made covers for our school books out of newspapers.

Theaters showed black and white newsreels, "The Eyes and Ears of the World," before the main feature. We viewed first-hand some of the bloody battles our men were fighting in Europe, North Africa and the South Pacific. News of thousands of casualties began to come in. We all displayed small American flags in the windows of our homes to show our patriotism. When a gold star appeared in the window, we knew the family lost a son or brother or father in battle. During this time, we were not even aware that Hitler was ordering the murder of millions of Jewish people in Europe in death camps and that such a Holocaust would continue for years.

Projecting ahead, the R.O.T.C. was a presence on the campus during my college years, and classmates were drilling in army uniforms and going on maneuvers. When I was a junior, President Roosevelt died. I was in a history class when the announcement came. Class was dismissed and everyone rushed to a radio to find out what would happen to our country on the loss of our leader in the midst of the terrible war.

After bitter allied fighting on many fronts, military successes were finally in view. By April of 1945, Hitler and Mussolini were dead. V-E Day in Europe was celebrated in May. Our new President, Harry Truman, ordered the newly tested atom bomb dropped on Hiroshima on August 6, then on Nagasaki shortly after. We had mixed feelings of shock and grief at the incredible loss of civilian life, even if it was that of our enemy, yet elation that the war might be about to end. Twenty-seven days later, Japan formally surrendered, V-J Day was declared and the war was over. The American casualty count was staggering.

I graduated from high school in 1943 and was glad to leave those days behind. I can't say that high school days were particularly happy days for me. I was still trying to find myself and was not sure about my identity. I was still an introvert, yet one who reached out to find acceptance among friends. I was only the second among all our relatives who wanted to go to college. My parents hoped I would attend Coe College, a local institution, and live at home, of course. As for me, I wanted to get as far away from home as possible. From childhood I seemed to possess a restless spirit, perhaps inherited from my ancestors, which drew me to leave my Iowa roots for unknown, uncharted ways—a path less traveled. I also wanted to leave behind my Czech connections and be recognized simply for who I was with no ethnic overtones.

17

A Glimpse
of The Artist's Plan.

I shared with the reader in the previous chapters primarily the *outward* things that happened in my early life, my environment and some events influencing my impressionable childhood. Equally or more important was what was going on *inwardly*—my personal response to those outward factors. The outward was only an overlay of my inner person. Both aspects shaped my future life.

I can't go further with my life story without revealing what influenced the direction of my life for the next three-quarters of a century. My decision would affect the lives of my *branches*—my children and my children's children, perhaps the lives of our future generations.

One of my favorite programs on Public Television is the demonstration of painting by a talented artist. One instructor is a bearded, soft-spoken artist who, in my estimation, is like a magi-

201

cian. He begins with a blank canvas, but the finished picture is already in his mind. He holds an artist's palette in one hand and has an array of paints and brushes at his disposal. He works in oils not water colors. He calls oils a "forgiving medium" because he can paint over any strokes that don't please him. He begins by applying a swishy neutral background with a big brush, sometimes using his hand. It looks like a mess and reminds me of a young child's random finger painting. Then he starts mixing the colors that are in his mind—new combinations of paint, new shades. He applies them here and there on the canvas. It certainly doesn't look like a masterpiece yet.

He applies dark sienna, midnight black, Van Dyke brown, fatal blue. Then by contrast he daubs brighter colors here and there calling them "little happy things." Occasionally, he changes brushes—big ones, small ones, round ones, flat ones, little liner ones for the details. Sometimes he picks up his knife and uses it to scrape some of the colors he has applied. Is he ruining his painting? Does it hurt the canvas? No, he does it so gently and always with purpose.

He layers paints to give dimension. He highlights the darker sections, putting finishing touches on what is finally beginning to look like a spectacular landscape with majestic mountains in the background, lofty pine trees, a happy babbling brook trickling into a sparkling lake. I can see the reflection of a deer bending to drink from a quiet pool. He hasn't left out the stones, even a few big boulders that rolled down from the mountain. I'm ready to "oo!" and "ah!"

I don't know what is coming when the artist begins. The canvas doesn't either. It just submits and trusts. But the artist knows.

No matter how many times the artist demonstrates his techniques to the TV audience, each of his canvases is an original masterpiece somewhat different from all the rest. When he finishes, he steps back and smiles at his handiwork. We know he is pleased. He even exclaims, "It is good!"

Each of our lives is like a canvas that God has prepared. He decides which colors to use—both dark and light—for the masterpiece He has in mind. The knife and the scraper come into play. He paints over sections that don't please Him. He contrasts bright, happy daubs with murky, shadowy parts.

When God prepared *my* life canvas and started to paint, I resented even the canvas. I disliked the colors He was choosing and protested loudly. "*NO!* I want a different canvas, brighter colors, no stones, no knife! I want the right to choose what the picture will be like!" It took me many years to learn not to complain about God's original painting that He has called *Leona* and not compare myself with other canvases. Not to resist the knife. Not to object to the stones which I thought were meant to stop me. Instead, to accept them as stepping stones toward God's loving and best purpose for my life.

I was guilty of resisting God's paint brush, knowingly and willfully, from childhood. I dug in my heels and objected, kicking and screaming, mostly within, in protest to the circumstances of my life. In some ways, I seemed to be born with a negative inclination and a bad attitude. God says that is true of all mankind, but I think I was born with an especially heavy dose of it.

That was in spite of being surrounded by love as a child, primarily through my grandma, Baba. Nevertheless, certain negatives, either real or perceived, developed in my young mind to convince me that my canvas was marred. I have already alluded to some in past chapters.

Very early in life, I began to resent the fact that both my parents spent all their waking hours working. I know now that it wasn't their fault, they were trying to make a living for us, and they didn't intend to neglect me. They had a strong work ethic which was admirable, and times were hard because of the Great

Depression. I felt that they didn't have time for me because whenever I wanted their attention, they scooted me off, gently, of course, with "Go to Baba." I became extremely shy and unsure of myself, insecure, feeling somewhat unwanted. I developed introvert qualities.

When I began school, I began to feel that I was different from my classmates because I was Czech. My surname was hard to pronounce, and my classmates mispronounced it deliberately and poked fun at me. I mentioned my reluctance to bring school friends home because I was embarrassed that Baba didn't speak English and Dad had a heavy European accent. I even hated my first name. I never heard of anyone named Leona. Why didn't my parents name me Mary or Dorothy, Betty, Jane or Sally—something ordinary?

From babyhood, I was fatter than most children and had a round, typically Czech face and a big-boned frame. At almost every grade level, I was the tallest and fattest. Yes, my parents were stout. But the dumplings, pork sausage, sauerkraut, mashed potatoes, rich gravies, sweet desserts, homemade butter, milk with cream direct from the cow—these only added to hereditary tendencies. I have mentioned my dread of the regular weighing and measuring by the nurse in school. This contributed to my aversion to recess. I was always the leftover one when kids chose sides for games. Thoughtless kids chanted at me, "Fatty, fatty, two by four, can't get through the kitchen door."

I mentioned my secret suspicion that Dad missed having the son he wanted and that's why he encouraged me to be a tomboy. Somehow I felt that I was his substitute boy and wondered whether he really loved me for myself. I know he did, and there was absolutely no reason for my doubts. But I still felt that way at times.

Our new little house in the city had only two bedrooms, so Baba and I not only shared one small room but one double bed until I was nearly 14. I dearly loved her. She was the most significant person in my life, but I complained to my parents that other kids at least had their own beds and some privacy.

Apparently I had a small, red, almost invisible, burst blood vessel on the side of my nose since I was born. That tiny dot didn't bother me, and I'm sure no one ever noticed it. But for some reason it bothered my mother, and she kept looking at it. She mentioned to other people in front of me that it would somehow "affect my future." I couldn't understand that, but it made me feel self-conscious and less than normal or flawed. Eventually, she took me to a doctor and had it "burned off." I know she meant well.

I already mentioned another secret "flaw" that I knew about since childhood but never mentioned to anyone—a spot in my left eye which kept me from seeing anything in focus with that eye. I kept it from everyone because I simply didn't want to draw attention to another way in which I was inferior and give my mother more to be worried about. My parents complained that I always had my nose in a book. I did, literally, because I couldn't see well.

Because I spent the first five years living in a house behind my parents' little lunch room, I had almost daily contact with their customers. Even as a pre-schooler, I perceived some class distinction between those who served other people for money and those who received such service. That was another factor that added to my self-consciousness. I couldn't verbalize it, but I didn't like being part of those who had to serve others. I thought we were somehow less worthy than the customers.

When I reached school age, Mother and Baba were still sewing my school dresses and play clothes. In those Depression years, anything store-bought was out of the question for our family budget. I know now that Mother couldn't help the fact that she didn't have much sense of style because she came from an immigrant family, and her mother paid scant attention to clothing except to be concerned that her children had enough to put on. This situation added another layer of self-consciousness to my shyness. I didn't grow up being taught how to coordinate outfits or select proper styles when it did become possible to buy ready-made clothing.

All the above caused me to dislike myself. Underneath my facade of a seemingly carefree and happy childhood, I was hiding "an attitude" in the negative sense. As the years went by, I became a complainer, a whiner, short-tempered, cocky and bad-mouthed. I was argumentative, talked back to my parents and seldom expressed appreciation for anything they did for me. When Baba talked to me, I would rudely answer in English, although I knew she wouldn't understand.

I don't recall ever being spanked or even reprimanded very often. I know my parents spoiled me, probably because I was an only child, perhaps also to compensate for having little time to spend with me because of their work. I got pretty much what I wanted anytime, although they must have sacrificed some of their own needs and wants to indulge me. I understand this in hindsight. When they gave me small chores to do around home, like dusting the furniture on Saturdays, feeding the dog, picking up my room, I had to be reminded many times and only reluctantly obeyed with grumbling.

As a discontented, restless child, at the same time, I longed for acceptance from my elders and my peers. My self-consciousness for the above mentioned perceptions resulted in a deep inferiority complex. I compared myself unfavorably in every aspect to my friends. I seemed to feel a void in my young life, but I didn't know what was missing. I was looking for something, but didn't know what it was. Intuitively, in my childish way, I began to seek after God as the missing ingredient in my life.

I now see God's hand on my life, not only from my infancy but from before I was conceived. "By Thee I have been sustained from my birth; Thou art He who took me from my mother's womb" (Psalm 71:6). God planned that I would not be born from my mother's previous marriage or else I would have been an entirely different person. After she married my dad, the brother I never knew died before birth. I was often reminded by Mother that both she and I nearly died when I was born. God's hand was clearly upon me—He planned that I should live.

I am convinced that the "faith of our fathers" practiced by some of my ancestors and their prayers down through the corridors of time "trickled down" to my grandmother, Baba, and eventually to me. My ancestors in Czechoslovakia, specifically from the region of Moravia where both sides of my family tree were planted, had a fearless faith in God that enabled them to endure persecution, even martyrdom, for the Christian faith. I found documentation that one ancestor of Baba's was martyred for his Christian faith in her village.

I can trace our religious heritage back to the Moravian Church and its courageous stand for the Word of God and freedom of worship under a repressive, persecuting politico-religious regime. That Church, in turn, was rooted in the teachings and martyrdom of Jan Hus, the famous early Reformer who was burned at the stake for his Christian beliefs. It is possible that such stalwart Christians prayed down through the centuries for their descendants and claimed such promises as Psalm 22:30, 31 "Posterity will serve Him; They shall tell of the Lord to the next generation. They will come and will declare His righteousness to a people yet to be born, that He has performed it."

God's goodness is promised to succeeding generations of those who love the Lord. "The plans of the Lord's heart are from generation to generation" (Psalm 33:11). I believe this reached all the way to me.

I know Baba prayed for me from before my birth. Her care and love and tender touch paved the way for God's Spirit to gradually begin His work in my heart long before I was aware of spiritual things. From the time I learned to speak my first words, she taught me in Czech to repeat with her the "Otce Nas," the Lord's Prayer. The lullabies she sang to put me to sleep from infancy were Czech hymns she learned in the Old Country. She brought me to the little Czech church with her from the time I was a toddler. Although I understood little, God's presence overshadowed me. He was there watching over this little fat child. Baba prayed that my young heart would be good soil and she faithfully sowed God's seeds in it for a later sure harvest.

After helping my mother with household matters, Baba spent most of her spare time reading her big Czech Bible and praying as she sat in our bedroom in her special chair by the window. I remember my dad and mother good-naturedly whispering behind Baba's back, commenting that she was "over pious." That confused me. I wanted to defend my precious grandmother against them, although I didn't even understand the issues. At the same time, I wanted the favor of my parents. I decided to do nothing about it and kept silent.

I still have Baba's Bible. She underlined many verses and some are from Psalm 139. "You, O Lord, formed my inward parts; You knit me together in my mother's womb....Your eyes saw my unformed substance, and in Your book all the days of my life were written, before ever they took shape, when as yet there was none of them." I would gradually come to realize years later that God planned my heritage *exactly as He wanted it* regardless of my rebellion against my ethnic roots. He had a Master Plan to unfold, and He was in no hurry. "The Lord will fulfill His purposes for me" (Psalm 138:8).

God was at work in me before I even knew it. In retrospect, I believe God chose the simple words of Christmas carols to give me my first clear, accurate concept of His plan of salvation. They presented sound, biblical theology. From the carols I learned:

Jesus was the Son of God, Messiah, King, born of a virgin in Bethlehem (and all the details).

He came to ransom captive Israel, and to set all men free. He had been expected for a long time.

Jesus is Lord and came to reconcile God and sinners. He is holy.

His coming brings joy to heaven and earth, but each heart has to receive Him. His own people didn't receive Him.

God sends angels to minister to men and announce God's plans. They proclaimed peace on earth.

The prophets foretold the coming new heaven and earth where Christ will reign.

Jesus was preexistent, left a throne in heaven, is truly God made flesh, is risen from the dead and will suddenly come again.

We must worship God and adore Him as the wise men from afar did who brought Him gifts.

Jesus was born to give men second birth, and then we will never die. He casts out our sin and enters into our hearts.

I don't remember ever knowingly or willfully rejecting anything I heard about God. I can't say that I disbelieved at some point and then turned around to believe. In my childhood innocence, I sought God. At the same time, I was so self-conscious that I didn't want anyone to know about my seeking. I was afraid to be teased for my interest in God and be considered "different" in yet another way. I didn't really know anyone else who talked about God except Baba. I didn't even confess my tender heart to Baba, who would have been overjoyed and encouraged to know her prayers were being answered. Nevertheless, secretly, whatever little bit I did hear about God, I immediately accepted without question and incorporated it in simple ways on my childish level of understanding.

By God's plan, when my 10 year old neighbor, June,

showed me how she was learning to play the piano, she did it from a hymnbook. She wasn't part of a church-going family, and it is strange that she even had a hymnbook. But she taught me the hymn, "The Old Rugged Cross." God saw to it that I learned about Jesus' suffering, crucifixion and death at a place called Calvary for a world of lost sinners—which included me. I was to love that old cross. This aspect of theology was added to my growing, basic belief system.

At church, someone gave Baba an English calendar with flip pages and illustrations of Bible scenes in color for each month. She pounded a nail on the wall by the side of our bed where I slept and hung it there. It was where I would constantly see it. The year began with a prayer poem by James Montgomery, "O Thou by whom we come to God, the Life, the Truth, the Way, the path of prayer Thyself hath trod. Lord, teach us how to pray." The picture with that prayer was of Jesus on his knees praying in Gethsemane. I memorized those words and God saw to it that the request to be taught to pray became part of me. I prayed that prayer constantly. I wasn't receiving any teaching from anyone since I didn't go to Sunday School, but God revealed Himself to me line upon line as I received each new truth I heard. The monthly pictures on that calendar each year walked me through biblical events.

Someone at Baba's church offered her a used copy of "Hurlburt's Story of the Bible" in English. The covers were nearly falling off and some pages were loose, but she eagerly accepted it, patched it up a bit and gave it to me. I learned to read in school by that time, and God saw to it that through that book I obtained considerable knowledge of Bible stories.

When I was about seven, Baba gave Mother some money to buy a small Bible in English for me. Mother found one in the ten cent store, and Baba wrapped it as my Christmas gift. I kept it to this day. My understanding of what I read was limited because of my age, because I had no one to teach me and because it was the King James version. That was the only version most people had in those days before the availability of all the new translations and paraphrases. I recall getting stuck in Leviticus and Numbers and sort of giving up. Nevertheless, whatever I did understand, I accepted. My heart was kept soft by years of Baba's prayers for me.

I do remember one occasion when my older cousin, Sylvia, and her friend, Alma, took me with them to Sunday School. It was my first experience. The students each had a Bible study workbook with a yellow cover in which they filled in answers to questions. Sylvia gave me an outdated one to take home, and I eagerly read it straight through. God was applying another level to my spiritual understanding.

Baba must have suggested to Mother that she should consider taking me to an English speaking church sometime. But it didn't happen until one Easter Sunday when I was about 12. Mother picked out a small Presbyterian church close to the street car line, and I had my first exposure to an English speaking church. I recall being restless and grumbling because I didn't get to sleep late that Sunday morning. A lady who noticed my figeting handed me a Sunday School story paper. That amused me for awhile. There were some Bible puzzles in it. The answer to one of the puzzles seemed to be in code, and I loved codes. "Matt. 21:22"

When I was alone at home, I took out the little Bible Baba had given me and started my search. I wasn't familiar enough with it to know there were two parts, the Old and New Testaments, so I started thumbing through from Genesis until I found the book of Matthew. Chapter 21, verse 22 sounded incredible. "Everything you ask in prayer, believing, you shall receive." Could this be true? I concluded that if Jesus said so and it was in the Bible, I would believe it. I thought it was something like rubbing Aladin's lamp and a genie would come out and grant your wish.

But what was I supposed to believe? I wondered. If Jesus meant believing in Him and His Father, God, I did believe that already. So perhaps I qualified.

There was something I really wanted to happen at that time, but it didn't seem probable. I decided I would try asking God for it based on that blanket promise. To my amazement, within a week it happened! I had taken another step in my spiritual understanding of God. He really answers prayers!

In my little Bible, I came across many instances where Jesus healed people. I took for granted that if He could do it back then, and since He was still alive and powerful, He could do it now. Many times in late childhood and teen years, I would pray for God to heal my various ills, and He graciously answered me. I took another step in my faith and have believed in God's healing power all my life.

Years later as an adult, I came across a collection of my writings scribbled on tablet paper with a pencil. They represented another level in my private search for God. Some were "I hereby believe" declarations of my childhood theology.

I wrote, "I believe in God and in Jesus, His Son. I believe in the Ten Commandments. I believe in the Bible, etc." Some were prayer poems written to God. (I remember burning candles in private and reading those prayers to God. I guess that's why I am somewhat of a "candle freak" to this day—the soft light of a candle makes me think of God.)

There were lists of my resolutions at self-improvement. I was becoming aware of my failures and my bad attitude. I wrote, "This is the Law of Leona Spryncl who lives at 42 degrees North Longitude, 92 degrees East Latitude, on 26th Street in Cedar Rapids, Iowa, Linn County, Central States, United States, North America, Earth, Universe. (I guess this came from a recent geography lesson! I wanted to let God know exactly where I was!) I will hereby strictly keep these resolutions: Read the Bible every day. Say my prayers every night. Don't go to a movie on Sunday. Do a good deed daily. Help Mother. Hold my temper. Study harder. Don't complain. Be more polite. Don't talk back to Dad. Hold my temper. (again!) Don't leave things lying around. Feed the dog. Live up to the Ten Commandments, etc."

I had penciled in "OK" or "Violated" beside each of 22 resolves. "Violated" appeared by nearly all of them. I remember my discouragement and self-loathing to realize that whatever things I wanted to do, I failed at, and the things I didn't want to do, I kept on doing. I concluded that I couldn't keep God's law or even my own resolutions. God probably didn't like me when I failed—and I failed all the time.

Mother eventually decided we should go to a different church where they might have a program for teens. From the Yellow Pages of the phone book she chose a large, prestigious, old Presbyterian church downtown. Unfortunately, people who went there were in a much higher income bracket than our family, and that again contributed to my self-consciousness. Nevertheless, God was moving me on to the next level of faith and understanding and this was not a detour.

There I learned reverence, the holiness of God and the great hymns and creeds of the church. Without question, I believed everything the robed minister preached, and I grew in my Christian knowledge. I started to go to Sunday School with my age group and joined the Youth Endeavor on Sunday nights. I was finally meeting other professing Christian teens. I went through instruction classes and became a member when I was 14. I didn't have to be baptized, they said, because I was "baptized" as an infant. I only needed to be "confirmed." (In my sixties, while on a tour of the Holy Land, I had the privilege of being baptized by immersion in the Jordan River at the traditional place where Jesus was baptized by John the Baptist.)

In retrospect, joining that church seemed to mean that you

assented to a creed and acknowledged it publicly. I admired the minister, learned a lot from the sermons, but the Bible didn't have much place in his preaching. He talked a lot about current events. Nevertheless, I was seeking God and whatever crumbs of Bible truth I heard, I believed and tried to live up to what light had been offered. But I still didn't feel that I had any power to live the Christian life.

At McKinley, a few of my classmates, one good friend, Harriet, in particular, went to another church of the same denomination and seemed to have a different view of the Christian experience. She spoke of Jesus in more personal terms and said He helped her in practical things of her daily life. That seemed more than just believing a creed.

Harriet invited me to go with her to church after school one Tuesday. She said her minister was teaching a small group study on Romans. I thought she said "romance" and decided that might be a fun thing to know more about. We met in the minister's study and I found out they called it the "Exegetes Class." (I couldn't imagine what "an exegete" was but the kids there seemed quite normal!) The minister was teaching a group of teens how to study the Bible by the "inductive" method. (Another strange term to me.) Verse by verse we studied the book of Romans to see what it really said, and it was deep, serious stuff.

At my own church, we didn't usually study the Bible. In our Sunday School class we discussed "situation ethics," moral questions, current events, how to make good choices—that sort of thing. In Youth Group the leader presented denominationally prepared programs that didn't require us to think very deeply. The main attraction was the social hour. But at Harriet's church things were different.

Harriet invited me to visit her Sunday School and church, to attend their Youth Group with her and participate in some fun activities they sponsored. At her church everyone brought their

Bibles to services and seemed to know where to find the references when the minister preached from it. Her Sunday School class was crowded with teenage girls eager to learn more about Jesus Christ. The teacher, Mrs. Templeman, took a personal interest in me. She even visited me at my home! Harriet's Youth Group was live wire and bursting with teens from more than one high school. They had great fun, but at the same time talked in a familiar way about "a personal relationship with Jesus" and being "born again." They used unfamiliar words like "saved" and "justified." I didn't hear that in my church. The other teens accepted me and warmly included me in their activities. (My Czech ethnic background didn't even come up!)

After a few months of visiting Harriet's church, I decided I had really been missing something important in my search for God. It wasn't long before I transferred my membership to Westminster Presbyterian Church.

The young, handsome minister, Rev. James H. Blackstone, Jr., invited the young people to make up the choir for Sunday night services. Sunday nights attracted as many people to church, including the youth, as came to morning worship. He always asked one of the young people to read the Scripture, another to pray and someone to "give a testimony" in the evening service. I had never heard of such a thing. They didn't read some prepared speech but talked from their hearts. The well-attended prayer meeting on Wednesday nights attracted not only adults but many young people. Everyone was invited to share their prayer requests and to pray extemporaneous prayers. As I began to participate in everything that church made available, my relationship with God became truly personal and real and very exciting.

I learned about and experienced the power of the Holy Spirit who enables me to live the Christian life, not in my own strength but through God's available strength and wisdom. I found out "born again" meant that I received the very life of God, His

DNA, and from that point I was "in Christ." I became a new person when I accepted Jesus into my heart and life. "If any person is in Christ, he is (a new creature altogether) a new creation; the old (previous moral and spiritual condition) has passed away. Behold, the fresh and new has come!" (2 Corinthians 5:17 from The Amplified Bible)

Yes, many times I still fell short of God's best for me, my attitude problems didn't disappear magically and the negative aspects of my personality didn't evaporate overnight. But I was on my way in God's direction. When I confessed to God my sins and my inability to please Him, I experienced God's love through His forgiveness. I found out that He wasn't mad at me when I blew it. He didn't hold it against me and reject me. He always gave me a clean slate to start again. I learned that was because of God's grace.

In Sunday School we studied the Westminster Shorter Catechism, and I became grounded in the historic faith of the Scriptures. The first question and answer has stayed with me for a lifetime. "What is the chief end (purpose) of man? Man's chief end is to glorify God and enjoy Him forever." That was a far cry from trying to keep either God's commandments or my resolutions, at which I had continually failed.

Our minister preached a series of sermons especially for youth based on Romans 12:1,2. "I appeal to you therefore, brethren, and beg of you in view of all the mercies of God, to make a decisive dedication of your bodies—presenting [all] your members and faculties—as a living sacrifice, holy (devoted, consecrated) and well pleasing to God, which is your reasonable (rational, intelligent) service and spiritual worship. Do not be conformed to this world—this age, fashioned after and adapted to its external, superficial customs. But be transformed (changed) by the [entire] renewal of your mind—by its new ideals and its new attitude—so that you may prove [for yourselves] what is the good and acceptable and perfect will of God, even the thing which is good and acceptable and perfect [in His sight for you]" (From The Amplified Bible).

No one ever pointed out to me before that God wanted me to give my body to Him, too. I thought He was just interested in my soul or spirit. If He really wanted my body, it would be only reasonable to dedicate it to Him because of all He had done on the cross to save me and was doing for me in my new spiritual life.

I tried to understand the implications of that. God wanted all *my* members and faculties? I figured He wouldn't be getting much in *my* case because I had a very low opinion of myself. Compared to my new friends, I still complained that I had no talents to offer Him. Other kids played the piano, were in the orchestra, acted in dramas, were good speakers, had nice person-alities, excelled in sports, were popular, smart in school, surely more physically attractive. But I was a "zero" in my estimation. I even borrowed books from the library on "How to develop a per-sonality." Besides, I was a fat and shy and uncoordinated girl from an ethnic minority—who had even thrown in the sponge on her miserable piano lessons. Why would God want someone like me? What could He do with me?

Nevertheless, I was in the habit of believing all God said in the Bible. In this verse it was promised that if I did give myself to Him totally, I would find out the will of God for me. And it would be good and perfect. It was beyond my comprehension that God noticed me, *Leona*, to the extent that He would have a plan for *my* life. Yes, He had already given me "new ideals and some new attitudes" so I knew He could do anything.

What it required on our parts as young people with our whole lives ahead of us, Pastor Blackstone explained to us, was "to make a decisive dedication," to surrender ourselves wholly to God. He invited those who were serious about doing that to come to the church altar and pray. Our action would let God know we were willing for Him to work in our lives to make us into what His special purpose was for each of us even before the world began. It blew my mind to think that God planned something *for insignificant me* from ages past!

Then Pastor made it clear. "God wants you to come *just as you are with nothing in your hands.* It doesn't matter whether you lack talents or abilities or are loaded with them. Jesus wants to be the one to make you into what He planned for you. He will provide you with all the resources to carry that out." *That was for me!*

Along with about a dozen other young people, I responded with all my heart.

Together we sang the hymn, "It may not be on the mountain's height or over the stormy sea; It may not be at the battle's front that my Lord will have need of me; But if by a still, small voice He calls to paths I do not know, I'll answer, dear Lord, with my hand in Thine, 'I'll go where You want me to go. I'll go where You want me to go, dear Lord, over mountain or plain or sea; I'll say what You want me to say, dear Lord, I'll be what You want me to be'." [1]

This personal surrender to God was the defining moment of my life. By my decision, I gave God blanket permission to work out His sovereign plan in my life. I was about 16 years old. I confessed to God, The Master Artist, that I had not liked either the canvas or the colors He started painting in my life. But I promised not to grab the brush out of His hand to keep Him from painting whatever He wanted to paint in my life—all the way to the final masterpiece. I realized that God had actually been painting all along. His hand was upon me and leading me from one level of faith to another by bringing circumstances and people into my life.

I thought I had chosen God. In fact, God had "chosen me" in Christ before the foundation of the world...predestined me...for His purpose" according to Ephesians, chapter one.

We, the Lord and I, were on our way to—wherever! The prayers of Baba and perhaps the prayers of godly Czech ancestors in Europe through the centuries were being answered as God's plan began to unfold in what I considered my insignificant life.

I wondered whether Baba knew about this in heaven?

Ted and Leona during ministry years in the U.S. and China

Leona traveling in China and leading tour groups

18

A Frame for my Painting

After my surrender to God in my 16th year, God accelerated the growth of His seeds planted in my life that would come
to harvests ten, twenty, thirty, forty, fifty, sixty and seventy years
later.

The mother of my friend, Ione, introduced me to some
books of deeper Christian experience from authors such as Andrew Murray, Ruth Paxson, S.D. Gordon, Frances Ridley
Havergal, D.L. Moody, R.A. Torrey, James McConkey, Amy
Carmichael, Hudson Taylor and other classic Christian writers.
The things I learned from them became part of my lifetime Christian experience. (Little could I imagine that about 50 years later, I
would be the biographer of Andrew Murray and write and publish
books based on the lives and teachings of some of those other
great evangelicals whose books I read in my teens.)

I read novels for young Christians written by Paul Hutchens
and others. From one of Murray's books I internalized his state-
ment, "God is ready to assume full responsibility for the life wholly

yielded to Him." I launched my life on that premise.

Pastor Blackstone was born to missionary parents in China. He often referred to events there and asked his congregation to pray for the Chinese people. When he first accepted the pastorate at Westminster, he and his beautiful wife, Jean, an accomplished pianist, sang a song in Chinese with their young children. About that time, the Christian world was shocked to hear the news that a young missionary couple in their mid-20s, John and Betty Stam, were martyred in China. Only their baby daughter was rescued from the hands of rebel bands of outlaws during the war. A book was published about them, *The Triumph of John and Betty Stam*, containing many poems and prayers Betty wrote in her younger years. One prayer became my life prayer:

"Lord, I give up all my own plans and purposes, all my own desires and hopes. I accept Thy will for my life. I give myself, my life, my all, utterly to Thee to be Thine forever. Fill me and seal me with Thy Holy Spirit. Use me as Thou wilt, send me where Thou wilt, and work out Thy whole will in my life at any cost, now and forever."

"At any cost" for Betty was to be beheaded in China at age 27. Pastor Blackstone challenged us during one Sunday evening service to consider giving our lives for missionary service, if God so led us. In the zeal of my youth, I promised God I would go to China some day, if He wanted me to. That was about the farthest away place I could imagine, and I didn't really think God would take me up on that.

The friendships I made at church were life changing. We teens spent much time at one another's homes just hanging out and talking on porch swings, at sleep overs with our girl friends and attending church activities and social events together. We were fun-loving teens yet serious about our Christian lives, encouraging each other in a warm support group. Together with friends in my youth group I went several summers to Christian camps, and those experiences strongly influenced my life.

The pastor started a group especially for those of us who responded to the call to surrender our lives to God. It was called "Life Work Recruits," and we met once a month at his home to discuss career plans and choices and to pray for one another. Joining the group didn't mean we were necessarily going into the ministry or Christian work or to the mission field but that we were open to God's leading in our lives. I believe that eventually out of the 20 or so of us, some did go into full time Christian work, others were witnesses for God within their careers or they married and established Christian homes. If I'm not mistaken, I was the only one who eventually went overseas in mission work.

I received valuable experience through the opportunities the pastor gave us youth to present talks, share about our camp experiences and speak of what was going on in our Christian lives from the pulpit on Sunday evenings. I received good leadership training by participating in and leading the programs of our youth fellowship. The shy, introverted girl was coming out of her shell. With several others, I sang and gave talks at the Sunshine Mission downtown and sang with a chorus over the local radio station on Sundays. Our "Singspirations" after evening services at the home of the pastor were the highlight of my week. In spite of homework from school, I usually went to midweek prayer meeting with other teens.

I moved in an entirely different peer group than before, with those who had a positive Christian attitude. That began to counteract the negatives in my life. I felt accepted by God, accepted by my friends, finally secure in God's love and confident of His guidance. My self-confidence began to rise. I was challenged to seek God's special plan for my life.

Then something came up to rattle my self-esteem. Dad and Mother ran a succession of restaurants rather unsuccessfully, then, worst case, Dad took a job to manage a tavern where they sold beer! That may not sound like a big deal, but at that point in my life, it embarrassed me in front of my new Christian friends far beyond what it should have. Old feelings of being different surfaced. We Christian teens were well-meaning and sincere in our code of conduct, but unfortunately we almost bent over backward in our legalism of "what we didn't do." I would say we were quite judgmental of the behavior of others, even of our elders, and not very open-minded. (I had a lot to learn in days and years to come.) My friends didn't criticize me for my dad's job, but I went through personal agonies about it. I'm afraid I wasn't very charitable and kind toward my parents. I was greatly relieved after Pearl Harbor when Dad got a job in a defense plant welding some kind of electronic parts for airplanes.

I often baby sat with the Blackstone children, and the Blackstones were genuine and transparent role models for my life. Pastor Blackstone was an accomplished singer, a faithful teacher of the Bible and a true gentle shepherd for his flock in Cedar Rapids. After Pearl Harbor in 1941, he volunteered as a Chaplain in the Navy and left the church.

It seemed that as soon as many of the teens in our youth fellowship graduated from high school, they headed for Wheaton College, a Christian liberal arts school not far from Chicago. They returned on holidays and during summers and several of them, Margaret Kikendall in particular, had a major influence on my life. After the Wheaton Men's Glee Club (40 handsome men!) sang at our church, several of us decided that was exactly where we wanted to go and nowhere else!

I graduated from high school before I turned 18 and continued in my determination to attend Wheaton College, although it was far beyond my parents' financial ability to send me. They wanted me to attend the college in our hometown and live at home, but I would hear none of it. Dad and Mom did finance my four year Wheaton education without college loans or personal loans but at great personal sacrifice, I'm sure. Although they both worked full time, I still can't imagine how they managed it. I worked part time at college and during the summers, but what I earned was not a great help toward my expenses. I am much indebted to them and wish I had expressed greater appreciation to them at the time.

When I entered Wheaton, I didn't have a strong inclination toward any specific major. My parents encouraged me toward a nursing career because "that's what girls do." I quickly abandoned that prospect after visiting Cook County Hospital in Chicago with a pre-nursing group. I began by majoring in Anthropology, but the head of the department was leaving and the department wasn't as strong as it should have been. "What can you do with Anthropology anyway?" my parents questioned. They weren't even sure what it was. Perhaps I would major in Archaeology. I would have loved going on a dig somewhere in Egypt. Same comment from my parents. I settled on Christian Education, although they weren't sure what I'd do with that either and whether I could earn a living.

In those days, career choices for girls seemed limited, a far cry from today when women enter any field. Usually girls majored in something they could later teach. If the college had offered a major in Communications, I might have gone in that direction because of my interest in writing, but that department wasn't established until much later. More and more through the influence of the Foreign Missions Fellowship at Wheaton and speakers from various overseas missions who came to report to our student body, I began to consider preparing for the mission field.

When I mentioned that to my parents, they objected even more strongly. I was their only child, and they couldn't imagine my leaving them for some far away country. They considered Iowa to be the Promised Land which they already reached. Why would anyone want to go anywhere else? Wasn't there plenty of Christian work I could do in this country, if that was the direction I insisted on going? They already thought I was "taking religion too seriously." "Why not let the people in other countries have their own religion?" they argued. "Moreover, there is no money in such a career. It would be a waste of your education. We sacrificed a lot to put you through college." Dad and Mother thoroughly rained on my parade—but I put up my umbrella.

Where would I go? I had no call from God to a specific location. My exposure to China in church during high school didn't seem to incline me in that direction. Africa? I didn't think so. I couldn't live with bugs and other larger creeping, crawling ferocious things. Those were the two main mission fields most people considered. I had to write a research paper on some country for a missions class. Since I didn't have a preference, I just opened up an Atlas and picked a country in South America—Paraguay, I think. As I remember, it was less than a mediocre project. I didn't have any passion for it.

While I was trying to decide on my future course, I wanted to develop a world view that would give me a satisfying perspective of life. I didn't want to simply accept the conclusions of others without examining the foundation of my Christian faith for myself. I wanted to be sure of its validity. Relativism didn't make sense to me. I want to find out whether there was absolute truth. I signed up for courses in Philosophy, Comparative Religion, Theism, Ethics, Archaeology, Anthropology, Introduction to Biblical Criticism, Apologetics as well as history, science and other exploratory subjects. I used up all my electives on these.

Two of the several dictionary definitions of *philosophy* are, "The rational investigation of the truths and principles of being, knowledge or conduct," and "A system of principles for guidance in practical affairs." That's what I was after.

I wanted to be sure my gradually growing experiential

Christian faith was authentic. Only if that were true and the Bible was a trustworthy historical document, could I accept its principles as a guide for all aspects of my lifestyle, career goals and human relationships.

I would describe my philosophy, which developed from this search, in part, in the words of a great European thinker, John Amos Comenius, who was a philosopher, author and scholar far ahead of his times. He was born in 1592, coincidentally in the same Moravian province in Czechoslovakia where all my ancestors were born. He became known world-wide as a progressive, educational reformer. He wrote:

"In this world and in all its affairs there is nothing but confusion and entanglement, floundering and drudgery, delusion and deception, misery and anxiety, and finally weariness and despair. But whoever rests at home in his heart alone with God comes to true and complete joy and peace of mind."

Because of my rational search, I concluded that the Christian faith was not merely one of many equally valid religions in the world, most of which may have worthy goals and worship a supreme being of some kind. I found that Christianity was unique in that God revealed Himself to the mankind He created and wanted to be known by them. The Christian faith was God reaching to man, not man attempting to reach God. It followed that if God did reveal Himself, the historical record, namely the Biblical record, would have to be proven trustworthy. I concluded from the evidence that the Bible was truly an authentic and reliable foundation for my faith and conduct, and I could base my world view on it.

I was affirmed in my understanding that one does not "join" Christianity like a club or organization, nor does one become a Christian merely because one's parents embrace that faith. Nor does church attendance or any of the rites of the church, like baptism, guarantee that a person is a Christian. It is a matter of not only accepting a body of doctrine but of heart commitment to the Person of Jesus Christ as the Son of God. Christianity is not ritual but a relationship.

I believed therefore, that God must have a plan for my life, and I was not only willing but eager to take my hands off the steering wheel and "let Him do the driving." That philosophy determined the courses I would study in college, choice of my career and who I would consider marrying. It influenced all my relationships, interests, goals and leisure time activities. If I ever married and had children, my Christian philosophy would determine the way I would handle those relationships.

I was satisfied that my examined faith would serve me well by providing all the answers to life that I would need and give me peace and contentment through any traumatic adversities or reverses or disappointments of life that were sure to come. My faith was already giving me great personal joy because I was discovering that God is a loving God, a good God. He was not a deity to be feared, waiting to punish us if we blew it or insisting that we appease Him by sacrifices. The Bible teaches that God is always planning for and working in the lives of His followers only the things which are good and ultimately for our welfare and the fulfillment of His sovereign purposes (Jeremiah 29:11).

I didn't delude myself that I now had all the answers. I knew there were many things I would never understand, questions of life to which my world view provided no pat or ready answers. I decided not to puzzle over the "whys" to which neither human history nor God had furnished answers or allow unsolved questions to shake my faith. I was content to leave them to the perfect knowledge of God who created the universe and our planet earth and who has a plan not only for all creation and history but for every individual life—including mine.

Beyond the Christian world view on which I settled, my philosophy, based on Biblical revelation, provided me with faith and hope for another life after this life, for eternal life beyond the death of the body. As a result of my studies in Biology, Zoology and Anthropology, I did not believe in human evolution. At the same time, I recognized the validity of natural changes within species. I believed that God created the material earth and mankind by a direct act of His omnipotent will and for a purpose. He created human beings with three distinct parts: body, soul, and spirit. With the body, we relate to the material, physical world. With our soul, we function in the mind, emotions and will. With a uniquely created and undying spirit, we can communicate with God. Therefore, a human being is not on the same low level as the animal world which lacks a spirit and can't communicate with its creator.

My Christian philosophy gave me the assurance that there is a literal place which the Bible calls heaven, wherever that may be in the spiritual realm, where those who have followed God through Jesus Christ will be conscious, joyful, fulfilled and eternally in the presence of God after death.

I believed that each person is free to make his or her own choice of a belief system. I had chosen mine. At the same time, I was free to share with others my beliefs and the answers to life that I found. I now had a solid basis for answering God's call, if He should make it clear, to go to another culture or another ethnic group to share my beliefs—not by coercion but by joyfully sharing the Christian faith.

On the first day I enrolled in a certain Anthropology class, the professor decided to assign students for the rest of the semester to whatever seat they took that first day. He said it would be easier for him to take attendance by noting the empty seats and counting those students absent. I happened to be a little late for class and rushed in after the large class was already seated. The professor pointed to me saying, "You, the girl back there, come up front and sit in this empty seat for the rest of the semester."

I did, and it happened to be in one of the front rows next

to a Chinese student, Ted Choy, whom I hadn't met before. We became acquainted very quickly, and I discovered a lot about him. His father was a businessman and Ted came from a Christian family and was already a third generation Christian. While a student in Hong Kong, he dedicated his life to the Lord for Christian service during meetings conducted by the famous young evangelist, Dr. John Sung, who earned his Ph.D. in America. God used Sung's preaching to deeply impact Ted's heart. He wanted to study in a seminary in America and the opportunity came in 1940.

Ted had less than $100 in his pocket when he arrived at the Evangelical Free Church Seminary in Chicago, Illinois. (That institution is now called Trinity Evangelical Divinity School and relocated to Deerfield, IL.) Knowing his financial need as an international student, the school didn't charge him tuition and gave him a free room. He earned his board by shoveling snow, shoveling coal for the heating system, painting houses and other odd jobs for the three years of his seminary training. He had opportunities to travel with gospel teams from the seminary to different churches of that denomination. He preached and played an accordion.

When Ted graduated from seminary, the war between China and Japan had escalated to the point where his family and church in Hong Kong strongly advised him not to return yet because it was dangerous. Although he was eager to return to China to begin his ministry, he had to pray about alternate plans.

He decided to take further studies at Wheaton College and realized he would have to work for his expenses there, too. Tuition, board and room, book fees and other necessities were especially high. Ted worked at every job he could find but income from part time work wasn't enough because he had to spend most of his time studying. Many times, he recalled, just at the last minute when some payment was due, he would find an anonymous envelope in his post office box with exactly the amount of money needed. Somehow the Lord provided all his needs year by year.

God really must have engineered that seating arrangement! I can't remember whether either of us got a very good grade in that class. We did write a lot of notes but they were the kind we passed to each other. However, I regarded him only as an interesting, cross-cultural friend and was surprised when, after a few weeks, he asked me for a date to attend some school function. I declined. He persisted in asking me to go to various events. I persisted in declining, saying I only wanted to be friends. Ted, however, let me know from the beginning that I was the girl he was going to marry—that God told him so. I replied that God didn't tell *me* any such thing!

I finally gave in and accepted a few dates with him to church and a banquet and we studied together occasionally. The campus didn't have any written regulations against it, but interracial dating was simply not practiced. Some nosey classmates, not even particularly close friends, took it upon themselves to advise us to stop dating. That shook me up more than a little. Because I was finally emerging from being self-conscious and insecure, to have other people criticize me and talk behind my back made me uncomfortable.

But opposition didn't upset Ted. In fact, it made him all the more determined to pursue me as his future wife. (He didn't tell me until later that the one thing his father warned him about when he left Hong Kong for study in America was, "Be sure you don't marry an American girl!" He replied, "Don't worry, father, I have no intention of doing that.")

When Ted finally saw that he wasn't getting anywhere with me, he said, whether jokingly or seriously, I didn't know at the time, "OK, I've decided to leave school and join the Marine Corps. If I get shot and never come back, you'll be sorry!" (His actual motivation was, he confessed to me after he returned, that since the war was still going on in Asia, he wanted to help America put an end to it.)

He did that very thing. With only one semester left to complete work for his degree, he volunteered for the Marine Corps. After boot camp at Camp Pendleton in California, he was sent as a Specialist Interpreter with the Intelligence to North China with the First Marine Division.

I didn't date a lot in college, but I did date several other fellows on campus and also at home during summer after Ted left. I thought that was the end of that, out of sight out of mind, and I'd probably never hear from Ted again. *Wrong!* Because he was allowed free postage as a member of the armed forces, Ted wrote me almost every day for the two years he was overseas. His letters to me filled boxes! Eventually, as I always reminded him, he simply "wore me down," and I began at least to consider the possibility that God might have a relationship here that I wasn't seeing.

When the war ended and he was mustered out, Ted returned to campus for his last semester. Meanwhile, I caught up with him, and I was in my senior year too. He arrived on campus in his dashing Marines uniform. I have always been a pushover for a uniform. By that time, I was willing to date him no matter what other people thought. I got to know Ted a lot better through all those letters and found that he was a man of character, vision and integrity. Certainly a man of perseverance! We decided to go together to ask counsel from some of the professors about the possibility of our relationship. One was the college president, Dr. V. Raymond Edman, who didn't oppose or discourage us because of racial difference. Instead, he gave us sound advice on goals, compatibility, backgrounds, Christian experience, personalities and the like and prayed that we would find God's wisdom and will in the matter. Another professor was Dr. Alexander Grigolia, the head of the Anthropology department (who seated us together in that first class!). We knew he would give us sound and realistic advise from the perspective of his field. He enthusiastically gave his blessing to us saying that the combination of Caucasian and Asian was an excellent one in every way.

To introduce Ted to my parents was a major hurdle. I had nightmares about it in advance. I chose Christmas vacation as the time for the bombshell. I asked my parents if I could bring a classmate home with me for a few days around Christmas. I probably should have prepared them in greater detail for meeting Ted—I only mentioned that he recently returned from serving in the Marines. Dad liked that bit of news since he had been in the army himself. I didn't tell them that he was a Chinese young man until the night before we arrived!

My practical, provincial, conservative parents nearly flipped with that news! They had visions of him being like the little laundryman down by the railroad tracks with a pigtail and speaking broken English—or at best like Charlie Chan from the detective movies. Actually, they had never met a Chinese person. When we arrived by train in my hometown and my parents met Ted, I'm sure they were still in shock but somewhat relieved to find a tall, handsome, young man in a business suit, soft spoken, with even a touch of British accent.

There were fireworks in private when they got me to themselves, but I will credit them with being polite to Ted's face. They strongly objected to our relationship, but they were no match for their stubborn daughter. We announced that we were already engaged and wanted to be married before leaving for ministry in Hong Kong. My parents were still reeling from the fact that we were going to be married when they were faced with the reality that I would be leaving them for "far off places with strange sounding names."

When we returned to campus, we rang the tower bell, as students customarily did to announce engagements or weddings. We decided that if some people objected, that was their problem not ours. I had come a long way in my self-esteem. Once we knew it was God's will and plan that we marry, we let the chips fall where they may.

I graduated in May, *cum laude*, and Ted continued in summer school to graduate in August.

My parents gave us a beautiful, large wedding on the 23rd of August in their own Czech church. Mother and Dad had become Christians during my Junior year at college and were members there. The church was crowded with many whom we suspected were simply curious. What most people remember about that 102 degree, sultry, summer day before air-conditioning was the sight of all the candles in both candelabra, between the banks of flowers at the altar, doubling over and melting from the heat! What I remember was the perspiration pouring down my back under my long, white, Chinese silk wedding gown and from my face under my wedding veil!

Three months later, loaded with crates and trunks and baggage, we left for the West Coast from the train station in Cedar Rapids. The cross country trip took us to San Francisco where we literally set sail on a slow boat to China that took a month. Because it was shortly after the war was over, many ships formerly used for troop transport were sold to shipping and transportation companies. The huge passenger ship on which we sailed was the S.S. General Meigs, an "unconverted" troop ship. By unconverted, I mean that the facilities were still intact from using it to transport soldiers—basic dormitory style with three-tier bunk beds. From the top one, to which I was assigned, I could touch the pipes on the ceiling. Because no cabin facilities were available for anyone, men were assigned to one deck, women to another. We were still supposed to be on our honeymoon! The only time we saw each other was at mealtimes and out on the deck! We were happy to arrive in the Hong Kong harbor the day after New Years 1948, ready for the next brush strokes of the Master Painter on the masterpiece He was creating in both of our lives.

I'm sure I didn't realize how difficult an adjustment it was for my parents to have me go so far away. Missionaries didn't fly back and forth frequently in those days as they do now. Little did any of us know that when we said goodbye at the train station, it would be the last time I would see Dad. He died unexpectedly at age 59 during our early ministry years in Hong Kong. He never got to see any of his grandchildren.

God's promise to me was from Luke 18:29 in the Amplified, "And [Jesus] said to them, I say to you, truly there is no one who has left house or wife or brothers or parents or children for the sake of the kingdom of God, who will not receive in return many times more in this world, and in the coming age eternal life." God has literally fulfilled that in my life in the many decades since then.

Looking back on my feelings at the time, I believe there was an underlying and lingering determination and relief to leave behind forever my Czech heritage and adopt a new identity in China. There it made no difference what my ethnic roots were. Besides, the Chinese people often laugh about all Caucasians looking alike to them, and we sometimes say the same about people from Asia—they all look alike to us! That is far from true, but at least it is a proverbial joke.

By marrying Ted, I adopted a totally new culture, a new language, a new country, a new ministry and gave my children-to-be a new heredity. China was about as far away as I could get from my Czech roots! Little did I suspect that about 40 years later, after fulfilling a lifetime of service in China and among the Chinese people, God would add broad, unexpected brush strokes to paint a new scene on my life masterpiece. God would give me a new, surprise assignment in my later, so-called retirement years. He would bring me full circle by giving me a love for, identification with, concern for and opportunities to bond with my Czech heritage!

I wouldn't have believed that as a young bride going to China in 1947!

Leona and Ted's wedding (1947) that drew a large crowd of curious guests

19

Brushing in the Details

I wrote and published the story of my 46 years of marriage and ministry with Ted in his biography, *My Dreams and Visions*. It includes Ted's ancestry, family, his childhood and early life, education and call to the ministry. I described many of our missionary adventures in Hong Kong, Singapore, China and the United States over a lifetime. In it I shared stories of over a dozen of my ministry trips to China after the normalization of diplomatic relations between China and the United States. I won't repeat all those thrilling details here. I hope you will read the book for yourself!

In another book, *Touching China: Close Encounters of the Christian Kind*, I chronicled more about China, its history, culture, the spread of Christianity in China, the revolutionary years of persecution and the imprisonment and martyrdom of many of China's faithful Christians. I included intimate stories of meeting Christian believers in China and the various possibilities of ministering there today. That information I will not repeat either.

But for the sake of continuity in this story of my life, in this chapter I will touch on the high points and sequence of events during those nearly 50 years. In the back of this book you will find a chronology and brief genealogical record of our families.

Ted's vision and plan upon our arrival in his home city of Hong Kong, at that time a British Colony through a one hundred year treaty between China and Britain, was for us to go to inland China to do mission work. However, the communists had gradually taken over all of China by the time we arrived, and all missionaries were on their way *out* of the country. God led us to remain in Hong Kong for ministry for the next six years.

Thus began an interesting and challenging new life adventure for me in a completely foreign environment. Ted's large and wonderful family welcomed me gladly, even (and especially) his father, who had warned him not to marry an American girl. We became good friends. Ted's mother didn't speak English, but we got along just fine with sign language and had many good laughs over our communication or miscommunication. I adapted quite rapidly to new customs, surroundings and the tropical climate, complete with typhoons. Ted's brothers and sisters soon became my warm friends, all spoke English and his nieces and nephews studied English at school. We lived in a house next door to his parents at Number 7 York Road in Kowloon Tong, which is on the peninsula across the harbor from the urban island of Hong Kong.

Soon after we arrived in Hong Kong, Ted's sister, Lillian, sailed for the United States to pursue her college education. We arranged for her to go to Coe College in my hometown and live with my parents, even to occupy my bedroom. That was like a family "exchange student" program. My parents appreciated having someone there to keep them from being lonely, and they embraced her to their hearts as if she were another daughter. For Lillian, it was an opportunity for a home away from home. Her presence with them gave me a sense of relief and hope that my parents wouldn't miss me too much. She lived with my parents throughout her college education and even after her fiancé, a medical student from China, joined her. They were married and lived with my parents for a time while Hong interned at a local hospital. They were still there to give Mother comfort when my dad suddenly died. The same month, Lillian gave birth to their first child.

Ted accepted the position as minister of the Swatow Christian Church in Kowloon where he had been a member before leaving for study in the U.S. During the time he served as pastor, the church grew, expanded and built a large new building on Prat Avenue in the Tsimshatsui district close to the harbor.

It was during that period that our first three sons were born—Richard, Clifford and Gary—all within three years! In the eyes of my friends, I always seemed to be pregnant! When they met me on the street, they asked whether that was still the same pregnancy as the last time we met! We did have household help with cooking, cleaning and shopping or else I wonder how I could have managed. When I had time, I taught Christian education classes for teachers and helped in the leadership of Child Evangelism meetings. After several years, Ted was invited to teach in a newly-established seminary in Singapore for a year. So when our youngest, Gary, was only three months old, we sailed for Singapore and another new adventure the Lord planned for our lives.

The children and I returned to the U.S. in 1952 because of the death of my dad and the illness and needs of my mother. Ted had to remain in Singapore for the duration of his teaching contract and couldn't return with us. Rick, the oldest child, was just over three, Cliff was two and a half and Gary was six months old. Mercifully, I can't remember many details of how I coped alone with all three on the month long voyage on a Dutch ship through the Suez Canal via England. Two were still in diapers and on bottles in the days before disposable diapers. The ship had no special facilities for children. In Southampton, we had to get off the ship with all our baggage and spend the night in a hostel of sorts. The next morning we boarded the QE I, the huge Queen Elizabeth, which actually docked next to the ship on which we arrived. About five days later, we sailed into New York harbor on a blustery cold and snowy Thanksgiving Day. My mother and Aunt Fan came from Iowa by train to meet us, and after a few days of adjusting to our land legs again by staying in a hotel, we boarded the train for the two day journey to Iowa. Our children went from sun suits to snowsuits, never having experienced bitter winter weather and snow. Colds and illness beset us the entire winter, but God surely cared for all of us in a special way while we were separated from Ted.

The children and I lived with Mother and my aunt, and the adjustments for all of us were tremendous. Noise and stress and the constant activity of three toddlers were probably more than my poor mother and aunt could endure confined in a small two-bedroom house in the winter. Mother, not in good health, was an unaccustomed "suddenly grandmother" of children who seemed to be almost triplets—and all boys! Aunt Fan had to get her sleep at night because she got up at five in the morning to go to work. That meant, "Kids! Be quiet!"—an almost impossible hope and command. Honestly, I don't even remember where we all slept! So many things God mercifully erased from my memory when time gives them distance.

Ted joined us after completing a year of seminary teaching in Singapore, and we added him to the mix of temporarily living with Mother and my aunt for another year. While waiting for the approval of his application to become a U.S. citizen, (he had traveled on his Chinese passport up to that point) Ted took further studies at the State University of Iowa and earned his M.A. degree from the School of Religion in 1955. I remember the endless typing of his research papers and reports "in my spare time" in the basement where we set up an old manual typewriter and makeshift office away from the children.

After his graduation, and while waiting for God's next marching orders, still hoping to return to Asia for mission work, Ted joined the staff of *International Students, Inc.* in Philadelphia. We moved there and became involved in an exciting and strategic ministry among many international scholars studying in the universities of that area. More and more his ministry became focused on the many thousands of Chinese students coming to study from different places in Southeast Asia. None were from communist China at that time because of government controls on travel and lack of diplomatic relations between our two countries.

Later we moved to Washington, D.C. to ISI headquarters, and Ted was given the opportunity to establish the Chinese Students Department of that organization. During the over six years we served with ISI, the ministry among Chinese students expanded across the country. There were many more Chinese students in comparison to other internationals and also many more Christians among them who needed spiritual encouragement. Ted traveled extensively to college towns and university centers to help establish Chinese Bible study groups on campuses and to assist the students however he could.

After we moved to Washington, we began gathering local Chinese Christians in our home for Bible studies and on Sundays for worship. On Sunday mornings, Ted would drive around to university dormitories and other places in the city to transport students to our Sunday meeting. We always had a Chinese potluck meal afterward for the students and families and this took place in our big four story house on 16th street Northwest. Some Chinese students lived with us while they attended local schools. We always had a house full.

As that meeting grew in numbers, it eventually gave birth to the *Chinese Christian Church of Greater Washington,* and at this writing, it continues as a thriving congregation with its own buildings on Piney Branch Road in Silver Spring, Maryland. We thanked God for the opportunity to help birth this lasting outreach to the Chinese community in the nation's capitol.

During that time, our 4th son, Jeffrey, was born and joined his three brothers in keeping our home lively and exciting. Besides taking care of our home and children, I assisted in the hospitality program for Chinese students and office work relating to the student ministry.

The work among Chinese students grew so extensive that in 1962 Ted resigned from ISI and three of us, Ted, Rev. Moses Chow, (who was by then pastor of our new Chinese church) and myself co-founded the independent new ministry for Chinese students and professionals in North America which we called *Ambassadors For Christ, Inc.* That ministry spread rapidly, eventually moving its headquarters from the nation's capitol to Paradise, Pennsylvania. It was located on property deeded to us by our Christian friends Christiana Tsai, Mary A. Leaman, her sister Lucy and their cousin, Mary W. Leaman. We built a new building for AFC headquarters and used the 112 acre property and farm house for a retreat center for Chinese Christian student activities and discipleship training. Our staff families moved to Paradise as well.

Ted served with AFC ministry until he retired, seeing it from its infancy to amazing growth on campuses across the country with an independent AFC ministry established in Canada. Many thriving Chinese Bible study groups throughout the U.S. eventually became Chinese churches. We rejoiced in the growing emphasis on missions to all the world by Chinese Christians. That led to the establishment of the triennial Chinese Missions convocations drawing hundreds of Chinese students to consider worldwide witness. After the normalization of diplomatic relations with

China, the flow of scholars from the People's Republic of China to the Western world, including the U.S., was like a flood. Both government-sponsored scholars and privately funded students poured into the U.S. It was a dream and vision come true—something we had prayed for from the time of our own student days.

That influx of students from the China Mainland gave rise to the unique opportunity Christians in America began to have for sharing their faith with thousands of scholars from China right in their own communities, although Westerners still couldn't go freely to China as missionaries. AFC established a substantial witness and literature ministry for those scholars from the People's Republic, and when Ted retired, we were happy and grateful to pass the torch to the younger generation of Chinese Christian workers at AFC.

Ted retired from AFC in 1981, but he didn't consider himself too old to continue direct involvement in mission work. He was still eager to actively pursue his initial call from the Lord to bring the gospel personally to China. The communist takeover of China in 1949 prevented our going inland after we arrived in Hong Kong and continued to prohibit any ministry to China for the next 30 years or so. When all missionaries had to leave China, the young Church in China was left to survive alone.

However, the Holy Spirit continued to work marvelously in China in the hearts of faithful Chinese Christians not only enabling them to survive but to grow to incredible numbers. The communist government closed churches, burned Bibles, sent pastors to labor camps and put many believers to death. Christians suffered great persecution and many, many thousands gave their lives as martyrs for Christ.

Through the quiet but fervent one-to-one witness of Chinese believers, whether they were thrown into prison, sent to labor camps, to "political rehabilitation" in the countryside or while working in factories or on farms, the Church in China increased to many millions of believers. Because churches were closed and public worship was forbidden by the government, Chinese believers had to meet secretly in homes or out-of-the-way places, giving rise to the term "house churches."

When China began to slightly open the "bamboo curtain" to allow selected persons to go in and out, Ted's vision and dream was to go to China and somehow help those struggling Christians with encouragement, prayer, Bibles, training materials or whatever their needs might be. After his retirement, he started a small, independent ministry called ETC "English Tutoring Center." His intent was to make personal contacts with people inside China, especially with young people. He believed that their eagerness to learn English could be a "friendship bridge" to witness to them with the gospel. On our repeated trips into China, we developed contacts and friendships with young people we met on streets, in hotels, in parks and at sightseeing locations. We linked them with Christian friends in America who wanted to use the pen-pal bridge to make friends in China and, as God would lead them, wisely witness to their Chinese friends about the Christian faith. Many letters were freely exchanged and American Christians were able to send books and other materials through the mail to them.

Through the years that we carried on this program, it proved to be a workable friendship and witness bridge for hundreds and hundreds of such contacts. We published some basic English learning materials, prepared cassettes and published a small magazine under the auspices of ETC.

Although China remained closed to any direct missionary work either by Westerners or by overseas Chinese Christians, the government allowed and welcomed experts in technology, science, business, education and the like who could benefit the people. China especially welcomed teachers of English.

Still more surprising was that it also became possible for Americans and people of other nationalities to visit China as tourists—something totally unanticipated. The grass roots people of China seemed eager to form friendships with outsiders since they had been isolated for so long. Both Ted and I, together and separately, followed through on this opportunity to establish friendships with China's young people by making a number of trips into China as visitors and tourists. We had unusual opportunities to witness for the Lord.

In the mid-80s, I enlisted and escorted a number of tour groups from the U.S. to China. Some groups were comprised of all Christians, some were general American tours to various major tourist sites in China for several weeks at a time. Other tours were made up of medical persons whom I took to visit hospitals and clinics, some were educational interest tours and I arranged for them to visit schools. On such tours I was able to make more friendship contacts and do further research on the situation in China for my writing. I traveled repeatedly to places in China like the Great Wall, the Forbidden City, the Ming Tombs, Tiananmen Square, the lakes of Hangzhou, the gardens of Suzhou, the misty mountains of Guilin, the archaeologic discoveries of Xian, famous cities like Beijing, Shanghai and Nanjing among other places. They became as familiar as my hometown to me. *What a privilege God has given me in my lifetime!*

China always did welcome Chinese who had been living overseas to visit their home villages because of generous funds they hoped might be invested there or spent by purchasing China's commodities. Overseas Chinese were free to travel virtually anywhere in China as tourists. Ted, considered an overseas Chinese, took full advantage of that welcome, and I was able to caboose on his opportunity. Traveling independently of any group, Ted and I made several trips together to far flung areas of China.

On such private trips by ourselves, we were overwhelmed with the privilege of meeting hundreds and hundreds of house church Christian believers in many locations, worshiping with them and learning how the Lord preserved them during the years of intense persecution and suffering. We marveled at the first century miracles they told us about, the power of their simple witness, the degree of their sacrifices and their boldness in proclaiming the gospel message under adverse political conditions. We got to know many of the Chinese believers intimately and kept in touch with them and prayed for them when we returned home. On subsequent trips, we were able to revisit some of them and bring them desperately needed Bibles and Christian training materials in the Chinese language.

I felt so privileged to travel with Ted at intervals during the entire decade of the 80s to many of the provinces of China— all the way north to Heilongjiang province, to Harbin, (in the dead of winter!) inland to Xian, South to Fujian and to many provinces, cities and villages between. We traveled by train, boat, plane, bus, pedicab, rickety ox carts, bicycles and often on foot. If I had not been with Ted, I would not have had such unique experiences as a non-Chinese.

Ted was especially burdened to witness for Christ on the island of Hainan off the Southern coast of China. I made several trips there with him of several months duration, traveling the length and breadth of the island, meeting with house church believers in villages and countryside and also with the Christians in registered churches. We always made it a point to visit universities and schools to make meaningful academic connections. Some of our contacts enabled us to find opportunities in universities and other institutions for American Christian teachers to apply for positions.

In 1979, Ted and I made a first visit to his hometown of Shantou (Swatow). He wondered what it would be like after more than a half century since he had seen it. Swatow was just beginning to wake up and stretch. There was a surprising amount of the old. But he was amazed that some things were still as he remembered them—dirty streets, houses and buildings in disrepair, primitive agriculture, lack of basic sanitation and careless health habits. In spite of communist propaganda that "new China" had become so progressive and self-sufficient, his hometown was far from a showcase.

However, between that first visit and our last visit a decade later, with several visits between, Swatow really began to shape up and quickly started to progress. In *My Dreams and Visions* I described Swatow as it was during our first trip to introduce it to generations who would never again be able to see it at that primitive stage. It was a slice of time that would never return.

One memorable incident from that first trip was Ted's search for the burial site of his precious grandmother who was one of the first Christians in their village. We crossed the river on a ferry, walked through the small village and up the tree-shaded, winding road. Ted was overjoyed to actually locate the site in a somewhat hidden spot, untouched, overgrown with weeds, next to a sturdy cement pavilion. The tall headstone was still firmly standing. Grandmother's name was inscribed, "Yang Hiang-sui," and the words "Mother and grandmother of the Choy family, 1846-1929."

Hers was one of the very few grave sites not destroyed during the Cultural Revolution. The communists demolished most burial sites to reclaim the land for cultivation. That was totally against the Chinese tradition of reverence for one's ancestors. Graves were never supposed to be disturbed, but the communists, although Chinese themselves, totally desecrated the cemeteries. Stone markers were especially valuable to hew into pieces for other uses—sometimes for stepping stones on paths, sometimes for building construction. It seemed that all the other grave markers in that area were destroyed except his grandmother's, which stood as straight as her living testimony. We took pictures at the site in memory of the oldest Christian in the Choy family ancestry.

Several reasons are possible for his grandmother's burial place not being destroyed. Hers was not in a cemetery but all by itself in a place outside the village. Moreover, we heard that some of the townspeople passed around the story that if anyone were to touch her tomb, someone close to them would take sick and die. That was superstitious hearsay, of course.

Our visit there was a solemn and holy experience. Ted remembered the godly heritage the Lord had given him and the rest of his brothers and sisters and families. He prayed that grandmother's prayers would be answered for our own generation—for the salvation of all the members of the Choy family and for our own four sons and their spouses to come to know the God of the Bible and Jesus Christ as their personal Savior and Lord. We prayed that our grandchildren and their children and descendants would, in their time, make the decision to follow the Christian faith of their parents and grandparents until the return of Jesus Christ. We prayed together that we might all be reunited in Heaven to give praise to God for His salvation and special care for our families throughout our lifetimes.

When Ted and I traveled in China early in the 1980s, before modernization and privatization and shirt-sleeve capitalism took over China like a flood, we wore dark Chinese jackets and trousers in order not to appear conspicuous when we traveled in the countryside. We visited some places where most of the villagers had never seen a foreigner. I always drew curious stares and interest and when I tried to converse with my limited Swatow-dialect conversation, they were surprised and pleased to hear my efforts. Although our "overseas-ness" was still evident, it didn't seem to hinder our welcome.

During his retirement, Ted was at last seeing the fulfillment of his prayers and his lifetime vision to have personal contacts with believers in China. He thanked God that he lived to see that day. During the height of the Cultural Revolution when the door to gospel witness in China from outside was totally closed, we heard reports that all religion in China had been eradicated by the communists. Many thought there would never again be any opportunity for Christian witness in China. All the while, the Holy Spirit was powerfully at work within the Chinese church!

Ted, reflecting the thinking of Chinese who have a background of thousands of years of history and culture, often said "everything passes, anything can change and eventually it does." As he prayed for China, he always maintained a faith attitude: "WHEN China opens again," not "IF China might open." But he confessed that he had not really expected to see such a thing in his lifetime or that he would experience personally what he saw during our travels in China after his retirement.

At this writing, The People's Republic of China is still not open to Western missionary activity in the same way it was before. Perhaps it never will be and never should be, because times have changed. That doesn't mean the Word of God is hindered and that the gospel cannot be spread by ardent believers within China to every province and throughout the cities and countryside. God has unique, creative ways to accomplish His purposes for world evangelism, and the Holy Spirit is powerfully at work in China.

We continued our contacts with Christians and with the youth of China after we moved from Paradise, Pennsylvania to Winchester, Virginia where we assisted our eldest son, Rick, establish a Christian radio station. Rick is founder, builder and C.E.O. of WTRM-FM (Southern Light Gospel Music Network) which has expanded from reaching parts of four states to eventually uplink on satellite with unlimited potential coverage across the country.

Ted was keenly aware that the Choy family received a godly heritage through God's wonderful, sovereign plan. God's love and salvation rescued them from the spiritual darkness in which their family was born. He was concerned that we be faithful to pray for those who follow us, our descendants, just as his beloved, blind grandmother's prayers followed her descendants down through the years and reached even to us. I felt the same way about the prayers of my grandmother, Baba. We shared a heritage. May it not be said that we failed to pass the torch.

What had *I* been doing in the decades when we were so involved in establishing the ministry among Chinese university students across the country? For many years I worked at AFC headquarters full time helping in administration and editorial work both while our headquarters was in Washington, D.C. and after it relocated to Paradise, PA. I was able to use my love for writing within the mission organization, and God was also multiplying that creative gift through freelance writing. I took a leave of absence from AFC which led eventually to devoting my full time to writing. Publishers were accepting my work for magazine articles, poetry submissions and book contracts. We were still living in Paradise, PA, and we had long before become empty-nesters. Two of our sons were married, and we were happily accumulating grandchildren.

It had been a long road from my complaint to God as a teen that I had no talents to offer Him. (No, I never did learn to play the piano!) That wasn't God's plan for me. He had other things in mind. With my early efforts at composing childish poems in secret, God fanned my desire to write. My voracious love for reading evolved into attempts to write for publication myself. While we were overseas as newlyweds and young parents, there was certainly no time to write. I could barely keep my head above water. But God has a time and season for everything, if we leave it with Him.

At age 27, when I returned to the U.S. from Singapore, exhausted from the tropical climate and with two toddlers and a baby in tow, it was possibly the worst of times to think about launching a writing career. Increasingly, however, even as a mom with my hands more than full, I sensed God's call to write. I had not taken any writing courses, and in those early years, we didn't have Christian writers conferences, how-to books on Christian writing, Christian market guides or instruction tapes.

I borrowed stacks of books from the public library and learned the writing craft between bottles and diaper changes. I joined a local writers group of university women in Cedar Rapids where we mercilessly critiqued each other's writings. I determined to try every writing genre until I got a sale in each category to see where God might be giving me more aptitude or interest. After accumulating many rejection slips, I actually achieved that goal. Journalism didn't appeal to me, but I was enthusiastic about creative writing, poetry and especially nonfiction. Of one thing I was sure, however—*no way would I ever write a book!* I was inclined to shorter manuscripts that didn't take so long. I guess the safest thing is *never to say never.* My autobiography is my 31st published book, and translations of my books or foreign language editions number well over a dozen.

I continued freelance writing while raising our four sons. Editing publications for our mission organization was good training and experience. Quite by accident, I found myself involved in "ghost writing" books (writing books for others). Invitations to be a "friendly ghost" still haunt me, but I try to limit my acceptance of those opportunities so I can invest my time in my own creative work. Successful ghosting led to my writing historical and missionary biographies, books on China, anthologies of my poetry, books on the craft and ministry of writing, parable-allegories, contemporizing classic works, short fiction, mission philosophy and devotional books. When the Master Painter added brush strokes of darker colors to my life canvas and I went through some of the traumas of life, among them my cancer surgery and widowhood, I wrote and published books to help others make it through with the help of God.

My early books were published through traditional publishing companies. Those were the days of manual and later electric typewriters when it was laborious to produce a clean, perfect manuscript to submit. When computer word processors were finally available and my writing became more prolific, the submit-and-wait-on-publishers-endlessly cycle seemed too slow and tedious. My potential for marketing grew during the years when I produced and broadcasted a daily radio program on station WTRM-FM, of which I was president from its founding to the present. Speaking in churches and writers conferences increased my visibility, my web site was active and through word of mouth by those who were helped by my books, I was reaching the niche readership I was targeting.

In more recent years, with our eldest son, Rick, I established *Golden Morning Publishing* primarily as an umbrella entity for my own books, although I have ghosted or edited several books for others through our company. We manage the entire process from writing to multiple editings, seemingly endless proof readings, to pagination and producing camera-ready copy through desktop publishing. We work with graphic artists for full-color covers, and we subcontract the printing. We aim for professional excellence because I write for the glory of God as a ministry, not as a business.

God is still in the process of multiplying that writing gift for His glory. *Hopefully, the best books are yet to come.*

20

My Ticket for Speeding

It is difficult to know where in my life story to insert this defining-moment chapter. The experience covers a span of many years and overlaps the previous chapter. If I didn't include it, I would not be honest. Because I first shared it when I spoke to a women's meeting in Pennsylvania in the early 1980s, I can best recount it in that format. It follows, approximately as I delivered it:

As your speaker, I could have been publicized as: "A woman who was arrested on two charges, was involved in a cover-up in Washington, D.C., [It was the era of the Watergate scandal] and was a former 'go-go' girl." That might have doubled our audience!

To dispel any shock, I will say at the beginning that God was the arresting officer, my addiction and cover up was spiritual and "*go-go*" was my Christian activity treadmill. Because I am a writer and story teller, I will relate my experience as a flashback in mini-chapters.

Chapter 1. After I became a Christian in my teens and sincerely surrendered my life to the Lord unreservedly, I began to climb a traditional, evangelical ladder of ministry. The first step was to consider full-time Christian service. Next, I was told that if I really wanted God's best in my life, I should be a missionary. There was nothing wrong with that sequence except the perception that accompanied it—that I was "saved to serve." Actually, serving God should be a byproduct of something more important—a love relationship with Jesus Christ as our motivation. With the emphasis on service, my hands, what I could *do*, became overly important.

Chapter 2. In college I was well trained in Christian Education and theology, married a minister and missionary and sailed off to Asia at the tender age of 21. I thought I was "equipped to serve" because I had sound doctrine and was armed with a "how to do it" list to get results. The truth was, I was like a car without gas. I was expected to fly, but had no wings. I tried to do God's work without His power tools and tried to live the Christian life in my own strength. I was spiritually impotent.

I confess that before long I realized that I was failing as a missionary. I blew it. I was not only disappointed in myself but disillusioned with Christian service and personally embarrassed. Defeat and depression set in. Like the disciples, I had toiled all night with rowing. Not only did I not catch any fish, but my boat had holes in it, was beginning to sink and I couldn't swim.

Facing such a dilemma, one alternative was to drop out of ministry—just quit, slink away, mumble the excuse that I was really "not called" to the ministry. But I couldn't do that. It would not have been honest. Besides, I married an "M and M"—a minister and missionary. I couldn't bear to let my husband "lose face" and allow his reputation in the ministry to be damaged. I had burned my bridges—said goodbye to everyone back home and cut all ties—no turning back or returning. Well, another legitimate way of escape would be to become ill or have a nervous breakdown, which I nearly did. I was so overwhelmed with my dismal, disappointing life and spiritual failure that I literally became ill.

I wish I could say my experience was a rare one, an exception on the mission field. It isn't. In the years since, I have met many Christian workers who have been sweating at the rowing in their likewise leaky boats without a catch of fish.

Since I couldn't drop out, I fell for one of the devil's prime tricks—the old cover-up game. If he can't keep you from doing God's work, he will put you on roller skates and give you a big push. Get busy—busy—busy in Christian work. You will look good on the outside, perhaps even be greatly admired. "How dedicated that *'go-go'* girl is!" You may be able to fool people, but you and God know that you are a hollow shell. You can then legitimately become weary in well-doing, and people will sympathize with you. But you will be stale spiritually, dry, without any Rivers of Living Water flowing through you because they are not flowing into you. I took that escape route to compensate for my lack of inward spiritual power.

Chapter 3. So began a 25 year cover-up, certainly much longer than the Watergate scandal. Bible study and prayer became only routine, a performance that lacked passion. I developed a professional approach to people's problems without feeling compassion. I couldn't shed any tears with or for others or for myself because I had a cold heart. The early joy of salvation and glow of God's presence faded. Church programs and activity were a reputable front, but I engaged in them without enthusiasm. I felt some wistfulness and longing for victory and for my previous burning heart, but they seemed illusive.

Because everything looked good on the outside, I advanced in missionary work. When we returned from Hong Kong and be-

255

gan a strategic ministry among Chinese university students across North America, I became immersed in administrative work, writing, speaking and reputable Christian activity. One *can* work for God in the flesh but it is not pleasing to Him. There may be results but not genuine spiritual fruit. I was very skilled at studying the Bible to teach it because I was trained in the inductive method and exegesis, able to "rightly divide the word of truth." But I didn't let God's Word bring me into the presence of God for intimate communion with Him. I prayed, of course, with my long list of requests for things I wanted God to do, similar to my own "to do" lists. I had slipped back into being lord of my own life. Intermittently, God tapped me on the shoulder, reminded me of His love and desire for my closer walk with Him, the promise and availability of His power and showed me glimpses of "from whence I had fallen." But because we have free will, it is possible for a Christian to continue to grieve the Holy Spirit and ignore His nudging.

Chapter 4. In the fullness of God's time, I was arrested for speeding. First, literally. I tend to have a somewhat heavy foot on the accelerator, and on one of my many commutes from AFC's Washington, D.C. headquarters to our ministry outreach in Pennsylvania, a state police officer pulled me aside. He showed no mercy. He wasn't willing to give me just a warning notice, but issued me a traffic ticket worth several points against my record, plus an unusually heavy fine.

I was the busiest I had ever been. Besides my family responsibilities with our children and my full time position as administrative assistant in our growing Chinese student ministry, I was editor of publications, writer, speaker, trainer of personnel, planner of retreats and itinerary for the staff and manager of our hospitality center for students. I was also in charge of building AFC's new headquarters in Paradise, PA. In that capacity, I was the designer, liaison with the architect, contractor, tradesmen and township supervisors. I was responsible for the interior decorating, landscaping, selling our property in Washington and simultaneously building our own new home in Paradise. I was commuting to Pennsylvania weekly to arrange for the packing and moving of our entire D.C. headquarters.

"Never say no" was my motto. I was proud of my dedicated Christian service. I probably worked so loudly that everyone heard me. Busy service was my safe place to hide my spiritual inadequacy.

Just before our move to Pennsylvania, I decided to take care of my routine dental and medical check ups. I planned to hurry through them and get on with my more important responsibilities.

But instead of receiving an expected clean bill of health, my doctor shocked me by scheduling surgery within ten days! God had set His radar trap. He was arresting me for my frantic pace and issuing me a speeding ticket.

X-rays and medical appointments spelled out the seriousness of the pending cancer surgery. The next three days passed in a daze and a haze. I went back and forth from panic to tears to depression, with anger sprinkled between. *Going to surgery? NO, LORD! I'm not done building Your Kingdom. I am indispensable to our ministry. My children need me. My husband needs me! We are in the middle of a building program.* (I was reminded of the man in Jesus' story in Luke 12 who was also in the midst of a building program. Jesus said that his life would terminate that night.)

The last straw—my surgery was scheduled for our moving day!

Chapter 5. God was speaking to me through a megaphone. I began to listen. I finally did turn to the Great Physician and asked Him for a diagnosis. God gave me a head to toe comprehensive check up. Then He gave me *ten points* against my life traffic record. Not in judgment, but with gentle love, the Lord said:

"Leona, you have a problem with your HEAD. You know much of My truth intellectually, but you don't live it out in obedience to Me.

You have a HEART problem. Your heart is cold and hard, it needs melting. You have lost your "first love" for Me.

I have a problem with your HANDS. They are overactive in service and hiding My face from you. They are not raised in worship because they are tied to Christian work.

You need a FACE-lift, lifted to Me, not with your nose to the grindstone.

There is something wrong with your EYES. You are blind to your own condition. You suffer from dry eyes because you have no compassion. Moreover, you don't see the big work I am doing by My Spirit in the world today.

You have a SPEECH problem. You are poor in one-to-one witness because you have no testimony of your relationship with Me. All you can talk about is mission strategy, church growth principles, contextualization and programs.

You have a WEIGHT problem. Like the biblical Martha, you are cumbered about with much serving. You have weights that so easily beset you—your "to do" lists, your own fleshly plans.

You have an ENERGY crisis. You lack My power to do My work. You have an oil crisis. Where is the Oil of the Holy Spirit in your life? You are tired because you are pushing everyone else as hard as you push yourself.

There is a problem with your BALANCE. An unsteady, ups and downs walk is not the expression of the abundant life I have available for you. You are not balancing your outside service with inward renewing.

You have a FOOT problem. You are not close enough to Me to hear My voice so I can't lead your feet where I want you to go."

Woe is me, I was undone! All those issues were symptoms of my work addiction. I was hooked on a good thing—service to God. I was focused on *doing* instead of *being*. I had become a professional Christian worker. With all my frantic activity, I was not bearing spiritual fruit. I was working *for* God instead of letting Him work *through* me. I needed a *cup-running-over* experience, but I was not even being filled. I was a dedicated empty pot! My attitude was, "If God doesn't seem to be doing anything, I'll have to do something myself!" Because I ignored God's previous warnings, He had to give me a shock treatment. Jesus was aware of and commended my good works, as He did the church in Ephesus (Revelation 2:2-5), but He wanted the one thing I wasn't giving Him, which He valued above all. I confessed that I lost my "first love" for Jesus.

"What shall I do? What do you really want from me, Lord?"

"I want YOU. I love YOU. I want your whole heart. Your hands are no substitute. I can build My kingdom without you. I created you for our mutual love and communication. You got off My main road onto a 'service road.' I know about the problem in your body. Long ago you presented your body to Me, and I accepted responsibility for it. I hold your breath, your health, your life in My hands. I want you to trust Me with your life."

At last my response was to open my heart to Him and cry in renewed surrender, *"Jesus Christ, You are Lord of my life!"*

Immediately He touched me—or re-touched, revived, renewed, restored me. The terminology isn't important, but the experience is essential. I already had the Holy Spirit living in me since the day I first became a Christian, but I had quenched and grieved Him. Now He poured His Holy Spirit into me and filled me to overflowing. Or baptized me in the Holy Spirit, whatever you wish to call it. I could say God released the Holy Spirit within me and filled me until Rivers of Living Water flowed through me. I could describe it both ways—I had more of Him and He had more of me.

Some people struggle over defining or labeling such a vital spiritual experience. Some call it the victorious life, the overcoming life, the fulfilled life, the crucified life, the higher life, dying to self, the baptism of the Holy Spirit, life on the highest plane, the second blessing, the Spirit-filled life, the overflowing life, the surrendered life, the abiding life and many more terms. Labels aren't important to me. It is a biblically accurate experience, and I simply accept it from God.

Had I been asked, I would have replied that it would probably take a long time to tenderize my heart or to replace my heart of stone with a heart of flesh, responsive and sensitive. But it was not a long, drawn out process—it was instant.

I tend to be rational rather than emotional. But God created our emotions to praise Him, too. We are not just big-headed, walking minds. God wants us to be passionate about Him. I was overwhelmed with love, joy, peace (are they not emotions?) all rolled up in the person of Jesus. I regained my "first love" for Him. From that point on, I couldn't even speak or sing or hear the name of Jesus without being awash with tears of joy. Laughing and crying were mingled. It was such a relief to be loved and mercifully forgiven by God and restored to a normal, intimate relationship with Jesus.

Any version of the Bible became "the living Bible" to me, no longer boring or to be studied only so I could teach a Bible class. I thought that only David the Psalmist and I had discovered praise! Demonstrative praise was not part of my traditional Christian upbringing nor of the churches in the context of our ministry. Worship was what we called the preliminary part of a Sunday service before the sermon—the singing of a few hymns, usually "the first, second and last verses," followed by a pastoral prayer and the offering. Church services were typically quiet and traditional. "Shhhh. This is God's House." Perhaps He doesn't like loud noise? Now, everything I read in the Bible motivated me to verbal praise and worship during my times of waiting on Him. David assured me, "His praise shall continually be in my mouth...rejoice and shout for joy...."

God was becoming very real to me again, the focus of my life. Because I was a slow learner, He lovingly had to use a life-threatening illness to get my attention. I don't believe God caused my illness, but He used it for His glory and my good. "Before I was afflicted, I went astray, but now I keep Thy word. Thou art good and doest good" (Psalm 119:67, 68).

The full joy of a restored relationship with God so overwhelmed me that I almost forgot about my pending surgery. A friend suggested that perhaps God wanted to heal me now. I wasn't so sure about that. I had always believed in healing because it was in the Bible, and in past years, God often healed me of minor difficulties. But this was a "biggy," and I didn't want to embarrass God in case He no longer did major miracles today. Nevertheless, I set about searching the Bible with childlike openness and came upon the book of James, chapter five, with the promise that when elders anoint the sick with oil, the sick would be healed. I read that many times before but never met any elders who practiced it. The only oil most churches had was in the cars in the parking lot or in the church heating systems.

Three days before my surgery, someone told me about a Presbyterian church that did practice that. Since I was familiar with that traditional denomination from my childhood, I thought it would be safe to go, and no one would know me there. It was the first time I was in a church service where they praised God freely and enthusiastically, even with upraised hands, yet a very orderly service. I felt at home because King David had taught me to do that. At the close of the service, the invitation was given for anyone who wanted prayer for healing to come to the altar. With others, I responded. Still a little embarrassed, I asked the elders for "prayer with oil." When an elder anointed me with oil, the pastor prayed very quietly that I would "be made whole." I was somewhat disappointed that he didn't pray specifically for my healing. I experienced no hot flashes, nor did I hear thunder or see lightning—I didn't even have goose bumps.

The following day was my final appointment before surgery. First one doctor and then another examined me, took another X-ray, compared it with the former one, then called me into his office. "It seems that the large lump on which we were going to operate is no longer there. We are canceling your surgery, Mrs. Choy." I shed tears of joy and gratitude to God. He does not always heal in the same way or instantly. Sometimes, for His sovereign reasons, He doesn't heal. In fact, in a later chapter I tell the story of the cancer surgery I did go through and the blessings that followed, because my experience gave me new compassion. God has enabled me to minister to others experiencing similar physical trials and to write several books on the topic.

Chapter 6. As I sought perspective on what happened to me, I received some insights from God. In retrospect, I saw how I had gradually drifted from the close, personal relationship I once had with Jesus in my early years. From the beginning, I became caught up (or rather dragged down) with the activities and programs of busy Christian ministry, as well as adapting to a new culture and family responsibilities and with giving birth to three children in three years. Gradually, I neglected the nourishment and cultivation of my inner spiritual life. That continued after our return to the U.S., when we became even more immersed in busy ministry. I lost sight of the simple truth that *Jesus loves me,* and His priority pleasure is for a continuing, daily, intimate relationship with me. My priorities had been out of order. My work *for* God came first, my family came second and time *with* God came last. God wanted me to put Him first, then my family, and my service *for* Him after that.

God promised never to forsake me, and He didn't, not even through the many years of my spiritual cover up. God created man with free will. That means I can wander from Him and follow my own way. But as long as I stay close to Him—Jesus called it "abiding in Him"—and am careful to continually nourish my spirit on His Words, I will live the normal, fruitful, abundant life which He desires for me.

Are refillings necessary? Most Christians, myself included, are leaky vessels and "cracked pots." The cares of this world, even legitimate ones, can cloud my relationship with God, unless I carefully nurture it. I also use up God's power through living for Him and serving Him, just as a car uses up gas and needs refilling. In the same way that the waitress keeps topping off my cup of coffee in a restaurant, so I must keep being filled with the Holy Spirit. One filling is not enough. The Bible instructs us, "be continually filled with the Holy Spirit"—an ongoing process (Ephesians 5:18). That is a command to be obeyed and indispensable for living the abundant, overflowing life in Christ. It is not an option. Why should we hesitate to ask one another whether we are filled with the Holy Spirit, a truth so clearly taught in Scripture?

Didn't I already know about and experience the filling of the Holy Spirit? Yes, I did. I had no excuse. I had known the sweetness of a totally surrendered life, read "deeper life" books, knew the biblical truths, tasted of His power. But once filled is no guarantee of continued power *unless I abide* continually in living contact with a living Jesus. Without spiritual maintenance, my branch withers on the vine, and I don't bear fruit. As long as I stay connected to Christ, the Vine, I bear fruit effortlessly through His

263

vital, supernatural life which flows into me and through me. A vine or tree doesn't have to use self-effort to produce fruit.

My problem was a strong, independent, capable attitude of "I can do it myself." If I can do something by expending my own energy and sweat, why do I need God? I fell into the trap of "self service" while God wants "full service." Jesus wants to do it all through me. I am to serve God out of His fullness. I am His channel. The more I am filled with self, the less there is of God in my life. The more of Him, the less of self. Does God want to cancel out my identity, creativity and service for Him? No, He wants me so full of His Spirit that, as my "Service Director," He can use me even more. That is the real secret of self-fulfillment.

When Christ said "Without Me, you can do nothing," He was in essence saying, "Whatever you do in your own strength counts for nothing." That is sobering. He counters that by saying, "With Me, all things are possible." It is my choice.

The experience I had, which God precipitated though my physical illness, was a major one for which I am thankful. It was a new beginning—or a renewal—launching me into a spiritually satisfying and fruitful lifestyle with many exciting ramifications for the rest of my life.

Chapter 7. Since my heart was now receptive to God, and my ears tuned to listen obediently to Him, I began to hear of mighty moves of the Holy Spirit in this country and in other parts of the world. Didn't Jesus promise that "greater works than I do shall you do because I go to My Father"? I became aware of many other people who were walking in the fullness of the Holy Spirit and discovered from them that God was moving in a powerful way, restoring and renewing His Church irrespective of denominations, traditions, cultures, political oppression or ecclesiastical labels. The little breeze of The Spirit I had just experienced was part of the Big Wind that was blowing worldwide. God was obviously making ready the Bride of Christ, the Church, for the return of Jesus Christ to claim that Bride. The Church for which Jesus was returning was not going to be a weak, sickly Bride, but a glorious, healthy, vigorous one through the Holy Spirit's preparation (Ephesians 5:26, 27).

A new revelation opened to me as a result of God's powerful touch on my life. A veil was taken from my eyes. I avoided labels then, as I do now, and didn't align myself with any of the Christian movements of those days or today. My only concern is that any teaching, experience or movement is Scriptural. I wanted to find out firsthand whether these things were so. Therefore, first I studied the Bible diligently to search out all aspects of the Holy Spirit's work in a Christian's life and in the Church. As a result, I had to unlearn some erroneous interpretations and go back to biblical basics.

I had paid scant attention to the Gifts of the Spirit which are so clearly taught in the writings of the Apostle Paul. I found nothing in the Scriptures or in church history to indicate that any of them were withdrawn, obsolete or unavailable today. To relegate them only to the early church age was not consistent exegetically or historically. If I rejected their validity, I would be guilty of picking and choosing or discarding parts of inspired Scripture. Here were the obviously available spiritual power tools provided by and appointed by the Holy Spirit for ministry *today*—as they were in the beginning. They were to be expressed by those who were *filled with the Fruit* of the Holy Spirit, thus insuring that they would be administered *with love*.

Next, I wanted to see for myself whether the worldwide movements of the Holy Spirit were real and how they were expressed transculturally. Since our children were now grown and out of the nest, and with the blessing of my husband, who continued his ministry with *Ambassadors For Christ, Inc.*, I set out on my search as an investigating committee of one. I traveled about

20,000 miles in the U.S. (10,000 of them driving) to attend trans-denominational conferences and seminars in churches, stadiums, universities and seminaries. I interviewed both leaders and ordinary Christians.

At the same time, I engaged in historical research on what the great men and women of past centuries, the evangelical giants of the faith, taught, experienced and wrote about the Holy Spirit and His work. I researched 88 books those leaders wrote and I (imaginatively) "interviewed them" on the subject. I let them "speak" for themselves from their writings. The results appear in my book *Powerlines* published by Christian Publications, Inc. I was satisfied that the work of the Holy Spirit going on in the world today was nothing strange or unbiblical or unexpected. It was a fresh Wind blowing more forcefully and widely in our times.

Next, I wanted to see with my own eyes how God's Spirit was working in other countries, especially Asia where we had ministered. God gave me a second chance to return "to the scene of my crime" in a sense, to the place where I had failed in my ministry because I lacked the Holy Spirit's power. I traveled for nearly four months in six countries of Asia, covering over 35,000 miles. Besides meeting with ordinary Christians and attending their gatherings, I met a cross-section of leaders—directors of missions, seminary presidents, bishops, deans, canons, priests, ministers, missionaries, teachers, faculty of colleges, radio and TV directors, editors and heads of publishing companies. Among others, I met the Christian Ambassador of Ghana, a British diplomat who was a missionary, workers with drug addicts and a converted witch.

I went to cathedrals, convents, hotels, orphanages, British military quarters, small village chapels, plush apartments, seashore gatherings, mountain churches, schools, YMCA, native villages, TV studios, a Catholic university and restaurant meetings with 12 course Chinese feasts. In contrast, I had an appointment with a Spirit-filled local Christian in a food stall with dirt floor surrounded by the noise of street vendors.

My travels took me to visit mission work near Mount Fuji in Japan, to Shinto shrines, to Sun-Moon lake and the Grande Hotel in Taiwan, to Buddhist temples in Thailand, to Waikiki beach and Pearl Harbor in Hawaii. I met people in boat ministries in Hong Kong, schools in the Philippines, ministries in high rise apartments in Singapore and churches in Macau. With missionary friends, I visited volcanos, tea houses, Japanese imperial gardens and native churches in all the countries. I slept in grass huts, in a trailer home in sub-zero weather with no heat, on Japanese style tatami floor mats, in the homes of missionaries and in elegant hotels.

China was not open for travel yet, but I was able to go to the border, look over and pray for God's Spirit to move mightily there. In later years, God gave me the wonderful opportunity to make 13 trips to Mainland China to see the incredible work of the Holy Spirit there, which I have described in another chapter.

An unforgettable experience was to be invited to speak in the world's largest church in Korea at midnight during their weekly all-night prayer meeting attended by 10,000 people. Then to visit Prayer Mountain in the company of devoted Christian Korean new friends.

God gave me the humble privilege of ministry to many powerless, discouraged, lonely, weary, overburdened missionaries who were in similar "leaky boats" as I had been in for so long. We talked and prayed into the midnight hours about how to hoist our sail to catch the Wind of the Spirit and maintain an abiding walk with God so we could bear genuine fruit for His Kingdom.

What did I learn? The Spirit of God, the Heavenly Wind, is indeed blowing all over the world—even more so at this writing! Sometimes the Wind blows to cool us when we are dry, weary and in need of times of refreshing. Sometimes the Wind supplies energy and power, like driving wind mills. Sometimes it is a hot Wind, full of fire, warming cold hearts like a blow heater. Sometimes the Wind is disturbing—blowing away our fleshly plans, changing our direction, lifting off roofs, collapsing walls, destroying fences. Once those ecclesiastical fences of separation are down, we should not try to build them again by attaching labels to the Spirit's work. God's Kingdom should be a united Kingdom.

Christians have built too many boxes isolating fellow believers into denominations, traditions and theological interpretations built on pet doctrines. The Holy Spirit is blowing the lids off such boxes and drawing Christians to come out and join hands for God's Harvest Task.

The present renewal of the Spirit, as I see it, involves four aspects of relationships: the individual believer to God—a return to "first love" with a heart surrender and joyful obedience; the Body of Christ, the Church, to God—a resurgence of worship and praise; the Body of Christ, to other parts of the Body—in the unity for which Christ prayed in John 17; the Body to the world—in compassionate witness and service.

Of course, many aspects of the renewal are far from perfect. We carry God's Treasure in earthen (fragile clay) vessels. Because flesh enters in, deviations, detours, extremes and tangents are unfortunately part of the scene. Lack of wisdom is disturbing, as is zeal without knowledge, and both over-emphasis and under-emphasis of certain biblical doctrines and teachings about the Holy Spirit. Some individuals and groups of believers feel threatened with any kind of change from their status quo. We fear the new, the different, and consider any departure from the traditional as divisive. But the Holy Spirit keeps moving in generation after generation, renewing, refiring, refreshing, empowering and bringing the Body of Christ to maturity.

Our need is for a balance of love and power. If we emphasize only the Word of God, we tend to dry up and become legalistic. If we emphasize only the work of the Holy Spirit, we tend to blow up, become too emotional. The two aspects must be like parallel tracks of a train that brings us to God's goal. We are safe if we lift up Jesus, not an experience, if we focus on the Giver, not the gifts. We are going in the right direction if we CLING TO THE WORD with diligent Bible study and openness to receive and obey all that God has revealed and commanded. At the same time we should RIDE THE WIND OF THE SPIRIT—hoist our sail instead of sweating at the rowing, flowing with His current, expecting surprises of His power. We should do it with THE HEART OF A BRIDE—in fervent "first love," anticipation, readiness, purity, holiness and responsiveness.

I believe there are two tragedies regarding the work of the Holy Spirit in the world today. The first is not to know about or recognize it. I was formerly in that category. Satan has various ways to blind our eyes, but God has merciful, unique and loving ways to enlighten our eyes. The second tragedy is to know about it, but not to become personally involved because of fear of change, misunderstanding, traditional or theological bias or outright rejection. I'm thankful I didn't miss it, although it took a traumatic experience to launch me into it.

Leona found Baba's and her father's old home in Radlice, Moravia

Leona found Baba's church in Velka Lhota, Moravia

21

Full Circle: Searching for My Roots

God surprised me with an unexpected scene He wanted to paint on my life canvas. After Ted retired and we moved from Paradise, Pennsylvania to Virginia, (we called it "Paradise Lost" and "Paradise Regained") the Lord reversed my feelings about my Czech heritage. It was as if He were saying, "You completed My assignment and call to the Chinese people. Now I have another assignment specifically for you regarding your own kinsmen in the flesh—your Czech heritage. That was in My plan from before your birth. *Get on with it.*"

With that revelation, God gave me an unanticipated, strong desire to identify with my own heritage similar to my identification with China. For most of my life, I wanted to forget my roots, forget the first language I spoke, forget my Czech ethnicity and get as far away from my hometown as I could. China *was* as far away as I could get! Now I had an exciting, even exhilarating "want to" in my spirit—not only to find out about my roots but to go to the land of my forefathers. Ted was as surprised as I was when I announced that after so many ministry years invested in China and our multiple trips there, I wanted "equal opportunity" to explore the homeland of my ancestors. However, he warmly agreed with me.

When I was a child, I didn't care a bit about asking for details about our roots from the direct source people in my life—my parents, grandparents and immigrant relatives. Sixty years had gone by, and most of those people were no longer living. I missed a never-to-be-recovered chance for inquiry. How I now regretted my indifference and the rejection of my heritage! Where would I find any information about my ancestors to eventually pass on to my children and grandchildren? I rummaged through boxes of old family records to see what I could find. The only thing I came up with was my dad's original baptismal certificate, which customarily served as a birth certificate in Europe, complete with the official seals. Well, it was a beginning.

From it I learned that my grandfather, Baba's husband, was named Jan (John) and at a certain point and for reasons unknown to me, the original spelling of his surname "Sprincl" (pronounced phonetically "Shprintzl") became Spryncl on later documents by the time I was born. Few Americans could pronounce it correctly. Usually people mispronounced it "Sprinkle," a mistake which haunted me even to the day I received my college degree. The Dean who handed out the graduation portfolios loudly mispronounced it "Sprinkle," although for four years he pronounced it correctly! I was happy to simplify it to "Choy" on my wedding day. Only four letters—that was a short and easy name that I thought surely no one could mispronounce. I was wrong—Americans can mispronounce anything!

The certificate stated that my grandmother Baba's name was Frantiska (pronounced "Frun-chee-shka") (Frances) and her maiden name was Plachy (pronounced "Plah-key." Their home village in Czechoslovakia was Radlice, (pronounced "rahd-lee-tzeh") in the county Dacice (pronounced "dah-chee-tzeh") in the province of Moravia.

My dad, Frantisek (pronounced "Frun-chee-shek") (Frank) was born on November 29, 1890. His place of birth is recorded as House #24 in Radlice, and he was baptized on December 9 at the Evangelical Reformed Church in the town of Velka Lhota, a few miles from Radlice.

I discovered a few other interesting and heretofore un-known to me pieces of information from this certificate. It lists my grandfather Jan's occupation as farm laborer and stone cutter. He is recorded as the "legitimate son" of Matej (Matthew) Sprincl and his mother's name as Marie Bednar from Studene. My grand-mother, Frantiska, is listed as "legitimate daughter" of Matej (Mat-thew) Plachy and his wife Anny Backak both from Radlice.

The godfather at my dad's baptism was Joseph Plachy, laborer, from the village of Novy Dvory, perhaps Baba's brother or uncle, whose wife was Marie. The midwife at my dad's birth was Marie Sarp of the village of Volfirova. The name of the priest-minister was Frank Novak of the West Moravia Diocese. The en-tire official paper was stated to be an excerpt from the records of the baptism book of the Evangelical Reform Group in Velka Lhota, in Part V, page folio 12, number 47.

The places meant little to me at the time, but I began to have a dream of tracing those roots in person before the end of my life. I had an urgent longing to find that little village, search for that church, perhaps even find a cemetery where some of my ancestors were buried. If I couldn't do it, perhaps some day some of our *branches* would fulfill my dream and become richer in their knowledge of our heritage.

A seemingly inconsistent notation is made on my dad's baptism certificate. It lists my grandfather Jan's religion as Roman Catholic and my grandmother's as Evangelical Reformed. I would search for the reason. I wish I had asked Baba.

I wanted to start digging for my roots immediately, but I doubted that anyone would still be alive who could shed light on my heritage. Then I remembered that Marie Soukup, a family friend who came to visit our home occasionally when I was a child, used to talk about "old times" with my dad and Baba. I didn't know whether she was still living since she already seemed old to me when I was a child. On one of my visits to Cedar Rapids the year God planted this desire in my heart, I inquired among my relatives. Yes, Marie was 81 and living right in Cedar Rapids! Marie was an educated business woman, well read, gentle, kind and caring. She never married and lived alone throughout her life, though she reached out in friendship to many people. I phoned to ask if I might visit her. She agreed, and I took Dad's baptismal certificate with me.

"You knew my dad when he was a child?" I asked incredulously.

"Our family lived right next door to your young grandparents and we knew the whole family. Some of their children were close in ages to children in our family," my precious informant told me. "We attended the same church." *This was better than I expected!*

I bombarded her with dozens of questions about my dad's roots in Czechoslovakia and she laughed, "Slow down! Write your questions and send them to me. I need more time to gather my thoughts and get some material together for you. Maybe I can rummage in the attic for some old photos."

"Just please tell me one thing, if you know the answer, and I'll hold the rest of my questions as you requested. Why is my dad's father listed as Catholic and my grandma Baba's religion as Protestant? How did Dad happen to be baptized in a Protestant church?"

Marie laughed. "That's quite a well-known story. I recall it well. When your grandmother and grandfather were very young, they fell in love and wanted to marry, but they were from families that differed strongly in religious convictions. In fact, the two religious communities were strongly antagonistic during those times. The Catholics were in the majority and in religious and political authority, but our village was predominantly Protestant. The only way your grandparents could resolve their differences was to sign what we would now call a "pre-nuptial contract." They agreed that your grandfather would go to his Catholic church and your grandmother to her Protestant church. When they had children, he would take the sons to his church, and she could take the daughters to hers.

"They had four sons, John, Joseph, Frank, who was your dad, and Charles. Their two daughters were Antonia and Mary. Apparently they carried out their arrangement. Your grandma took the girls and went in one direction on Sunday morning, and your grandfather took the boys and went the other way. That is, until your grandfather's very early death, probably from emphysema. He was a stone-cutter and your grandma said that the fine dust from his occupation filled his lungs and was a fatal hazard. Workmen were not protected for their health as they would be now.

"Free of her pre-nuptial promise to her husband, your grandma brought all the children over to the Evangelical Reformed church. When grown, none of the children, as I remember, had deep religious convictions until your dad, later in life, expressed his faith through his regular church attendance. He affirmed his faith during our conversations together.

"The apparent inconsistency on your father's birth certificate seems to be that his baptism took place in a Protestant church instead of the Catholic church according to his parents' agreement for their sons. The clue might be on the reverse side of the certificate with a later notation that is not entirely legible. It seems to read, 'Became Roman Catholic according to transcription from county office in Dacice September 7, 18?? (illegible date), Number 11957.' That event must have taken place at least a year later, perhaps much later. So it looked as if your grandfather had his cake but your grandma ate it too!"

I thanked Marie with all my heart and followed through by sending her a sheet of questions, after I returned home to the East Coast. Then I heard nothing from Marie for two years! I was afraid she died, and I had missed obtaining information from the last person who could provide anything for me to share with our *branches*. I was so excited when eventually two bulky envelopes arrived, one with photos identified by numbers and the other with about 20 pages of handwritten recollections from dear Marie—in beautiful penmanship—with a detailed map! She had even done some research for me from books written in Czech, which I could not have read. I am tremendously grateful and indebted to her, and I wrote to tell her so.

Dear Marie died soon afterward, and I didn't have the chance to thank her in person for her assistance—but I will later. She was a committed Christian believer who spoke openly and lovingly of her faith in Jesus Christ and her assurance of salvation. She looked upon heaven as only a step away. She might be talking with Baba and my dad right now in heaven, and they might be chuckling in disbelief at my struggling efforts to dig up my roots after all these years so I could pass on our legacy to our *branches*. They might be discussing with each other, *Why didn't Leonka ask us when she had a chance?* Chalk it up to foolish, childish immaturity and not recognizing the value of our heritage.

Marie finished her letter with the comment, "I'm so glad that 'the little fat girl' (thanks, I didn't need that!) is serving the Lord. I know your grandma is rejoicing in heaven when she sees how her prayers were answered. I doubt it ever occurred to her that you would contemplate writing about her life and family, authoring books, becoming a missionary to China or making a trip to her beloved homeland. I hope you get to do that. God bless you in your work for Him. May He give you strength and health to carry on." I never heard from Marie again.

She had known me since I was a baby in the crib so I've forgiven her for the above remark about my lifelong "chubbiness!"

In order to retain the flavor of an eye-witness, this chapter records Marie's word for word recollections. She duplicated and confirmed some information I have already written about, but approached it from a personal perspective.

The following are Marie's recollections:

"Your grandfather, Jan Sprincl, was a tall, broad-shouldered man, a stone mason by trade. They owned a house near our home and also a small field outside the village. My mother always spoke of grandfather Sprincl as a very strict man, very honest and well-respected in the village. He did not know what it was to put anything off. When there was a job to be done, he did it right away, especially to help people.

"One of the photos I am giving you pictures him in a military uniform. I don't know exactly what war he would have been connected with. At that time, Bohemia (there was no Czechoslovakia yet, but I am using the term for convenience) was under the Austrian empire. All men drafted into service while young still had to go for military duty for about six weeks during summers, at which time they went on maneuvers. It was sort of like the reserves or National Guard. It's possible that the photo was taken on such an occasion. At that time, Austria ruled Bosnia and Hercegovina, too. Those countries now belong to other countries. Part of them became Yugoslavia. But during your grandfather's time, there was considerable fighting when Austria took over those countries to claim them as part of the Austrian Empire. A great many Czech soldiers fought and died there—in other people's wars. That was about 1860-70, I think.

"After your grandfather died so young, your grandmother was left with six children to raise, most of them too young to go to work and help out the family. But your exceptionally courageous grandmother, relying on her great faith in the Lord, was willing to work hard and somehow managed to raise them all. The children helped, as soon as they were able, by finding work with other farmers in the village or traveling further from home, if work was scarce locally. Many of the young folks of the village did likewise.

"Their oldest daughter, Antonia, went to work in a town nearby. I remember her coming home to visit. She married Jacob Slavik, and they came to this country in 1912 when their only son, Godfrey, was a year old. They visited us at Lucerne, Iowa, and settled in Cedar Rapids. She was exceptionally close to her mother, your grandma, all her life. I knew the family well because when I arrived in America to continue my education, I lived at the Slavik home for six years. It was really a welcome home away from home for me.

"I remember your oldest uncle, John, while we were still in Czechoslovakia. He often visited our home because my brother, Charles, was about the same age as John, and they were good friends. My family left for the U.S. in 1903. When it was time for John to be drafted into the Austrian army, he did the same as my two brothers—he figured it was time to leave and "sneaked away" without fanfare to America. I think it was about 1905. We were living in Cedar Rapids at that time, and he visited us after he arrived.

"John later married Anna Dvorak of Walker, Iowa, where they farmed for some time. Later they moved to Cedar Rapids. They had three children—Lillian, who passed away during the terrible flu epidemic at the age of 13, and Frances and Jerry who are still living in town.

"I have little recollection of Joseph in the homeland except that he was a handsome, rather quiet and reserved young man. When I met him after he came to the U.S., he was already married to Mary Jasa. They had three daughters—Ruth, Esther and Maxine.

"Your dad's sister, Mary, married John Kasparek in Czechoslovakia when she was only 16 years old. He was about twice her age. It was not a happy marriage and did not last. The last time I heard of Mary, she was living in Chicago, had remarried, had children and I lost track of her. She did not seem very close to your grandma or to the rest of the family.

"Their youngest, Charlie, was my schoolmate in the old country. He visited us after coming to America when we were living near Lucerne. I felt he had a lot of potential, although he was always a very sensitive youth, easily hurt or discouraged. He died very young.

"I think your father, Frank, came to America after John. He came to visit us when we were living on the farm near Lucerne. He married Marie Rompot Warner, and they had one daughter—you!

"I last saw Radlice on September 26, 1903. The village is built on a slope and in somewhat of a valley. The Sprincl home was located at the lower end of the village. I believe you can still find it there even a hundred years later. It is the village custom to retain the name of the original owner in connection with each dwelling. Therefore, regardless of who may be living in it now, and recording their own surname on the deed or lease, I'm sure it's still referred to as "Sprinclova chalupa" (Sprincl's cottage). The Sprincl home was to the right of our home as you would enter from our front gate.

"Our old home is probably still known as 'Macku dum' (Macku's house) although there hasn't been a Macku living there for many, many years. Some changes of names take place, like your surname and ours. My brothers and sisters changed our name to Macek which was easier for Americans to pronounce and spell. I'm not sure yours got any easier with that slight vowel change!

"The buildings of each farm were joined together, and there was a front gate and a back gate. When the gates were closed at night, no one could enter by the large front gate without some loud pounding. Closer to the home building was a smaller garden gate used by members of the family.

"Judging from letters I've received from my friends there through the years, many changes have taken place, but some places may be recognizable. The reason the houses are still likely to be there was because of the construction—mostly of stone, some walls three feet thick! I remember sitting on the deep stone window sill in the kitchen as a child and watching my mother preparing a meal.

"There was a pond in front of our houses. Perhaps you will find it's still there. That was an ideal place for ice skating for all the children of the village and many of the adults as well. The winters were long and very cold. When the ice was thick enough, some of the village fathers would get together, bore a hole in the middle of the ice and put a big wooden farm wheel on a pole. As each skater held on to a rope at the spokes, boy, did that ever furnish a fast skating merry-go-round! But if one didn't hang on tight enough, once the whirling started it was just too bad—he went flying off on his skates and didn't stop until he hit the bank of the pond! Ouch! The older skaters didn't like the smaller ones taking part in this sport because the smaller ones couldn't whirl as fast, and the bigger ones had to pull them along.

"I remember very well the time your father, Frankie, when quite a little lad, was sliding around on the pond alone when the ice was really too thin. He was a daring chap. The ice could not hold him, and he fell through the ice. He paddled through the icy water to our pier and pulled himself up on the bank. I looked out the window and saw him just standing there so forlornly, dripping and freezing. I can still see that pitiful little boy shivering and bewildered. He was peering into the slush and water to see if he could recover his lost foot gear—"pantofle" (clogs). How he must have dreaded going home to tell his mother. That meant she would have to order new ones made for him, and money was so scarce. But there was no way to retrieve the pantofle from the deep pond. Little Frankie had to face the music—and it wouldn't be fun. He knew punishment awaited him from his strict father, when he came home from work.

"Whatever was used for amusement was always something that cost very little or nothing at all. There was little or no money to be spent on toys and frivolous things. Usually it was something home made but it was enjoyed greatly by the children. For the skaters, this sport never lasted long enough. When the ice got too thin and springtime was around the corner, it was time to take out the wheel again because the ice would no longer be safe.

"In the summertime there was much less time for sport, but the children were still welcome to swim in the pond to cool off. There were always some chores to do, poultry to be fed, eggs gathered, cattle to be herded to the grazing areas before and after school and barn chores. Children who were too small to herd cattle would be assigned to keep an eye on the family geese and prevent them from sneaking off into the grain patches. Grain was often planted in fields close to the village and the geese were tempted to help themselves.

"The church where your grandmother worshiped was in the nearby village of Velka Lhota. In the picture I am giving you, you will see two churches right across the road from each other. Your grandmother's church is to the right. It was the Reformed Church, the same one our family attended. On the other side was the Lutheran Church. When the Reformed Church was dedicated on October 17, 1873, my mother was a girl of 14 years. She recited a prepared speech and carried the key which she handed to the official of the church, who had come to Velka Lhota for the dedication. He was Ferdinand Cisar, one of the last of the Czech nobility.

"Religion was taught in the village school by the schoolmaster along with other subjects. The minister, called the "Farrar," occasionally came to question the pupils as to their knowledge of the Bible and Christian doctrines. There were no Catholic children in our village of Radlice, which was primarily a Protestant community.

"Every child who approached the age of 14 years went to church for further training. I don't remember if this was on a daily basis. Parents of children who lived too far away or where there was no church in their area went to live with relatives or friends in our village during that period of religious training, so they would not miss out on any of the classes. Some of the less fortunate children "hired themselves out" to work so they could afford the Christian training.

"When they completed their classes, Confirmation Day came next—the great and important day when all the confirmants stood in the front of the church facing the minister. He asked questions from the catechism. He skipped through the book here and there and students were expected to know the right answers. This brought some anxious moments, not only for the pupils, but for the parents sitting in the congregation. Afterward, the minister invited them to partake of the Lord's Supper, or Communion, for the first time. Upon such occasions, if at all possible, everyone dressed in his or her best clothes for the confirmation service. The girls wore wreaths in their hair. It was a memorable day for those young adults.

"I have been advised that the school house in Radlice is still there but no longer used as a school. There has been some consolidation, and children are bussed to the village of Volfirov, which, when we lived there, was a predominantly Catholic village. Of course, religion is no longer allowed to be taught in any of the schools in my homeland since the communist government took over, according to information I last received. (Marie wrote this at the time of the Russian occupation.)

"The quarries where your grandfather worked were located near the village of Mrakotin, my mother's birthplace. My grandfather owned a large shop that manufactured tools for the stone masons and kept them in good repair. Stone masons worked very hard, and the process was slow and strenuous because nearly everything was done by hand. The workers didn't have proper protection from the stone dust such as they have now, and many died young from lung disease.

"Most families worked very hard at haying time. Cows were used to pull the wagon loads. The government requisitioned all the horses for their own use, so any cattle that were left had to be used for field work. Constant wars and harsh government controls seriously affected the rural areas.

"A very memorable spot to all those who truly love the Lord is the "Studanka Pane" (the Well of the Lord). The place is named after an occasion when Christians, who were being persecuted, were surprised by enemies while partaking of the Lord's Supper, and they fled into the forest. The minister threw the Communion Cup into a nearby well to hide it. The cup was never recovered. Around this well in the deep pine forest near Velka Lhota, courageous Christians who were forbidden by the government to worship the Lord according to their conscience and the way they believed the Bible taught, nevertheless dared to worship in their homes or in secret places in the forest. The stone table, around which the Christians stood to partake of the Communion, may still be on that spot. Those who persecuted the Christians attempted to destroy all evidence of that place, which to this day is precious and sacred to many. But they will never erase the memory of those who participated in this secret worship.

"The communist regime is also attempting to suppress Christian faith. Sometimes it is by outright persecution and imprisonment and sometimes by making it impossible through imposing pressures and limitations on Christians. Especially where young people are concerned. Their education and jobs and advancement opportunities are in peril if they are Christians.

"There were still evidences of bombings during the war near Radlice as late as 1944, just over the hill from the village of Brandlin. My relatives took pictures of shattered roofs and holes in the ground where bombs were dropped on non-military targets. One bomb dropped in 1944 was near the schoolhouse. It shattered windows and made a big crater in the ground, and of course it frightened the children. But the hardy Czechs never lose their good humor and soon made light of it. They joked about the possibility that the German pilot got his directions confused and thought he was dropping a bomb on Berlin instead of Brandlin. Perhaps he could not "read the signs"?

"My cousin said that for some unknown reason enemy planes would sometimes zoom low and drop an empty gasoline tank or can. Did they run out of bombs? Those did no damage if they landed near a person, except to frighten him half to death while he was waiting for the explosion."

Marie did considerable research on the history of the church where my grandmother worshiped and where my dad and probably all his brothers and sisters were baptized. I studied her material carefully, because I felt it would be valuable if I ever fulfilled my dream to visit that place of my roots. I hoped to find that historic church, to actually sit in the pews and pray and to visit the cemetery where some of my ancestors are buried. I imagined how wonderful it would be if I could find some descendants of my ancestors who still have my grandparents' surnames. The following is a greatly abbreviated summary of the history of grandma

Baba's church.

In 1422 the Hussites gained control of the Town of Jemnice (Yem-nitz-eh), and the Christian teachings of Jan Hus were practiced there and in the surrounding area. Protestant families predominated, and it was not until after the great tragedy in 1620 at "Bila Hora" (White Mountain) that Catholicism was again established in that area, about 1624. By that year, about 31 Protestant families lived in the district of Dacice. However, Catholicism grew, and in 1754 a Catholic church was built there. Every day one could see people making a pilgrimage to the church, fingering their rosaries as they walked along to pay homage to the Virgin Mary.

Near the village of Radlice and not far from Velka Lhota is the village of Volfirov which, at one time, was a totally Protestant village. In spite of great persecution and the burning of their Bibles, Protestants still courageously met for worship in barns, caves, in the woods and sometimes in a home, if the house was situated in the deep woods and not easily detected.

The region of Moravia and surrounding provinces of Bohemia and Slezko were all under the Austrian empire and the Catholic church was established as the state church. Finally in 1781, after many years of persecution, Emperor Josef II, son of Marie Teresia, issued the now famous "Proclamation of Tolerance" allowing Protestants to worship and serve God according to the Bible. The government gave them permission to build a place of worship in Velka Lhota.

The congregation was asked by the church officials to make a choice whether to follow the Reformed or Lutheran form of worship. Not being well enough informed about either one, they brought with them to the meeting a book known as Jan Amos Komensky's (Comenius) "Praxis." The official scanned the book hurriedly and advised them that it would be difficult to find a minister who would follow the Bible that closely. Nevertheless, in

1787 a congregation was formed which became known as the Reformed Church, and it was decided that the church would serve both the Reformed and the Lutheran congregations with services conducted at different times. Both congregations agreed to make every effort to live in peace together. The two ministers who served the separate congregations lived in the same manse. The children of the two congregations continued to attend school together in the manse. Later the Reformed Church congregation decided to build a school of their own in Radlice. Eventually it became a public school but the Protestant religion continued to be taught.

The building of a new church was begun in 1872, and through many hardships and sacrifices of the congregation, which was mostly made up of farmers and tradesmen who were poor in worldly goods, the building project was completed.

On October 21, 1873, the bells of both churches tolled long and loud to announce to the members and to the whole countryside that it was the day of dedication of the Reformed Church and the installation of the new minister. It was a day of rejoicing and thanksgiving as can be appreciated only by such brave souls as those who endured much suffering and persecution for their faith.

******

My parents and grandparents chose to leave their ancestral village to begin new lives in America. Time moves on, and I live in the second century after some of them emigrated. The world they left behind in the Old Country has ceased to exist. The people who didn't come with them are long gone. Some of their descendants walk (probably drive) the village roads and live in some of the same houses as my forefathers. Are the geographic landmarks still there? The churches, the school, the fields, the forest, the houses and the pond?

I wondered whether God would allow me to fulfill my new dream of actually going to "Czech my roots."

22

The Artist Daubs Dark Colors

Providentially, not coincidentally, the year when God gave me the desire to travel to the land of my roots would have been my dad's one hundredth birthday and exactly a half-century since my precious grandma, Baba, celebrated her arrival in heaven. Her prayers, I know, have followed my life and ministry. *Somehow it all seemed to be coming together in 1990.*

I reached age 65 that year, but had no retirement thoughts nor do I have such plans 12 years later. I was continuing full-speed ahead immersed in lifelong ministry toward China and the writing of books and articles interpreting the Christian situation there. I could hardly keep up with my current opportunities for writing, publishing and speaking, plus producing daily radio broadcasts.

Earlier in the year, I remember casually asking the Lord whether He had anything else He wanted to fulfill through me during my lifetime. It was my habit since my teens, after I committed my life to the Lord, to ask God for guidance in major and even in seemingly minor things. I wasn't asking for anything special at that time and certainly wasn't expecting any spectacular answer. But I guess you don't mention anything to God "casually"—He takes it seriously.

Was I like Caleb in the Bible who dared to "ask for another mountain" in his advanced years? The incident in Joshua chapter 14 records Caleb's unfulfilled dream to go into the Promised Land according to God's original mandate to him and his people a whole generation earlier. For the people of Israel, their entry into the Land was delayed so many years because of their disobedience. Caleb, however, "followed the Lord his God fully." God never canceled His plan for the giants and the fortified cities to be conquered by His people. Caleb didn't forget about it either. Now the fullness of God's time came. Apparently it is never too late, although that certainly seemed to be the case for Caleb. He waited 45 years and was now 85 years old. Obviously, God recognizes no impossible time frame. I figured that both Caleb and I were in pretty good shape—strong, healthy and available to the Lord, and not too old.

Clearly but surely the conviction came to me—a kind of predestined feeling—that God was also showing me "another mountain," new paths "prepared beforehand (foreordained) that we should walk in them" (Ephesians 2:10). What? God wanted to send me to *Czechoslovakia*, the land of my roots, where I had never been? To the heritage I spent a lifetime trying to forget? I could hardly believe it!

I knew I must obey and arrange my life and priorities to be in sync with God's apparent new plan. I was no longer dragging my feet with reluctance, but with great joy I began to anticipate the adventure and ministry that seemed to lie ahead in August to journey to the land of my "kinsmen in the flesh." That country recently experienced a new measure of freedom through their "Velvet Revolution" and with the exodus of the Russian occupation troops. The timing seemed so right.

Moreover, as some kind of confirmation, our four sons surprised me with a birthday gift of the round trip airfare to Czechoslovakia! (Good thing it wasn't a *one-way* ticket or I would have had some cause to wonder!)

My plan was simply to go wherever God wanted me to go and do what He wanted me to do. I didn't need to know details because God was my "Master (in) Charge." When Ted and I first traveled to the People's Republic of China in 1979, after a measure of freedom was being experienced there, too, I couldn't have imagined that I would make 14 trips to China during the following decade! I began to wonder if perhaps this trip to Czechoslovakia might only be the *first*.

Ted was unable to accompany me on this journey, but he gave me his enthusiastic blessing to go. I planned to wing it alone with the Lord. No tour group, just praying and planning to whatever extent I was able with the sparse contacts I had.

God is full of surprises. Initially, I thought that I no longer had relatives there. My parents and grandparents left Czechoslovakia about 85 years before, and there were no contacts left there that I knew about. I only knew the names of the two native villages of our family on both sides of my family tree. I had one lead, an old address from decades ago. I wrote a "hello, is anybody there?" letter to that address, and after a few months I received a reply. I was delighted to find a cluster of relatives with my mother's maiden name and friendly connections! My correspondent in Policka, Moravia, Czechoslovakia—well, here's how it went: his paternal grandfather and my maternal grandfather were *brothers!* They generously offered me hospitality and chauffeuring around the country. How God provides! But they warned me—other than one teenage granddaughter, no one spoke English!

From the old photo that my family friend, Marie, gave me, I thought I knew where to look for the church where my grandma, Baba, worshiped and could possibly find the house where they used to live in Radlice, Moravia. I planned to be off to dig a few roots while I was there. God would lead, of that I was certain. I was ready for surprises and eager to see how the prayers of Baba would be answered when she prayed for the generations that would come after her.

As I prepared for the trip, I tried to crash-program enough Czech language into my mind in the short weeks before I was to leave, so that when people talked to me in Czech, my tongue wouldn't automatically answer in Chinese! I tried to temporarily brainwash my mind of the Chinese language. Although I spoke Czech as my first language from infancy, I had not heard it spoken since my early teens. I was afraid I didn't remember enough to get along. I regretted not having more time to study before leaving. I wasn't sure whether, according to the proverb, you could teach an old dog new tricks.

My suitcases were packed, my ticket was purchased, my itinerary finalized. All I had to do was show up at the doctor's office for my routine annual check up, blood profile, mammogram and a routine chest X-ray. (The scenario reminded me of a similar situation years ago when we were getting ready to relocate to Pennsylvania.)

Major STOP SIGN *again!* My check up was anything but routine.

Within a week, I was scheduled for lung surgery with an uncertain outcome. The chest X-ray revealed a spot on one lung which the doctor said required immediate removal. Cancer was suspected, but the surgeon said the prognosis would not be definitive until surgery was in progress. He told me that the extent of the surgery could also not be determined until then. The surgeon soberly walked me through all the distressing possibilities.

I canceled my plane ticket, informed all my contacts in Czechoslovakia, unpacked my suitcases and entered Columbia University Hospital in Missouri. During the operation, cancer was found, and a third of one lung was removed. This was a valley of the shadow of death experience for me. But by God's mercy, I came through minus one rib and the addition of a series of permanent inner staples. Cause of my cancer was unknown. I had never even been around second hand smoke. Ted suspected that our many travels in China's pollution and the multiple bad-air plane trips were contributing factors.

The surgeon told me I'd require at least a year of gradual recuperation. I couldn't accept that. I was always in good health, and the only hospital experiences I ever had were for the delivery of our four babies. The doctor proved to be right. My recovery was slow for such a major ordeal. He also advised me that lung cancer has the lowest survival rate for five years—only 13 percent. Thanks for that good news, doctor!

The Master Painter was brushing in some dark colors but they were only meant to enhance the masterpiece He already had in His mind. I thanked God for the robust, Czech body that I never liked, but which God planned from the beginning.

I wrestled with the common questions: why me? why now? and what now? Why did God so clearly seem to give me a new assignment, an unanticipated new love for and identity with my Czech heritage, lead me to prepare for and nearly embark on my trip to Europe and then stop me at the very last minute? Why didn't He let me know earlier, if that was not exactly the time He wanted me to go?

Those were unanswerable questions. I couldn't second guess God and shouldn't try. He was looking for my right response. He didn't want me to doubt or complain but to trust Him. God never allows anything into the lives of His children without a purpose. I determined to rest in Him and take one step at a time.

This was certainly a bend in the road, and I couldn't see around the corner. I grappled with a new sense of my own mortality. I had always been strong. Now I knew I was vulnerable, and life was fragile. Since I didn't know how long my life might last, I had a new sense of celebrating each day as a gift from God. I decided to look at this interruption not as a disruption but as an opportunity for growth, to squeeze every bit of learning from this serious tap on the shoulder.

The extended time of recovery provided me with the opportunity to evaluate my life before God in quietness and inactivity. All my life I tended to drive myself, to require the utmost of myself, to concentrate on *doing* and producing. I interpreted this pause as another signal to put more value on *being*. I thought I had already learned that lesson thoroughly, but I found that it is a lifelong learning process. God occasionally has to bring such interruptions into my life to bring me up short. He wants me to focus totally on Himself.

Because I had always been healthy, I didn't have the sensitivity and empathy for persons who were ill or weak. God used my serious illness and surgery to develop more compassion in me for the sick and the suffering, and launched me in another new direction of help ministry. I began writing several books to assist others to walk through such experiences with God. *Are You Mad at Me, God?* and *Hospital Gowns Don't Have Pockets* were published within the next few years. God had proved Himself faithful to me, and I offered my embrace to other hurting people. I asked God, through His continued mercy and lovingkindness, to give me some bonus time to keep fulfilling His plan for my life, to serve Him, to write and share God's faithfulness with others.

The forced waiting time also gave me a longer opportunity to refresh my Czech language ability in case God would heal me to the extent that I could still make that dream trip to check my roots. I found it difficult to study the grammar and learn to read because that was not the way I initially learned the language. The diacritical markings above many of the letters were not familiar to me. When you learn a language as a child, you depend on your ears to hear it and your mouth to imitate it, not your eyes to see it written. That is why it's easier for young children to learn languages. Now I had to sound out all the words on paper so that my ears could hear them. Then they became familiar again. I taught myself to read at about a third grade level. I did have a tongue to pronounce Czech well since it had been my first language.

Because it was a whole year before I could travel, it turned out to be God's perfect time after all because now Ted and I could go together. When we got to Czechoslovakia, I realized how extremely difficult the trip would have been for me the year before without Ted. God knew. I'm certain He directs in all major events and minor details of our lives, if we are obediently under His control. I could never have managed the heavy luggage, even if I had been healthy. We were obliged to wrestle with it by ourselves en route. The transfers between planes and trains would have been almost impossible for me alone. Ted added a wonderful measure of fun, companionship, support and protection.

This was to be more than an ordinary overseas trip—it was a *pilgrimage* to the land of my forefathers. I'm sure I experienced the same feelings Ted did upon return to his homeland for the first time. Both were fulfillments of long-deferred dreams.

The Lord had been in control of the timing all along. My surgery and a year of recovery was not a road block, not a detour, not a permanent change in plan but simply a God-planned delay to put in motion more perfectly what God originally intended.

I was to "get ready," then "get set" for a year, *then "go!"*

Leona's maternal ancestral home in Siroky Dul, Moravia
The name means "Wide Valley"

Leona's maternal ancestral home in Siroky Dul, Moravia

23

My Turn at Last!

As we prepared to go to Czechoslovakia, we were given some tips on visiting homes there.

"It's nice to bring flowers when you visit but never a dozen or even just two because even numbers are only for funerals. Until recently, dried flowers were only used for the deceased. Be prepared to take your shoes off at the door. Your hosts will probably insist that you don't have to, but they will most likely furnish slippers. Don't admire anything. Czechs will take it off the wall or shelf and it's yours! Drinking "palenka" (brandy) or "slivovice" (plum brandy) is a national tradition. Even if you don't drink, take a sip. It saves arguments and really kills sore throat germs. Whatever you're drinking, don't drain the glass empty because that's the signal for a refill. Before a meal, your host will say "Dobrow Choot" (spelled phonetically) and you should respond with the same. It's like "Bon Appetit!" Lay your napkin on the table as you use it. If you put it into our lap, they'll give you another one.

"Don't be surprised when no one in the family sits and

eats with you in their homes. Usually they feed you, then every-body sits around and talks. They often eat first. Restrooms in homes usually are two rooms with separate doors. Washing is done in the room with a sink, the toilet is in a separate room. Pull the suspended string to flush. Close the door when you leave. Don't leave it open like you do at home. If you make a mistake about anything, just laugh and they will laugh with you."

I'm indebted to an article by Hellene Cincebeaux for those tips. We found many of them to be true.

Off we went on a new adventure that was to be quite dif-ferent from our travels in China. We were not nervous or anxious about what we would encounter because we never traveled abroad without the assurance of the specific, daily prayers of our good friends across the country.

"Jsme doma" (We're home!) we cabled after our first trip to assure relatives now so dear to us in the Czech & Slovak Fed-erative Republic (CSFR: new name for Czechoslovakia as of 1990.) Because of schedule and airline changes, the delays and rerouting were incredible and tiring. It turned out to be a 38 hour return trip from our relatives' home in the central region of Moravia, until we pulled into our driveway in Virginia at nearly midnight a day later. But all the inconvenience was forgotten as we recalled the unique joys and surprises of a month of superbly God-planned adventures.

October 1991 was "touch down at last" for me in the coun-try of my roots! I was afraid that I'd be adrift in Czechoslovakia with my inadequate Czech language ability. After the first day of culture and language shock in a totally non-English-speaking en-vironment, God answered prayer—my mental computer began to express from my mouth rapidly and easily all the language pro-grammed into it when I was a child. My newly acquired Czech reading ability from the past year's difficult self-study supplemented that. The success of our trip depended on my language facility.

Day after day, I improved in my speaking ability and I was thrilled to communicate hours on end with everyone—as if I spoke Czech every day instead of *not at all for more than 50 years!* I understood possibly 90 percent, and I think they understood *all* (although I must have butchered the complicated Czech grammar!) My Czech/English dictionary was always in my hand. I'm not bragging—just thankful to God.

Everyone there was relieved and overjoyed, too. They confessed to being afraid we'd just have to sit and stare at each other and smile and wouldn't be able to communicate! Even those who could speak some English, soon asked me to speak *entirely in Czech*—and away we went! Some days I spoke no English except with poor Ted, who learned a few "necessary" words, then just smiled and nodded (or dozed off!) for hours. Believe it or not, I interpreted for Ted—sightseeing explanations, sermons, directions, conversation. I even became so bold as to speak entirely in Czech before a large congregation, when they called on me to bring greetings during a Czech church service. I treasure the Czech hymnbook my relatives bought for me. Everyone carries his own Bible and hymnbook to church. Worshiping with them and hearing them sing the Psalms with all Czech tunes is an experience I valued more than all the sightseeing we did. I am a debtor to "the faith of my (Czech) fathers, living still...."

"Home base" was our relatives' home in Siroky Dul near Policka, where my maternal grandfather was born in 1865. When I started the search for my roots a year or so before, I had no idea whether any descendants of the family were still there. I wrote in English to an old address an Iowa relative gave me, explaining who I was and my possible connection with anyone who might be living in that area. Because the letter was in English and no one could read it at the address where it arrived, they gave it to their teenage granddaughter, Jitka, who was just starting to learn English in school. Prior to the Russian troop withdrawal, children were forced to learn Russian and were forbidden to study or speak English. With the help of her Czech/English dictionary, she composed a letter to me, which I received months later. She conveyed the news that scores of relatives by my mother's surname were still there and welcomed my visit!

We felt as if we were stepping back in time. Village and farm life that my ancestors experienced *in the very same house and village* seemed to be unchanged, although the house had been enlarged and remodeled. The village school and church were still there. I could walk the same fields and paths and look across the wide valley. The village was named Siroky Dul, which means "wide valley." The landscape was much like our Shenandoah Valley in Virginia. TV antennas and cars were seen everywhere, but my relatives still milked their one cow, churned homemade butter, baked their bread and cooked on their wood stove all the Czech foods I relished as a child growing up in a Czech community in Iowa.

We grew close to "dedecek and babicka" (grandpa and grandma), Adolf and Miloslava, the patriarch and matriarch of the family. My grandfather, Antonin, and grandpa Adolf's grandfather were brothers. We all shed tears upon our arrival and again at parting. We also became close to their four adult children and their families They are similar I age to our four sons and our grandchildren. We were shuttled from one set of relatives to another for meals, hours of small talk, questions, sharing photos and comparing news and facts about our mutual family tree. They took us around to visit other neighbors and friends. Ted and I were not treated as "outsiders" but were "hugged in" to their daily lives.

We visited their workplaces, worshiped in their churches, shopped with them, played with the children and chatted with the neighbors. We found our own way around the village and spent days in Policka roaming by ourselves. All our relatives were openhearted and enthusiastic about our visit. Being accepted as an intimate part of this extended, blood-related family, whom I had not even known existed, was an unforgettable high point of our pilgrimage.

(I will combine some observations about their family life gleaned from all three of my trips so the reader can get a feeling for everyday life in the village of our heritage.)

In general, our relatives seem to be quite well off, which is surprising seeing that their salaries were frozen at a low level during the years of the communist occupation. That period represented the entire lifetime of the mid-generation and the younger children. Most men of the family were laborers with their hands. Each family seemed to have a nice home with basic modern conveniences, even in the village. The old folks live in the huge ancestral house that appeared to have had continual additions to the structure. Probably in earlier years, more families lived together there. Apparently they owned a lot of really nice furniture, and Adolf said the communists took it all. That was why the huge rooms on the second and third floors were mostly empty.

The old folks lived in just the bedroom and kitchen area with old furniture and on a lower living standard than their grown children and families. I think it was by their own choice. They don't spend much on themselves and their own living quarters because I believe they helped each of their sons and daughter get established, build and furnish their own houses, perhaps loaned or gave them money. On our first trip, one of their sons with his wife and two daughters lived in an apartment in the main house, but otherwise the rest of the house was empty. They turned off the furnace at night to save heat, and everyone crawled under his goose down quilt. The youngest son built a beautiful new house for his family of four in Svartouch, but recently lost his job as a welder.

Adolf farmed all his life on his very fertile land. Their daughter with her husband and sons lives in a house a short distance behind them. Perhaps her husband farms all the land now. A daughter and a daughter-in-law work in town at day care facilities where they bake and prepares meals for children.

The families see each other often. It seems that their daughter stops in every afternoon when she comes from work in town. When we went to their home for dinner, it was already dark. We made our way through the woods with flashlights, about a ten minute walk on a little path. Another son, Jitka's dad, works in the fields on the village co-op and runs heavy machinery. He lives with his family at the bottom of the steep hill.

All the sons have cars, Czech made, somewhat smaller than U.S. cars. They told us that when they buy a car, it lasts for a lifetime. No trading in for newer models. Gas prices are high, so if they can walk or take a bus, they do so.

They all eat well and fed us sumptuously. We did miss fresh vegetables on our first trip but they may have been scarce since it was nearly winter. Meals were mostly meat and potatoes and dumplings. They always eat their main meal at noon and supper is lighter, usually just sliced bread or rolls with some salami pieces, a slice of tomato, a bit of green pepper, an olive, a bit of cheese—sort of open-faced sandwiches. A hot soup appears at every meal. Their coffee is "espresso." They pour boiling water on the powdered stuff and just stir it, although it still settles like mud at the bottom. Mostly they drink coffee black, which we weren't accustomed to. We were relieved when they brought out top cream from fresh milk and sugar cubes. It was still strong— probably a hundred percent caffeine!

The grandma has diabetes but doesn't watch her diet too carefully. We brought several big boxes of artificial sweetener packets as a gift without realizing that she would need it. She never heard of it. She bakes a lot, is a typically good Czech cook, a very "babicka" person, warm and earthy, gentle and soft-spoken. The grandpa sort of nags her and commands her, even criticizes her sometime, but she just smiles it off! Grandpa likes soft foods since he is missing most of his teeth, so Grandma cooks special food for him. He likes to sit with his back against the tiled oven to keep warm in the kitchen. He walks with a cane but still does the barn work, cuts grass with a big scythe and tends his garden. A wood stove is burning all the time in the kitchen. That's where they stay most of the day and where the children and grand-children gather when they visit. Their bedroom is unheated.

Grandma is up at five in the morning, milks the cow and does the chores. She also gardens and grows flowers in pots on the wide window sill. Through the window Grandpa looks out toward the village and watches people walk by on the road. The family had no phone on our first trip, and in an emergency they would use the next door neighbor's phone.

Grandma made sweet plum dumplings for us one day at lunch, the kind I remembered from my childhood. She served us breakfast every morning—a couple of thick slices from a big round loaf of home baked rye bread, home churned butter, cheese and hot espresso. No such thing as dried cereals or orange juice. We didn't taste any citrus for the entire month.

If we were at home in the evening, we'd usually linger in one of the son's apartment chatting or looking at pictures and just lounging around. Each family has a TV, and they receive many American programs that are dubbed in Czech. We watched CNN but the dubbing went too fast for me to understand it. They wanted to learn some English words in exchange for teaching Ted some Czech words. They had some good laughs together over Ted's pronunciation of Czech words. He showed the young people how to use the chopsticks we brought in quantity to give as souvenirs to them.

The families always generously served us huge helpings of foods. We couldn't possibly eat that much. We didn't want to offend them, nor did we want to waste food. We would ask for an extra plate so we could scoop off half of everything and share it. They laughed at us and assured us that there was enough food to go around and that we should eat it all and not try to share it. They never got used to the idea that we simply couldn't eat such large quantities. Sure enough, they didn't eat with us, and they all sat around talking and looking at us while we ate!

We brought a lot of things in our big suitcases that we guessed they might not be able to get there. We were right. From the packages of Jell-O we made finger Jell-O, which was a big hit. The peanut butter required a lot of unexpected explanation. They never tasted it before. We had lots of fun with the popcorn we brought. One night we gave the entire gathered family all the vitamins and medicines we brought along, and the son-in-law, who knew a little English, wrote the dosage and what it was for in Czech on the packages. We all laughed to tears when I tried to explain in Czech and sign language some of the symptoms for which they might take the medicines—especially ones for diarrhea! Antihistamines, cough suppressants, Tylenol, aspirin and vitamins are very expensive there.

The previous year, when I had to cancel my trip, I sent 80 pounds of books and gifts to them by a friend who was traveling to Czechoslovakia. Among other things we brought new clothing, baseball caps, tee shirts, panty hose, aluminum foil, plastic wrap, zip lock bags, straws, packages of gum, film, costume jewelry, scarves, games, Scrabble, jigsaw puzzles, some Chinese art weavings, Chinese fans, chopsticks, embroidered hankies, school supplies and cassette music tapes.

They were all thrilled and excited by the 800 packets of flower seeds and vegetable seeds we bought for a few cents each at the end of the season because they were out dated. They didn't take up much weight or space in our suitcases. Each family took a number of packets to share with neighbors and friends. They planned to grow "American gardens" in the spring! They never heard of some of the vegetables like broccoli, okra and egg plant. What fun I had trying to explain in my elementary Czech how they could be cooked and what they tasted like.

On my second trip in 1993, I was amazed and pleased to be shown the flourishing gardens of each of the families where splendid splashes of color of every variety of flowers were growing. They already gathered several generations of seeds from the original packets and shared them with the whole village! Apparently, all the vegetable seeds we gave them grew bumper crops, so new vegetable varieties were introduced to that area. I felt that I had been able to give back a simple gift of my love and appreciation to the place of my heritage.

We brought Christian books and cassettes and other Christian literature for the Bible school and churches we visited. That was what made our suitcases so heavy. Everything was so well received, appreciated and needed, that we felt satisfied and privileged to invest in the Christian cause there.

When we were ready to return home, we emptied our big suitcases of all our own clothes and gave them to our relatives. We returned home with only the clothes on our backs. What we left behind included shoes, jackets, shirts, skirts, socks, ties, suits, bathrobes, nightwear, jeans—everything. The family members were overjoyed to get them and we had such fun leaving them behind. We even left our cosmetics and toilet articles, (not our toothbrushes, of course!) hair spray, rollers, shampoo, cologne and any medications we brought for our own use. We did the same when we traveled in China and stayed with Christian friends. We gave away everything and brought back light suitcases except for all the research books and Chinese novels translated into English which I always purchased. Ted tried to keep me away from bookstores toward the end of our trip to Czechoslovakia, but I still managed to purchase books when I did last minute shopping with our relatives.

We *hoped* our return suitcases would be light because we had been physically exhausted transporting them there. But at the last minute, when we were all packed and ready to leave, suitcases already closed, everyone began giving *us* gifts. Not only were our suitcases jammed full again, but we had to buy an additional suitcase. We had to struggle and hand carry them again to the plane! Our relatives were very generous to us, giving us lovely Czech mementos, and we did appreciate everything. These included Czech crystal goblets, dishes and other breakables that we had to hand carry on the plane and keep on our laps!

One of Grandpa's sons insisted on giving us four bottles of Czech beer to bring to our four sons, but we finally talked him out of it with the logic that they might get broken on the plane and then what? But our relatives did stop on the way out of the village to buy a still hot, fresh baked, five pound round loaf of rye bread for us to put in our carry-on case along with a large, long salami. Those attracted many curious sniffers on our return flight!

We traveled to other cities on our own after I learned how to take trains, long-distance buses, trolleys and the sleek metro system in the capital, Prague. Our relatives took time off from work to drive us to some cities at quite a distance. We stayed in a variety of places: a village inn, a hostel, homes of new friends in a high rise in Prague and on a farm where the bedroom had its own pot-bellied stove for heating. There we had to find our way with a flashlight through the barnyard to the outhouse during the night. Always our beds were piled high with goose feather comforters and immense feather pillows where we disappeared from sight at bedtime.

We learned how to order and eat on our own in villages and towns—inexpensive and tasty—the equivalent of 60 cents U.S. for a full course meal. We survived the fat and cholesterol assault with anti-acid tablets we brought along.

Thank God, we remained healthy during the entire extremely strenuous trip, although just before we left, winter arrived early, and the weather was incredibly cold, often rainy, with bitter wind and snow. We were prepared with winter jackets, scarves and gloves, but I appear in every photo wearing my ski cap! The final week we experienced total "germ warfare" because wherever we accepted hospitality, it seemed that someone was sick, their kids were out of school coughing or they had fevers. We had to keep smiling, breathe the same air and pray! We asked God for the special protection of Psalm 28:7, "The Lord is my *strength* and *shield*...." asking for God's invisible shield from the germ attacks, especially because of my lung sensitivity only a year after surgery. Miraculously, we arrived home unscathed.

On each of my three trips, I visited my paternal grandparents' village of Radlice in Moravia where my dad was born in 1890. The little village of perhaps 60 houses was apparently much the same as before the turn of the century (1900). I did walk the same dirt paths and saw the pond where my dad fished, swam and ice-skated as a child. I found the number on the house where my grandparents lived (though the house was now rebuilt) and saw the old schoolhouse where my dad and his siblings attended. We watched herds of deer in the fields adjoining the thick forests and went into the picturesque white church on the hill in Velka Lhota where Baba and her family worshiped. *It was all just as our dear friend, Marie, had described it* when she left the village for America early in the 20th century.

We stayed overnight with "a grandma" of the village, also named Marie. I contacted her before our trip when someone who knew English responded on her behalf to my "to whom it may concern" search-letter sent to Radlice. Three generations of her family lived in that village and they doubtless knew Baba's family. She showed us a huge, 200 year old oak tree that they would have seen—and possibly my dad tried to climb as a child. That night, under my feather comforter, I dreamed dreams of my ancestors *in that very place.* God fulfilled His promise to bring me there.

Both in Velka Lhota and Siroky Dul, we visited old cemeteries with gravestones inscribed with my ancestors' surnames, and we took pictures of them. I felt as if I had come full circle in my life—just as Ted felt when we visited his grandmother's grave in an obscure China village. Both of us are heirs and stewards of a godly Christian heritage from generations past.

We exposed ten rolls of color film to record every experience we had. The photos all came out beautifully and make up part of our memorable heritage saga.

Ted and I spent part of a week alone in the Czech capital, Prague, trying to find our way around with a map. We climbed the hill to the 1100 year old Hradcany Castle, the seat of government where President Vaclav Havel carries on matters of state. We were awed at the magnificence of the multi-spired, stained glass windowed, massive St. Vitus Cathedral. Back and forth we strolled the famous Charles IV bridge built in the 1300s over the Vltava river.

Several times we came upon a brass band playing lively, traditional Czech and Moravian music on the streets to enthusiastic crowds and passersby. We were fascinated by street performers in Czech costumes—talented young people playing instruments, singing and dancing for the crowd—not for money, just for the pleasure of performing. It was all a contrast of culture from what we had seen in China and Asia.

In the cemetery of the Old Jewish Synagogue we saw centuries old, ancient tombstones leaning helter-skelter. We were intrigued to hear that the cemetery site was 10 layers deep with burial at all the levels. People wrote prayers on little pieces of paper and tucked them into the crevices of the stones. Snow already lay against the markers giving them a ghostly appearance. Several times we joined the crowd waiting to hear the 15th century astronomical clock on the Old Town Hall strike the hour.

We repeatedly walked around famous Wenceslaus Square, the site of protests through the centuries. The mass demonstration for "Prague Spring" in 1968 and the 1989 "Velvet Revolution" which toppled the communist government took place on this bustling boulevard. It is the hub of New Town. Below the imposing statue of King Wenceslaus on his horse at the high end of the Square, was an informal shrine in memory of Jan Palach, the student who set himself on fire to protest the Soviet invasion of 1968. It was surrounded with fresh flowers and burning candles.

The modern metro system sped us underground to destinations of our choice. We learned to get on and off at the right stops—sometimes! Stops were only announced very rapidly in Czech. We were obliged to find our way to the American Express office where we wasted time replacing Travelers' Checks after a thief stole Ted's wallet (also his I.D., credit cards, driver's license and cash) somewhere in the press of people on the street. Our relatives warned us too late about the light-fingered gypsies. "Most Prague tourists are robbed!" the American Embassy consoled us!

We traveled by bus to Bratislava, capitol of Slovakia. It is situated along the Danube river—which *wasn't* blue! I struggled with the somewhat different Slovak dialect. We sensed a tense political atmosphere as rumblings were heard everywhere advocating the separation of Slovakia from the Czech regions of CSFR. We visited the city square where candle light demonstrations and fasting vigils were taking place against a backdrop of protest placards and angry voices. From the high Bratislava castle, marking settlements as far back at 3000 B.C., we could see across to Austria and Hungary. Old Town displayed its ancient palaces, cathedrals, museums and galleries. Memories of Mozart and Beethoven and famous Czech composers followed us through ancient alleyways where they lived and performed. We saw combinations of Gothic, Renaissance, Baroque and Romanesque architecture everywhere.

In Bratislava, we worshiped in a large church which provided English translation headsets and where we participated in
the service. Most of the churches we visited were by denomination the Church of the Brethren and the Evangelical Church of
Czech Brethren. The latter is the one to which my maternal relatives belong. It is a union of Lutheran and Czech Reformed
churches. The Reformed church was the one my grandma, Baba,
belonged to in Velka Lhota.

The Catholic church is the largest religious group in
Czechoslovakia with nearly 10 million members out of a total
Czech population of approximately 15 million. The Slovakian regions were traditionally Catholic. The Bohemian region was the
cradle of the Protestant Reformation in the 15th century. There
are varying shades of Catholicism from the orthodox to the char-
ismatic. An underground church emerged during past decades
comprised of both Catholics and Protestants who engaged in secret Bible study, prayer and witness with many youth and laity
involved, meeting in private homes.

We had the privilege of staying with a young Catholic
couple in Slovakia who were in the forefront of that renewal movement. They were enthusiastic and truly born again Christians, as
were the members of their youth group in whose mountain retreat we participated. They were engaged in publishing and widely
distributing their own evangelical Bible studies and chorus books
and translating some excellent English (Protestant!) Christian
books. They were active in evangelism.

Through correspondence before we came, we arranged
to meet the key youth pastor of a Brethren church who was involved in extensive translating and publishing of Christian books
on issues and problems facing Christians in Czechoslovakia. By
previous arrangement, we brought along for him, also sent in advance by post, a large quantity of Christian books, basic Bible
studies, Christian tapes, music and other Christian helps. We were

satisfied that we planted them where God wanted them to reproduce.

We spent a memorable day and night with friends in Kutna Hora, a short bus ride from Prague, where we visited the massive, splendid, towering Cathedral of St. Barbara. The "grandma" of the family, age 96, was a friend of my grandma, Baba, and remembered me as a toddler in Iowa. Her husband was minister of the little Czech church where Baba worshiped.

In Olomouc we visited a newly re-opened Bible School filled with enthusiastic young Czech students. The teachers asked us to speak to them in their classroom. Ted showed them what Chinese writing looked like and wrote a Bible verse on the blackboard. They sang for us and we prayed with them, leaving behind more books, tapes and other Christian literature. Our hosts were the president of the school, his wife and a teacher from America.

Ted and I visited different churches each Sunday, typically European style where they sang hymns with traditional Czech tunes, many of them based on the Psalms. Our first experience was on a bitterly cold morning in the unheated Evangelical Brethren church at Svartouch where some of the family worships. You could see your breath inside! We sat for a lengthy service on narrow wooden pews where you could only sit ramrod straight. The minister climbed a steep, narrow staircase to preach from a tall, raised pulpit with a canopy top fastened against the wall. We joined the congregation at the front for the Bread and the Wine, feeling at home in warm Christian bonds.

On another occasion, we worshiped at the Evangelical Brethren church in Borova, which my relatives attend and where Adolph's son-in-law is a presiding deacon. Rather than in their unheated main sanctuary, during the winter they worship in the church house. There a pot-bellied stove kept us from freezing. Our relatives in Siroky Dul host a bi-weekly "house meeting" in their home which their young, bearded pastor from Borova comes to conduct. He leads the singing accompanied by his keyboard set on the kitchen table. That is preceded in another part of the house by a lively meeting for the children and youth of their extended family, to which they also invite neighborhood kids. The pastor brings along his guitar for the singing.

During our short time in Prague, we participated in a Bible study and prayer meeting, also in a week night youth meeting with about 80 young people. Guitars accompanied the lively singing, and some of the choruses were familiar. They asked Ted to speak to the group.

Some of our younger relatives took us to other historic places of interest—to deep limestone caves with their boiling mudpools and geysers, where one could take a boat ride on an underground river. Vesely Kopec near Drevikov and Mozdenice is a restored historical old pioneer settlement representative of rural life in past centuries. We saw folk culture, log cabins, thatched roofs, granaries, sheep sheds, pigsties, barns and spring houses as they used to be. Smithies were working with anvils, joiners and cabinet makers were demonstrating their skills. The overhead door frames of the old cottages were so low—people must have been shorter in those days.

Jan and his wife, Vera, also helped us to find the old house, No. 45, in Martinice, near Prosec, not far from Siroky Dul and Svitavy, in which my grandfather Antonin was born. Doubtless great-grandfather Josef Rompotl lived there with his family. It was now remodeled and occupied by a doctor from Prague whose family used it as a getaway vacation home.

We missed the famous spas—you can't see everything. The country has about 900 healing springs and approximately 50 spas, four of which are counted among the world's most famous. Ordinary people as well as the rich and prominent from all over the world come to recuperate in the hot springs and take advantage of their medicinal effect.

We saw one of our first castles, an imposing, ancient structure in Litomysl. Unfortunately, it was closed for the winter, but our young relative, Jan, knew the caretaker. We were given a VIP guided tour of the majestic castle with full explanations (in Czech, which I interpreted for Ted). She even gave us a mini-concert of Mozart's music which she played on the harpsichord in the castle's private theater. International music festivals are held in the castle courtyard in summer. Jan, the vice principal of a large technical and agricultural high school, took us to visit his school.

Generally, the Czech people seem more laid back and less intense than in urban Asian settings. Many stores close for a long lunch siesta. Except for the supermarkets, all of them close before dinner in the evening. Most are closed on Saturday and Sunday. People stay at home on weekends to enjoy their families or take off for the countryside or mountains where they have small A-frame chalets called "chaty." Some have refurbished large, old farm cottages called "chalupy." Such structures cluster by mill-ponds or nestle in forests of silver spruce. They are refreshing "getaways" to help them endure their weekday grind of work. We were delighted to visit one in the forest.

People seem to be breathing sighs of relief with the demise of communism. Many considered the communists to have been worse than the Hitler occupation of their country. Not only stripping our relatives' home of all possessions, the Russian communists took away cattle and other livestock from them and from all the other villagers. They forced the people to work for them. Private farms were lumped into co-operatives, and former owners were paid a meager wage. Their jobs were secure, but all decisions of life were made on their behalf. Because minimal health care was provided and education was paid for by the state, the Czechs were basically pretty well off compared to the rest of Europe. But the high price tag was the lack of freedom.

On our first visit, privatization was slowly returning, but

jobs were scarce. People lacked money and experience to do their own thing. They realized that soon everyone would have to start paying for his own health care, and students would have to pay for their own education. The transition period was bringing hardship and frustration. All was not coming up roses. Apprehension and dissatisfaction were bubbling to the surface. The economy was in a slump, commodities cost more and prices were escalating. Everyone was speculating on what would lie ahead if the Czechs and the Slovaks had a political split. The man on the street sincerely hoped it would not come to bloodshed and civil war like it did in Yugoslavia. We didn't understand all the issues, but we were able to empathize and pray with more love and understanding because we lived with them for a month and listened to their problems.

(By my second trip, the split between the two parts of the country had taken place peacefully and everyone was drawing a breath of relief.)

The new religious freedom was a real plus. Previously, the Czechoslovakian communist-controlled government followed a policy of religious repression that denied its citizens everything but the most rudimentary elements of religious life. It completely controlled every religious body. Recently, the Ministry of Education had even authorized the placement of New Testaments in schools throughout the country. Ministers were invited into the public school system to introduce the Christian faith to students! Churches were free to develop their own evangelistic programs without harassment. Radio and TV time was available for religious programming. The Bible was again being published by their Bible Society, although Christian literature was still a critical need.

Now seems to be a window of opportunity for the Christian gospel, but a caution directed at zealous Christian Westerners was set forth in a recent article. "Many people faithfully kept religious traditions [during the time of communist government persecution] and we must be very respectful. There are a lot of unchurched people, but we ought not act imperialistic and push American-style 'churchianity' in a country that has a long-established religious heritage."

Obviously, the need is for an indigenous revival of faith and for training of the country's own Christian leadership—along with our support by prayer, finances and help for *their* endeavors.

As "Travelers Czechs," (me by heritage and Ted by adoption) we treasured and soaked up our Czech experience. But I felt that I only scratched the surface. I wanted to return and spend in-depth time there to understand even better the heritage I now value highly for myself and for our *branches*. Would God give me opportunities to return in years to come?

Leona's four "Chinese Czechers" sons:
Rick, Gary, (Leona in center) Jeff, with Cliff in foreground

24

An Encore Journey

Little did I know that I would be a widow in less than a year from the time Ted and I traveled to my heritage homeland for the first time. Ted died suddenly in 1992 without suffering any illness. Our trip to Czechoslovakia was the last overseas trip he took. He was, in fact, packed and ready to leave for California the following day for a family reunion with his brother and sisters. Two years before, when I was packed to leave for Czechoslovakia, God interrupted my plan and I went through cancer surgery. This time God interrupted Ted's earthly flight plan, and he left peacefully for heaven.

That traumatic experience was nothing I could have prepared for. I went through the process of grief with the help of God, thankful for our 46 happy years of marriage, parenthood, grandparenthood and ministry together at home and abroad. God was my ever-present help and comfort as I made my way through sorrow to adjustment and moving on. I had to get accustomed to a single life, living as a single parent to my four grown sons and as a single grandparent to my grandchildren. I began to live alone for the first time in my life. As a child I lived with my parents and Baba, in college I lived in a dorm or with roommates. Then I married and had children. The house was always full of family and for many years full of international students. Now I was entirely alone and it was sadly quiet.

Because of lessons I previously learned when God used darker colors to paint my life canvas, I trusted that God was in control and nothing caught Him by surprise. He helped me walk through the process of heartache and taught me as I went along. Because writing is a natural part of my life, I wrote books to help others cope with the experience of losing a loved one. Eventually I published three books: *Singled Out for God's Assignment, A Widow's Might* and *Walk the Green Valley.* In the years since, I am thankful God has been using those books to help many people throughout the country.

As I spoke to myself through those books, God confirmed that He had a continuing assignment for me which didn't terminate with the death of my husband. God had a plan for me before I met Ted, a plan for us together, now an agenda for me at this new point in my life. The Master Artist was adding more dark colors to the masterpiece of my life, but I had learned not to push away His hand with the brush dipped in darker paint or complain about my aloneness. When I responded as a teen to surrender my life totally to God, I didn't put any time limit on my commitment to His plan and purpose, nor was any "retirement program" built in. I decided to joyfully go forward until the Lord completed His purpose through me.

At our request, our son, Rick, was in the process of building a little chalet in the woods of Virginia for Ted and me. It is on five acres of Rick's property adjoining the five acres where he built his own home. Although Ted died during its construction, when it was finished, I moved in and occupied the chalet by myself. I call it my little "chalupa" hideaway like the Czechs go to on weekends—but this is my year-round, cozy nest. Rick outfitted me with the latest in computer equipment, as he continues to do, and I went forward in the direction of God's continuing call to a writing ministry. My home is secluded and convenient as a residence and writing studio with floor to ceiling big windows on all sides, so I can look out on a wrap-around woodland in all seasons. I don't feel isolated—God gave me many friends and opportunities to speak at conferences for Christian writers. I continue to travel for writing research and to visit my families.

In 1993, Martha Warner, a cousin on my mother's side with the same maiden name as all my maternal relatives, invited me to accompany her on her first trip to Czechoslovakia. She wanted to visit our mutual relatives and see the places of her roots, too. She spoke Czech better than I did. She was an energetic 84 year old and so peppy that she ran circles around all of us. I had a hard time keeping up with her! (Marty made another trip alone to revisit our relatives when she was 91!) We left from her home near Chicago and flew directly to Prague.

We spent more time with the extended families of our mutual Rompotl heritage, and our relatives took us to some places I didn't see before—castles, caves and historic and cultural sites. I learned more about the background of Siroky Dul, the village where my maternal roots went deep. Its history is worth documenting to give the reader the flavor of small village tradition and present life. Because of the smallness of the village, at present only about 350 residents, one may overlook its importance. All out of proportion to its size, it is the place from which many forefathers of Czech-Americans came, especially those who settled in Iowa.

This seemingly insignificant village is one of the oldest communities in the region of the town of Policka located near the Northern border of the Bohemian-Moravian Uplands. The first written record can be found in the provincial archives at the city of Litomysl. According to those ancient documents, the village already existed in the year 1269!

It is named for its location in the broad valley along the brook called Jalovy Potok, "Barren Brook." The village has always been divided into two sections by this brook. In the early days, the town had two magistrate's houses. On the left of the brook, (Litomysl Dominion) it was at the place where house No. 61 presently stands; on the right side of the brook, (Policka Dominion) it was where house No. 20 stands. The place of our heritage is house No. 36.

Geologically, the village can be divided into the "Hill" area and the "Plain." The bed of the higher elevation is of volcanic origin, and the stone underlying it is similar to granite. The lower part lies on a sea sediment where frequent traces of primeval sea shells are found in the argillite. Moreover, the fertility of the soil in both parts is different.

The most significant historical structure of Siroky Dul is probably the small Catholic church which was founded in the first half of the 14th century. Old documents reveal that the first vicar was Nicholas of Litomysl in 1347. The vestry portal of the Gothic style church is characteristic of the first half of the 16th century, and in the 17th century the nave was rebuilt and elongated. Whenever any renovation or repair of the spire took place, valuable historical documents and coins were placed inside. These provide precious insight into the history and development of the village.

Old documents chronicle for us that Siroky Dul was the village of the king's dowry in the town of Policka. Its people took part in the rebellion of the Protestant nobility in 1619. After the Battle of Bila Hora, great suffering fell upon the region, especially on the Protestants. At that point, many decided to emigrate. The Napoleonic wars, and several years later the Prussian war, greatly affected this small village. One Prussian general is said to have taken his lunch on the "Hill" of Siroky Dul.

In the second half of the 19th century, continuing through the beginning of the 20th century, the emigration of people from this village was intensive. Not only young single men and women but whole families moved abroad, mainly to America—including many of our ancestors.

The residents of Siroky Dul were hit hard by World War I when all able-bodied men were called to arms. Many lost their lives and were unable to take part in the joyful rise of the Czechoslovak Republic formed after the war in 1918. World War II brought still more suffering and hardship for many residents, even deportation to a fascist concentration camp.

The church and the schoolhouse are always distinct elements of Czech and Moravian villages. In Siroky Dul, the school was constructed under the reign of Emperor Joseph the Second when there was an effort to extend education in Bohemia. Before that, pupils were taught in various cottages of the village. Because money was in short supply, construction was delayed. In 1858, the small school opened its doors to students for the first time. Before long, it became clear that the building was too small and had to be enlarged. They were forced to hold two sessions since 1888. The building was repaired and modernized several times. During its heyday, the school produced many fine citizens, teachers and notable persons who took their place in the economic, cultural and spiritual life of the village and further afield. That was undoubtedly the school which our ancestors attended, including my grandfather, maternal uncles and aunts, and Marty's dad. We had a delightful time visiting it on this trip. It was like a step back into time. Since 1978, all the children of the village attend school in Policka and no longer in their little community. At present, the schoolhouse is used by the Local Citizens Board of Representatives.

The Voluntary Firemen Brigade of this village celebrated

its one hundredth anniversary in 1991. In its history, not only have numerous serious fires been successfully put out, but the activities of the firemen have enhanced the public life of the village. Throughout the years, these public-spirited citizens of the Fire Brigade were involved in nearly every event of community improvement and development.

The Agricultural Cooperative is an important aspect of this village. In 1975, it was combined with the cooperative of the neighboring village of Lubna, which resulted in a large and prosperous farm. After Czechoslovakia's transformation to free market conditions, the co-op provided many jobs for Siroky Dul residents, among them Jitka's dad. Those who do not work on the farm have jobs in the vicinity in the towns of Policka, Svitavy, Litomysl, etc. I visited some of those work places on my third visit.

During the last several decades, the face of the village has changed considerably. Many families were able to modernize and enlarge their homes, and new houses were built. A new road connects both parts of the village, now uniting the "Hill" and the "Plain." (That hill is a formidable one, so steep that it is impassable in the winter except on foot, although ideal for children's sledding! I can imagine my grandfather doing so as a child. Cars have to change gears when approaching the top. When I climbed it on foot in the hot summer, I was totally exhausted when I reached the summit where our relatives' house is located. Once was enough!) The village has a new water supply and a tall television relay tower at the highest point just behind the home of our relatives. A more spacious and modern fire station now provides a place for community meetings and more room to store fire trucks. A new grocery store was built on the "Plain." The brook has a more stable bed for its flow, and other new facilities have developed.

In community elections in 1990, a new Local Citizens

Board of Representatives and its chairman were elected. This relatively young body makes every effort to continue beneficial activities and bring the noble ideas resulting from the "Velvet Revolution" to practical reality in this village.

The village opens its arms of welcome, especially each summer, to American descendants of Siroky Dul forefathers. Planned special activities and sightseeing make this "journey to their roots" an unforgettable experience, as it was for me on my three trips.

I felt strangely at home in Siroky Dul. I touched my roots and felt a deep satisfaction at having completed another delightful chapter in my life, which God kept in reserve as a surprise for me. Those experiences and the new relationships formed with blood kinsmen were daubs of bright colors on the canvas of my life.

I am documenting some of these historic details because it's probable that they will be lost or changed with time, and I feel they are valuable not only for our heritage but for those who share a similar Czech background in that part of Czechoslovakia. Not everyone will have the opportunity to check their roots in person and to walk the roads where their ancestors walked. Therefore, if I don't write about it, perhaps no one else will. Or if they do, it will be from their perspective, not mine. If I don't do it now, the sense of recall will begin to fade, the opportunity may slip by and some people will have passed on, including myself. I can't do it from heaven!

I continue to regret that while many members of the older generations were alive, I didn't ask them questions or encourage them to tell stories of their past. It would have been fascinating and historically significant. Now there is no one left to ask, and all those interesting experiences are lost. We usually don't value our heritage while we are young.

Sometimes I ask myself, who cares? Although even some of our *branches* may not be vitally interested in their roots at the moment, I have recorded what I wish my forefathers had. I have written of the events and times of my own era, dipped into the past to dig for our heritage and recorded the results as best I could. I believe the reader will know me from this slice of our family history as I have followed our "root canals."

I had such warm and friendly experiences by finding present day relatives abroad. They, in turn, have all been exceptionally appreciative and excited to be in touch with the American side of their heritage. I opened a new world to them. They are down-to-earth people, both fun-loving and serious, joking and hospitable. They seemed to be waiting for someone to contact them and they also regreted that someone didn't do it a long time ago. Too many years wasted, they always say. The many family photos I brought along on each visit intrigued them, and they were so excited to see the rough draft of our genealogy chart to find out where we all fit in. I gleaned more information from their recall.

Since the initial visit Ted and I made in 1991, some of our relatives in the U.S. have traveled through the door we opened, and several of the younger generation in Czechoslovakia also traveled to the U.S. Mutual relationships became even richer. The result can only be good when people reach out to touch one another and learn to understand each other, although they grew up on continents far apart.

On my second trip, I had an unusual experience relevant to another ancestor around whose roots I had not dug yet. It was a tragic hidden discovery. My relatives took us to a famous historical spot equally as famous as the village of Lidice, which was totally destroyed by Hitler's troops in revenge. We arrived at the quiet little village of Lezaky, about an hour's drive from Policka.

We toured the museum set on a hill, the highest point in the area. No other tourists or visitors were around that day. It was like a ghost town. We could almost feel the pathos and grief resulting from what had so tragically happened there. In one of the rooms of the museum, we saw pictures of each of the families who lived in that secluded little hamlet of only nine houses. The total population was 54 up to June 23, 1942.

One of the families was the Josefa Bohac family, and the first five photos under the glass in the case were of that family, identified by name. It is probable that Frantisek (Frank) Bohac (1865-1949) was born in that village. He might have immigrated to the U.S. in about 1885 and settled in the West Branch area of Iowa. He married Louise Drapela (1870-1938) who was my cousin Blanche Lovetinsky Seigling's grandmother. Frank Bohac Sr. was her grandfather. Louise Drapela would have been the sister of my maternal grandmother, Anastasia Drapela Rompot.

In the peaceful little settlement of Lezaky in the charming countryside, life was hard but happy and undisturbed until March 15, 1939. From the earliest days of the Nazi occupation of the Czech lands, a resistance movement against the German enemy formed there.

A group of parachutists called "Silver A" was dropped into the region of Eastern Bohemia at the end of 1941. The radio-telegraph operator of that group found a welcome among the Czech villagers and a place of hiding for himself and his transmitter, which he called "Libuse." First it was hidden in Lezaky and later in the Hluboka quarry. He kept the transmitter busy. From January 1, 1942 almost daily up to the assassination of Heydrich, it sent out its reports and received messages. The results achieved by the "Silver A" group were remarkable.

After the assassination of Heydrich, the Gestapo found its way to Lezaky too. SS-man Gerhard Clages asked for and received the consent of Prague Gestapo headquarters for the liquidation of the entire little village in retaliation for their resistance to Hitler's troops and the Nazi advance. The massacre was planned for June 24, 1942. The hamlet was surrounded and the people were powerless to defend themselves. Everyone, including the children, was carried off to the Mansion House at Pardubice. After the troops robbed and plundered to their satisfaction, the houses of Lezaky were burned to the ground. All adults in Lezaky were immediately and mercilessly executed. Soldiers took the children to concentration camps for retraining. Only two little girls survived, apart from one or two persons who were sent to forced labor in the Reich.

Later, the ruins of the burned-out houses were leveled to the ground by the Fascists. In memory of the brave villagers, no community was ever again built on that spot. We saw only the outlines of the foundations where the houses stood. The hush that surrounded them was eerie. There were commemorative plaques or monuments at each location with the number of the house engraved in gold along with the family's name.

A monument at the crossroads of the village proclaims: "The Hamlet of Lezaky once stood here. On June 1942 it was burned to the ground by the Fascists and its population executed."

We solemnly walked through the wooded area through which a small road passes. The wind whispered in the tree tops. All was silent except for some workmen cutting grass and repairing some of the landmarks. A small foot-bridge spanned the stream intersecting the village where the houses once stood. A "rybnik" (a fish pond) was nearby. As mentioned, typically, each village in Bohemia raised and still raises its own fish for the community's consumption. We walked from monument to monument reading the names of the families whose houses once stood on that spot. Each large monument had a Christian cross engraved in the center. Up one hill and down another we walked, trying to find the marker for the Bohac home. We had nearly given up when we saw one more marker at the very top of the hill bordering the forest which surrounded the village. Finally! It had "Dum 23" on it (House #23) and "Rodina (family of) Josefa Bohace a (and)

Rodina Bretislava Bohace." We took a picture. It was a solemn, tearful moment to remember the suffering of our own ancestors as they endured many wars, one after the other for centuries, trying to peacefully survive on their small plot of land and worship God in whom they maintained their steadfast faith.

I feel intensely about my Czech roots now. In those contacts with my blood relatives, I learned that on both sides of my family, my ancestors had a strong Christian faith and worshiped God who helped them endure countless adversities. Not all had this faith, of course, but the roots were there. Through the years of the Austria-Hungary occupation, the oppressive Hitler years and the communist tyranny, their Christian faith sustained them and gave them courage. The Czechs are a tough bunch, accustomed to hardship. Some, like Baba, brought their Christian faith with them to the "New World," and God gave them hope and wisdom to settle in a strange country and make a living.

Some of our ancestors who did not have that Christian faith to sustain them, struggled aimlessly, gave in to depression, lost hope and purpose, succumbed to alcoholism and some to suicide. They set their hearts on the pursuit of material things and their search ended in disappointment. Our Czech relatives told me many such stories. That was as true for those who stayed in the Old Country as for those who settled in the New World. It is not always a pretty picture, but I must tell it truthfully.

The present young generation is going through the same struggles. Faith in God will see them through, but if they go their own way, they may lose their direction. I thank God for the opportunity to get to know the younger generation of our relatives and hopefully to encourage them to follow the Christian faith.

My grandmother, Baba, passed on the Christian faith to me from my childhood. She was one who brought that faith in God with her from the Old Country and endured many hardships both there and here. Baba never preached in public nor led a Bible study. She didn't teach me to memorize Scripture or even read her Czech Bible to me. She didn't explain the way of salvation or lead me to personal faith by asking me to "make a decision to accept Jesus." She didn't counsel me on my life choices. But she loved me unconditionally, faithfully prayed for me and lived a quiet, authentic Christian life before me. I had to accept that faith for myself, which I did in God's perfect time. Since searching for and finding my roots, I appreciate her more and more as the pivotal person in my life.

25
Hometowns of My Ancestors

On each trip to Czechoslovakia, I tried to visit some of the hometowns of my ancestors as well as villages and cities in the immediate vicinity where some of my more distant forefathers were said to have originated. On my father's side, in the vicinity of Radlice where he was born, I explored Velka Lhota, Dacice, Telc, Jihlava, Trebic and other small villages in the surrounding countryside. On my maternal side, my ancestors came from around Policka. I was told that other ancestors lived in Litomysl, Svitavy, Brno, Borova, Svartouch, Oldris, Pomezi, Sadek, Teleci, Pusta Rybna, Sebranice, Svojanov and Brezova. These are villages in the vicinity of Siroky Dul where our current relatives still live, which I have already described. People usually married spouses from regions not too far from their places of birth.

Because I have been led to believe that Policka (pronounced Po-lich-ka) figures so largely in my ancestry for many generations, I spent as much time as possible leisurely walking its streets. I wanted to breathe in some of my family history. What

327

happened there through past centuries is probably bound up with the day-by-day lives of my ancestors. I found it fascinating to learn of the town's history and asked my relatives to tell me about its background.

"Are we still in the region of Moravia?" I wondered as we walked around studying the map.

"The town lies in the Bohemian-Moravian Highlands close to the border between the two regions. Many of us go back and forth between the two in a day's time. There's really no distinct border except on the map. In the early days, a trade route passed through Policka connecting Bohemia and Moravia. That brought prosperity to the settlement."

"How old is the town?"

"Written documents date back to 1265 when it was founded at the request of Premysl Ottokar II, King of Bohemia. He was also Duke of Austria and Styria and Moravian Margrave, so he wanted to extend his sovereign power to the farthest corner of East Bohemia."

We were strolling the cobblestone streets along with other local citizens who had come to market or shop. The scent of freshly baked goodies filled the air and we stopped at a small cafe for coffee and some traditional Czech fruit-filled kolaches. I marveled to see small babies in carriages left at the door while mothers shopped inside stores. "Won't someone kidnap the babies?" I wondered. "In the United States you couldn't do that safely."

"It's quite common just to park the little ones outside. People have such close knit relationships here that someone would have a hard time wheeling off a baby that didn't belong to her without drawing immediate attention. See that big dog tied to the carriage? He is trained to watch out for the baby." The child was chewing on a crescent roll and cooing happily.

We walked toward the park where I wanted a close look at the ancient wall. I was told that the town was built in an oval shape. Massive stone walls encircled it with multi-storied spires. The drawbridge was designed to protect against enemy attacks centuries ago. The thick stone walls were strengthened by 19 semi-cylindrical fortifications, and the rotundas were built in a pre-Romanesque style which originated in the Frankish Empire. The town was entered by four gates, they explained, each of which led to roads going toward different towns.

In time it became a dowry town of Bohemian queens and started to flourish during the reign of Charles IV. Stone houses several stories high, as well as a Gothic town hall, were built in the center of town. When I marveled at the good condition of the old cobblestone paving, my cousin told me that the streets were first paved in the second half of the 14th century. The town maintains them well.

"Everywhere I go I hear about the wonders of king Charles IV. He must have left a lasting impression on this country."

"He reigned for three decades, and Policka prospered along with the rest of the country. He was considered a genius and far ahead of his times because he linked traditions of Western civilization with the East. Instead of fighting wars like most of the previous kings, he invested national funds to build up the Czech Lands. Prague became his capital. Do you remember seeing some of his amazing cultural treasures when we visited Hradcany Castle and St Vitus Cathedral? He founded Charles University, the oldest institution of higher learning north of the Alps and east of the Rhine."

"What was Policka's position during the Reformation of Jan Hus and the upheavals that followed his martyrdom?"

"At the start of the Hussite wars, Policka supported the queen. But when Jan Zizka, the warrior at the head of the Hussite troops, reached here, the town opened its gates in welcome to him. The townspeople supported the Prague reformation movement. The Catholic German element was driven out, and the town became truly Bohemian and reformed. But trouble followed. Not long after, in 1421, the Hungarian army of Sigismund attacked, conquered and plundered our town. It took a long time for Policka to recover. When the town fathers rejoined the Prague reform movement, they decided not to involve themselves very closely in further Hussite revolts. They decided to reinforce the town's defense system by building a second moat and more fortifications to protect the gates. Of course, it was all ground warfare in those days and that would have helped to protect the town."

"I noticed many different styles of architecture around, sort of a hodge-podge."

"Around the middle of the 16th century, the Renaissance style began to appear in town, and the outside and inside of the buildings were almost totally rebuilt to reflect it. But one disaster after another came on the town. Property was confiscated and fines were imposed. As a result, the town deteriorated. In 1613 a fire swept through and destroyed most of the houses, three town gates and 11 bastions."

"Was anything left of the town?"

"Only the town hall and the southwest part of the town were spared. St. Michael's Church was the only other major structure that survived. Things went from bad to worse with the Swedish army occupying the town three times. The devastation was almost total. Shortly after, the town again took part in the revolt against the Habsburgs and was once more severely punished with great losses."

"How did Policka make out in that famous Thirty Years War? It seems that every place I visit they still talk about the battle of the White Mountain."

"Yes, that was the conflict between Catholicism and Protestantism which ended with that battle. It nearly crushed the country and wiped out a third of the people in the Czech Lands. People were forced either to convert to Catholicism or leave their homeland. Many decided for exile. After those people left, their property was confiscated and sold to those who were loyal to the House of Hapsburg. The economy of the whole country suffered greatly, and much of its cultural heritage was looted or destroyed. Policka suffered as well, and the town remained almost deserted until the 18th century. They say that in 1654 only 90 people were recorded by the king's magistrate."

"The people must have suffered one blow after another. I can't imagine how our ancestors lived through those terrible times."

"Hard to believe, but again the town slowly recovered from all the losses suffered in the war. Finally, in the second half of the 17th century and into the 18th century, Policka entered a boom period known as its Golden Age. That's why you noticed Baroque architecture around. Music and the arts began to thrive. The town became known as one of the most attractive of Bohemian towns and prospered economically. Most of the houses were restored in Baroque style, and St. James church was re-decorated at great cost.

"What is the significance of that huge monument in the middle of the Palacky Square?"

"You've probably heard of the disastrous plague epidemic that swept Europe in 1713 with many thousands of deaths. It affected nearly every other town and the countryside but Policka's people were miraculously spared. In gratitude to God, a Plague Column 22 meters high was erected during 1727-31 in the center of our town square. It is one of the outstanding features of the town today. You notice it pictured on our literature. The foremost Bohemian architect, F. M. Kanka, designed it, and the large sculptures of saints decorating the column are the work of Jiri Pacak of Litomysl. In the opinion of experts, there is nothing to equal it in all Bohemia. Do you see the other statues decorating the Square by the fountain? Those are by Pacak, too."

We walked over to the impressive town hall. It is a two-storied building with an attic roof and spire. Ornamental ledges and other elaborate carvings are above the windows.

"This isn't the original building. A new town hall was constructed in the Baroque style and took the place of the original Gothic one which had been destroyed in some of those catastrophes."

Our next stop was the St. James Church, one of the clearly dominant features of the town built in Neo-Gothic style. "Is that one the original structure?"

"No, it was rebuilt in the years 1853-1865 after the old church burned down in another huge fire in 1845. In that fire, the largest yet, of the 237 buildings standing in the center of town, only four remained undamaged. The Baroque image of the town was quite lost because the houses were repaired in Classicist style. After that tragedy, a fire-watcher's room was established in the high tower of the Church."

"Is that the place I have been hearing about where the famous composer, Bohuslav Martinu was born?"

"That's one of the outstanding attractions to visit, if you can climb the narrow, circular staircase inside the tower. Are you ready for the steps?" (She didn't tell me how many!)

I said I was ready, and after a tedious climb, we reached the room and stopped to catch our breath. It remained furnished as it had been during the family's occupancy long ago. A round dining table was covered with a crocheted white tablecloth, and four chairs stood around it. Narrow single beds, a desk-like table, chairs, antique clock and framed family pictures on the old-fashioned, wall-papered walls gave it an Old World atmosphere. An iron contraption in the garret was part of his father's equipment for shoemaking and repair, his occupation. You could see the entire town and far away to the distant horizon from the windows. The view was worth the climb. Martinu once compared his tower to a lighthouse. He spent his first 12 years living there. (I imagined his mother saying, "Run out to play." That would be 384 steps round trip!) He claimed that this living space played a major role in forming his whole attitude to composing.

From the western side of the tower gallery we looked over the rusty red roof of St. Michael's Church. I asked whether we could visit the cemetery adjoining it. The church itself was built in 1572-76 and is Gothic outside but entirely Renaissance inside. Not far from the iron gate entrance to the cemetery is the tomb of the Martinu family where the composer is buried. A massive, horizontal gravestone was placed over the plot in 1984. We strolled through the meticulously kept graveyard pausing to read the ancient dates on the markers.

A few minutes walk along a pleasant alley between Synsky pond and the southern front of the town walls, we reached the park where a larger than life bronze statue of Martinu towers over the landscape. This tribute was unveiled in 1990, the work of Milan Knobloch. We walked through the spacious park with its 104 species of plants and flowers, all of which are identified by plaques. A pamphlet is available with numbers to locate each variety. Its many walkways are lined with tall trees, a quiet haven right in the middle of town.

My relatives pointed out a steel on stone war memorial to commemorate local citizens who sacrificed their lives after the occupation of Bohemia and Moravia on March 15, 1930. Policka was "liberated" on May 9, 1945, when soldiers of the Red Army and the First Czechoslovak Army Corps entered the town. My relatives showed me a special area with a flourishing flower garden and manicured lawn which is a popular place for wedding parties to have pictures taken.

We walked down Masaryk Street and stopped at house No. 8, the private music school where Martinu taught violin and piano before 1920. Considerably further along Hus Street is a Music School which bears his name. Even after Martinu lived in

Paris, New York, the American countryside, Rome and Switzerland, he often returned to a small garret room near the southwest outskirts of his hometown.

I was eager to see the Martinu Memorial Exhibition. The collection of compiled documentary material introduces visitors to the life and work of the composer. Photographs, slides, drawings and models of stage scenery, costume designs and original billboard posters of his performances are displayed in the various rooms. To me, the highlight of our visit was to sit in a thick-carpeted room with modern audio-visual facilities to view a film about his life. At the request of visitors, some of his recorded works are played. The piano on which he performed is prominently displayed in the room. I bought a number of CD recordings of his works, especially my favorites for cello and piano. Martinu may be less well known than his compatriots, Dvorak, Smetana and Janacek, but his output was large and ranged from chamber music to symphonies and operas. Martinu holds a special place in my mind because he was born in the same year as my dad—1890.

I may sound like the local Chamber of Commerce, but I am proud of modern Policka, which has much to delight a pilgrim to one of the significant hometowns of Czech ancestry. The Art Gallery in the Town Hall exhibits old and new art. The unique carved gates and house doors, rare examples of woodwork in Classicist style, originate from the time after the fire of 1845. Burghers' houses in various styles, restaurants ranging from the cozy cafes and pubs to elegant hotel dining and theaters—all are sure to please the visitor. For the sports inclined, Policka offers numerous nearby fishing lakes and ponds, tennis courts, indoor and outdoor Olympic size modern swimming pools, saunas, fitness centers, an indoor climbing wall, gymnasium, tourist footpaths, cycling, winter sports, an ice hockey stadium and an ice rink.

I have been intrigued with castles since my childhood when

I read the story of "The Little Lame Prince" in one of my first books, *The Child's Garden of Verses*. On my trips to the Czech lands, I visited castles in at least a dozen cities. I still have the desire to spend the night in a real castle and listen for ghosts of knights and fair ladies! Policka owns the nearby Early Gothic castle of Svojanov which was built in the 13th century to protect the trade routes. It is a tourist hostel with 50 beds and a dining room seating 40. The oldest in the Czech territory, it is dominated by a watch tower and a well preserved fortification system. A permanent exhibition of the history of the castle is said to be outstanding. An overnight stay in this castle is on the agenda for my next trip!

Several other cities in the vicinity of my maternal forefathers' origin have some distinctiveness. Svitavy is the birthplace of Oskar Schindler, brought to the world's attention by the Steven Spielberg movie *Schindler's List*. On one of my walks in that city I saw the modest memorial at the edge of the town park in front of a house where he lived. It was unveiled on the occasion of the film's first run in the Czech Republic. The response of Svitavy residents is mixed. To the townspeople, he had been known as "an easygoing skirt-chaser, bragging drinker, gambler, self-seeker and wheeler-dealer." Allegedly, he even had a poor start by being expelled from grammar school because of a document forgery. By the time of his marriage, he was said to have had a few illegitimate children. He always managed to avoid complete tragedy, thanks to some trick or bribery, and could play two sides against each other in war or business or relationships. But his claim to fame was, as the memorial states, "To the unforgotten savior of the lives of 1200 persecuted Jews" during the Nazi era.

Litomysl, where some of our ancestors originated, is a cultural and historical center on the Loucna river founded along the important commercial route connecting Bohemia and Moravia. The town dates back to the 10th century and was built around the original castle mentioned in the Cosmas Chronicles of 981. It became an important center of the Czech Brethren church. Its history was later closely related to the monastery built in the 12th century. During the 16th century, the castle was rebuilt as a Renaissance Chateau with a college and cathedral as part of the complex. The castle is distinctive for the 8000 remarkable sgraffitos (three dimensional, ornamental carved blocks) that make up its facade. In 1824 Bedrich Smetana, the famous composer, was born in the castle brewery. A museum documenting his life draws visitors. You can see the piano on which he composed some of his famous works. Alois Jirasek, the Czech writer, also lived there. The city hosts international festivals of classical music, operas and chorus competitions in the open courtyard. Litomysl Square is one of the largest in the country with its many arcades, vaulted ground-floor rooms and houses in Renaissance and Baroque style.

Borova, where I worshiped with some of our relatives in the 18th century Evangelical Reformed church, was established as a parish village in 1349. The names of the small towns in our ancestral area are derived from some characteristic of that settlement. Lubna was named for a certain kind of thin, bended strips of wood called "luby" which are found in the surrounding forests. A new rococo style castle ("hrad" means castle) gave Nove Hrady its name. Oldris was first settled in the 9th century by duke Oldrich. Pusta Rybna, the birthplace of some of our relatives, probably derives its name from the plentiful fish ("ryba" means fish) in the local streams. Sebranice is named for the fact that it was settled by people who were collected ("sebrani" means gathered) from a wide area as early as the 13th century. Teleci, founded in the 1600s, was a storehouse of salt used for cattle licks. "Tele" is the word for calves. Makov was named for the vast fields of wild poppies or "mak" growing near the village. Policka, our town of origin, apparently had many small fields or "pole" adjoining the settlement.

The hometowns of some of my ancestors are so picturesque that many artists and writers were lured to spend time in them and composed some of their works there. I, too, with a small claim to being a writer, absorbed its quiet, ancient atmosphere on each trip and dreamed of my forefathers who walked the same cobblestone streets and somehow survived the fires and wars that were Policka's lot for so many centuries. Waterwheel powered flour mills and sawmills, fish ponds, rolling hills and deep forests lend a unique beauty to the villages. The woody odor of forests mingles with the scent of hay on freshly mown meadows. Local people say you can hear a cricket and church bells at the same time in this region that is now at peace.

I was at peace, too, while strolling the countryside of my ancestors. I had a warm sense of belonging there, having found my roots at last.

Leona's writing studio/chalet in the woods,
Shenandoah Valley, Winchester, Virginia

26

Prague, the Shining Jewel

I had three goals for my third trip that were related to finishing the search for my roots in the homeland of my ancestors. First, I wanted to spend leisurely, in-depth time soaking up the history and culture of Prague, the Czech capitol. I felt the same about repeated trips to China—walking the Great Wall, strolling through Tienanmen Square, the Forbidden City in Beijing, around the lakes of Hangzhou or viewing the mystic mountains of Guilin. I especially felt that way about Ted's birthplace. The first visit is only a brief, exciting exposure; the second time, you are more aware of details. Subsequent times, you gain a still greater perspective and appreciation as you take your time to immerse yourself in its history, breathe in the atmosphere and let the experience permeate you.

My second goal was to do the same in the villages of my ancestors, extending my relationships to the younger generation who, now 10 years after my first trip, were working or married and establishing their own families. I also wanted to spend more time with the older generation and understand their lives under the new political freedoms the country was experiencing.

My third goal was to research and relate to some of the historic religious roots that were foundational to the faith of my fathers, namely Jan Hus (1373-1415), Jan Amos Comenius (1592-1671) and the Moravian movement related to Count Nikolaus Ludwig Von Zinzendorf (1700-1760). That path would take me to Germany, to the small, famous town of Herrnhut.

Thank God, I accomplished each goal and I returned with an appreciation of the richness of both my cultural heritage and my religious roots.

"Babo, have you ever been to Praha (Prague)?" I remember asking in the latter days of her life. Baba's blue-grey eyes took on a faraway look. "I visited it once—as a young girl. And again as I left my homeland for the trip to America. But I can still see it in my dreams—the castle, Charles Bridge...."

"Did you name Uncle Charles after famous King Charles?" I asked. We had been studying about that brilliant king in a history class. A wistful smile, then tears, kept her from answering. I didn't pursue my question because I didn't want to see my beloved grandmother crying. What was the mystery? No one ever talked about it. The family changed the subject whenever I asked about the uncle I never knew. I loved mysteries, but I never found the solution to this one until after Baba's death.

I learned from a relative about the tragic death of Baba's 20 year old son who accompanied her on the long voyage to America as a teen, her youngest child, born not long before my grandfather died. My uncle "Karel" (Charles), who died before I was born, committed suicide in despondency over a love affair. A relative showed me an old, yellowed newspaper clipping about the story—reported in gross details. "Young Man Ends Own Life With Cheap Revolver. Fires Shot into His Brain. Body Found on Grave of Former Sweetheart's Kin."

He shot himself at the Czech cemetery. Authorities found a suicide note in his pocket along with several letters addressed to his girlfriend and mother. The newspaper went into other gory details which I will not repeat. The body was, in fact, misidentified as someone else, and that man's relatives were notified. When the "difficult to decipher" letters were finally read, it became clear the man was Karel. I can't imagine Baba's grief when she received his letter. "Dearest Parents, Brothers and Sisters: I must lose my life for my girl, Emma. Do not blame me for killing myself. I cannot live this life without her. Your affectionate son, Karel." That must have been a traumatic loss for Baba, one of the many griefs she experienced in her new homeland of America.

From that old newspaper clipping I discovered another tragedy in Baba's life that I never knew about. It listed Uncle Karel's stepfather and gave his name and the address where Baba and he were living in Luzerne, Iowa. It must have been an unhappy marriage between a widow and a widower. I don't know how long it lasted or any details. After Baba was divorced, she came to live with us to care for me from the time I was born.

Another heartache was the estrangement from her youngest daughter, Mary, only a year older than Charlie. After she emigrated to America, she seemed to drop out of sight. Baba had tears in her eyes whenever anyone mentioned Mary. Her daughter married two or three more times after coming to the U.S., and had been married once in her teens while still in Radlice. She lived somewhere in Chicago with her family. Baba missed knowing those grandchildren. I don't remember the family visiting Baba during my childhood, although I could be wrong. I do recall that they came to her funeral.

Still another misfortune had come upon her son, Joseph, who may have come to the U.S. after Baba was already here. He had an auto accident early in his married life in which the early model car he was driving was hit and demolished by an interurban train. His wife and a neighbor were passengers, and the neighbor was killed. The trauma so upset his mental condition that he was institutionalized for the rest of his long life. He died at the age of 75, more than 20 years after Baba died.

I vividly remember that our family, with Baba and sometimes other relatives, visited him while he was in the institution in Independence, Iowa. He was free to have picnics with us on the grounds. Mother always brought a full course meal in a big dinner basket for all of us to share with Uncle Joe. She gave a box of candy, gum and other goodies to him when we left. I recall climbing on Uncle Joe's lap and playing tag with him on the grounds. He did not seem any different to me. He was gentle, smiling, but sat silently a lot and didn't enter into our conversations. I'm not sure whether he recognized his mother, Baba. She always cried as we drove home. After Baba died and he was transferred to the County Farm for the remainder of his life, Mother continued to visit him with some members of our family, always bringing treats to him. During my teen years, I accompanied her occasionally. We were not sure he really knew who we were, but Mother said that didn't matter, that we would continue to visit him.

Baba's final heartache the year before she died was the untimely death of Aunt Tony, her eldest daughter, at age 56. She came to the U.S. with her husband and year old son, Godfrey, after Baba was already living here.

Baba's 31 years of life in her adopted homeland was not without griefs and difficulties, but she always found comfort and strength in her intimate relationship with God. Her faith and trust in Him never wavered. As a child, when I snuggled in the security and affection of the big apron on her lap, how little I knew of the heartaches Baba kept hidden in her heart!

As long as I can remember, I was aware of the restless blood that ran in my veins from my immigrant heritage. I wanted to grow up quickly and leave the settled life of heartland America and *go somewhere, anywhere, far away.* It didn't matter where, as long as it was "away." Although I rejected my Czech heritage during my childhood and youth because I wanted to fit in with my peer group of "ordinary kids," in the back of my mind God planted the desire to someday walk over that historic Charles Bridge. Ted and I finally did that together in 1991, just as we shared a similar experience walking the Great Wall of China when he traced his heritage.

I set off on my third trip to Czechoslovakia, now officially called The Czech Republic after the official division of the country into two parts. So many changes of names for the same country within a hundred year period! I deliberately timed my arrival in Prague to be on August first, 2001.

My guide for the next few weeks was Jitka Rompotlova. During my first trip, she was the teenage granddaughter of my relatives—my only English-speaking contact. Since then, she graduated from a university, was now a beautiful, sophisticated, professional, 26 year old career teacher of English at a school in Prague. I called her "My Lady of Prague!" She volunteered to devote her vacation time to accompany me anywhere I wanted to go. I really lucked out! I hoped to talk nothing but Czech with her for the first two weeks so I could brush up on my language skills. She, however, had something else in mind—she insisted we speak only English so that she could acquire new idioms and vocabulary to enhance her teaching skills. She called the shots!

We bunked in her tiny room at the English school, "Skola Jitrn," on the outskirts of Prague, at least a 45 minute return trip by metro, tram, bus and then by foot from anywhere in Prague where we were sightseeing during the day. Her Spartan accommodations mattered little because, after an average long day extending into the evening before our return, sometimes having walked up to ten miles a day, we could do nothing more than quickly shower and flop exhausted into bed. The lodging for me was free, a real perk in a city where hotel prices are off the charts.

We spent ten saturation days visiting cultural and historic places in Prague. Our standing joke was that we *walked* our way through Prague and *ate* our way through it. Since Jitka's little room had no kitchen facilities, we happily ate all our meals out. Jitka found all the terrific restaurants of both traditional Czech and international foods. We indulged ourselves without feeling guilty because we certainly walked off any extra calories we delectably took in.

More than a dozen bridges of stone, iron and concrete span the Vltava river. Charles Bridge, of course, with its Gothic arches and at least thirty imposing Baroque statues of stern looking saints and martyrs lining both sides, is a main attraction. The statues proclaim the triumph of the Catholic Hapsburgs over Protestant Prague during the Renaissance. You must cross this bridge on foot because cars, buses and trams are banned. Here young Czech artists display for sale their engravings, oils, water colors or sketches of Prague life. The old street lamps look like the gas lamps on Christmas cards of carolers with top hats and scarves singing "God rest ye merry gentlemen." We took a cruise down the Vltava River and looked at the bridges from underneath and seeing the grand landscape of Prague from river level. Fresh brewed coffee and pastries were served on board as we listened to a professional guide explain the sights in several languages.

The genius of King Charles IV is in evidence everywhere. As Holy Roman Emperor and King of Bohemia, Charles was really the builder of Gothic Prague, of the famous Charles University, modeled on the Sorbonne, of Charles Bridge, St. Vitus Cathedral, and of his crowning achievement, the Karlstejn castle. To this day, he is revered in Prague for the sense of national identity he brought to Bohemia.

We climbed to Hradcany Castle's heights and I learned far more than when Ted and I stumbled through trying to explore on our own. The massive structure displays architectural styles of all kinds. The view of the entire "Golden City of a Hundred Spires" from the castle set on a rocky hill is spectacular. We toured the majestic St. Vitus Metropolitan Cathedral there, the most important sacred building in the country. Building began under Emperor Charles IV in 1344 but was not completed until 1929. A long building program! The big rose window portrays the creation of the world, another shows scenes from the lives of saints Cyril and Methodius, which I was particularly interested in photographing. They were the ones who originally systematized the Czech language and brought the Christian faith to this country.

Prague is still one of the great cultural cities of the world. Many of the historic buildings are being cleaned and restored. The city that Mozart loved still has much to offer music lovers. Adoring Czechs virtually made him an honorary Praguer. The first performance of Mozart's *Don Giovanni* was in the Tyl Theater in 1787 where the movie *Amadeus* was also filmed. Tickets to places of musical entertainment from classical concerts to modern rock are sold on the streets.

Jitka and I dressed up one night and made reservations in a famous concert hall for an evening of symphony orchestra and ballet performance of Mozart and Strauss music. The musicians appeared in exquisite period costumes including powdered wigs. Always there are a wide variety of films and plays from all over the world going on—not just from the European bloc. Jitka and I took in a film one afternoon, a current American movie with Czech subtitles. I got dizzy listening to the English dialogue while trying to follow the words in Czech to upgrade my language skills. The Czechs seem happily obsessed with music, literature and the theater, and we went with the flow.

Czechs are not a loud people; they are gentle and polite. Moderation in behavior is expected. Nevertheless, they are a merry people and the annual Music Festivals are a time to display their talents not only in formal theater settings but in public. How we enjoyed the street musicians in Old Town Square as we sat on benches indulging in our daily ice cream cones and resting our tired feet!

The tale of Faust had its real-life origin in Prague, where you can still visit the "Faust House." They say the real glory of Prague is the Gothic and Baroque atmosphere of its ancient quarters, which we had fun exploring.

In the beginning, Prague was not a unified whole but five separate towns that came together about 1794. Old Town, "Stare Mesto," is the medieval nucleus of the city which dates back to 1120. On each trip, I wanted to stand in the Square again with the crowd to wait for the magnificent, early 15th century Astronomical Clock to strike the hour. The Grim Reaper strikes the bell and turns an hour-glass upside down. That's the cue for a mechanical cock to crow and the Twelve Apostles to march by, one by one, at two windows high up in the facade of the Old Town hall. A cock flaps its wings and crows. By the side of the Grim Reaper, a Turk shakes his head to indicate he's not ready for death. Two other figures symbolize human greed and vanity. The upper part of the clock contains a sphere showing the time and positions of the sun and moon in the Zodiac. The lower part is a calendar with signs of the Zodiac and scenes from the seasons. This famous clock was the genius work of clock-maker Mikulas of Kadan and the astronomer Jan Sindel.

Gothic and older former residences, all topped with spires and turrets, border the Square. A group of colossal statues stands on an island in the Square, the most prominent of which is Jan Hus, the martyred reformer churchman whose story I had come to research. The statue was unveiled in 1915 to mark the 500th anniversary of his death. Jitka and I often sat on the benches in the shadow of this great man.

St. George's Basilica, the magnificent National Theater,

St. Wenceslaus Chapel, whose walls glow softly in the light of votive candles, all beckoned to us. One of the Catholic churches in Cedar Rapids was named for St. Wenceslaus. Wenceslaus Square is the main artery of Prague, 750 meters long, with the huge statue of St. Wenceslaus on his horse towering over the Square. (Baba told me she had seen that.) The remains of this famous king are buried in the castle. The imposing National Museum built in the neo-Renaissance style tops the Square. The entire tree-lined area, when lit up at night, is a never-to-be-forgotten sight. Sometimes we sat resting on benches there, too, watching people of all ages from all nations strolling by on the cobblestone walks.

In the midst of the hustle and bustle of this great metropolis, Jitka often guided us to the very heart of Prague to the incredibly quiet Frantiskanska Garden and Park where flowers bloomed everywhere. Public benches were available and classical music played in the background from a little pavilion. We felt as if we were in the calm and serene eye of the storm. Another favorite place for our ice cream cone breaks!

We climbed hills with hundreds of broad, stone steps (I counted one typical set—490 steps!) to reach parks, rose gardens, monasteries, more cathedrals and up Petrin Hill to view the intriguing, massive Metronome at Letna. Whatever you climbed up, you had to climb down—even harder on the calves of your legs and your poor toes. As a matter of trivia, I wore out one pair of Rebocks, and before my trip was over, I discovered that I would probably lose the toe nails on two already black and blue bruised toes as a result of all the Prague trekking!

Jitka and I got caught in a downpour without an umbrella on one of our hilltop excursions, and I suffered for the rest of my trip from a bruised elbow that I scraped against a castle wall during our slippery flight to shelter. But from an overlook of the entire city, when the rain stopped and the sun emerged to dazzle us and dry us off, we saw a sight that will remain forever in my

347

memory—the biggest and most brilliant rainbow I had ever seen stretched across the entire horizon with one end anchored behind Hradcany castle! Of course I snapped the picture! I decided that God staged this spectacular display just for us as a finale to my Prague adventure!

On previous trips, I was delighted to visit several major castles. Czechoslovakia is reputed to have about 3000 ancient castles and mansions, and during my three trips, I saw my share of them. Strictly speaking, the Czechs call a major castle a "hrad," a chateau is called a "zamek" and a "chram" is more like a cathedral. St. Barbara's cathedral in Kutna Hora is an example of a "chram." St. Barbara is the patron saint of miners—the town mined silver in the 14th century. Some of these historic, national cultural monuments are restored as museums and art galleries filled with period furniture, paintings, sculptures and other priceless exhibits of long ago. They are usually closed in winter—no wonder, imagine trying to heat a castle! Others are ghostly ruins on top of deserted, sheer, rocky outcrops in the forest. They are marvels of engineering from early centuries. Many of the restored ones have parks and gardens surrounding them, the grounds sometimes being used for exhibitions, concerts and plays.

I visited Pernstejn, a medieval fortress castle that looks exactly like what I imagined a "real" fairy tale castle should look like. Regarded as unassailable, its ancient towers and ramparts rise straight up from high rocks. It is full of dank dungeons and passageways. I'd hate to be left behind when they close the door at night! Movies are often filmed at this castle. On my visit there I met several modern Czechs dressed in knight's armor and elaborate period costumes—probably for the benefit of tourists. They were more than happy to pose for photos with us. The Landstejn castle, on the other hand, is a massive ruin with an outstanding exhibition of medieval weapons.

Karlstejn, not far from Prague, the largest and most visited castle in Bohemia, was founded by Charles IV in 1348. It looms up in a spectacular setting on a green hilltop in a forested area. The king held court there and made it a repository for the crown jewels, church relics and spectacular paintings. Everywhere I went I learned more about this enlightened monarch who lived before the age of enlightenment. He was fluent in five languages, wrote his autobiography in Latin and gathered about him a court of astronomers, writers, theologians and intellectuals.

Legend has it that six centuries ago, Charles IV was on a hunt chasing a deer in the dense forest and came upon remarkable bubbling hot springs. He called it "Karlovy Vary," literally, "Charles' Boiling Place," or as we know it, Karlsbad. This famous spa has lured into its waters emperors, kings and noted people from all over the world including America. Especially musicians—Bach, Beethoven, Brahms, Liszt, Paganini, Wagner, Tchaikovsky and of course the famous Czech musician, Smetana— chose to come and lie around in the warm, healing waters at some point in their lives. Ordinary Czech people and tourists avail themselves of this natural wonder as well. Antonin Dvorak selected that location for the first performance of his made-in-the-U.S.A. symphony, called *From the New World*.

Praguers spend long lunch hours and coffee breaks leisurely snacking delicacies and conversing over rich, aromatic coffee. We went with that flow too, sampling a variety of sumptuous baked goods and pastries at sidewalk coffee houses. Jitka knew exactly where to find good Cappuccino and tall glasses of iced coffee. We were willing to walk out of our way to indulge ourselves. If you go by recent statistics, there are 424 pubs, 134 wine bars and 466 restaurants in Prague. That probably doesn't count the several McDonalds and KFCs. We "Czeched" out those too— not the pubs but the fast food! The world famous Czech beer is distinctive, drawn directly from wooden kegs and served in ornate mugs indoors or outdoors under awnings at small sidewalk eateries or beer gardens in the parks. Jitka and I did not "Czech" on those.

Why have I included this personal travelogue? So that the reader might walk with me through a fulfillment of my desires and dreams and complete with me the circle of my heritage. I also hope to whet the reader's appetite to follow his dreams to discover and explore for himself or herself this ancient, brilliant jewel city in Europe.

My second goal of spending quality time with my Czech relatives in their home village was happily realized. Jitka and I traveled several hours by bus from Prague to her home in Siroky Dul where I enjoyed the hospitality of her family in their home for my accommodations this time. Various relatives royally entertained me with home cooked Czech delicacies and traditional fare, with outdoor fish fries and chicken barbecue picnics. Time and again we strolled the streets of Policka, a 15 minute bus ride from Jitka's home, shopping in quaint stores and snacking in favorite cafes.

I appreciated a more laid back pace after our intensive urban excursions in Prague. I enjoyed more time with both the older generation, Adolf and Miloslava, and the younger ones. Many more of them could speak English by this time and their standard of living was quite luxurious. They had many modern conveniences and the latest appliances and electronic gadgetry. Jitka and her sister wanted me to bring them American cold cereals, so I lined my suitcases with the little variety boxes. Vitamins and medications were still welcome and I came prepared again.

My relatives kindly drove me to Radlice once more because I continue to feel drawn to visit Baba's church. Major renovation had been completed, and the sanctuary is beautiful. This time, the minister's wife took us on a guided tour, and Jitka interpreted for me. On our first trip we saw scaffolding and dropcloths everywhere and were unable to appreciate its historic grandeur. Now I was able to sit in the very pews where Baba sat and worshiped. Most probably she sat there as a child, a young girl, a bride, a mother and as a widow left with six children to raise. It was a sacred moment to me.

How did she feel the last time she worshiped there before leaving her homeland forever? I thought of the many heartaches that awaited her in America. Did she regret the transplanting of her entire family to a new country? Leaving behind all the familiar places and people? I don't think she did. She surely must have sought guidance from God and received His assurance that He was leading her and her family to His Promised Land for them. I am one of the grateful beneficiaries of her momentous choice.

Once more I visited the elderly Radlice neighbor, Maria, who welcomed us so warmly when Ted and I stayed with her. Maria's daughter, Stana, and husband, Gerhard, had driven from their home in Austria to meet us ten years ago. Ted shared the hobby of collecting postage stamps with young Petr, their shy, blond grandson, who showed off his pet rooster. Today we saw pictures of tall, handsome Petr taken when he graduated from the university as an engineer. He posed with his stunning fiancé, Nina, who was an architect. On that first visit we also met Petr's sister, Jana, an attractive, talented young teen who wanted to study music at the conservatory. Last year I received an e-mail from someone in Prague who relayed shocking news. Stana wanted to let me know that her daughter committed suicide after graduating from the university.

Stana had driven over again from Austria especially to see me. She brought me privately into Maria's bedroom and shut the door. She wanted to show me the last pictures of Jana at her graduation. We embraced for a long time and shed tears together.

My third goal for the trip, the fascinating Moravian research journey to Germany for the Hus-Comenius-Zinzendorf connection, is so important that it requires separate chapters.

*Jan Hus—martyr for the Christian faith.
Bethlehem Chapel in the background*

27

Digging Deeper and Further

The faith of my grandmother and our other ancestors is rooted in the Moravian Church, which is so called because of its origins in the Moravia region of the Czech lands. That Church, in turn, had its roots in the teachings of Jan Hus, the early Czech reformer. Because those foundations are so integral to the Christian faith as it was expressed in my ancestors' homeland and in Baba's faith, I wanted to follow the trail of our faith all the way back to its source. On my third trip, I investigated the Jan Hus connection still further by traveling to the German location where the Moravian refugees from religious persecution were welcomed to settle on the estate of Count Nicolaus Ludwig von Zinzendorf.

To prepare myself, I did considerable pre-trip research in archives of libraries, on the Internet, in books from the Moravian Theological Seminary and the Moravian Board of World Missions in Bethlehem, Pennsylvania and videos on the lives of those great men. I also had access to the personal libraries and recollections of former Moravian missionaries and clergy.

Because of the importance of those Christian roots to my own faith and heritage and that of my *branches*, I will recap some background of Christianity in the Czech lands to make the context clear. Our roots go deep. Christianity came to Bohemia and Moravia shortly before 800 A.D. After that, Germanic missionaries from the West intensively evangelized the country. In an effort to moderate this Germanic influence, the Great Moravian prince Rastislav invited Greek missionaries from Constantinople, the brothers Constantine (later called Cyril) and Methodius from Salonica. They introduced a new script, the Cyrillic, modified from the Greek alphabet. Their important contribution was to translate many important passages from the Bible into the dialect which was easily understood by the Czechs, thus laying foundations for the Czechs' own literature and culture.

Not long after the decline of the Great Moravian Empire, the Czech lands once again came under the influence of Germanic Latin Christianity and Western culture. In the 10th century, the famous Prince Vaclav (known also as "Good King Wenceslaus") of the House of Premysl became the most important representative of a peaceable Christian piety. A beloved hero, he was later canonized as the patron saint of the Czech nation. The most outstanding Czech Christian medieval figure was the pious Emperor Charles IV who established the University of Prague in 1348, the first university in central Europe. Under his reign, the capital, Prague, became the third most important city in Europe, and Bohemia became one of the most developed Christian cultural lands.

By the end of the 14th century, an intense spiritual and social tension appeared within the Czech nation between those who pursued true Christian renewal and reform and the Roman Papal Church. A revival movement grew under the preaching and teaching of Czech spiritual leaders. This reached its peak in the preaching of God's Word in the Czech language by Master Jan

Hus, a Catholic priest, in the pulpit of Bethlehem Chapel founded in the very heart of Prague in 1391. I would have liked to write an entire book on the life of Jan Hus, but I must limit myself to this brief chapter to capture his importance even to my own life. My parents were members of a local church in my hometown called Jan Hus Memorial Church, the same church where Ted and I were married. At that time, I had no idea of how pivotal and significant that reformer was to my heritage.

Born in 1372 in Husinec, an obscure village in Moravia, Jan (John) took his surname from the name of that village in the days when few people had surnames. He studied for the Catholic priesthood since that was one of the few ways for any poor young man to climb up the ladder of economic and social success. Otherwise, a boy was expected to follow in the craft or occupation of his father. Hus climbed that ladder at the University of Prague to become a professor and then dean of the philosophical faculty. Soon he became rector of the university as well as attaining his priesthood. That qualified him for appointment as preacher of the large Bethlehem Chapel, the most popular church in the city, and brought him into the reform movement. Strongly influenced by John Wycliffe, (1320-1384) the English theologian, reformer and Bible translator, Hus became the recognized leader and spokesman of that movement in his own country. That period also marked what Hus called his true spiritual conversion—all within 13 years of leaving his little village.

Hus declared that all his teaching was grounded in the Bible alone as the source of truth and rule of faith in all spheres of life. He believed that only God, not priests, could forgive sins and only after a man met all God's required conditions could a priest declare anyone's sins forgiven. This was a blatant protest against the widespread corrupt practice of the Papal church to sell the forgiveness of sins to anyone who paid money for slips of paper called "indulgences." In 1411, the new Pope called Europe to a war and used that means to raise the necessary funds to wage it. He sent papal agents throughout Europe to set up stands in town squares and ordered every church to sell the forgiveness of sins. All churches complied except Bethlehem Chapel in Prague, where Hus preached strongly against it. "God alone can forgive sins through Christ, forgiveness cannot be bought and sold and God pardons the penitent only."

Hus preached sermons in the Czech language of the common people, not in Latin as the Papal Church required. He pioneered spiritual revival through the singing of religious hymns by the whole congregation. That was a radical departure from the Catholic mass. He also defined the true church as a spiritual fellowship including any who possessed the spirit of Christ, not a legal corporation or society with a membership which one entered in some formal religious way. He claimed that there were other true Christian groups in the world—the Greek Orthodox, the national churches of the near eastern countries, all of whom possessed their own history, structure and independence. As far as Hus was concerned, true Christians were in all those groups and not exclusively in the Catholic Church. All these made up the one, universal church of Christ, the Body of Christ. This threatened the very foundations of the Papal Church. Bethlehem Chapel became a rallying point for thousands of Czech Christians who were earnestly seeking to learn the truth of God for themselves from the Word of God. This heralded the beginning of the Hussite reformation movement, the true forerunner of the Reformation, a full one hundred years before Martin Luther in Germany and John Calvin in Switzerland.

The queen was a faithful worshiper in the Chapel, and the king admired the courage of Hus and defended him against criticism. The Papal Church, however, turned its anger against Hus forbidding him to preach, publicly burning more than 200 volumes of Wycliffe's writings and beheading three of the Chapel's

Christian men who called the indulgences a fraud. The Pope excommunicated Hus, forbidding anyone to give him food or drink or a place of refuge. He ordered him seized and held prisoner, pronouncing an everlasting curse against him. Hus was protected against armed seizure by his faithful congregation but agreed, upon the wise advice of the king, to withdraw from the city for awhile. That period of exile gave him time to write important works to encourage Christians in the biblical principles of what he was preaching.

The Pope called for a council of the Church to deal with abuses of his authority and to expose heresies. Prince Sigismund, the successor son of the aged good king Wenceslaus, summoned Hus to appear and guaranteed him safe conduct to go and return. Hus agreed, although his followers strongly advised him not to go. His protection turned out to be violated. Upon the arrival of Hus at Constance, soldiers threw him in a prison cell and chained him in a dungeon under the Dominican convent next to the sewer system. The Synod Council was in no hurry to consider his case, so after he became gravely ill and nearly died, they transferred him to a kind of cage at the top of one of the towers of the castle. That exposed him both to the burning sun and cold night winds. He bravely endured the abuse and agony for two more months. The prince ordered Hus set free, but because wily cardinals persuaded him it wasn't necessary to keep promises to heretics, he changed his mind and kept silent.

Finally Hus was taken to a trial which lasted a month. When he attempted to defend himself, he was shouted down and ignored. On July 6, Hus was brought to the cathedral where the prince was also in attendance. In the presence of bishops and cardinals arrayed in their glorious religious robes, Hus was forced to sit on a high stool and listen to his funeral sermon. That was followed by the reading of 31 charges of heresy against him, while he was ordered to remain silent. He was asked to recant, which he refused to do. Thus Hus was not condemned for his own words or views, since they didn't allow him to express or defend them from the Scriptures, but for what others said he taught. They clothed him with vestments of a priest (officially Hus was still a Catholic) and put a communion cup in his hands. Then they tore off the garments one by one; lastly the communion cup was jerked from his fingers with the words, "We take from thee, thou Judas, this cup of salvation!"

The reply of Hus was distinctly heard this time: "But God does not take it from me. I shall drink it today in His Kingdom."

Soldiers placed on his head a tall fool's cap decorated with a picture of three devils fighting for his soul, and marched him to the place of execution. A thousand soldiers cleared the way for the procession. They passed a huge bonfire where Hus could see copies of his precious books being burned. The whole scene, the mock trial, the false accusations, the robes put upon him and the public execution are reminiscent of the unjust trial of Jesus. His writings during imprisonment to encourage and instruct his disciples reminds us of the apostle Paul. A man who would later become a Pope admitted that "not a word escaped Hus which gave indication of the least weakness."

They took Hus to an open field outside the city, as the Romans had taken Jesus outside the city to His crucifixion, tied him with wet ropes to a stake in the ground and piled straw and wood around him. He was given one last chance to recant his heresies. "I shall die with joy," he declared, "in the faith of the gospel which I have preached."

At the clap of an officer's hands, the burning torch lit the straw and flames engulfed him. Hus began to sing one of the chants of the Church: "Christ, Thou Son of the Living God, have mercy upon me!" And so, upon "a chariot of fire," the spirit of John Hus rose to heaven on July 6th, 1415. To prevent his followers from keeping any of his remains as relics, soldiers gathered his ashes and threw them into the Rhine river.

Later historians, both Protestant and Roman Catholic, agreed that Hus didn't receive a fair trial according to the procedures of the times, and that the basic content of his ideas and teachings were not heretical. But what was done was done. History can't be tidied up in some neat fashion. Far from stamping out the reform movement, the martyrdom of Hus gave it an even stronger momentum, and the basic tenets of what he taught spread all the more widely.

On my first and third trips to Czechoslovakia, I found my way to Bethlehem Chapel and spent much time there. Not a small place, it is large enough to accommodate 3000 people. I felt that I was truly on sacred ground as I walked through various museum rooms displaying historical documents and full color paintings depicting the entire life and ministry of Jan Hus and illustrating his part in the Reformation. Each painting was identified by which year the events took place. Silently, with tears blurring my eyes, I traced those events from start to finish, then sat for a long time on a stone window seat in a museum room. I pondered this slice of life from my Christian heritage. I was captivated by a huge, lifelike painting of the trial—Hus was pictured as the central figure. I was absorbed by the several graphic canvases of the execution scene. I stopped by a tiny, plain room with stone walls, more like a prison cell. On one wall was a large, ornate-lettered plaque that proclaimed "Zde bydlel Mistr Jan Hus" (Here lived Master Jan Hus). Below the words was a round, bronze relief of the profile of Jan Hus wearing an honored university professor's mortar board cap—not the heretic's cap his accusers forced him to wear before his execution. I left by way of the sanctuary again, pausing before the raised podium from which Hus loudly preached the truths of our faith in Czech. I took many pictures to remind me of that solemn experience. I wondered whether Baba had ever been there. She talked often and reverently of Jan Hus.

Some Hussite followers became militant after his martyrdom, assembled armed troops and won some resounding victories against the Roman Church. That forced the Church to negotiate with the "Czech heretics." Among the Hussite demands was for the chalice of wine to be available also to laymen during the administration of Communion, a practice heretofore forbidden by the Papal Church. (The chalice, the cup, not the cross, became the distinguishing symbol of the Reformation. I saw it displayed everywhere today on Protestant Churches, hymnbooks, prayer books and Christian literature. In Czechoslovakia, if a cross is seen, it is a Catholic symbol.) Before long, almost all of the Czech nation adhered to Hussite ideas.

In the mid-15th century, a group of Hussite Christians separated from the rest to form a congregation of brethren according to the example of the Early Church. They were non-militant, called "people with no sword," and emphasized the uncompromising following of Jesus Christ as the "Silent King" and the "Lamb of God." After ten preparatory years, they elected their first priests, calling themselves *The Unity of Brethren (Unitas Fratrum)*. Although a minority group, they deepened in many respects the original reforming concepts of Hussitism, stood for an exemplary Christian life and represented the peak of the Czech Reformation. Among their theological and cultural endeavors, the *Kralice Bible*, translated from original texts in the late 1500s, was a notable achievement. They produced many editions of hymnbooks, confessions of faith, catechisms and church orders. The Unity of Brethren represented the most significant phenomenon of Czech spiritual life in the 16th and 17th centuries.

During difficult times, the Czech Reformation received considerable spiritual support from those involved in the German Reformation. The German Christians soon found those evangelical brethren to be of like faith, so they supported the original principles of Jan Hus to subordinate all things to the obedience of the

Holy Scriptures. The publishing of the Augsburg Confession was soon followed by the Brethren Confession. After Luther's death, the Brethren resumed good contacts with the Swiss Reformation, having found the simple reformed doctrines and the presbyterian church order very close to their own concepts.

In the second half of the 16th century, the Protestants in Bohemia and Moravia came under persecution during the reign of the Catholic Habsburgs. The Counter-Reformation activities of the Roman Catholic Church grew intense and were zealously carried out by Jesuit priests. The Protestants united their factions in a consistent front of spiritual unity in the questions of faith and confession. Attempts to establish full confessional liberty and a guarantee of legal and equal rights of Protestants with Roman Catholics appeared to be succeeding. During what was later called the "Golden Age" of Christian literature, Bibles and religious evangelical books were widely published. Those hopeful times, however, only lasted about 11 years.

The Bohemian Revolt in 1618 against the Roman Catholic Habsburg Emperor, Ferdinand II, was unsuccessful and led to the outbreak of the Thirty Years' War. The evangelicals were defeated in the famous Battle of the White Mountain (which I've mentioned so often) near Prague on November 8, 1620. It was a major turning point. Religious and national liberty of the Czech people was subsequently lost for the next 300 years, although 90 percent of the Czech people at that time were of evangelical faith.

A day of bloodshed and martyrdom followed on June 21, 1621 in which 27 Protestant leaders of the revolt were executed in the Old Town Square in Prague. "A field of blood" continued for six years. The population was reduced from three million to one million by persecution and killing. Nobles who refused to renounce their faith were forced into exile, and their property was confiscated. By military power combined with Jesuit intrigues, the rest of the general population was ordered by the sword to accept the Roman Catholic faith.

The Moravian Brethren church was broken and scattered. A hundred years of continuous suffering would elapse before they would admit that their cause in their homeland was lost. They had to make the heartbreaking decision to leave their country as exiles. Their church was driven underground for the next hundred years. There was a question whether the church would ever be revived in her native land or whether it would ever be resuscitated elsewhere.

The Westphalian Peace of 1648 ended the Thirty Years' War but brought no relief to the Czechs at home or to those scattered abroad. That period of 160 years of the merciless Counter-Reformation was appropriately called the "Age of Darkness." It looked as if no Protestants would remain in the country of Jan Hus and that his martyrdom was in vain.

Nevertheless, the spark of evangelical faith within the Czech people never died. In spite of continuous persecutions, small groups of faithful Protestants called "The Quiet in the Land" or "The Hidden Seed" gathered for secret worship in remote places in forests and caves. They were spiritually cheered and uplifted by Czech preachers in exile who secretly come from neighboring Saxony, Germany and Poland. Protestants kept their Bibles and religious books hidden in secluded places to save them from the searching Jesuits and soldiers. New religious books were later printed in German lands and brought clandestinely to the faithful Czech Christians.

That was the period I described in chapter 21, reflected in my ancestors' sufferings for their faith in the area of Moravia where my grandmother, Baba, lived. My relatives told me that Bibles were sometimes baked into bread, hidden under the floor boards of their houses, under the straw in barns or buried in the fields. The elderly lady with whom we stayed during several visits to Radlice, gave me a precious, hand-printed copy of a book in Czech documenting 300 years of suffering and faithfulness to God by the people who lived in Baba's small village. Some of our family surnames appear in that record, among them a martyr for his faith from Baba's ancestry.

During that period, a brilliant Christian, Jan Amos Comenius (Komensky) came on the scene (1592-1671). As part of my Christian heritage, he is another person about whom I would have liked to write an entire book. He was a famous Czech theologian, philosopher, educationalist and pacifist who achieved worldwide fame. One of the many outstanding thinkers and leaders of the Unity of the Brethren, he was the last Czech Senior Bishop of the scattered Moravian Brethren. For half his life he was forced to live abroad as an exile, yet he became, on the ground of his outstanding writings and revolutionary teaching methods, one of the greatest men of his time. His spiritual heritage and educational innovations are still relevant and appreciated by modern educators.

Comenius started out as a poor student and a slow learner who hated school. He was so quiet and shy that some thought him to be slightly retarded. He later wrote that he suffered at the hands of cruel and thoughtless teachers, and that is the reason he determined to spend his life introducing new teaching methods. Coming from a background of the Moravian evangelical movement, from childhood he developed a deep, personal love for Jesus Christ. An intensely spiritual and highly educated man, he believed Christ could and should be seen in all knowledge, and that every academic discipline should honor Him. He had a world view based on his conviction that only a knowledge of Christ can bring peace among nations. Because he believed that the Great Commission could best be fulfilled through schools founded on the gospel in every nation, he set about training teachers who would impart to students a love for knowledge, a delight in learning and a love for God.

Living in a time of continual wars, persecutions and personal and national tragedies, time and again Comenius lost all his published books and unpublished manuscripts. Repeatedly, he had to start from scratch in his writing. He published more than 90 books in days when publishing was primitive and laborious. His works on education helped set the course of modern civilization, gave new life to the church and laid a groundwork for modern democratic movements.

Some of Comenius' pioneer contributions to education, which are echoed throughout the world in schools today, were that women should have equal opportunity for an education, (a truly revolutionary idea in his time!) that children of all classes should be educated and that a varied curriculum including history, geography, science, music, drama, civics and handiwork should be offered. He advocated the use of all five senses in the learning process and produced children's books with pictures—another startling departure from the unattractive literature of his day. He encouraged play time for children, prescribed no more than four hours a day of academic work for them and insisted on attractive, cheerful classrooms. He championed learning by doing and required children who had mastered a skill to teach younger children. Reproducing leaders by apprentice teaching from within the school was one of his goals. Time at home with one's parents was high on his list of ways for children to achieve a healthy balance in their lives. Comenius insisted on high qualifications for his teachers in morals, attitude, training, diligence and personal spirituality. He was far ahead of his times in the 16th century.

The Moravian evangelical church had a healthy spiritual birth dating from the era of Jan Hus and undergirded by Jan Amos Comenius and other reformers. But they were now diminished by unceasing persecution and oppression. Christian leadership was almost totally annihilated, martyrdom was widespread, clergy were separated from their congregations and Christians were scattered.

The church was intermixed unfavorably with the state. There was confusion of Christian values, dilution of testimony, rigid control of religion by the state and repression of all religious expression outside of Catholic worship.

Before Comenius and the small band of exiles left Moravia, God gave him a remarkable prophetic word. He encouraged his followers by declaring that the "hidden seed" of which Jan Hus spoke would grow and bear fruit *in a hundred years*. Although that seemed like a distant dream, Comenius planned a long-term strategy by dedicating his life to the Christian education of the young. He had far reaching vision and faith. Another confirming prophecy was given later that something would happen to restore the Moravian church. An 83 year old Christian, George Jaeschke, one of the few witnesses to the truth at that time, on his deathbed spoke:

"It may seem as though the end of the Brethren's Church has come. But, my beloved children, you will see a great deliverance. A remnant will be saved. I do not know whether this deliverance will come to pass here in Moravia or whether you will have to go out of 'Babylon.' But I do know it will transpire not very long hence. I am inclined to believe that an *exodus* will take place and a *refuge* will be offered on a spot where you will be able, without fear, to serve the Lord according to His holy Word."

The hundred years of which Comenius prophesied eventually passed, and God began to put the events in motion to fulfill his prophecy and that of Jaeschke!

*Count Nicolaus Ludwig von Zinzendorf, the rich,
young ruler who did say "Yes" to God*

28

The Moravians: Poured Upon and Poured Forth

God had prepared a place in which to plant the precious "Hidden Seed!" It was offered to the persecuted Moravians *outside* their own region of Moravia and in another country. I consider the story to follow of such importance to our faith that I want to share the exciting details. They are relevant to my trip to Germany in 2001 when I went to the precise locations where the events below were dramatically played out hundreds of years ago. Those happenings are part of my faith roots.

On a personal level, I recognize the loving and sovereign hand of God upon me when He saved my life at birth because He had a call on my life that was channeled through my heritage. My Czech background, my surrender to God's plan for my life, my subsequent call to missionary ministry in China—I believe that all were part of the canvas of my life on which the Divine Artist was painting. The historic faith of my fathers ran in my blood and the prayers of my ancestors have followed me. The Moravian story is part of that mosaic.

Count Nicolaus Ludwig von Zinzendorf, a wealthy young Christian nobleman and a Lutheran Pietist, opened his heart and offered his material resources to the Moravian Protestant refugees who came to his estate in Saxony, Germany. They were descendants of the Old Unity of Brethren in Moravia who would soon experience rebirth into the "Renewed Unity of Brethren" to continue the faithful legacy of the Czech Reformation.

Zinzendorf was born into a powerful European family and destined for a career in the Emperor's court. As a child, he had a passionate love for Jesus, prayed ardently, wrote love letters to Jesus and developed a deep love for the study of the Scriptures. Educated in the most prestigious schools, universities, law schools and theological institutions, he was well-traveled and able to move with ease and reputation among the highest people in society and government. As part of the Pietistic movement, he was more interested in the renewal of individuals than institutions. He wanted to apply the biblical truths of the Reformation to practical life. Personal faith and intimacy with Christ, he believed, were where sound doctrine should lead people. An outstanding man of prayer, Zinzendorf had superb writing and preaching skills and an extraordinary creative gift for composing poems and hymns. When the time came for a career decision, he turned from a life in the court to study for the ministry, viewing matters of the kingdom of God a higher calling than matters of the state. He is sometimes referred to as "the rich, young ruler who said 'Yes'" in contrast to the one who refused to follow Jesus.

His marriage to Countess Erdmuth Dorethea von Reuss, a highly educated and spiritual woman, united both of them in a lifelong commitment to advance the kingdom of God in whatever way God might lead them. His wife had remarkable abilities to manage finances and administer their extensive estates as well as all practical household and domestic matters (including their twelve children!) That freed her husband to give himself fully to the ministry. Zinzendorf was able to go on long missionary journeys abroad, some lasting for years.

God set the stage and chose the characters for a great Kingdom drama that would affect the evangelization of the world for centuries. It began with a single young Christian from Moravia named Christian David, who found his way to Zinzendorf's estate while looking for a place of refuge for his persecuted Czech brethren. He was brought up a Catholic, but pursued further truth through his study of a German Bible. That resulted in his spiritual conversion. While making evangelistic trips into Moravia to encourage the persecuted Christians, he found remnants of the Brethren who were longing for a true New Testament church. They were praying for the fulfillment of the legacy of Hus and the prophetic words of Comenius and Jaeschke that such a church would be reborn. When he found a welcome at Herrnhut, whose name meant "Under the watch of the Lord," he made ten secret and dangerous trips back over the border to bring small groups of oppressed, courageous Moravian Christians to migrate there. They totaled only about 200, later still no more than 300 people. God had appointed Christian David, like the biblical Joshua, to lead the people into a "Promised Land."

The Moravians shared the premises of Zinzendorf's estate with all sorts of other religious refugees and malcontents who took advantage of the Count's generous hospitality. The spirit of discord was everywhere in this mixed multitude, and the settlement was in danger of becoming a splintered and sectarian community. Misunderstandings, prejudices and secret divisions were common. A false teacher moved in and stirred up further trouble. Even Christian David was for a time influenced by the fanatical wrong teaching. At this critical point, the Count stepped in and declared that he would have no makers of sects on his estate.

With all their faults, he believed that the Moravian settlers were at heart broad-minded, sincere Christian people. Once the rubbish was cleared away, the gold would be found underneath. He recognized Christian David's honest heart and knew he could lead him in the right direction.

The Count asserted his authority to enforce control of the quarreling dissenters. He prayed for them with compassion and persuaded them as a father would to unity and disciplined obedience. He dealt with them firmly but lovingly, first as a unit, then going house to house to pray with and counsel each family from the Scriptures. After time and patience, a spirit of cooperation and love began to genuinely unite the people. With the leaders, Zinzendorf drafted a "Brotherly Agreement" between the people and the Lord. They elected responsible leadership by elders, then the people were divided into affinity groups to care for one another's needs, to study the Bible and pray.

About this time, a pivotal event happened. Zinzendorf discovered in the archives of a German library an ancient copy of the constitution of the *Unitas Fratrum* written by Jan Amos Comenius. This confirmed to him that the Moravian Brethren were historically a "fully established church" and even predated the establishment of his Lutheran Church. He was amazed at the similarities between that document and their recently adopted "Brotherly Agreement." After translating parts of it, he shared it enthusiastically with the Moravians, including his discovery of the prophecy of Comenius regarding the one hundred year span of time until the Church's rebirth. *The time had come!* Zinzendorf and the Moravians were inspired and encouraged with a new sense of God's destiny for them as they traced the hand of God that had so obviously and sovereignly brought them to that moment in time.

The Moravian forebears of these refugees had been pure and bold upholders of the faith. Now this remnant group rediscovered their godly roots while in exile. Recognizing the guidance of God in their history, they re-embraced the solid, biblical beliefs and lifestyle of their spiritual fathers in the historic Church of the Brethren. Although the Count was actually not a part of their group, he resolved, "As far as I can, I will help bring about this spiritual renewal. Though I have to sacrifice my earthly possessions, my honors and my life, as long as I live, I will do my utmost to see to it that this little flock of the Lord shall be preserved for Him until He comes." Thus an outside leader, by God's enlightenment, recognized the destiny of a people. God used him as a channel for its protection, renewal and missions outreach.

A loving unity began to solidify the Herrnhut community. The presence of the Holy Spirit was heavy among them. The leaders began to visit each house to share Christ with the families and prepare them for the Communion service which was to celebrate their unity, not achieve it. It was to be their first Communion since the new realization of their destiny. A hushed sense of anticipation settled over the people.

The very men who had been called a nest of scheming dissenters now formed little groups for intense prayer and praise to God. As the evening shadows lengthened across the Square, the whole settlement met to pray and praise God and fellowship with each other like brothers and sisters of one family. They came to the point of heart searching and reconciliation where everyone surrendered himself to be taught by the Holy Spirit and committed himself to follow the will of God wherever and however He would lead.

On the fifth of August, the Count spent the whole night in "watching before the Lord" in the company of about 12 or 14 of the Moravian brethren. At midnight, a large meeting was held on the Hutberg for the purpose of prayer at which great emotion toward God was expressed.

Many authors wrote about those events, their accounts confirm each other and their writings overlap. Therefore, it is difficult to continually distinguish and identify the sources in my story. I will do so only in a few cases. The quotations that follow are from various historians which I list in the resources section of this book.

An eye witness recorded, "On Sunday August 10th about noon, while Pastor Rothe was holding the meeting at Herrnhut, he felt himself overwhelmed by a wonderful and irresistible power of the Lord and sank down to the floor before God. With him sank down the whole assembled congregation in an ecstasy of feeling. In this frame of mind, they continued until midnight, engaged in prayer and singing, weeping and supplication."

Dr. J. Kenneth Pfohl, a Moravian pastor, wrote in *The Moravian*, "The great Moravian Pentecost was not a shower of blessing out of a cloudless sky. It did come suddenly, as suddenly as the blessing of its greater predecessor in Jerusalem when the Christian Church was born. Yet for long there had been signs of abundance of rain, though many recognized them not. In short, the blessing of August 13th was diligently and earnestly prepared for. We know of no annals of Church history which evidence greater desire for an outpouring of the Holy Spirit and more patient and persistent effort in that direction than those of our own church between the years 1725 and 1727.

"Two distinct lines of preparation and spiritual effort for the blessing are evident. One was prayer, the other was individual work with individuals. We are told that men and women met for prayer and praise at one another's homes, and the Church of Berthelsdorf was also crowded out. Then the Spirit came in great power. The entire company experienced the blessing at one and the same time."

The outpouring of the Holy Spirit upon the group (or the baptism in the Holy Spirit, as many historians refer to it) took place at the 11 o'clock Communion service. Not only were the Christians renewed and empowered, but people were saved both during the meeting and subsequently.

Eyewitnesses reported, "The sense of awe was overpowering. As the Brethren walked down the slope, [from Herrnhut to the Berthelsdorf Church] all felt that the supreme occasion had arrived. All who quarreled in days gone by made a covenant of loyalty and love. At the door of the Church, the strange sense of awe was thrilling. They entered the building and the service began. The 'Confession' was offered by the Count, two young girls were confirmed and the congregation knelt to sing: *My soul before Thee prostrate lies, to Thee, its source, my spirit flies.*

"Then, at one and the same moment, all present, rapt in deep devotion, were stirred by the mystic, wondrous touch of a power which none could define or understand. There, in Berthelsdorf Parish Church, they attained at last the firm conviction that they were one in Christ. There, above all, they believed and felt that on them, as on the disciples at the Day of Pentecost, had rested the purifying fire of the Holy Ghost."

Count Zinzendorf summarized the happenings, "...It was a sense of the nearness of Christ bestowed in a single moment upon all the members present; it was so unanimous that two members at work 20 miles away, [among them Christian David, who was fulfilling his work assignment] unaware that the meeting was being held, became at the same time deeply conscious of the same blessing." Emotional aspects were not foremost. The Count commented, "The whole movement was calm, strong, deep and abiding."

Some of the manifestations listed by historians were "signs and wonders....During the singing, there was great weeping of repentance and joy....They were conscious during the singing meetings of a strange, overwhelming power....Prayer often continued until after midnight....It passed into continual praise....There was great grace in the whole neighborhood....Each of us in great measure was lifted up beyond himself...." It is recorded that the sense of revival continued for four years following the initial outpouring of the Holy Spirit.

"On that day," wrote the Count, "the Savior permitted to come upon us a Spirit of whom we had hitherto not had any experience or knowledge. Hitherto we had been the leaders and helpers. Now the Holy Spirit Himself took full control of everything and everybody. These members were all laity, though at a later time, ministers and missionaries, deacons, presbyters and bishops arose out of the wonderfully blessed assemblage...yet in another sense, they were all ministers of Christ, 'a holy priesthood....'"

"The entire congregation was youthful. Zinzendorf was only 27, and if a census had been taken, it would have been found that his age was approximately the average of the whole company. Throughout the story of the early labors of the Renewed Church, we are impressed with the comparative youth of the men and women who made such wonderful ventures of faith for Jesus Christ."

Another wrote, "The breezes of the Spirit pervaded at that time equally upon young and old....The spirit of prayer and supplication poured out upon the children was so powerful and efficacious that it is impossible to give an adequate description of it in words....The spiritually awakened children began a plan of intercessory prayer similar to the adults...." The girls met in one place and the boys in another. On one occasion after the outpouring, they met from 10 at night until one the following morning praying, singing and weeping on the Hutberg.

A later event took place in 1741 that set its seal on the chief characteristic of the Moravians—devotion to the Lord Jesus. Leonhard Dober had for some years been the chief elder (the title is the Eldest) of the Church. He and others felt that his special gifts fitted him more for other work. But as the Brethren in synod looked around, they felt it would be difficult to find a suitable person to fill his place.

A historian wrote, "At once the thought was suggested to many to ask *the Savior* to be the Eldest of His little Church. In answer to prayer, they received the assurance that He would accept the charge. Their one desire was that He would do all that the chief elder hitherto had to do—would take them as His special possession, concern Himself about every member individually and care for all their needs. They promised to love and honor Him, to give Him the confidence of their hearts, to know no man as head in the things of the Spirit, and as children, to be guided by His mind and will.

"On November 13th, they had an inauguration day 'for our dear and tenderly beloved Sovereign and Eldest....The impression was so deep that at first great stillness fell upon all, which soon changed into tears of wonder and joy....The Church had now attained its maturity."

How should they conserve the blessing that they so wonderfully received? For that purpose, a few days after the outpouring of the Spirit, the Brethren began a system of Hourly Intercession that remained unbroken for one hundred years. That is what enabled them to maintain their deep spiritual life and gave them power for world evangelism. Their concern was, "To see that the blessing was not lost....As the fire on the altar in the Jewish Temple was never allowed to go out, so the Brethren resolved that in this new temple of the Lord, the incense of intercessory prayer should rise continually day and night. Henceforth, Herrnhut in very truth should be 'the Watch of the Lord.' The whole day was carefully mapped out and each brother or sister took his or her turn. Of all the prayer unions ever organized, surely this was one of the most remarkable."

Another reason for continual prayer was because they recognized "how needful it is that our Church, which is yet in its infancy and has in Satan such a mighty enemy, should guard itself against one who never slumbers day or night and have an unceasing holy watch kept against him. We resolved, therefore, to light a freewill offering of intercession which should burn night and day, leaving the matter for the present to God's working in the hearts of the Brethren.

"By August 26th the plan had ripened. Twenty-four brethren and an equal number of sisters engaged each to spend an hour, as fixed for them by the 'lot,' to bring before God all the needs and interests of those around them. They could pray in their own room or wherever else they might be. The number was soon increased. But we wished to leave everything to free grace and have nothing forced, so we agreed that when anyone from poverty of spirit or special business could not spend the whole hour in prayer, he might instead praise God in spiritual songs and so bring the sacrifice of praise or of prayer for himself and all saints. These watchers unto prayer met together once a week, at which time all news received from far or near concerning the need of persons, congregations or nations was communicated. The purpose was to stir them to praise for answers given and lead to more hearty and definite prayer."

The 24 hour prayer chain became known as "The Hourly Intercession." Prayer of that intense and disciplined kind always leads to action. In this case, it kindled a burning desire to make Christ's salvation known to the unevangelized. In the months following the revival, "some of the Brethren were continually going to places near and more distant preaching the love of Christ. Their thoughts were continually occupied with the object for which God had so blessed them." That led to the beginning of modern foreign missions.

The Count divided the people into age and stage of life classifications called "choirs," (not in a musical sense) so they could concentrate on Christ and His work at their level. For example: married people, single brethren, widows, widowers, youths, the older girls, the younger boys, the younger girls, etc. The purpose was division, organization, efficiency and order. He declared, "For each class the Master has a special message, therefore each class must have its special meetings and study its special duties. Each has its own president, special services, festival day, love feasts, etc."

The Count's characteristic was compassion. He shed tears. He cared. His love for God burned in Him and burned out to the people. His leadership was fatherly, strong, definite and persistent. He presented to the people the needs of the fields of the world as they came to his attention. "He stood in communication with all parts of the world and did not fail to communicate what he heard. He had a tender, childlike passionate love for Jesus. His love melted the people into one body. A historian wrote, "The Count had an intense sense of the need and value of fellowship. He found himself multiplied in each one." Zinzendorf believed, "Men become interested not so much in abstract ideas as in individuals who represent their ideas. Victories are won because men follow some leader whom they have learned to love...."

The Count was, in a unique way, an instigator in thrusting the Moravians out in missionary witness. "He was a man of intense missionary zeal. As the woman who found the lost piece of silver invited her friends and neighbors to share in her joy, so he wished all Christians to share in the treasure (the Moravians) which he had discovered on his own field—at Herrnhut. He believed that the Brethren were called to a worldwide mission. 'I have no sympathy,' he said, 'with those comfortable people who sit warming themselves before the fire of the future life.' So he brought before the now Spirit-filled Moravians, information about the needs of the nations of the world and allowed the Spirit to touch their hearts with specific calls. Then he stepped back to watch the Lord 'thrust the laborers into His harvest.'"

Monthly Saturday meetings were scheduled to hear reports of evangelistic work in other districts given by traveling missionaries or visitors from some distant land. "It fostered broadness of mind and put an end to spiritual pride. They rejoiced to hear of the good done by others. They prayed not only for their own narrow circle but for all rulers, all churches and all people that on earth do dwell. The Count was the missionary catalyst for the Moravians at those Saturday missionary meetings. There he was in his element. He would keep his audience enthralled for hours at a time. First he would read them a piece of news in a vivid, dramatic style. Then he would suddenly strike up a missionary hymn. Then he would give them a little more information. Thus he taught them to take an interest in lands beyond the sea."

During the first ten years, young Moravian missionaries went to St. Croix, Greenland, Surinam, Guinea, South Africa, Lapland, Algeria, Ceylon, Romania, Constantinople and North and South America. Before long, they had gone to nearly every country in Europe and on to Asia and Africa. Their first mission was to the Negroes in the West Indies, only five years after the outpouring of the Spirit.

Despite extremely difficult and primitive means of travel and communication, no modern media and small financial resources, they gave birth to the modern missionary movement 50 years before William Carey, who was influenced by the example of the Moravians. Those youthful missionaries were not highly trained academically, other than through the School of the Holy Spirit and disciplined Christian living in a closely knit community at Herrnhut. That was the part of the Body of Christ which gave them birth and supported them in every way.

Their example directly or indirectly influenced such prominent men of God as George Whitfield and John and Charles Wesley who, in turn, possibly kept the French Revolution from England through the revivals they sparked. Those spiritual awakenings influenced the revivals in America and elsewhere and stemmed the tide of evil for several generations.

Andrew Murray, the missionary statesman, suggested, "If the appeal to the example of the Moravian Brethren is to exercise any influence and the Church be aroused to follow their footsteps, we must find out: 1) what the principles were that animated them, 2) where they obtained the power that enabled them to do so much and especially 3) how God fitted them for doing that work. We cannot have like effects without like causes. As the conditions of their successes are discovered, the cause of failure in the Church of today and the path to restoration may be found."

What were some of the reasons those Moravians made successful missionaries?

Historically, the Moravians had been a disciplined church, solid in their stand on the Word of God, wholeheartedly devoted to Christ and brought through the crucible of great and prolonged suffering and persecution. However, it was not their doctrine but their life; not their theory but their practice that gave them such power.

Instructions given to their missionaries can be summarized in one sentence—to see and be led by the Spirit in all things. They set off on foot with nothing but a few shillings in their pocket but strong in the faith of God and His care. One of their principles in missions was not to interfere with other men's labors; thus they were found evangelizing on the outskirts of society, to peoples unreached and uncared for. They went to the remote and unfrequented wilderness motivated by their love for the Lord.

Moravian missionaries were sent to wherever others were not willing to go. They understood that their mission was to break up the ground and sow the seed so others could continue to water and reap. They never competed with other works in the same location. They were content even to turn over their work to other denominations who would continue it. They happily moved on to unreached areas. Their goal was not to establish the Moravian Church as a large denomination. Mass evangelism was not their method; they dealt with one person at a time. Count Zinzendorf taught them the principle of looking for a heart already prepared by the Holy Spirit, then patiently planting the seed of the gospel there.

Their motivation was clear. "Making the Lord's suffering (Isaiah 53:10-12) the spur of all our activity, our missionary battle cry is: 'To win for the Lamb that was slain, the reward of His sufferings.' We feel that we must compensate Him in some way for the awful sufferings which He endured to obtain our salvation. The only way we can reward Him is by bringing souls to Him. When we bring Him souls, that is compensation for the travail of His soul. In no other way can we so effectively bring the suffering Savior the reward of His passion as by missionary labor, whether we go ourselves or enable others to go. Get this burning thought of 'personal love for the Savior who redeemed me' into the hearts of all Christians and you have the most powerful incentive for missionary effort."

The targets of their missionary burden were simultaneously their own Moravian countrymen in their homeland, (later called Czechoslovakia) people of the land in which they had taken refuge (Germany) and cross-culturally the people of all nations—in the same pattern as the Early Church was commissioned by the Lord after its Pentecost.

The Moravians themselves were literally strangers and pilgrims on earth, so they had a detachment from the world and its hopes. They knew how it felt to be refugees and homeless, were familiar with the thought and spirit of sacrifice, had experience in enduring hardship and looking to God alone in every trouble. Add to this, the discipline they inherited as a lifestyle from their ancestors and to which they were led to yield themselves so completely at Herrnhut. They were rooted in the view that to the Christian, his faith is the all important thing. Everything is secondary to the one great consideration—to know and do the will of God and walk in the footsteps of Jesus Christ. For the sake of this, they were ready to submit to the care and correction of those appointed to watch over them. Their fellowship made them strong; when they were sent out, they were ready to help each other, to depend upon and to submit to one another.

God prepared them well. They weren't hasty. They met together for nearly five years from the time of the first outpouring of the Spirit to the time the first missionaries went out. During that time, they were continually worshiping the Son of God, offering themselves to Him and waiting for Him to make known what He would have His Church do. Each one held himself in readiness to go or to support those who went. They continued in the experiences of the deep move of the Holy Spirit during the following years. A historian wrote, "This was mostly when they gathered in prayer before the Lord. Because of their strong belief in direct answers to prayer, they customarily used the 'lot' to make decisions. Once the 'lot' has been consulted, everyone accepted the decision as absolute and binding. Prayer had been answered, the Lord had spoken and the servant must now obey."

The above events in Herrnhut happened over 275 years ago. The connection to Jan Hus was still more distant, almost 600 years ago. What does this have to do with the contemporary Christian missions enterprise or with me personally? What had God laid on my heart as a result of this research into my Christian roots?

I encountered many references to the Moravians while doing research for other books I have written. For my book *Powerlines*, published by *Christian Publications, Inc.*, I noted recurring references to the Moravians by Bible teachers, evangelists and revivalists of past generations, even to the present day. The example of the Moravian Christians apparently influenced many of them.

John Wesley's conversion was in the context of meeting

Moravian missionaries on a ship to America. He went on to found the Methodist movement. William Carey was stirred to foreign missions work by their example and used the Moravian experience as a model. He often referred to them for inspiration. Andrew Murray devoted a chapter to the Moravian revival in his major book, *The Key to the Missionary Problem,* which I contemporized before its republication by *Christian Literature Crusade.* In my research for writing the biography: *Andrew and Emma Murray, An Intimate Portrait of Their Marriage and Ministry,* published in 2000 by *Christian Publications, Inc.,* I found significance in Murray's desire, after having written 240 books, to write one more book in his latter years. He wanted to write about the outpouring of the Holy Spirit upon the Moravians and Count Zinzendorf's involvement! After having gathered many resources, Murray died before he could write it.

I believe today's worldwide Church stands at a crossroads of history and will face end-times prophetic events either with spiritual impotence or with mighty power that only a fresh outpouring of the Holy Spirit can provide. That revival or outpouring could catapult today's Christians into a final missionary thrust of a magnitude hitherto unknown. As 21st century Christians, we can glean valuable transferable spiritual principles from the Moravian Christians for our modern era of missions.

Today we have incredible transportation and communication ease and multi-technological resources for world evangelization. Limited to primitive means, in the first 20 years after the outpouring of the Holy Spirit in 1727, the Moravian Church sent out more missionaries than the entire Protestant Church in 200 years. And it kept up its spiritual impetus with success for years to come. *God's power is still the same.* A new outpouring of The Holy Spirit will enable today's Christians to do the same and "greater works than these" as Jesus promised.

******

I wanted to travel to Herrnhut, to walk that mile from its town Square to the Lutheran Church in the village of Berthelsdorf where the Moravians worshiped and where the outpouring of the Holy Spirit took place. I wanted to visit the cemetery where Count Zinzendorf, his family and the early Moravian missionaries are buried. I wanted to meet present day Moravian Christians in Herrnhut to see whether the passionate love for Christ was in any of their hearts, whether there was a vision for intercession and whether the fire for missions was still burning. *I wanted to be there exactly on August 13th, the precise date 272 years after the first defining event happened.*

God granted me that desire because it was His loving plan for me to be able to personally touch those roots of my faith! *Another chapter....*

"That which we have heard and known,
and our fathers have told us,
we will not conceal them from (our) children,
But tell to the generation to come the praises of the Lord
and His strength and the wonderful works
that He has done.
So that the generation to come might know,
even the children yet to be born, that they may arise
and tell them to their children,
That they should put their confidence in God,
and not forget the works of God."

(Psalm 78:3,4,6,7)

"Posterity will serve him;
future generations will be told about the Lord.
They will proclaim His righteousness
to a people yet unborn—for He has done it."

(Psalm 22:30,31)

29

Appointment—Herrnhut

Before I left home, I spent several months trying to establish a personal contact in Herrnhut. Jitka and I would need a place to stay for a few days over the August 13 weekend and someone to guide me to see what I wanted to see. Each contact seemed to be a blind lead, and I continued to pray for a breakthrough. Finally, in a roundabout way by one person suggesting another and that person suggesting still another possibility, I obtained an e-mail address of an unknown person in Herrnhut. God directed me to the absolutely best contact I could make—a minister in Herrnhut whose first name was Christian.

After several attempts to communicate, (I didn't understand German and Christian didn't understand English) we had some e-mail exchanges through his daughter who could e-mail me in English. To my great relief, he said he would arrange overnight accommodations for us, and he and his wife would meet us when the train to which we would have to transfer from Dresden arrived at the station in Lobau. I knew no further details.

After our intensive sightseeing in Prague, Jitka and I set off for our adventure to Germany. We were to catch the first city bus of the morning near her school, but Jitka forgot that the Saturday bus schedule was different. We were almost late for all our subsequent connections. We quickly transferred to the metro and finally half ran the rest of the way to the central train station in Prague while carrying our bags. Jitka had made reservations on the train to Dresden, and we ran the last flights of stairs to breathlessly board at the last minute before the train pulled away from the city heading north.

After a pleasant several hours riding through the countryside and small towns of the Czech Republic, then over the border to Germany, we reached Dresden. We had more than an hour layover before boarding the train to Lobau. Since neither of us spoke German, we weren't able to ask information from anyone or read the German signs in the station. None of the signs were sub-titled in English as they are in Prague. We finally located what we hoped was our Lobau connection and departure time on the huge overhead electronic board. We decided to take no chances on missing that train, so we waited on a bench close to the tracks from which it would leave. Were we to miss it, we didn't know how to use the phones in Germany nor had we been able to exchange any money to German currency. We departed on time and after more than an hour's ride, arrived at our destination. I had no idea what Christian and his wife looked like nor did they know what we looked like.

God prepared the way for us. I spotted a tall, heavy set German man with a neatly trimmed beard and a lady at his side. They were anxiously looking over the passengers getting off. They welcomed us warmly, took our bags and ushered us to their small German car. We depended on Christian's wife, Maren, with her limited English, for our communication. After about a half-hour's drive through the countryside, much like our Virginia countryside but without mountains in the distance, we reached Herrnhut, still a small town of about 700. Many of the surrounding towns are larger and older, dating back to the 1500s. I had to pinch myself to realize that I was actually at the location of the events that had become so familiar through my research. I wanted to absorb all the historic atmosphere and pile up the memories to think about later.

We arrived at their large, multi-storied home on August-Bebel Street, which they called "The Herrnhut House of Prayer." It may have been built centuries ago but was beautifully renovated for modern living. All houses on the block had window boxes with flowers in abundance and lace curtains at the windows. The ground level of The House of Prayer served as a meeting place for their church. Folding chairs were set up, instruments were in place for a music ministry, and we noticed an elaborate sound system. Adjoining was a large, attractive dining room, modern kitchen, bathrooms, all tastefully furnished and cheerfully decorated. Off to one side was a room being remodeled as a prayer chapel. Several other rooms served as Christian's study, library and smaller meeting or study rooms. On the next level were living quarters for Christian's family, which included a son in his early 20s and a daughter who was a senior in high school. All rooms were spotlessly clean and well-furnished. A winding staircase led us up another level to several modern apartments which they keep available for Christians who came from all over the world individually or in a group specifically for Prayer or Intercession Conferences.

Jitka and I had separate rooms with a fully equipped, up-to-date kitchen, dining area and modern bathroom. We felt we were in the lap of luxury! Fresh flowers were in vases and fresh fruit and little dishes filled with candies and cookies were on the table. Maren told us to help ourselves from a stocked refrigerator and cupboards of food. She soon appeared with fresh bread and

387

buns, milk and more fresh vegetables, cheese and cold cuts. Nothing was lacking in their generous hospitality.

After giving us time to freshen up, Maren invited us down to their apartment for tea and coffee which turned out to be almost a lunch. We met their son and daughter, who could speak passable English, and served as my interpreter when I eagerly asked Christian many questions. After our tea, Christian said he had arranged for an English speaking young student from Australia, who was studying at a Bible school in Holland, to be our interpreter. Christian himself would take us around Herrnhut on a tour of historic places. My anticipation mounted.

A light mist began to fall and a chilly wind greeted us as we left on our tour. I tape recorded the explanations and took pictures everywhere in spite of the unusually blustery and overcast weather. We walked across several streets and along cobblestone sidewalks to the town Square where the Moravian Church stood. It was almost in sight of Christian's house. Christian confirmed many things I learned from my research, but added much background, human interest and new information which made the historic events come alive to me.

At the Square under shade trees, a bust of Zinzendorf overlooked a garden. I paused before it, remembering the nobility, the strength and vision of this rich, young, estate owner who dared to give asylum to those some called homeless "riff-raff" from Moravia. God opened his eyes to view them through His eyes. He understood that God chose him to help transform those people, with the Holy Spirit's empowering, into one of the most dynamic and strategic missionary groups since the Early Church. His estate, the very place where I was standing, would be the launching pad for this missionary outreach. Far from resembling a somber monastic community of celibates, the historic Moravian community was largely made up of laity—men and women who married and raised families. They were nicknamed "God's Happy

People." Everyone considered himself a missionary available to go overseas or to support by financial means and prayer those who went. The spread of the Christian message throughout the world was their common objective.

Not satisfied simply to encourage the Moravian settlers to go to abroad with the gospel, Zinzendorf himself went to many foreign lands, including colonial America. While there, he legally renounced his royal titles as a nobleman because he found them a hindrance to his witness to the Indians and the colonists. Benjamin Franklin and the Governor of Pennsylvania witnessed that ceremony which was conducted in Latin. He wanted to approach everyone as their equal. Slave converts, Indian converts, all were regarded the same in fellowship and leadership. Even his own denomination severely criticized and opposed Zinzendorf for allowing women to preach and hold leadership roles in the church, but he held fast to his convictions on biblical grounds.

We walked around looking at the remains of some of the buildings that had been burned or bombed in the war. Christian took us into the large, beautiful Moravian Church meeting house furnished very simply but with a grand pipe organ in the balcony. At intervals during our tour, we heard the church bell ringing the hours and half hours. All the homes, church meeting houses and community buildings were built within a short walking distance of the Square for the convenience of early Moravians who met for five or six meetings a day.

It had begun to rain and the wind picked up as Christian led us down another road toward the outskirts of town. When we arrived at the Moravian cemetery, I was shivering and chilled to the bone without a heavy jacket or umbrella, but I was willing to endure anything just for the wonderful privilege of being in this celebrated place. We walked the grassy rows between hundreds of flat gravestones while reading aloud the names and dates of so many people about whom I studied. I brushed the leaves off the markers to see them more clearly—Leonhard Dober, David Nitschmann (the first two missionaries to go to St. Thomas in the West Indies in 1732). Nearby were markers of Christian David, the Zinzendorfs and even some of the native converts from far-away places who returned with the missionaries. I knew I was on sacred ground. Those young Christians, constrained by the sacrifice of Christ and their fervent love for Him, went gladly to the toughest places under the most deplorable conditions. Dober and Nitschmann were willing to sell themselves as slaves when they found out that was the only way to gain access to the slaves on St. Thomas. Of the 18 who went to that first mission field, half of them died within the first nine months. The more who died, the more who volunteered to replace them.

With the exception of the Zinzendorf family, people were not buried next to the graves of their family members. They were buried according to the Moravian custom--in the order in which they died. None was honored more or less in this cemetery. All were equal.

Before we left the cemetery, Christian led the way for us to climb the spiral staircase to the circular mezzanine at the top of a wooden watch tower built in 1790 which overlooked Herrnhut, the surrounding villages and the rolling countryside. The warm sun came out briefly, and from this vantage point, we could see all the way beyond the southeastern border of Germany into The Czech Republic and as far as Poland. Christian informed us that contrary to what some thought, this was not a prayer tower. The hundred year continuous prayer vigil was carried on elsewhere, wherever Moravian Christians lived or worked. Each prayed at the hour designated for him regardless of where he was. Nor did they have long lists of requests to pray for, he said. They spent the time in the presence of God with worship, praise, singing, intercession or however God led them.

Such round-the-clock prayer sustained the fires of evangelism and supported the missionaries who went to faraway places. Their motto was: "No one works unless someone prays." Christian said the idea for nonstop prayer actually began with the zeal of the children after the August 13th revival. At four o'clock in the summer and five o'clock in winter, a watchman's song awakened the town, and everyone assembled in the Great Hall for morning prayers and singing.

That evening we joined the regular Saturday night "Singing" held in the Church meeting house for all ages of Moravians in the community. Christian's daughter accompanied us and instructed us to slide along the polished wooden pew to sit close to other people with no gaps between. It was a Moravian tradition that demonstrated close fellowship in Christ with no distance between anyone. The walls, ceiling, pews and all furnishings were painted in gloss white with no decorations. The windows were plain without any stained glass. For an hour the congregation sang one hymn after another from the hymnbook without interruption. The sequence and number were indicated on a leaflet we received as we came in.

They sang traditional hymns in German which seemed familiar to everyone but totally unfamiliar to me. The Moravian church has a rich store of hymnody, many of the songs composed by Zinzendorf himself, who was a gifted poet from his youth. It is said that he often composed a new hymn of many verses, all rhymed in German, while a worship service was in progress. By the time the congregation finished singing one verse, he would lead them in another newly composed verse. He was said to have extemporaneously sung many "spiritual songs" under the guidance of the Holy Spirit.

An organist accompanied the Saturday "Singing." A lady, perhaps a Moravian deaconess, sat behind a plain table at the front of the large auditorium, although she didn't seem to be leading the singing. I tape recorded the hour for my memories.

Christian told me many details that weren't found in the research books I read. He had come upon old books in the attic of the archives building, some of which dated back to the early days of Herrnhut, from which he was discovering new information. He even found a handwritten list of the hours and names of the early intercessors who lived in the Sisters' house. Christian was searching for information that might have been overlooked by early historians in order to write a book himself. He told me there were records of some prophecies from the early days of the settlement which came to pass in later years. Herman Heitz, the manager of Zinzendorf's estate, who initially welcomed the Moravian refugees, expressed a prophetic word about their future on the day Christian David felled the first tree to build the first house. Christian spoke of finding records of signs and wonders and manifestations of the Holy Spirit experienced by the Herrnhut Christians.

Some of the gifts of the Holy Spirit listed in the New Testament were apparently exercised in the normal course of the lives of Herrnhut Christians—especially in Count Zinzendorf's experience. It was recorded that God often gave him the gift of special, intuitive knowledge about situations. He seemed to hear from God in an intimate way. When asked what his experience was in that regard, Zinzendorf said that when faced with a decision or a need to know about some problem, he would first search his own heart before God to see whether he had any sin that would hinder hearing God's voice. If the Lord revealed some sin to him, he would immediately confess it, repent and be assured of God's forgiveness. When all was clear before the Lord, he would ask God how to solve the particular problem and often received remarkable wisdom. If God didn't give him the solution, he said, God nevertheless gave him great peace about it as he trusted the matter into God's hands. Christian gave me several examples of situations involving the exercise of Zinzendorf's special gift which turned up in his research.

I asked Christian why some of those stories never came to light before. He said that in the early years, the leaders felt that outsiders wouldn't understand. Zinzendorf was meticulous in keeping diaries or journals of everything that happened throughout his life. But he ordered all his personal diaries destroyed before his death, particularly those describing detailed events and experiences at Herrnhut during the outpouring of the Holy Spirit. The reason again: apparently he thought people wouldn't believe or would misunderstand, especially since he was still part of the traditional Lutheran Church.

I thought it strange when Christian told me that the Russians senselessly burned the Moravian church and other main buildings in the heart of Herrnhut *after* the war was over. The little town had no political, military or economic significance, but on the last day of World War II, it was captured by the Soviet Army. Christian explained that when the soldiers arrived, no men were left in the town to defend it. Therefore, the few people who had not fled could offer no resistance. The Russian soldiers got drunk during the night and probably didn't even know what they were doing or just wanted some entertainment. They deliberately set fire to the buildings and destroyed so much history.

Why would God allow such a thing, I wondered. Christian's opinion was that it could have been God's judgment on the Moravian church. He said that one possible reason God may have lifted His hand of protection from them was because the Moravians had not courageously taken a clear stand against the Nazis. Moreover, they were silent about Hitler's persecution of the Jews.

I was still looking for some answers. Why did the hundred year prayer vigil stop? Was it by a deliberate decision of the Moravian Church or was it simply dropped from lack of motivation or waning fervor of devotion to God and their original vision? Has the Moravian blazing fire for missions outreach continued with the same zeal as in the first hundred years? Is there any correlation between the two? Christian said he was still looking into the annals of their church history for the answers. He shared some keen insights with me that were relevant to my other questions. I concluded that my own research is not finished—I have more homework to do.

As the bell tolled the hour again, it reminded Christian to tell us the story of the bell. The only part of the Moravian church building that remained after the devastating fire was the bell tower we were now looking at in the courtyard. The three original bells were carried off by the Germans to melt down for military use. After the war ended, the Moravian Christians hoped that at least one bell would be recovered. They were overjoyed to find one in another part of Germany. They knew it was authentic because of the quotation by Zinzendorf inscribed on it. It was clearly a prophetic word: "Herrnhut should only continue as long as the purposes of God go forth unhindered." That was the bell we heard tolling today, restored in the old bell tower that was left intact. "This may throw some light on your unanswered questions," Christian offered.

The night before my memorable adventure in Herrnhut ended, Christian and Maren came up to our apartment and I had the privilege of laying my hands on both of them to bless them and pray for the strategic ministry God has committed to them. Christian shared his clear vision from the Lord to expand their ministry of the Herrnhut House of Prayer in order to welcome more groups of intercessors from all over the world who are led to come to this small, historic town to renew their spiritual lives. His burden is that they will carry the vision of reinstating the round-the-clock prayer vigil to their own churches.

Christian and his present day Moravian Christian group in Herrnhut believe such sustained worldwide prayer may once again thrust God's messengers from every nation to every nation to spark a glorious, end-times revival before the return of Jesus Christ.

They are asking God for faith, favor and funds to purchase the large hospital facility just off the Square in Herrnhut for an expanded House of Prayer to accommodate larger groups. There would be ample space there for more meeting rooms, dormitories, apartments, kitchens, dining rooms, library, prayer and study rooms and auditorium. The building is for sale because the hospital will relocate to another town. That structure happens, in the providence of God, to date back to the founding of Herrnhut—it is the original Moravian "Brothers House" exactly where the hundred year prayer vigil began!

The next morning at dawn, Christian and Maren drove us to our train where we had a tearful parting. We had grown to love one another in a short weekend because our hearts were spiritually knit together.

I was full of gratitude to God for granting me this experience of a lifetime to personally touch another aspect of my Christian roots—*roots that were sprouting again. Ancient wells of revival were beginning to flow again!*

> *"Bless the Lord, O my soul;*
> *and all that is within me,*
> *bless His holy name.*
> *Bless the Lord, O my soul,*
> *and forget none of His benefits;*
> *Who pardons all your sins;*
> *and heals all your diseases;*
> *Who redeems your life from the pit;*
> *and crowns you with love and compassion;*
> *Who satisfies your years with good things,*
> *So that your youth is renewed like the eagle. "*
>
> (Psalm 103: 1-5)

30

View from the Summit

The top of a mountain should be the best place to see the entire 380 degree panorama of life. The look backward should be satisfying—not proud, not disappointing, but grateful. The look around should be one of contentment and joy. The look ahead should be exhilarating with anticipation. *That is largely true of my life as of this writing in the latter half of my seventh decade.*

Being at the *summit* also implies *summary*—what I learned from the long, steep climb. If I can't summarize what I learned, 75 plus years were a wasted trip. But since the Lord has been my Master Teacher, I learned a lot.

A children's song goes something like this, if I remember correctly:

"The bear went over the mountain...(repeat)
...to see what he could see...(repeat)."
(Next verse) "The other side of the mountain
...was all that he could see...." (repeat)

Early in life, I decided I didn't want to be like that frustrated, disappointed bear who wasted his time and energy on such a climb only to find nothing at the top—or on the other side. I would try to evaluate my life as I went along to be sure I had the right goals in view, and that my ladder was leaning against the right house.

For years, I've tried to live the examined life, which Plato said was the only life worth living. I didn't want to arrive at my chronological top of the mountain with a backpack full of regrets, nor view the other side of the mountain with disillusionment, despair or dread. At intervals, at least once a year, I try to take time out to ask myself specific, searching questions and write them in a journal. My answers aren't for anyone else but God to see. He is the Searcher of hearts.

I wish I had begun that self-evaluation practice earlier. Had I done so, and continued it more regularly, I could have kept myself from taking some detours for which I do have regrets. However, I deliberately don't focus on those now. I confessed them, repented of them, turned from them and have the assurance God has forgiven me. Both God and I remember them no more. I keep moving on.

Among the questions I ask myself are:

Do I know God's purpose for my life? What talents, capabilities, skills and gifts has God given me to carry out that purpose? What have been my five specific life goals? Are they realistic, measurable and attainable? Am I certain they are God's goals *for me* to pursue? Have I been achieving my potential based on resources and opportunities God has given me? What obstacles have I faced? Are they real or imagined? What are my current limitations? Can I do anything about them, to what degree have I come to terms with them, or am I accepting them joyfully? How does God measure success, am I in line with that, or do I try to live up to my own or other people's standards? Do I define my self-worth in terms of my productivity and accomplishments or my character? What cause, issue or calling am I passionate about? Is it from God, from my own ambition, or imposed by others? Am I more concerned about personal satisfaction and happiness or how I can serve and encourage others? What are the darkest events or periods of my life? Did I grow through them or did they set me back? Do I see God's hand in them for my good?

The closer I came to the top of my chronological mountain, the more time-sensitive my self-evaluation became. I began to ask myself:

From the perspective of an average life span, how many physically, mentally and spiritually productive or alert years might realistically lie ahead? In view of that, on what priorities should I be focusing? What "things of the world" or "cares of life" hinder my pursuit of eternal values and sap my time and strength? What could I eliminate or limit? Is there anything significant I am missing in my life? Should I still go for it or accept its absence? What benefits and bonus blessings has God given me at this time of my life for which I should specifically thank Him? Is my life characterized by joy and optimism or by complaint, negativism, defeat, depression or regrets? Do I have a grateful, contented heart toward God, or am I frustrated about unfinished work, unfulfilled goals, broken dreams or unsatisfactory relationships? Is Christ truly still the center of my life, or am I focused on a cause, ministry, person or my own desires? Am I satisfied with what I have become and with what God painted on the canvas of my life?

Such questions go to the core of my authentic self, my inner person, my eternal spirit created by God. I struggle over the honesty of my answers and what they expose of my inner life. My answers stir me to redeem the time God is allotting me. Some answers cause me to shout with a grateful heart when I see how wisely God leads me, especially when I have been prone to go off on a detour. He often lovingly jerks my leash and (sometimes not so gently but firmly) guides me into His best ways. Always I am energized by God's absolute goodness and sovereign work in my life.

God has been the Potter; I have been the clay. He had something specific in mind for this insignificant, chubby little child hiding shyly behind her immigrant grandmother's apron. He worked on the clay of my life, sometimes when it was still un-yielding, or when I tried to squirm out of His hand. Sometimes the clay was broken—even while in His hands.

"...I went down to the potter's house, and there he was, making something on the wheel. But the vessel that he was mak-ing of clay was spoiled in the hand of the potter; so he remade it into another vessel, as it pleased the potter to make" (Jeremiah 18:3,4).

God gives us second chances and third and fourth chances, whatever it takes for Him to accomplish His purpose through His children. It is never too late; the clay is not ruined forever. I have made major mess ups many times. In my early years, I complained about my life, talked back to God, disliked what I thought was my misshapen lump of clay that could never amount to anything.

"Who are you, a mere man, to criticize and contradict and answer back to God...Why did you make me like this? Does not the potter have a right over the clay...?" (Romans 9:20) "Yet, O Lord, thou art our Father; we are the clay, and thou art our potter; we are all the work of thy hand" (Isaiah 64:8).

MY POTTER

Lord, You are my Potter
I am the clay
so do with me today
as You may

for You have a plan for every man
and, as All-knowing,
You can see it through.

I'm a vessel of earth
one that is made.
The price for me is paid
and Your hand is laid on me
to fashion as You will
for I am still incomplete and marred
sometimes brittle and hard.

You do not ask me
to "shape up" by myself
to be acceptable to Deity
nor do I dare question
what You are making
or criticize Your task, how long it's taking
or fret at the pressure on my clay.

I truly know and trust
that You shape me for Your pleasure
with Your touch of love
to make of me ultimately
a vessel unto honor
Your honor, glory, praise
for You are my Potter.[1]

Changing the metaphor, I was wrong when I pushed the
Master Artist's brush away, when He painted a background I didn't
like on the canvas of my life. I thought He was unfair, that I had
been short-changed in my ethnic identity, in the body He gave me,
in my family and my lack of abilities and talents. I liked other
canvases better and wanted mine to be a carbon copy (photo copy,
in today's terms). But God didn't give up on the pouting, sullen
little girl. He was painting an original which He would consider
His masterpiece because He planned it from before the founda-

tion of the world (Ephesians 1:4). There would never be another like me.

    The Master Artist's canvas is nearly complete now. The picture is taking shape as He is putting finishing touches on it. I don't know how long that will take, but He knows. This I have learned: God is not in a hurry. Radishes only take a couple of weeks to mature. Oak trees take considerably longer. God waited to put some unexpected finishing touches on my painting late in my life. He still keeps coming up with surprises—more "little happy things," bright color daubs on my canvas. He alternates with darker colors that I didn't think were necessary. But after His brush applies them, my painting is enriched. All the colors give dimension and perspective.

MY REQUEST

"God, I demand a canvas big enough
on which to paint all my ambitions.
Give me a durable piece of cloth.
Provide me with a spacious studio.
I require a complete spectrum of colors.
I must have quality oil paints.
Plenty of time is essential
to accomplish my life's masterpiece."

God provided me instead a fragile easel,
a small palette of primary water colors,
confined me in what I thought was a cramped room
without a sure promise that I'd even have
threescore and ten years
in which to emblazon my dreams
on a miniature, disposable canvas.

"That isn't fair, God!" I complained.

"My Beloved Son, in only thirty-three years

in an obscure corner of an oppressed land
among hostile people and misunderstanding friends
without media blitz or published books
reconciled heaven and earth
interpreted Eternity to man
and declared, 'IT IS FINISHED!'"

I fell at His feet ashamed of my impertinence.
"Your Majesty! Lord of my days!
Accept my praise for whatever You grant me.
Help me understand
Your perfect plan for mortal man
and for *me*
that I might accept joyfully and soberly
both my limitations and opportunities.
So teach me to number my days
that I might apply my heart unto wisdom
and learn to paint by their number."²

"Teach us to number our days and recognize how few they are; help us to spend them as we should" (Psalm 90:12 Amplified).

Because I am a writer and think in visual terms, another simile comes to mind as I stand on the summit. My life is like a box of jigsaw puzzle pieces. God gradually gives me more pieces but withholds from me the top of the box on which is pictured what the assembled pieces should look like. My picture is unique. It takes a lifetime to put it together. It is incomplete at any point, even now. Sometimes it seems as if there are too many dark pieces and they are hard for me to fit in. Where could cancer and widowhood fit in? No experience is wasted in God's picture. A lot of pieces are small and some are look-alikes, the routines of daily life. But if one piece is missing, the puzzle can't be completed.

Putting together puzzles was one of the traditional fun things we did with our family of four boys. Sometimes our pet dog would find a piece that dropped under the table and chew it up! When children are small, they start with puzzles of only a few large simple pieces. Our family worked up to puzzles of a 1000 or more pieces. Now you can buy circular puzzles, 3-D puzzles and other complicated variations. I think my life is more like those.

My puzzle will eventually be complete. "In Him [God] you have been made complete" (Colossians 1:10. "He [God] who began...will complete..." (Philippians 1:6). "I [Jesus] am the Alpha [A] and the Omega [Z], the first and the last, the beginning and the end" (Revelation 22:13).

I may not see the finished picture until God Himself fits in the final surprising piece and I view it from "the other side of the mountain" in Eternity. I will understand that every piece had its purpose and place. Without a doubt, I will see that under God's control, my life turned out just like the picture on His box.

"For I know the thoughts and plans that I have for you, says the Lord, thoughts and plans for welfare and peace, and not for evil, to give you hope in your final outcome" (Jeremiah 29:11 Amplified).

I will see then how God answered Baba's prayers for her little granddaughter and how her prayers continued to be effectual as they reached all the way to our children and grandchildren and on through the generations. Scores of years after her death, I am still influenced by her godly life and prayers.

MY PUZZLE

My life is like a jigsaw puzzle.
I don't know what the finished picture
should look like because
the pieces of my life puzzle
don't come packaged
and sealed in a cardboard box
with the picture on the cover.
I'm only given pieces to assemble.

Since many are look-alikes
sometimes I foolishly try to force them
into places where they don't fit.
The life puzzles of my friends
are not the same as mine
so they aren't much help.
It's awesome to think
that God made my puzzle unique
and that it has never-ever
been put together before!

As each year passes
the pieces fit together better—but not always.
Why so many dark pieces
when I like bright, colorful ones?
What is their meaning?
I want to see the finished puzzle
right away—now!

Only God knows
what my finished life puzzle should look like
so I think I'd better ask
for His help day-by-day
to work my life puzzle
in His perfect way!³

Dr. Phillip C. McGraw, in his best seller, *Self Matters,* offered some suggestions for self-understanding that coincided with my self-evaluation questions. He urged readers to list their ten *defining moments,* their seven *critical choices* and their five *pivotal people.* That is an excellent exercise in perceiving what defines a person. In short, what and who made me the person I am? That is what I attempted to do in writing my autobiography—one of the most rewarding, creative, meaningful "workouts" (I use the word deliberately) of my life. I am the one who benefited most from tracing God's hand on my life and on my heritage before I was born. The insights I gained give me perspective on what still lies ahead. I will adapt some of McGraw's framework into my own life summary but lump all his categories under *"Defining Choices/Events/Learnings"* and ignore how many there may be.

Looking back from my summit, I realize that all my defining moments and pivotal people have resulted from my *choices,* the *decisions* I made and their consequences.

Decision: I would choose my own direction in life. I was a strong-willed, stubborn child. I determined I would be the one to choose whose expectations I would try to meet, and they wouldn't be the expectations of my parents. From the time I was very young, I resolved to leave my hometown as soon as I grew up and go to "some other place." Perhaps it was the immigrant blood in my veins. I didn't want to pursue the settled "comfort zone" that my parents valued and urged on me. I believe God put this desire in me.

Without a doubt, a major defining choice was when I found God. That determined my entire life direction. Because of my godly generational roots, which I knew nothing about, coupled with my grandmother's prayers for her little charge, I was restless and searching from my earliest recollection. Instinctively, I seemed to know it was God for whom I was searching. He would fill the void in my young life.

I recognize now that my choice, too, was the work of the Holy Spirit. *God was actually pursuing me, but I thought I found Him.* That was still part of my insistence on self-determination. *I* wanted to decide whom I would follow. When I discovered who God really was, and what He had done for me, I was eager to submit myself to the Lordship of Jesus Christ. I surrendered my way to His without reservation and forever. That commitment gave me security and direction and, at the same time, catapulted me into a life of adventure and risk. God didn't instantly change my life, my negative attitude, my distorted view of my heritage or my low self-esteem. God accepted my surrender, turned me around in the right direction and began the process of transformation.

Decision: To finally accept myself "as is." Because I had been ultra-critical of myself, my imperfect body, my shy, introvert temperament, always comparing myself unfavorably with others, that was a pivotal decision. I found out that God loved me and accepted me unconditionally. Moreover, He fashioned in detail and according to His deliberate plan, all parts of my body while I was still in my mother's womb (Psalm 139). I was finally on the road to liking my authentic self and being comfortable with myself. I had the sense that God was in the process of changing me to the core, including my attitudes and perceptions, to align me toward His best for my life. I became a new person in Christ right away, but the outworking of that newness would take a lifetime.

Decision: To find my identity. When I was young, I struggled with that search, as most people do. It takes a lifetime because "what you will be, you are still becoming," and that is a process. Now I believe that I know who I am, and I'm at peace with that discovery. Putting it simply, from the Bible I learned that *I am who God says I am*—loved by Him, forgiven, cleansed and righteous because He made me righteous through Jesus' death on the Cross. It is not because of my goodness, the lack of it, or my works. *I can have what He says I can have* through the awesome promises in the Scriptures. God is generous and lavish in His provision of all I need. *I can do what He says I can do* by relying on His strength, channeled through me by the Holy Spirit. That has required a lifetime of serious but joyful study of the Scriptures.

Decision: To follow God's plan for my life, not mine. Before I left high school, I began to understand that God has some divine purpose for me. My sense of mission became strong and was a defining factor for my future decisions. That gave meaning to my life. Although I couldn't have defined my purpose in life in my early years, as time went on it became clearer. God Himself and what He wants to do in my life is central to my thinking, ambitions, desires and goals. I would say that I never lost the awareness of God's purpose for me, even at this latter stage of my life.

Decision: To find a world view and live by it. College was a defining period in my life when I sought for and formulated a world view based on sincere inquiry into the basis for my Christian faith. That provided me with a satisfactory frame for the picture that would be my life.

Decision: Not to care what people say or think, if I know clearly what God wants me to do. That was a major decision with far reaching consequences that flew in the face of my strong desire and need to be approved by others and accepted by my peer group. It was hard on my inferiority complex to become still more "different" when I married someone from another culture and expected to spend a lifetime identifying with it.

Decision: To stop whining about my lack of talents and gifts (forget the piano!) and accept with joy God's gift to me of creative writing. That bolstered my self-worth and enabled me to have a fruitful lifetime of service for God. In embracing my gift, developing, exercising and passing it on, I discovered not only one gift but a cluster of gifts. Writing led to speaking, teaching, traveling, publishing and other help ministries—even now I am unwrapping new gifts within that one gift from God.

Decision: I would marry and have children. That choice opened a whole world of joy. God's decision, in turn, was to give me the bonus of four wonderful sons whom I thoroughly enjoy, respect and value at every age and stage of their lives from infancy to manhood. Each one of my six foot tall "Chinese Czechers" is The Master Artist's "original," blessed and gifted by the Creator in unique ways. That led to the absolute delight in my daughters-in-law (I call them "daughters-in-love") and my ten (current count) grandchildren.

Decision: I would agree with God that my character is more important than my accomplishments. I began to understand, during my years of active ministry, that God values my *being* more than my *doing*, even if the *doing* is serving Him. I'm sure that the truism given to us Christian teens in our church: *"Only one life, it will soon be past; only what's done for Christ will last"* was well-intentioned. The basic truth is there, but the subtle difference took me a long time to understand. *We were created by God primarily to be in His presence, to communicate with Him as His highest desire for us.* He wants time with His children—to talk with them and listen to them. God did not create us primarily to be His servants. He can call ministering angels to do His work, if He wants to. God desires above all my "first love" and values time spent in His presence waiting on Him, more than busy Christian activity (Revelation 2:2-4). That doesn't demean service for God but puts it in its proper place. I am still learning this lesson.

Decision. I wouldn't—because I couldn't—be able to live up to God's standards. I discovered in my late childhood and early teens that in spite of my will power and good intentions, I could never live up to my endless good resolutions. I failed over and over. I wanted to do better, but I didn't have the power in myself to do so. I thought I had to work really hard to live up to His commandments—not only the original Ten but the thousands of others in the Bible. Then I found out from the Scriptures that being "born again" meant that God implants His new, supernatural life within me and provides me with the power to please Him. He never intended for me to conjure up my own goodness. God's Law and commandments were only meant to show me that I couldn't do it on my own. On the cross, Jesus Christ already did everything that needed to be done to pay for my sins and to obtain my salvation. It was "a done deal." I realized that truth early in life, but the process of living it out continues. God has to teach me the same difficult lesson again and again.

Overlaying that truth, there is another critical one: The filling of the Holy Spirit, as taught in Scripture, is essential for living victoriously and abundantly and serving God with power. Whatever theological terms one may use to describe that filling, God wants us to pursue it and continue in that fullness as a priority.

Decision: I accept the fact that I can't solve everything, understand everything or fix everything. I tend to try mending or correcting every situation or relationship that seems broken. A long life and watching God do His work in His own way is teaching me to relax, step back, pray, be available, but "leave the driving to God." He may want to allow people to go through some difficult circumstances to teach them His own lessons. God has not appointed me the #1 leader of His Rescue Squad. I don't have to retrieve every ball that someone drops.

Decision: I refused to live with regrets or guilt about my mistakes, failures or sins of the past or present. God wants me to view them as He does—forgiven, gone, erased, remembered no more—after I have repented and confessed them. If I don't forget them and move on, I hinder my dreams for the future. I made mistakes even in later years when I should have known better. I am still making them and still learning. God is incredibly loving and patient with me. I never ask for His justice but for His mercy. I may not be writing the last chapter in my life story yet. In fact, I may not really have reached the summit of my mountain. I am still climbing. Certainly I haven't attained, but I press on toward God's high calling in Christ Jesus (Philippians 4:12-14). The slogan is so true: "PBPWMGNFWMY" (Please Be Patient With Me, God's Not Finished With Me Yet!)

Decision: I would sacrifice whatever God wanted. But I discovered that God always more than compensates me for anything I might give up. He is a God of increase, not deprivation. Whatever sacrifices I've made are not worthy to compare with the generous "exceedingly, abundantly above all I could ask or even think" blessings that God has showered on me (Ephesians 3:20). To hold back anything from God is to lose it. To give up my life for His sake, Jesus said, is to save it (Mark 8:35). In Mark 10:29,30 Jesus promised that if anyone "left houses or brothers or sisters or mother or father or children or lands for His sake and for the gospel's sake" he would receive "a hundred times as much now in the present age and in the age to come eternal life." I have proven this true in the past, and it is still being fulfilled in my life. Jesus said that if I seek first His kingdom and righteousness, all material things I need will be added to me (Matthew 6:25). Literally true.

As only one example of God's generosity and compensation, when I left my hometown, He gave me opportunities to travel. Besides living in Hong Kong and Singapore, among other places I have been privileged to travel are Egypt, Israel, Malaysia, the Philippines, Korea, Japan, Taiwan, England, Scotland, Canada, Holland, Germany, Czechoslovakia, Thailand and extensively in China—so far. (But not to forget my roots, I try to make an annual pilgrimage back to my hometown, which I now value as a part of my rich heritage.)

Decision: Not to allow a potentially terminal illness to interrupt God's purpose for my life. When I developed cancer, a defining moment was my decision *to become a survivor not a victim*. I learned that "goodness and mercy (lovingkindness)" (Psalm 23:6) does follow us all the days of our lives through adversities, valleys of the shadow of death and other hurtful and painful experiences. Whatever has come into my life, I've learned to genuinely say, "Thanks, Lord, I needed that!" God developed compassion in me through those God-ordained events. Each such experience enabled me to write another book to minister to others who walk similar paths. My adversities launched me into new ways to encourage others. I learned to celebrate each day of life as a gift from God while He continues to give me bonus time to live, serve, write and speak.

Decision: I wouldn't let widowhood define my life. It was my choice to move forward and continue with God's assignment when my beloved husband died. God had a purpose for our lives together as a couple and for our ministry together. That purpose was completed after 46 years. Nevertheless, God still has a purpose and agenda for me as a single woman again, as a single mom and a single grandparent. He has a continuing ministry and a fulfilling life for me that was part of His original plan. I am not living in "Plan B" now. Nor am I only half a person—I am still "complete in Christ." My new status allows me to minister to others who are walking life's path alone and enabled me to write several books to help them.

Decision: To accept my Czech heritage as God's perfect arrangement. A defining event late in life was my surprising discovery, through the adventure of searching for my roots, of the meaning of my ethnic heritage and where it fit into my life puzzle. I now joyfully identify with it, value it, and understand God's sovereign intent to enrich my life through this appreciation. I began to pursue my ethnic identity more fully after Ted died because that event seemed to put some measure of closure on my total involvement with Chinese culture and ministry. I thank God, however, that while Ted was still living, we were able to share the beginning experience of exploring my Czech heritage. I knew I had his blessing in my pursuit.

If I could live life over again, would I make any radically different choices? Perhaps. I definitely wouldn't want to repeat some mistakes I've made. I might change some secondary choices. But no—I haven't regretted any of my major life decisions. I have no complaint about the colors God chose to paint on my life canvas. "Father [God] knows best."

Decision: A critical, defining choice I am making right now

is to ignore the trivial limitations of aging and live fully each day of the rest of my life. I want to live in anticipation that "The best is yet to come!" I look forward to *living on the summit.*

"O Lord, You have searched me and known me....
Even before there is a word on my tongue,
You know it completely, O Lord;
You hem me in—behind and before;
You have laid Your hand upon me;
You created my inmost being;
You knit me together in my mother's womb;
Your eyes saw my unformed body.
All the days ordained for me were written in your book
before one of them came to be.
How precious to me are Your thoughts, O God!
How vast is the sum of them!"

(Psalm 139: 1,4,5,13,16,17 NIV)

31

Living on the Summit

How then shall I live on my chronological summit for as long as God gives me life on Planet Earth?

The summit of a mountain isn't usually a plateau. I don't believe the summit of my life is a place to settle or let down my guard. As I look around my mountain top, I see more peaks to climb. My life is not yet spent—I'm still spending it, even if I have only one day left.

If I don't keep growing, climbing, moving, I will slide backward. Doctors say that this applies to both the aging body and mind. "You have to use it or you'll lose it." If I don't keep my mind alert, it will deteriorate in the same way as my body. The latest medical research gives us some previously unknown and unexpected good news. Even in older age, the neurons (nerve cells) in the brain can renew themselves and new stem cells can grow! That's not news to God—He created us with that capacity and expects us to "be transformed by the renewing of your mind" daily (Romans 12:2). Therefore, I want to push the horizons of my mind and spirit further and remain on the cutting edge of life. The more I stretch, the higher I can reach. I don't want to miss anything God sovereignly planned for me.

Suddenly, so it seems, I am the eldest in our family, the "matriarch!" That role carries with it serious responsibility. I am supposed to be wise by this time, and matriarchs should pass on their godly wisdom. Some who reach mature age unfortunately become foolish instead. I am happy in my continuity role as the *trunk* in our family tree, as the connection between the *roots* (our heritage) and the *branches* (our children and grandchildren). When I was a child, my grandmother, Baba, was the trunk and the matriarch. I was a little branch, *just a twig*. Now I feel honored to be the trunk, and I pray that I might be a strong one to support and encourage our multiple *branches* as long as I can.

At whatever season or stage of life I find myself, I want to live in it fully. Statistically, realistically and chronologically, I know I am in the last season of my life. I don't look at it as the tail end or as being in the caboose of life's train; perhaps I can say that I am in the graduating class. If I haven't reached fulfillment and satisfaction in life by now, chances are I never will. *I believe I have, and it feels good!* My cup is running over, and I'm happy to overflow on others!

Dr. V. Raymond Edman, the president of Wheaton College at the time I attended, challenged the students every semester at exam time to do everything "Not somehow, but triumphantly." Every season of life, including aging, is an exam time of some sort to which I should apply that maxim. I want to pass that exam, too. Do I dare to aim for *magna cum laude?* If my motivation is to please the Lord, why not?

When I reached my 75 year milestone a couple of years ago, I waited on God for His marching orders for "the rest of the way." Summit time is my opportunity to thank God for blessings of the *past*, celebrate the *present* and anticipate the *future*. The following is my philosophy of life at this chronological season. I shall "put my house in order" not to *retire or expire* but to *refire*. I spelled it out for myself in these major areas:

Focus on keeping the *main thing* the main thing.
Simplify my material "stuff."
Prioritize my goals and time and efforts as though I had little time left.
Anticipate that God will still give me generous time to live for, serve and glorify Him.
Obey fully and do promptly whatever God reveals as His will and purpose for me.
Keep *sowing and reaping* at the same time.
Celebrate each day as a gift from God.

That *main thing* that I shall keep in focus is to put God and His Kingdom first by coming into His presence and seeking His face each day. Then living in His presence throughout the day. I want to keep hungering and thirsting for an ever higher and deeper relationship with God, to know Him more intimately. I want to pursue the abundant life Jesus came to give (John 10:10). My priority shall be to see that I'm filled with the Spirit daily (Ephesians 3:19-21). I want to go deeper and be more serious in my prayer life and intercession in order to partner with God in accomplishing His purpose on earth as it is in heaven.

As to any "stuff" of this world, I shall hold it loosely and not let my time be taken up with acquiring it or taking care of it. For a lifetime of accumulated "stuff," I shall simplify it by gradually giving it generously away or decisively throwing it away.

To adjust my priorities, I shall *eliminate or limit* pursuits which are no longer relevant to life goals that God gave me. I shall *surrender* any cares of this world that hinder me from following the Lord fully. *I shall seek God's specific wisdom* to know where and how I should continue to press forward and where I should cut myself some slack and smell those roses. Because I'm inclined to push myself, I have to remind myself often to loosen the ropes and relax.

I shall delete the word "busy" from my vocabulary and substitute "fruit bearing." It has taken me a lifetime to learn that a flurry of activity, even self-powered service for God, is not in the mainstream of God's will. I need to discern whether or not my daily doings are bearing fruit for the Lord. In my advancing years, that distinction is all the more critical because, at best, my time is shorter than it is for those who are younger.

God expects me to concentrate on fruit bearing in my aging years (Psalm 92) instead of letting my fruit wither or dry up. In fact, He expects me to "flourish," to stay "full of sap and very green." The date palm tree is the example for us that God gave in Scripture. It continues to grow about one foot a year for the first 50 years, after which the rate still continues but more slowly. New fronds (branches) keep developing. The annual yield of dates of a single tree may reach 600 pounds, and fruit bearing continues for over one hundred years. *I want to be a date palm, too!*

I shall take time *to smell the roses* by setting aside some "be good to myself" days of quiet and enjoyment, not pushing so hard toward self-imposed deadlines and goals. That is my ongoing struggle in God's classroom of my life—even at the summit. I absolutely *love life* and want to live it enthusiastically. I'm so glad that God planned for Everlasting Life after this earthly life. Each day isn't long enough for me. I really do enjoy sleeping, but I'm eager to get up in the morning to find out what God planned for my day—but I don't mean outside activities.

It may seem strange that the exciting days to which I look forward are those I spend at home alone! (Other than my extended travel times to visit my family or related to my writing, speaking or other ministry, I'm usually happily at home.) Of course, I appreciate being with friends and family, *but I love God's silence*. I'm at peace with myself and God. I'm thrilled with entire days that I can spend quietly enjoying God's presence, not even reading or studying, simply thinking and being aware of the miracle of living. Perhaps walking in my woods and sitting by the pond. This is my time of life to smile at God and enjoy His smile of pleasure at me, just to be contented and express, "Whatever my lot, Thou hast taught me to say, 'It is well, it is well with my soul.'" [1]

Living on the summit, I shall seek rest in the Lord rather than give in to stress. REST is made up of the rearranged first four letters of STREss—the better part. People and circumstances have pressured us toward stress for a lifetime. Only God can give rest. I shall not strain and be restless for achievement, yet still press on in my chief purpose: "to glorify God and enjoy Him forever." Living on the summit, I have an opportunity to practice more fully the waiting on the Lord that enables me to mount up with wings as an eagle, to run and not be weary, to walk and not faint (Isaiah 40:31). In the process, God promised that He will "satisfy our years with good things" (Psalm 103:5). I plan to fly on that promise!

How *long* do I anticipate living on the summit? That is in God's hands and He doesn't tell me. I have always been a goal-setter and will probably not consider myself "finished" when my earthly life is over. I'll still have lots of exciting things left on the back burner—more that I want to do, to become, to write, to express, to learn, to enjoy, to reach for. But God, who planned every one of my days before the foundation of the world (Ephesians 2:10) and their number, when He decides to, will count my assignment in life "complete."

I thank God He has already given me long life, much longer than most members of my generational family. After potentially terminal illness, I thank God for giving me bonus time to live. I hope I've made use of those years for His glory. But I'm asking God for more years to satisfy me (Psalm 91:16) and to accomplish what He has planned for me. If He grants my desire, it is good. My *sooner or later* time to leave Planet Earth is up to God. If my entry into heaven is sooner, that's obviously His best and perfect plan—my life work will be finished. Either way is *A-OK* with me.

Because I belong to the Lord, it is His responsibility, not mine, to accomplish what concerns me. Would He terminate my life before *He* is done? Cut it short earlier than *He* eternally planned? I don't think so. Satan is the one who tries to intimidate me with the fear of having an aborted, unfinished life. What God began He will finish (Philippians 1:6), and He will do it in His time frame. Meanwhile, I look forward to each day on earth. But I know beyond any doubt that the reality of Eternity with Jesus will be far, far better than this life. When I leave behind my *earth suit*, my body, it will be a time for celebration. At last I will be made whole—*really complete!*

Meanwhile, how shall I deal realistically with the deteriorating *earth suit* which God decided to issue me many years ago? In His Word, God calls my physical body a temporary dwelling, a temple, a building, a sanctuary, a house, a tent. My body is the tent I am most familiar with because I've lived in it for so many years. God has plans to transform it into a wonderful new model in Eternity. For the time being, I have to accept its aging, mortal limitations and inevitably increasing frailties. I shall try to overlook the aging "inconveniences" that are common to everyone.

At the same time, I am responsible to continue *maintenance procedures* so I can live in maximum health as long as my eternal spirit needs this *earth suit*. That means I must do my part to eat nourishing foods, get enough exercise and rest, go for annual checkups and take whatever supplements or medications are necessary. Later in life, I am learning how to choose and eat only the foods that build up my body and keep it in good health. I am learning that God's plan for the human body includes both discipline on my part and the availability of God's healing when I need it. I believe that God heals both through divine and natural means.

I shall *obey* what God tells me by continuing to be a faithful steward—but only of what He has given me, not of what He gave someone else. When I surrendered my life into His hands as a teen, I came empty-handed. God began to generously give me specific abilities, gifts, opportunities, experiences and relationships which He expected me to use responsibly. I'm still accountable to use them. God hasn't let me off the hook because of my age. I haven't lacked anything that God knew I needed in order to fulfill His purposes through me. God promised He would "not withhold any good thing from those who walk uprightly" (Psalm 84:11).

God gave me the gift of creative writing in which I find great joy. I also have pleasure in trying to inspire and guide other writers to develop their gift. Expressing myself in writing is as easy as breathing for me. I believe that I have revealed myself most fully through my free verse poems in my Poetry Trilogy, *Celebrate This Moment: Prime Time is NOW!*

I shall continue to *both sow and reap*. Living on the summit, I am happy to be enjoying some of the harvest, eating the fruit of my planting. But I shall keep generously sowing for God into the lives of others. According to God's promise, I can always expect a harvest from sowing, whether I live to see it or not. I'm finding great joy in giving, not only of myself but of anything I have. It all belongs to God anyway. One of life's paradoxes is that I can only keep what I give away.

I am rich in friends all over the world, delighted to keep precious, old friends and eager to make new ones. I shall sow into the lives of others by sharing the riches of Christ-life with others, especially young people. The Bible says that older women (I think

I qualify by now!) should teach the younger. I'm so optimistic about the new generation! I want to be open to redemptive relationships with my family, friends and whomever God brings into the orbit of my daily life. Every morning I ask God to schedule my day in detail, to bring into my life that day only the people and the events that He wills. Nothing, therefore, is an interruption to fret about.

By people coming into my *orbit,* I mean into my *circle of my daily life.* That may be through a phone call, letter, e-mail, an impression, thought, a Scripture passage or meeting someone somewhere. I look at nothing as chance. When someone enters my life in these ways, I believe God planned for me to bless them or be blessed by them. I try to pray for them immediately, however briefly, and ask God whether He has a word of encouragement for them through me. That includes affirming whatever good I see in their lives, expressing my love for them in words and sharing God's love. Also by listening, by concern and being available to them.

While living on the summit, I shall practice *lightening up.* Is a sense of humor a gift? If so, I have continued to enjoy that gift for a lifetime. In my high school yearbook, my classmates voted me "the student with the best sense of humor." (Did they intend to say that I was "the most humorous"?) In my early teens, my wit may have started out as a cover up or compensation for my inferiority complex, but it developed into a lifelong asset. I try to see the humor even in difficult circumstances. Lightening up helps me to avoid stress. Unlike my medications from the pharmacy, a merry heart doesn't cost anything and contributes to my health!

Every day I shall say to the Lord, "You are welcome to come *today!* Feel free to interrupt anything I am doing which I may think is so important." The promise of Jesus Christ's return to this earth at any time is becoming increasingly real to me. He clearly promised that He will come again (John 14:2,3). Having said that, I want to keep redeeming the time I still have. God doesn't want me to be idle while waiting for Him.

I don't want this last season of my life to be a time of regret and remorse for what I should have done for the Lord or sadness because I missed His best. Yes, there were times I missed the mark and failed to follow God fully, *but I still have today.* I don't want to let any more time slip by and be sorry that I wasted my opportunity. I've spent yesterday; it is a canceled check. The future is a promissory note from God backed by all the riches in His heavenly bank. I'm sure I'll receive what God promised either in days to come while I'm still on earth or in Eternity. I can wake up each day with a clean slate. Lord willing, I still have time to make a few good marks on it to please the Lord.

I shall try to roll with the punches and meet changes of life head on with courage and trust in God. Changes are inevitable, and they come thick and fast as we grow older. They are part of the Heavenly Potter's maturing, finishing process, shaping us like clay until the final day of life. Changes move me further along as I am being transformed into the image of my Lord Jesus Christ from glory to glory. Changes that God brings into my life are not accidental or incidental. They are God's appointments for my good and for His glory.

Older people tend to resist changes, even in themselves. Our negative attitudes and habits become more pronounced as we grow older. We become rigid and think it is too late to change. That isn't true. I lose a blessing if I refuse to change. I gain and progress when I accept changes as new challenges and opportunities to grow. Even while living on the summit, I can still change so that my "rest of my way" will be more pleasing to the Lord. I shall face life's changes anchored to the Unchanging One, the Lord who is "the same yesterday, today and forever."

I still have a long way to go to achieve balance in all the above areas, but these attitudes are what I aspire to. I look forward to the coming years, however long or short, as the best ones of my life—closest to God, closest to my family and the most productive yet for the Lord.

But I know that the summit is not a permanent place for me to camp. That isn't God's life plan for humans. Nevertheless, it is a good place from which to take off when I'm ready to fly....

I NEED TO FLY

Jesus, I know You understand
my need to fly.
You walked the dusty Judean hills
earthbound for a season
yet You walked on the water, too
eventually You flew into the heavens
before the invention of planes
and space shuttles.

My spirit was born with wings
but the ordinariness of life
keeps them clipped, or at best
locked behind me with handcuffs
preventing my take off
into the sky lanes.

I hunger for free flight
for newness and ecstasy
for breaking loose from gravity.
I live with the urge
to explore the uncharted
and search for tantalizing treasures.

I yearn for abandon to kick off my shoes
run barefoot through fields wet with dew
and not worry about snakes and thorns
or who's watching you.

I'm tired of mediocre achieving
I'm weary of plugging along
resigning myself to grey life.
I'd rather move toward risk.

Lord, have compassion upon my unrest.
I'm hard pressed to settle for the humdrum.

I don't ask for swift descent
from the pinnacle of a temple
with the safe arrangement
of a catch-net at the bottom
in case the angels are on coffee break.

You talked about it Yourself, Lord--
You promised a life of *more*
You offered *abundance*.
Whatever it means
that's what I'm looking for!

If I'm not asking too much
would You let me enroll
in Your class on *Water Walking 101?*[2]

> *"For You have been my hope, O Sovereign Lord,*
> *My confidence since my youth;*
> *From birth I have relied upon You;*
> *You brought me forth from my mother's womb;*
> *I will always praise You.*
> *Since my youth, O God, You have taught me;*
> *And to this day I declare Your marvelous deeds;*
> *Even when I am old and gray,*
> *do not forsake me, O God till I declare Your power*
> *to the next generation,*
> *Your might to all who are to come."*
> (Psalm 71: 5,6,17,18 NIV)

32

Unfinished Symphony

I can't write the last chapter(s) of my life because I haven't lived them yet!

I'm on tiptoe of anticipation to discover what gold God still has for me in my original treasure chest—how much I can keep learning, how close to God I can become and what fruit I can still bear for Him....

To change the metaphor once again, my life at this point is an "Unfinished Symphony."

MUSIC SCORE

The last score of the song
of my earthly life
will it be in a major key?
A majestic symphony?
I'd like that, Lord!
To crescendo fortissimo
with a sustained final note

followed by thunderous applause
maybe an encore or two
a standing ovation
to climax my performance
with glorious elation!

But it just may be
that You've chosen for me
a simple closing melody
in a minor key, not melancholy
but plaintive and gentle
generous with rests
and closing pianissimo.

I cannot chose my life score.
Both lyrics and chords
are selected in advance
by You, my Divine Conductor.
You have the floor. What's more—
I don't perform alone.
The orchestra has many players
not just me
whose melodies You bring in
to achieve Your perfect harmony.

But the *finale* is assured:
The ovation is for *YOU!*
The "Hallelujah Chorus"
echoes throughout Your creation.

So I'll watch Your eye
I'll heed Your hand
I'll play or be silent
at Your command and be content
with the musical score
You've prepared for me
from ages before.[1]

Epilogue

I dug as deep as I could in my search for our roots, but I didn't attempt a detailed genealogical chart. Through my life story, I wanted to pass on more than names of people and how they were related. I aimed for a human interest saga to convey how I *felt* at different stages of my life—my responses, my dreams, hopes and struggles through the years. I did the same for my parents and grandparents insofar as I could. I hope such insights will enrich our *branches* and other readers.

In an awesome and unique way, both Ted and I inherited a rich legacy brought from both the continents we represented. That bequest is incomparably more valuable than money or any buried treasure because it wasn't buried—it was freely shared.

The Christian heritage each of our grandparents left to us, although they spoke different languages and grew up far apart on this Planet, was no accident or coincidence. We believe it was appointed by God for His eternal, sovereign purposes. *That's* the legacy we want to leave.

LEGACY

I anticipate leaving Planet Earth some day.
Sooner or later this body of clay
will pass away
but that's OK
because I'll be
happily Elsewhere
and won't need it anyway.

But I have a longing to leave
something of worth behind
something the next generation will find
of value, some kind
of stepping stones on life's road

to help steady
their uncertain feet
as they walk in uncharted ways
and carry heavy loads.

I can bequeath no greater assets
when I leave this transient life
than the *legacy of spiritual wealth*
which I've received from The King.
And wonder of wonders—
each one of my heirs
may claim *the whole estate*
and inherit *EVERYTHING!*[1]

Apparently Patrick Henry couldn't leave much of a material inheritance to his family, so he concluded his Last Will and Testament with the following words, with which I agree:

"This is all the inheritance I can give to my dear family. The religion of Christ can give them one which will make them rich indeed!"

Religion is only a family tradition to some people, and my husband and I were not interested in simply passing on religion. That is not *the* rich treasure. Our hope was to pass on *faith*, the true faith in Jesus Christ, the son of God, who lived in the hearts of our forefathers. Only God knows in how many of our ancestors' "root canals" Christ also lived in past centuries. We may find out later *when we are in our Father's House.*

Obviously, the Christian faith played a major part in my life story. Faith in Christ, however, can't be passed on like genetic traits. In that sense, no one can inherit it. It is not simply a tradition to follow. Someone has rightly said, "God has no grandchildren, *only children,* each one born again directly." True Christian faith is not like belonging to a political party or joining a club or organization—even joining a church. *It is a relationship with God,* a matter of each person's inward response. It includes a rational decision of the mind and will as well as the heart.

Since we can never pass on our faith to our children or grandchildren, any more than it was actually passed on to us, we can only point the way and assure them that the direction is right, and it *does* lead to God. We must caution them that it is not a smooth road without difficulties and struggles. But it is *the* "yellow brick (gold) road" to give meaning and purpose to their lives and lead them to Eternal Life at the end of that road.

Ted and I have proved throughout our lifetimes that this is true: God exists, He has revealed Himself to man and He invites communication with Himself through a personal relationship with Jesus Christ which lasts throughout Eternity. God put a spirit within each of us. That is what makes human beings different from the animal world. Through our spirits we can communicate with God through His Son, Jesus Christ, who said no one can come to the Father but through Him (John 14:6).

Although we can't pass on our faith, there is a very real sense in which the promised blessing of God is passed on and is available to succeeding generations of those who have a personal faith in Him. God specifically promises that in the Bible. Ted and I were glad receivers of that blessing in the spiritual bloodline from our godly ancestors. God made a covenant with those who belong to Him: their "children and children's children" will be blessed because of parental faith and obedience. Our faith and obedience can never be perfect, but God is always faithful in spite of our unfaithfulness.

Receiving generational blessing is, however, conditional upon one's personal decision to exercise that faith. Neither church membership or baptism or being born in a Christian family guarantees eternal life. Each of our children and grandchildren (as well as each reader) needs to make his or her own decision regarding accepting the "faith of our fathers" (and mothers). It is not automatic. When anyone does so, that puts him in line to receive and enjoy God's specially promised *generational blessings and favor.*

After I dug for our heritage roots and examined the soil in which our family trees grew, I concluded that it certainly wasn't fertile ground to begin with. Both sides of our family tree on two continents were planted in soil that was rough, stony and unfavorable, and family relationships were far from ideal. But in His sovereignty, God stepped in and nourished both of our families in that inhospitable ground with the warmth of His Son, the rain of His goodness and the nutrients of His mercy. It turned out that both Ted and I *did* grow up in the *good ground* of God's love and according to His predestined plan.

Our family tree became strong and fruitful under God's care—but not without the painful and necessary furrows of God's cultivation and transplanting. God was there all the time tending its growth, pruning, nurturing and protecting it. He lovingly continues to care for and watch over our spreading family tree from the trunk upward and outward to the furthest *branches* and young twigs. *To Him be all the glory!*

Memorable Genealogical Dates
Spryncl - Choy Heritage

Family Statistics BEFORE the turn of the century 1900

Leona Spryncl's *maternal* line: (Rompotl a.k.a. Rompot)

Jan Rompotl (dates unknown, born approx 1799)
Married to Terezie (Theresa) Zahradnickova (dates unknown)
Son: Josef Rompotl born 1822
Married Terezie (Theresa) Vtipilova
Son: Antonin Rompotl 1865-1904 (Leona's maternal grandfather)
Married Anastazie Drapelova 1875-1933
Daughter: Marie Rompot 1892-1965 (Leona's mother)
Married Frank Sprincl 1890-1950 (Leona's father)
Daughter: Leona Spryncl 1925-
Married Theodore Choy 1916-1992

Leona Spryncl's *paternal* line: (Spryncl a.k.a. Sprincl)

Matthew Sprincl (dates unknown)
Married Marie Bednar (dates unknown)
Son: Jan Sprincl approx. 1858-approx. 1899
Married Frantiska (Frances) Plachy 1861-1940
(Parents of Frantiska:Matej (Matthew) Plachy
married Anny Backak)
Son: Frank Sprincl 1890-1950 born in Czechoslovakia
Married Marie Rompot 1890-1950 born in Iowa
Daughter: Leona Spryncl, born in Iowa

Theodore (Ted) Choy's *paternal* line: (Choy a.k.a. Chua, Tsai, Tsoi, Choi)

Yang Hiang Sui (Grandmother of the Chua heritage) 1846-1929
Married: (surname Chua but given name and dates unknown)
Son: Choy Hon Yuen 1873-1953 (Ted's father)
Married: Chan Wang Fong 1883-1969 (Ted's mother)
Son: Theodore (Sih Hui) Choy, born in China

Some Family Events In The 20th Century

1907 Approximate date Leona's dad, Frank, arrived in the U.S. from
   Radlice, Moravia, Austria *(Later known as Czechoslovakia, currently
   The Czech Republic)*
1909 Approximate date Leona's paternal grandmother arrived in the U.S.
1916 Ted was born in Swatow, China
1919 Leona's parents were married
1925 Leona was born in Cedar Rapids, Iowa
1930 Leona started kindergarten at Buchanan Elementary School
1937-39 Ted studied at Canton Bible Institute in China and Hong Kong
1940 Ted age 24 arrived in U.S. to attend Evangelical Free Church Seminary
   in Chicago
1943 Leona graduated from McKinley High School and entered Wheaton
   College, IL
1943 Ted finished Seminary and enrolled at Wheaton College
1945-46 Ted enlisted and served in the U.S. Marine Corps in North China
1943-1947 Ted and Leona studied at Wheaton College receiving B.A.s
1947 Ted and Leona were married on August 23 in Cedar Rapids and moved
   to Hong Kong
1948-1952 Ted pastored the Swatow Christian Church in Tsimshatsui,
   Hong Kong
1949 Son Theodore Richard Choy born in Hong Kong
1951 Son Clifford Arthur Choy born in Hong Kong
1952 Son Gary Frank Choy born in Hong Kong
1952 The family moved to Singapore where Ted taught at Singapore
   Theological College
1952 Leona and 3 sons returned to U.S., Ted continued to teach in Singapore
1953 Ted arrived in U.S. to join his family in Iowa
1955 Ted received M.A. from the University of Iowa and the family moved to
   Philadelphia.
1955-62 Ted and Leona on the staff of International Students, Inc.
1957 Family moved to Washington, D.C. in service with I.S.I. among
   Chinese students
1957 Ted became a Naturalized U.S. citizen in Rockville, Maryland
1958 Son Jeffrey Mark Choy born in Kensington, Maryland
1958 Three oldest sons received their Certificate of U.S. Citizenship in
   Baltimore, Maryland

1958 Ted established the Chinese Christian Church of Washington, D.C.

1963 Ted and Leona co-founded Ambassadors for Christ, Inc. in Wash. D.C. with Moses Chow

1966 Christiana Tsai and Leaman family deeded their property in Paradise, PA to A.F.C.

1974 A.F.C. Headquarters built in Paradise, PA

1974 Ted and Leona with Jeffrey moved to Paradise, PA

1979 With Leona, Ted made his first trip back to China after a half-century absence

1981 Ted retired from A.F.C. and continued independent ministry to China

1983 Ted and Leona moved to Winchester, VA

1985 Radio station WTRM went on the air, Leona and Ted helping son Rick to establish it.

1979-1989 Ted and Leona made multiple ministry trips to China (Leona also led tour groups there)

1991 Ted and Leona made a first trip to Czechoslovakia to visit her heritage places and relatives

1992 Ted died at age 76

1993 Leona made a second trip to what was renamed The Czech Republic (The remainder of the century Leona continued living and writing in Winchester, VA)

2001 Leona made a third trip to The Czech Republic and Germany

Selected Bibliography of Resources

Andrews, Clarence, *This is Iowa, A Cavalcade of the Tall Corn State*, Iowa City: Midwest Heritage Publishing Co., 1982

Bacha, Leo, *Czech Immigration*, Vol. 1, Hallettsville, TX: Old Homestead Publ. Co. 1983

The Brotherly Agreement of the Moravian Church, Adopted by the Northern and Southern Province Synods of 1966 and 1971, Moravian Church in America, Bethlehem (undated)

Brownstone, David M. And Franck, Irene M., *Island of Hope, Island of Tears*, New York: Rawson, Wade Publ. Inc., 1979

Chapek, Thomas, *The Czechs (Bohemians) in America*, New York: AMS Press, 1969

Choy, Leona, *Andrew and Emma Murray: An Intimate Portrait of Their Marriage and Ministry*, Winchester: Golden Morning Publishing, 2000 Christian History Magazine, Carol Stream, IL: Issues: *Jan Hus, Comenius, Zinzendorf, The Moravians*, Vol. 1, No. 1, 1982; Vol. 19, No. 4; Vol. 6, No. 1

Clements, Ralph, *Tales of the Town, Little-known Anecdotes of life in Cedar Rapids*, Cedar Rapids: Stamats Publishing Co, 1967

Czechoslovakia, Prospect New Europe Guides, Prague: Hawker Publications Ltd and Orbis, 1991

Danek, Ernie, Cedar Rapids, *Tall Corn and High Technology*, Woodland Hills, CA: Windsor Publications, 1980

Engle, Paul and others, *Portrait of Iowa*, Minneapolis: Adams Press, 1974

Fodor's 90 *Eastern Europe*, New York: Fodor's Travel Publications, Inc. 1990

Forell, George W. Translator and Editor, *Nicholaus Ludwig Count von Zinzendorf, Nine Public Lectures on Important Subjects in Religion*, Iowa City: University of Iowa Press, 1973

Fradin, Dennis B., *Iowa in Words and Pictures*, Chicago: Children's Press, 1980

Gauslin, Dawn, *The Moravians, God's Hidden Seed*, (Article) 20th Century Disciple, No. 1, 1977

Greenfield, John, *Power from on High*, Minneapolis: Bethany Fellowship, Inc. 1928 (also published under *When the Spirit Came*, 1967

Griffith, Martha E., *The History of Czechs in Cedar Rapids, Vol. I 1852-1942*, Reprinted from The Iowa Journal of History and Politics, Iowa City: The Division of The State Historical Society
Griffith, Martha E., *The History of Czechs in Cedar Rapids, Vol. II 1942-1982*, Cedar Rapids: The Czech Heritage Foundation Inc. Lilly Printing Co., 1982
Goll, Jim W., *The Lost Art of Intercession: Restoring the Power and Passion of the Watch of the Lord*, Shippensburg: Revival Press, 1997
Hall, Elvajean, *The Land and People of Czechoslovakia*, New York: J.B. Lippincott Co. 1966
Hamilton, J. Taylor and Kenneth G., *History of the Moravian Church*, Bethlehem: 1967
Hamilton, Carl (Editor) *Pure Nostalgia, Memories of Early Iowa*, Ames: Iowa State University Press, 1979
Hayman, Simon, *Guide to Czechoslovakia*, New York: Hippocrene Books Inc. 1987
Hutton, J.E., *A History of the Moravian Church*, 1909
The Hymnal and Liturgies of the Moravian Church, Moravian Church of America, Chicago, 1969
Internet Sites: EKD Bulletin; Moravian.edu; Moravian.org; Zinzendorf.com, etc.
Jan Amos Komensky, Teacher of Nations, (Morava Krasna Magazine), Vol. 2, No. 2, Fall 1995
Lewis, A.J., *Zinzendorf The Ecumenical Pioneer: A Study in the Moravian Contribution to Christian Mission and Unity*, Philadelphia: Westminster Press, 1962
Martin, Pat (Compiler) *The Czech Book—Recipes and Traditions*, Iowa City: Penfield Press, 1981
Martin, Pat (Compiler) *Czechoslovak Wit and Wisdom*, Iowa City: Penfield Press, 1984
Mills, George, *Rogues and Heroes from Iowa's Amazing Past*, Ames: Iowa State University Press, 1972
Murray, Andrew, *The Key to the Missionary Problem*, Fort Washington: Christian Literature Crusade, 1979
Nagel's Encyclopedia-Guide: *Czechoslovakia*, New York: Cowles Education Corp., 1968
Otter, Jiri, *Evangelical Church of Czech Brethren*, Prague: Synodal Council of the Evangelical Church of Czech Brethren, 1985

Peterson, Rodney L., *Holy Warrior of God, John Hus, Witness and Martyr*, (Article, Voices Magazine, undated)

Rican, Rudolf, *The History of the Unity of Brethren, A Protestant Hussite Church in Bohemia and Moravia*, Bethlehem: The Moravian Church in America, 1992

Sawyer, Edwin A., *All About the Moravians: History, Beliefs, and Practices of a Worldwide Church*, Bethlehem: The Moravian Church, 1990

Schattschneider, Allen W., *Through Five Hundred Years: A Popular History of the Moravian Church*, Bethlehem, PA: Comenius Press, 1956, revised 1974

Schattschneider, David A., *John Hus...and Us*, booklet, reprint from July-August 1979 issue of The North American Moravian.

Seton-Watson, *History of the Czechs and Slovaks*, Hamden, CN: Archon Books, 1965

Sjolund, Angela and Richard, *Iowa*, Fenton, MI: McRoberts Publishing Inc., 1975

Spinka, Matthew, *John Hus, A Biography*, Princeton: Princeton University Press, 1968

Spinka, Matthew, *John Amos Comenius, That Incomparable Moravian*, New York: Macmillan, 1943, reissued by Russell and Russell with University of Chicago Press, New York, 1967

The Story of Our Church in Text and Pictures, The Moravian Magazine, March 1957

Thompson, Augustus C., *Moravian Missions*, New York: Charles Scribner's Sons, 1882

Thompson, Steve, *Herrnhut—A Prophetic Warning*, (Article) The Morning Star Journal, Vol. 9, No. 4, 1999

Videos: Gateway Video. Worcester, PA: Christian History Institute, *Jan Hus, Zinzendorf, Comenius, the Moravians*

Walters, Philip (Editor), *World Christianity: Eastern Europe*, Monrovia, CA: MARC, 1988

Weinlick, John R., *Count Zinzendorf: The Story of His Life and Leadership in the Renewed Moravian Church*: Bethlehem, Moravian Church, 1984

Wellauer, Maralyn A., *Tracing Your Czech and Slovak Roots*, Milwaukee

Zeman, Jarold Knox, *Renewal of Church and Society in the Hussite Reformation*, Bethlehem: Moravian Theological Seminary, 1984

Endnotes by Chapters

Chapter 1

1 *Trunk Destiny*—by Leona Choy. Celebrate This Moment, (Winchester, VA: Golden Morning Publishing, 1996) Part 1, p.17.
2 *Find Us Faithful*—Words and music by Jon Mohr. ©1987 Jonathan Mark Music ASCAP and Birdwing Music ASCAP. All rights reserved.
3 *Stage of Generations*—by Leona Choy. Celebrate This Moment, Ibid., p. 3

Chapter 17

1 *I'll Go Where You Want Me to Go*—Text: Mary Brown; Music: Carrie E. Rounsefell. All rights reserved.

Chapter 30

1 *My Potter*—by Leona Choy. Celebrate This Moment, p.186
2 *My Request*—by Leona Choy. Ibid., p. 3
3 *My Puzzle*—by Leona Choy. Ibid., p. 53

Chapter 31

1 *It is Well with My Soul.* Hymn text by Horatio G. Spafford; Music: Philip P. Bliss
2 *I Need to Fly*—by Leona Choy. Celebrate This Moment. p.41

Chapter 32

1 *Music Score*—by Leona Choy. Celebrate This Moment. p. 7

Epilogue

1 *Legacy*—by Leona Choy. Celebrate This Moment. p. 72